Classical Astrology for Modern Living:

From Ptolemy to Psychology & Back Again

J. Lee Lehman, Ph.D.

A division of Schiffer Publishing, Ltd.
77 Lower Valley Road
Atglen, Pennsylvania 19310 USA

Copyright © 1996
by J. Lee Lehman

All rights reserved. No part of this work may be reproduced
or used in any forms or by any means--graphic, electronic, or
mechanical, including photocopying or information storage
and retrieval systems—without written permission from the
copyright holder.

Printed in the United States of America

ISBN: 0-924608-24-2

Published by Whitford Press
A Division of Schiffer Publishing, Ltd.
77 Lower Valley Road
Atglen, PA 19310
Phone: (610) 593-1777
Fax: (610) 593-2002

Please write for a free catalog.
This book may be purchased from the publisher.
Please include $2.95 for shipping.
Try your bookstore first.

We are interested in hearing from authors with book
ideas on related subjects.

Contents

Preface	7
1. Introduction: Why Classical?	10
2. Have you forgotten what the Sky looks like at night? The Babylonian Captivity	14
3. Elements, Qualities and Triplicities	26
4. Historical Context: From the Fall of Rome to the End of the Renaissance	47
Historical Interlude: The Cyclic New Ages	67
5. Essential Dignities	85
6. Accidental Dignities	112
7. Everything you ever wanted to know about Sect...	135
8.The Part of Fortune	164
9.When a Quincunx (or Semi-sextile) is not Inconjunct	187
10.The Nodal Cycle: from Ptolemy to Rudhyar	202
11.What is Mutual Reception, anyway?	219
12.The Ancient Medical Model and its Meaning in Wellness & Psychology	231
13.Beyond Aspects: How to Read A House	248
14.Profections: The Easy Way to Spin the Chart	261
15.Changes	286
References	296
Appendix. Classical Sources Index	302
Charts	330

Table of Charts

The Spiritualist New Age	81
The Current New Age	82
Nicholas II	330
Mary Godwin Shelley	331
Prince Charles	332
Sunrise before Nicholas II	333
Sunset before Mary Godwin Shelley	334
Aleister Crowley	335
Catherine De Medici	336

Muhammad Ali   337
George Foreman   338
Union Carbide   339
Union Carbide 1st Trade   340
Bhopal Gas Leak   341
Circle of Athla: Nicholas II   342
Circle of Athla: Mary Godwin Shelley   342
Circle of Athla: Prince Charles   342
Circle of Athla: Aleister Crowley   343
Circle of Athla: Muhammad Ali   343
Circle of Athla: Union Carbide   344
Circle of Athla: Phopal Gas Leak   344
Camille Paglia   345
Ludwig II of Bavaria   346
Mickey Mantle   347
Mantle's Liver Transplant Operation   348
Mantle's Death   349
Nancy Hastings and Nancy Hasting's Death   350

Table of Tables

Chapter 2.
Sidereal Periods for the Traditional Planets   18
Synodic Periods for the Traditional Planets   18
Successive Mars Retrograde Period Comparisons   19
Goal Periods for the Planets. Late Babylonian Period   20

Chapter 3.
Traditional Qualities of the Planets   30
Aristotelian Changes between Elements: Being and Becoming 31
Hippocrates' Regimen for the Four Seasons   32
Qualities of the Cyclic Process of Human Development   32
The Seasons: Being and Becoming   33
The Elements: Being and Becoming   33
The Seasons and Elements: Being and Becoming   33
The Stoic System of Elements   34
Time Line for the Principal Philosophers Discussed   36
Schools of Philosophy   37
Compass Directions   38
The Humors   39
The Seasons and the Humors   39
Humors, Fluids, and Organs   40
The Humoral Temperaments   41

Christiansen-Carnap's Cosmopsychological Types 42
The Ebertin Point System for evaluating Cosmopsychological
    Types 43
Elements, Signs and Temperament Types 43
Elements, Signs, Qualities, Seasonal Components/Hemisphere 43

Chapter 4
A Brief Chronology of the Middle Ages and Renaissance 51
Astrologers publishing on Eclipses & Grand Conjunctions
    1400-1500 57

Chapter 5
Essential Dignities and Debilities: Whole Sign Types 86
Triplicities as given by Ptolemy and William Lilly 88
Ptolemaic and Egyptian Terms 88
The Faces (Chaldean Decanates) 89
Keywords associated with the five Essential Dignities 92
Almuten Rulers by Degree: Day 93
Almuten Rulers by Degree: Night 94
Nicholas II's Temperament Types 98
Mary Wollstonecraft Godwin Shelley's Temperament Types 102
Prince Charles' Temperament Types 106

Chapter 6
Accidental Dignities & Debilities 113
Qualities of Planets depending on Orientality/Occidentality 118
Qualities of the Moon according to her phase 121
Occidental & Oriental Planets of Nicholas II 124
Aleister Crowley's Temperament Types 126
Catherine de Medici's Temperament Types 127
Occidental & Oriental Planets of Mary Godwin Shelley 129
Occidental & Oriental Planets of Prince Charles 130

Chapter 7.
Assignment of Day or Night Condition of the Planets and
    Luminaries 136
Ptolemy's Planetary Attributions of Sect and Sex 138
Nicholas II's Planets by Sect 139
Mary Shelley's Planets by Sect 140
Prince Charles' Planets by Sect 140
Aleister Crowley's Planets by Sect 141
Catherine de Medici's Planets by Sect 142
Muhammad Ali's Temperament Types 142
Occidental & Oriental Planets of Muhammed Ali 143

George Foreman's Temperament Types 144
Muhammad Ali's Planets by Sect 145
George Foreman's Planets by Sect 146
Chi-square Values for Gauquelin Professional Data by Sect 151
Summary of Hayz & Out-of-Sect Placements for 8
    Gauquelin Professions 154
Summary of Chart Sect-*Halb* and Out-of-Chart Sect-*Halb*
    Placements for 8 Gauquelin Professions 155

Chapter 8.
The Relationship of Part of Fortune to Angular Separation 166
Manilius' meanings of the Lots 170
A Table of Fortitudes and Debilities of Fortuna 173
Union Carbide's Temperament Types 174
Union Carbide's Planets by Sect 176
Bhopal Gas Leak's Temperament Types 177
Bhopal Gas Leak's Planets by Sect 178
Union Carbide 1st Trade's Temperament Types 179
Union Carbide 1st Trade's Planets by Sect 180

Chapter 9.
Antiscial & contra-antiscial signs 191
Nomenclature for quincunx & semi-sextile types, & aspects 196

Chapter 12.
Camille Paglia's Temperament Types 236
Camille Paglia's Planets by Sect 239
Ludwig II's Temperament Types 243
Ludwig II's Planets by Sect 243

Chapter 13.
Length of Life from the condition of the Alchocoden 253

Chapter 14.
Correspondence between House Rulership and Age in
    Profection Calculation 263
Profected Houses for Lee Lehman's 42nd Year 264
Significant Dates in Nancy Hasting's Life 265
Profected Houses for any Year 266
Events in Prince Charles' Life 268
Events in the life of Muhammad Ali 270
Events in the life of Catherine de Medici 273
Events in the life of Mickey Mantle 278

Preface

No work is conceived in isolation without the intellectual contributions of others, intentional or not. It is my purpose in this Preface to acknowledge the sources of whom I am aware, and to state my own approach to this subject.

First, my thanks go back to M. Louise Crawford, the friend who got me interested in Astrology in the first place. The first few years, I learned my Astrology from books and from Louise's chart file, which included most of the women that I was working with politically in the mid-Seventies. I discovered Astrologers in New York through N.A.S.O., and the seminars and conferences put on by Barbara Somerfield. The two biggest influences at this time were Betty Lundsted and Doris Hebel. From N.A.S.O. I discovered *Mercury Hour* and the National Council for Geocosmic Research.

Mercury Hour and Edie Custer provided an introduction for me, and many others, to a host of other Astrologers. Where else (in those pre-Internet days) could *any* Astrologer dialog with any other one, regardless of relative fame or geographic location?

The introduction to the National Council for Geocosmic Research proved to be of profound importance to my development as an astrologer. NCGR has been a haven for techno-freaks since its inception in 1971. NCGR's educational focus has challenged many Astrologers to go beyond the Astrology they originally learned. NCGR has always welcomed new ideas, techniques, and approaches thorough its publications and people. Thus, it was under NCGR's aegis that I was able to develop friendships and working relationships with people such as Diana K. Rosenberg, Rob Hand, and Robert Zoller, who have all had profound impact on my thinking—and hopefully that impact has been in both directions.

NCGR was responsible for providing the forum for my first astrology trips abroad. It was through these trips that I came to be acquainted with the British horary astrologers who have also impacted my thinking: Olivia Barclay, Clive Kavan, Geoffrey Cornelius, and Maggie Hyde. These trips also led to my continuing interest in, and enjoyment of, many individual Astrologers, as well as the publications of the Astrological Association of Great Britain and the Astrological Lodge of London. Nick Campion especially has been most helpful, by fax and e-mail, in keeping me up to date with what's happening in the U.K.

It was at the A.A. Conference in Nottingham that I first had the opportunity to make connections with the Australian Astrologers, through the agency of Bernadette Brady and Darrelyn Gunzburg. Bernadette and Darrelyn have been kind enough to show me around a bit of Australia, and to introduce me to a number of other Aussies.

It would be truly remiss to fail to mention the software developers, an integral part of our communication circles. Mark Pottenger developed a horary page in CCRS beginning in 1989 which calculated the essential dignities and the planetary hours. Rob Hand incorporated these techniques into Print Wheels in 1992. In parallel circles, Allen Edwall developed Horary Helper, and Matrix added a classical tab page. Graham Dawson incorporated classical techniques into the general astrology program, Solar Fire 3.0, and also into the research program Jigsaw. Finally, Rob Hand may have finally achieved overkill in the awesome variety of classical techniques that he has embedded into Chart Wheels 3. In my opinion, without computer tools, we cannot expect any technique to take root anymore, unless it is so simple that it doesn't require additional calculation!

Throughout all these adventures, Margaret M. Meister has edited my books and articles, argued concepts, and asked for more examples, footnotes, and illustrations. *None* of my books would be as good as they are without her.

Five people in particular have contributed to this work. Marie Faure, one of the Reference Librarians at the Franklin T. DeGroodt Memorial Library in Palm Bay, Florida, has chased down dates and references, saving me hours of work. Carol Wiggers, Editor of *The Horary Practitioner*, was kind enough to read this manuscript, as was Carol Garlick, one of the Steering Committee members of the Association for Astrological Networking. Sarajane Garten also read a portion. Finally, I wish to thank Clara Darr. Clara was interested in Classical Astrology long before I had even discovered *any* Astrology. Sadly, her eyesight no longer allows her to enjoy the original works she had collected, many of which she sold to me for far below their official value. I can never even begin to repay this kindness. There are probably a host of others I should thank. I beg their forgiveness for omitting them by name. But I cannot omit the names of the three feline members of the household, who serve to remind us of truly higher values: Spaz, Staghorn, and Mischief.

I published earlier versions of two of the Chapters in this work. The material in Chapters 9 and 10 was originally published in "Aspects." Chapter 8 has never been published, but I began giving it as a lecture in 1990.

Finally, let me mention a couple of things about my approach to this material. It has become increasingly clear as we study ancient Astrology that there was a host of techniques that were, until recently, forgotten. The task of Classical Astrology today is twofold: to recover these techniques, but also to evaluate and understand them within a modern context.

The intellectual challenge of this Astrology is not through the invention of new concepts. This flies in the face of the last couple generations of astrological dogma. Now, the source and pedigree of a technique is interesting and essential. Having said this, there is still room for innovation, but it is the innovation of understanding, clarification, and extension.

I am also taking a fundamentally different approach in this work than that taken by Project Hindsight in their translations. (See Chapter 1 for a description of Project Hindsight.) Rob Hand and Robert Schmidt have taken the position, especially when it comes to the Greek translations, that many of the technical terms are too ambiguous to be translated at this time, so they are relying on anglicized Greek or literal translation to convey the meaning of terms such as *zoidion* (sign) or *pivot point* (angle). While this may be true, I believe that in the interim, the use of such words makes the concepts more off-putting than they need to be. Consequently, I have chosen to use or invent common English terms, which may somewhat sacrifice technical correctness, but which should help clarity of understanding. I am somewhat reminded of the frustration for Westerners who peruse Oriental studies when confronted with transliterated Sanskrit words. Such transliteration usually stops the comprehension, rather than clarifying it.

I believe that the study of classical concepts can radically improve *all* Astrology, regardless of whether the practitioner chooses to adopt a Classical or Neo-classical approach. All the techniques presented here can be successfully incorporated into a modern delineation. I would challenge the Reader to consider not merely the techniques, but the logic behind them, as well as the philosophical matrix from which the techniques spring.

Perhaps the biggest demand upon our comprehension as we explore these concepts is that Astrology is intrinsically part of the way of delineating a sacred system of living. Astrology is alive when every moment is sacred, which is to say, every moment has meaning. We seldom manage to live our lives with that level of awareness, but at the crisis times, it is there. Charts become seared into our existence just when we align with the Cosmos. There is Choice, but there is also Destiny.

──── Chapter One ────
Why Classical?

In 1980, Robert Zoller launched the latest classical revolution in astrology when he published *The Lost Key to Prediction*. Almost none of us knew it at the time. In fact, I wrote a review of it for *C.A.O. Times* in which I questioned the relevance of Medieval material and methods for a modern delineation. It was a good question, but my answer at the time was noticeably weak in retrospect.

This is not to say that others did not appreciate classical works before Bob. Clara Darr, for one, had collected classical texts, and reprinted John Gadbury's *The Nativity of King Charls* in 1974. The American Federation of Astrologers had doggedly kept Manilius and Bonatti in print.

We must also hasten to add that this revolution, such as it is, is a reference to English-speaking countries only, because at least a variant of classical methods has been taught continuously since at least the 19th Century in France and Germany, as well as other Romance language countries.[1] It is curious that although Astrology dropped out of the Romance countries more thoroughly in the 18th Century than was the case in English-speaking countries, when it revived, it did so with the strong influence of the 17th Century contemporary of William Lilly, Jean Baptiste Morin de Villefranche, known as Morinus. We have a hint of this in English through two English translations of Morinus which appeared in the '70s: one by Schwickert & Weiss (albeit of a volume originally published in German in the 1940s); the other by Lucy Little. We shall have more to say about this later.

My own revolution came when I was researching my second book, *Essential Dignities*. I was forced to re-examine my own prejudices as a modern natal astrologer. The modern rulerships provided little interesting information for a reading. Yet here was this incredibly rich classical system which added considerable scope to a consultation. No... it changed the very essence of the process of reading a chart. All it required was abandoning ideas which, I discovered, had only become entrenched since the early 19th Century. Being a triple Virgo, I find that occasional revolutions in thought patterns are not difficult at all!

In the early 1980s another piece was being played out in England. Geoffrey Cornelius had begun lecturing from a copy of William Lilly's *Christian Astrology*, a work that was also picked up and appreciated by Olivia Barclay. Both worked with Clive Kavan to help produce the 1985 Regulus Edition of that work.

Lilly was initially appreciated mainly by horary astrologers. At this time, horary was often trivialized, or even looked down upon, as a specialty which was way off the beaten track. Furthermore, many of the early enthusiasts of Lilly were women, and I doubt that sexism was irrelevant. Serious men were still doing *real* astrology, which is to say, natal, or perhaps mundane.

I shared this prejudice against horary, an almost inevitable result of the conquest of astrology by secular psychology. As a so-called science, psychology has tended to emphasize the importance of free will, actually a religious position inherited from the previous Christian religious establishment. Free will was important in Christianity because the individual had to choose damnation or salvation.[2] Free will was important to psychologists, because the improvement represented by therapy is produced by the individual *choosing* to take charge of his or her life, and to transcend habit patterns which are the antithesis of free will.

As Cornelius pointed out as early as 1985,[3] horary is intrinsically divinatory. It is hard to disguise horary's predictive nature, although some have tried. Thus, the success of horary prediction implies that free will, if it exists at all, isn't exercised very often. This perspective can be very challenging to the modern mind, accustomed as we are to belief in growth at will, and such concepts as choice-centered psychology or astrology!

Because I had always seen myself as a natal astrologer, my interest in horary was at best lukewarm. However, I began to study classical horary, supposedly, *I thought*, in order to learn and apply classical techniques more consistently. The joke was on me! Again, circumstances called for a readjustment of my perspective as I was bitten by the bug.

The classical horary that was being developed in England was very strongly Lilly-biased, with occasional references to Ptolemy and al-Biruni. There is no question that Lilly's work is the best textbook of horary that we have, in great part because of the example charts. However, I began to explore other sources, aided to a great degree by the reprint service provided by John Ballentrae. John has made available xerographic editions of many classical works that are *much* less expensive than collecting 17th Century originals, no matter how satisfying those moldy oldies may be.

However, as late as 1992, classical astrology was still an area for specialists and iconoclasts. The major watershed occurred at the United Astrology Congress (UAC) in Washington, D.C. with the founding of A.R.H.A.T. (Association for the Retrieval of Historic Astrological Texts), and subsequently, Project Hindsight. Originally a joint project of Rob Hand, Robert Schmidt, and Robert Zoller, Project Hindsight took on the task of providing translations of astrological texts, many of which had never been translated into English. Furthermore, they chose to organize this bold idea as a commercial venture, that would sink or swim, depending on financial support from the Astrological Community. It didn't fail.

In the three years between UAC conventions (1992-1995), interest had grown to the point where the classical lectures at UAC '95 constituted the most popular "track," more than doubling attendance from UAC '92. In 1995 Project Hindsight received the Regulus Award for Astrological Research.

Since 1987, my own classical interest has been to elucidate various classical methods, and in the process, to apply these techniques to delineation, whether in natal, horary, electional, or mundane. I do *not* propose to throw out the modern style of reading, but rather, to enhance the power of that reading. My original doubt about the modern relevance of Zoller's work (and other classical work as well) remains. An astrological client in the late 20th Century does not come to us for the same type of natal reading that a person would in the Middle Ages, or even the Renaissance.[4] However, in many respects the expectations are not as different as we may wish to believe: since love, family matters, work, and health still frame much of our existence.

Thus, recovering the texts and techniques is only the first step. In its march forward, Astrology leaves behind a graveyard of abandoned techniques. Many were abandoned for very good reasons: they didn't work, or more precisely, they only worked for the person who invented the technique. Others were abandoned either because people didn't understand the technique, or because the computations involved in applying it were too complex. This is the category of most interest to us, since computational complexity has been completely eliminated as an excuse in our computerized era. A final issue addresses whether the technique is still relevant, or at least, how important it is in our changed life circumstances. For example, in classical texts a great deal of emphasis was placed on methods of calculating the length of life. This is not an issue which concerns most of my clients, unless they have already been diagnosed with a fatal condition!

As an exercise in scholarship and philosophical understanding, I am delighted that the folks at Project Hindsight are devoting their efforts to translating this material and attempting to correctly reconstruct the techniques. I suspect, however, that this idea of predicting the length of life will simply be an interesting exercise until we achieve a more fundamental revolution: the full re-integration of Hippocratic medicine and its concepts into our understanding of wellness, health, and disease.

Having gotten this far, where does this revolution leave psychologically-based astrology? Changed, perhaps. I do not mean to imply that psychology has no place in astrology. I am concerned about Astrology becoming too dependent on psychology. Astrology has many dimensions: psychological, metaphysical, philosophical, medical, or even biological. I will address some of these connections in the later chapters of this book.

First, however, comes the major purpose of this book: to teach the reader how to *think* classically. I will be demonstrating various techniques in the following chapters. My method may seem maddening to those people who prefer one particular classical period, because I will run the gamut from Babylonian to the 17th Century C.E., without giving any period necessary preference. However, I don't believe in golden ages either:[5] thus, I do not believe that there was *ever* one period which had the best techniques, as well as all the answers.

While the methods I demonstrate are ones I have found especially compelling, they are not the point. The point is that there are certain primary ways of approaching astrological delineation which underpin the entire classical system. About half of the methods which we will examine fall into this category. Before we examine these techniques, however, we shall begin with a survey of some ideas—astrological, cultural, and philosophical—which are important to the understanding of all that follows.

Endnotes

[1] c.f., Julevno, Ely Star.

[2] For a full discussion of the positions of Augustine and Thomas Aquinas in these matters, see Choisnard.

[3] Geoffrey Cornelius. 1985. The Moment of Astrology. Astrology 59(1): 42-49.

[4] I think a very good argument can be made that a horary reading does not differ in very many fundamentals between Classical and Modern times, except for the obvious change in the method of *asking* questions: namely, the possibility of simultaneous understanding at a distance (the telephone), and instantaneous written communication via fax or e-mail.

[5] nor the Easter Bunny, nor the perfect chart!

——— CHAPTER TWO ———

HAVE YOU FORGOTTEN WHAT THE SKY LOOKS LIKE AT NIGHT?

THE BABYLONIAN CAPTIVITY

Who would deny the sacrilege of grasping an unwilling heaven, enslaving it, as it were, in its own domain, and fetching it to Earth?

Manilius, page 93

It began with the sky. Can we ever recapture the wonder, the awe, of the night sky?

If you go out tonight to observe the sky (assuming that you can see it at all!) what would you see? If you went out at Sunset, and you could see the Western horizon, more or less, you would see the Sun sink slowly out of sight. But it would still be light! Astrologically, you just saw the Sun move from the 7th to the 6th House.

Gradually, twilight would give way to darkness. In the twilight, you might begin to be able to see any planets still visible in the Western sky, *Occidental* to the Sun, meaning those that set *after* the Sun. And gradually, you would be able to see the stars. Hundreds of stars. Thousands of stars.

If you come back outside two hours later, the stars and any planets would appear to have moved. It would seem as if the whole sky had rotated. Each time you would come back out on this hypothetical night, the bowl would seem to have rotated some more.

Eventually, it would be almost dawn. Now, any *Oriental* planets would be visible near the Eastern horizon. Gradually, the amount of light increases, until finally the Sun becomes visible. You have now watched the Sun go from the 1st House to the 12th House.

If you repeated this exercise night after night, you would notice several things. First, the length of the night itself would change. Between the Winter Solstice and the Summer Solstice, the total length of the night would be decreasing. If it was between the Summer Solstice and the Winter Solstice, the length of the night would be increasing. You might also notice a slight change in which stars were visible. Every day there is about a 1° shift in the position which rises. This may not be very apparent from day to day, but week to week it becomes more obvious. The planets also shift places. While the Moon's movement is the most apparent, but the other planets shift as well.

Suppose you could tabulate these changes over time. Maybe you could also note the weather conditions, or unusual phenomena, like the appearance of a ring around the Moon, a shooting star, a drought, or an especially good harvest, or the birth of twins...

If you did this, you would be repeating the gift that the Babylonians gave to astrology. We call them Babylonians, or Chaldeans, but they could be called (correctly) by many names.[1]

So let us set the stage. First, we know that the Babylonians used a lunar calendar that was periodically adjusted to bring it back into sync with the solar seasons. We know that they named many of the constellations that we still know today, including the zodiac, a grouping of 12, 30° equal-length signs, which was probably invented in about the 4th Century B.C.E. Neugebauer notes that the invention of the zodiac was essentially a matter of mathematical convenience for the Babylonians, because they continued to express position in reference to the fixed stars, not to this hypothetical zodiac.[2]

The Babylonians named the planets for the gods and goddesses with which they were associated. Their early "astrology" was essentially a system of omens: observation of certain conditions had a meaning that could be interpreted. Working in teams,[3] they recorded and interpreted these observations, and this information was then passed on to the king. Among those conditions noted was whether the Moon was visible on the first day of the month. This condition which *should* be true, but often wasn't, because of the difficulty of keeping the calendar accurate: the lunar month in fact is not really 30 days. Thus, the Moon appearing on the first day of the month was a good omen, as if to say all was in order between heaven and earth. Other sample observations:

No. 39. Happy welfare to the land, the Moon will smite the foe. The Moon has occulted Mercury.

No. 49. When the Moon rides in a chariot in the month of Sililiti, the rule of the king of Akkad will prosper and his hand will overcome the enemy...[4]

Despite our modern fantasy that even the skies were clearer in earlier, pre-industrial times, conditions for observation were hardly ideal.
As Neugebauer reminds us:

> ... the almost proverbial brilliance of the Babylonian sky is more
> a literary cliché, than an actual fact. The closeness of the desert
> with its sand storms frequently obscures the horizon. This is the
> more essential as the majority of problems in which the
> Babylonian astronomers were interested are phenomena close
> to the horizon. The lunar calendar requires observation of the
> first visibility of the new crescent in the western horizon.... Dis-
> appearance and reappearance of the planets are phenomena close
> to the horizon and it seems also "opposition" of a planet was
> defined as rising or setting at sunset and sunrise respectively.
> Only eclipses and occultations will usually be observable under
> favorable conditions. It is certainly the result of this situation
> that Ptolemy states that practically complete lists of eclipses are
> available from the reign of Nabonassar (747 B.C.) while he com-
> plains about the lack of reliable planetary observations.[5]

We learn from Neugebauer exactly how much of the Babylonian
system was horizon-based. This is a form of observation that has become almost totally foreign to us. It survives today mainly as *angularity*, a form of *accidental dignity*, which we shall revisit in Chapter 6. A
horizon-based system (*i.e.*, one that relies heavily on the observation of
the rising and setting of planets and star groups) makes sense from an
observational standpoint. These kinds of observations are easy to explain and teach to new observers. The problems in practice with such a
system are manifold. For example, we *now* know that the planets move
around the Sun in elliptical orbits,[6] and the same for the Moon's movement around the Earth (actually the Earth-Moon barycenter). In practice, this means that, from the standpoint of an Earth-based system, the
speed of the planets will appear variable. Why does this matter? It means
that since the Moon has a daily motion from about 10° to 14°, the change
in the Moon's position from day to day is variable. Further, since there
is the change in the compass angle of sunrise and sunset throughout the
calendar year[7], not to mention changes in the latitude of all bodies *except* the Sun, this combination results in variability in the *timing* of the
rise and set of various bodies, especially the Moon, throughout the
year. With a calendar which assumes a constant month, this is a problem! That the Babylonians were able to solve these problems *at all* is
truly remarkable.

So what exactly were the components of the Babylonian astronomical and astrological systems? We have already seen that the Babylonians
had named the planets, many fixed stars, and computed the rudiments
of planetary orbit components. We have seen that planetary position

was expressed in reference to location within a constellation, an asterism within a constellation, or near to a fixed star.

Six observations were taken concerning the Moon in each month, the observations that Sachs called the Lunar Sixes.[8] These were:

- First visibility of the new crescent, which was the start of the lunar month
- Time from moonset to sunrise near full Moon
- Time from sunrise to moonset near full Moon
- Time from moonrise to sunset near full Moon
- Time from sunset to moonrise near full Moon
- Last visibility of the Moon before the next New Moon

The positions were noted in reference to 31 standard reference stars, all of which are located within 10° of the ecliptic. These 31 stars included most of the major fixed stars used in astrological delineation to this day, including Aldebaran, Regulus, Spica, and Antares. They were not at fixed intervals, however, but somewhat clustered.

The Outer or Superior Planets (Mars through Saturn) were observed through their phases. Here their positions were recorded by sign. These phases were:

- First appearance
- First station (retrograde)
- Opposition
- Second station (direct)
- Last appearance

We know, of course, that the Superior planets, Mars through Pluto (at the moment), are those planets with orbits outside the Earth's, relative to the Sun. Superior planets do not appear geocentrically the same as inferior ones. Superior planets:

- appear as evening stars at opposition
- disappear from the evening sky as they approach conjunction
- go retrograde as they approach opposition
- are brightest at opposition to the Sun
- enter the evening sky in the East

By contrast, Inferior planets (Mercury and Venus):

- appear to oscillate around the Sun
- are faster on the Earth's side of their orbit (fastest at inferior conjunction, when they are between the Earth and the Sun)
- are slower when the Sun is between the Earth and the inferior planet (i.e., slowest at superior conjunction)
- move swiftly when they first appear in the morning sky, slowing down before leaving it
- move slowly when they first appear in the evening sky, speeding up before leaving it
- are brightest at conjunction with the Sun

- enter the evening sky in the West

With this number of contrasts between Inferior and Superior planets, it is not surprising that the Babylonians had to track additional items for the inferior planets, where the phases were:
- First visibility in the East (morning)
- Station point in the morning
- Last visibility in the morning
- First visibility in the West (evening)
- Station point in the evening
- Last visibility in the evening

Over time, the Babylonians were able to derive the synodic and sidereal periods of the planets, what they called the goal years. Goal years? (Listen, astronomy is easy when the equations have already been worked out for you!) First let's review our definitions.

The *sidereal period* of a planet is the time it takes that planet to complete exactly one orbit, measured by its recurrent alignment to a fixed star. The *synodic period* of a planet is the time that it takes that planet to complete exactly one orbit, measured from one conjunction of the Sun to the next. Now obviously, the Sun moves, while the amount of movement relative to a fixed star is trivial. Thus, the synodic period by definition, *should* be longer for inferior planets, and shorter for superior planets, right? Let's see!

Table One. Sidereal Periods for the Traditional planets.

	Modern Value	Ancient Value
Mercury	88 days	46 years
Venus	224 days	8 years
Mars	1 year 322 days	47 years
Jupiter	11 years 315 days	83 years
Saturn	29 years 167 days	59 years

Table Two. Synodic Periods for the Traditional planets

	Modern Value	Ancient Value
Mercury	116 days	46 years
Venus	1 year 220 days	8 years
Mars	2 years 289 days	79 years
Jupiter	1 year 34 days	71 years
Saturn	1 year 13 days	59 years

Why are the goal years—the synodic and sidereal periods—so different between ancient and modern, apart from the obvious fact that the Babylonians did not know that these planets traveled around the Sun, not the Earth? We can find out the answer to this by examining some modern data about Mars. The idea for this answer, however, was derived from Hinze.

Table 3 shows data for nine successive retrograde periods of Mars. Figure 1 shows the longitude positions of three successive cycles. We have to remember that the Babylonians were attempting to derive a way to *predict* the position of Mars in the future, as well as to prognosticate from the conditions observed at the time of a significant Mars phase change. This table uses two of the phase changes: the two station points. We observe that the length of the Mars retrograde cycle varies from cycle to cycle, a phenomenon we have already discussed as due, in part, to the nature of elliptical orbits.

Table 3. Successive Mars Retrograde Period Comparisons

Dates	Station 1	Station 2	Difference	Length
1999: Mar 17-Jun 4	12♏12	24♎27	19° 45'	78 days
1997: Feb 6 - Apr 27	5♎55	16♍44	19° 11'	79 days
1995: Jan 2-Mar 24	2♍14	13♌10	19° 04	80 days
1992: Nov 28-Feb 15 1993	27♋37	8♋40	18° 57'	78 days
1990: Oct 20-Jan 1 1991	14♊34	27♉45	16° 49'	72 days
1988: Aug 26-Oct 28	11♈28	29♓53	11° 35'	62 days
1986: Jun 8-Aug 12	23♑06	11♑25	11° 41'	64 days
1984: Apr 5-Jun 9	28♏21	11♏42	16° 39'	64 days
1982: Feb 20-May 11	19♎11	0♎23	18° 48'	79 days

A word about "accuracy." How close does a return have to be to constitute a return to the same "point?" For the earlier part of astronomical history, the answer is 10°, because the asterisms that later became the decanates[9] were the general unit of measure.[10] Here in nine cycles, or seventeen years, there has been no such repeat! In 1952, 47 years before 1999, there was a Mars retrograde cycle that began on March 25 at 18 ♏ 29. Similarly, in 2046, there will be a Mars retrograde cycle starting on March 11 at 6 ♏ 14. Now these are by no means exact according to our modern standards. But there still is one additional factor to consider.

We occasionally see a diagram of a retrograde loop. If you were to plot the ecliptic longitude and latitude of Mars on successive nights during a retrograde period, you would see a loop. But not all loops are the same shape! What transpires over the course of the cycle between "goal years" is a sequence of differently-shaped loops, from fat loops, to elongated loops, to S-shaped curves. *This is the sequence that repeats in the synodic sequence: the shape of the successive retrograde curves.*

If you didn't have equations to do the job for you, and you had observations going back for a long enough period of time, it would be extremely useful to know in advance what the retrograde cycle would "look" like! Thus, the development of the longer sidereal and synodic periods actually provided useful information which seems less than obvious—especially for the inner planets—from our modern heliocentric perspective. It also is obvious from Table 1 that we have adopted the *modern heliocentric* sidereal periods in our interpretation of the Saturn Return, the Jupiter Return, or even the Mars Return.

The "goal texts" of the Babylonians were one of two major categories of astrological writings; the "goal" being to successfully predict a future astronomical occurrence! With this idea in mind, the Babylonians assigned periods to the planets which could be used for prediction. This was performed by looking up records of previous positions of the planets, and applying them to the present cycles as shown in Table Four, taken from O'Neil.[11]

In other words, you could "predict" the position of Venus next week by taking the date, finding an observation from 8 years previously, and then subtracting 4 days. Where more than one period is given, each cycle was used for different values, such as the station date versus the actual longitude.

Let's review the generic observations that the Babylonians considered important:
- First visibility
- Station point (retrograde)
- Last visibility
- Station point (direct)

Table Four. Goal Periods of the Planets. Late Babylonian Period.

Saturn	59 years	minus 6 days
Jupiter	71 years	same date
	83 years	subtract 13 days, or add 17 days
Mars	47 years	add 2 days
	79 years	add 7 days
Venus	8 years	minus 4 days
Mercury	6 years	add 14 days, or subtract 16 days
	13 years	minus 4 days
	46 years	minus 1 day

If we translate these concepts into modern parlance, we are really looking at two different concepts which have survived to a greater or lesser extent. The station points are, of course, the boundary points in the retrograde cycle of a planet. We still recognize the importance of retrogradation. We all know astrologers who can get downright obsessive about Mercury retrograde. However, our general concept of the *meaning* of a retrograde planet has gotten a little obscure, so let me remind the reader of the classical horary approach as seen in Lilly and other sources. Retrograde planets:

- bring confusion[12]
- auger discord and contradiction[13]
- bring delay[14]
- can bring results suddenly[15]
- can bring return of a lost object[16]
- can bring a surprise outcome[17]

All this for a planet which is, by definition, changing *direction*. The meaning of a retrograde planet is thus a logical extension of exactly what such a planet is doing in the sky: contradicting itself in its direction of motion.

The meaning of the other two phases (or four phases in the case of Mercury and Venus) is perhaps less obvious, but still clear upon consideration. What is "first" or "last" appearance? These are phases related to the proximity of the planet in question to the Sun.

Planets are not visible in the day. Only the Moon can be seen in the light of the Sun—for part of her cycle. First appearance is basically a measure of being far enough away from the Sun to be seen. In the morning, this means that the planet is *Oriental*, or rising before the Sun. If the planet rises *after* the Sun, then the planet is simply invisible in the daylight. Similarly, at night, the planet needs to be *Occidental* in order to be seen. It must rise *after* the Sun. But how much before or after? This varies by planet, since the different planets have differing degrees of brightness.

As a convention, an orb of about 8° to the Sun is about the rule-of-thumb for the condition that we refer to as *combustion*. A combust planet cannot be seen. We shall explore this concept further in Chapter 6. For now, we will simply add that the next level of visibility is *Under the Sun's beams*, which extends out to roughly 17°. When a planet is under the beams, it can be seen, but not under all conditions.

Thus, we see two more concepts inherited from our Chaldean forbears. But before we transfer our attention from the Tigris and Euphrates to Mount Olympus, we should perhaps consider one of the biases betrayed by our astrology: a bias from the temperate zone.

Everything we have covered so far about Babylonian astrology fits one criterion: what was recorded as significant *astrologically* could be readily observed *astronomically*. And the converse was true as well! Any astronomically "interesting" event must have an astrological meaning. Thus, we see the developments in Babylonian astrology: the naming and location conventions of the constellations, asterisms, and later signs; the identification of the planets and certain qualities about them; and the identification of changes in the "normal" progress of the planets, be they the retrograde stations, or eclipses.

The various Babylonian Empires were situated around 30–34° North latitude, about the latitude of Northern California to Virginia in the United States. As such, they were North of the Tropic of Cancer, which is located at 23°. So what? There are three very different regions of the globe astronomically: the Tropics, the Poles, and the Temperate Zones. Perhaps you are aware that most house systems break down within the Arctic and Antarctic Circles because those regions have periods of constant light or constant dark, hence there is no sunrise and sunset, and therefore, no Ascendant and Descendant.

The difference in the Tropics is this. In the temperate zones, go out at night and watch the sky. A star or a planet rises in the Eastern portion of the sky (not due East, unless it's equinox time). Then, its motion through the sky is *oblique*. It does not rise "straight up." There is a horizontal as well as a vertical displacement. We know this horizontal displacement is showing the ecliptic: the path of the Sun which is tilted 23° from the plane of the Earth's axis. In addition to the stars that rise and set, there are the circumpolar stars, like Polaris, that never rise and set. These occupy a circle with a radius equal to the observer's latitude on Earth. So in our example above, the circumpolar stars occupy a circle of radius 30–34°. As the latitude increases, the portion of the sky occupied by the cirumpolars increases until finally, at the pole, there are *only* circumpolar stars.

But in the Tropics that is not how stars and planets appear to act. Here, there are virtually *no* circumpolar stars (atmosphere refraction can produce a minor circumpolar effect), and planets and stars appear to rise completely vertically: there is no oblique component. This has a major advantage.

Suppose you are living on a tropical island (don't you wish!) and you want to visit the next island. If you can look in the direction of that next island and you see a star rising over it, you can steer in the direction of the star! You could *not* do this in the temperate zone, because as soon as that star rose, the oblique component would begin as soon as you attempted to steer in that direction, and your direction would be off, and it would continue to get worse the higher that star rose in the sky. If it is Summer in the Northern Hemisphere and you were attempting to travel East, you would have steered too far North, because the tilt of the Ecliptic would have added a Northern lateral component to the direction "pointed" by the star. How "severe" is the error? In the temperate zone, the altitude of the celestial Pole is the same as the geographical latitude. Thus, the degree of error isn't even constant in the temperate zone, yet one more complication to navigating by the stars! In the Tropics, ocean-going people developed "horizontal" constellations: stars that rose in the same degree, but sequentially. That way, when one navigational star rose too high in the sky to be useful, the next in its horizontal sequence would rise, and the navigation could continue.

One side element—this component of oblique motion in the temperate zone, which prevented direct celestial navigation from developing any degree of sophistication—also puts an interesting spin on the story of the Three Wise Men (now finally translated *Astrologers* in some versions) from the Christian Gospels. The Astrologers could *not* have used the so-called Christmas Star to navigate to Jesus. They must have used either some form of locational astrology, or found where a previous eclipse or major conjunction was angular!

At this point, we have to bring in a second component: the *zenith*. The zenith is that point in the celestial sphere directly above the observer. The Sun only culminates at the zenith on the longest day of the year. Virtually all tropical cultures evolved an astronomy and astrology based on the horizon and zenith, while temperate cultures evolved systems that had to consider oblique ascension, which is much more difficult to measure. Still, as we recall from Neugebauer, the early Babylonian system was much more horizon-based than the later Western systems. While a horizon-based system makes complete sense in the Temperate Zone, Neugebauer also informs us of the ramifications of that choice of coordinates:

> The Babylonians were primarily interested in the appearance and disappearance of the planets in analogy to the first and last visibility of fixed stars—e.g. Sirius—and of the moon. It was the periodic recurrence of these phenomena and their fluctuations which they primarily attempted to determine. When Ptolemy developed his planetary theory, he had already at his disposal the geometrical methods by means of which solar and lunar anomalies were explained very satisfactorily, and similar models had been used also for an at least qualitative explanation of the apparent planetary orbits. Thus it had become an obvious goal of theoretical astronomy to offer a strictly geometrical theory of the planetary motions as a whole and the

characteristic phenomena lost much of their specific interest, especially after Greek astronomers had developed enough observational experience to realize that horizon phenomena were the worst possible choice to provide the necessary empirical data.[18]

Clearly, which components of the sky are important depends on where the observer lives. This difference, while it certainly includes cultural differences, also includes the appearance of the sky. As we proceed more deeply into the Western interpretation of astrology promulgated by the Greeks, Astrology unabashedly entered into, then melded with, various philosophical interpretations of human life, and the meaning thereof. However, let us remember that *no* astrology is universal, even on Earth. We don't have to wait to confront the issue of universality until we have the *Enterprise-1700* or its successors!

Figure 1. Mars longitude positions of three successive retrograde cycles.

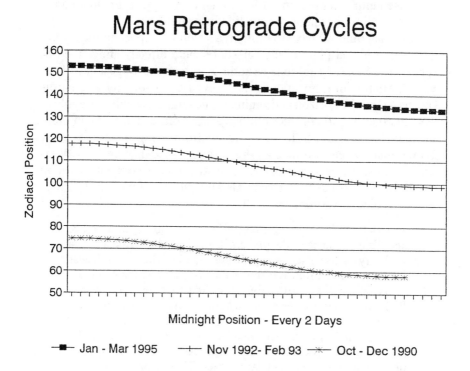

Endnotes

[1] And no! We are not going to get into the specifics of which period should be called Assyrian, or Sumerian, etc. For our purposes here, we shall restrict our vocabulary to the admittedly vague "Babylonians." Also see Hand's Introduction in Schmidt (1995) as a good overview of this period.

[2] Neugebauer, pp 102–103. What is especially significant about this idea is that it is truly irrelevant whether the Babylonians used a "sidereal" or a "tropical" zodiac. If they continued to use the fixed stars as the basis for expressing positions, and the zodiac was simply used as a computational convenience, then it really has little in the way of justification for the "correctness" of any later system.

[3] *op. cit.*, Oppenheim.

[4] All from Thompson.

[5] Neugebauer, p. 98.

[6] What is the effect of elliptical orbits? It means that the Sun appears to move more rapidly at certain times of the year than it does at others. To be more precise, the Sun appears to move most rapidly in January in the Northern Hemisphere when the apparent motion is 61', and least rapidly in July, when the rate slows to 57'.

The Sun occupies one of the two focal points of the elliptical orbit of each planet. Planets move fastest when they are closest to the Sun and slowest when they are furthest away from the Sun. The magnitude of the difference between the aphelion speed and the perihelion speed is a function of the eccentricity, or degree of curvature of the ellipse. The Earth's orbit is close to circular. Only the orbits of Venus and Neptune are more so. The orbits of Mercury and Pluto are the least circular.

[7] At the equinox, the Sun does rise in the East and set in the West, with the day and night of equal length. (At the poles there is no East and West, so these systems never work properly there.)

At the summer solstice in the North latitudes, the Sun rises in the Northeast and sets in the Northwest, with the exact degree varying with the latitude, the angle increasing towards the Arctic Circle, where day lasts 24 hours.

At the winter solstice in the Northern Hemisphere, the situation is reversed. The Sun rises in the Southeast, setting in the Southwest, with the angle decreasing towards the North Pole, which experiences night for the full sidereal period.

Our astrological diagrams only resemble the exception: the equinoxes in temperate latitudes. The astrological axes *do* represent a correct *projection* of the plane of the ecliptic (i.e., the zodiac). At most times of the year in most locations, sunrise does *not* take place at a point opposite (i.e., at 180°) to sunset. Yet by our astrological conventions the descendant is opposite the ascendant by definition. Our conventions are distorted in time. We have defined our ecliptic (house) coordinates so that sunrise is opposite sunset. But temporally and spatially they are not.

The effect of time is shown more obliquely in astrological systems through the concept of signs of short and long ascension: the elapsed time of Cancer rising is greater than that of Capricorn rising.

[8] This material on the types of lunar and planetary observations taken is from Aaboe.

[9] An Egyptian concept. The decanates originates as nighttime hour markers: the time it took particular stars to rise was used to mark off the twelve (unequal) hours of the night. They were called decans because the groups of stars used changed every ten days.

[10] The decans are as old as 2100 B.C. according to Neugebauer (1983), p 205.

[11] *Op. cit.*, page 27.

[12] al-Biruni, page 60.

[13] Lilly *CA*, page 299.

[14] *Ibid.*, page 4

[15] *Ibid*, pp 107, 198, 211, 406.

[16] *Ibid.*, pp 211, 357.

[17] *Ibid.*, page 211.

[18] Neugebauer, page 127.

——— CHAPTER THREE ———
ElEMENTS, QUAliTiES ANd TRiPliciTiES

*Life is short, the Art long, opportunity fleeting, experiment
treacherous, judgment difficult.*

Hippocrates[1]

In this chapter we take up the theory of the signs and planets as
developed during the Classical Greek Period and in the later Hellenistic Period. Astrology appeared as an intellectual force in Greece *after*
much of cosmology and medicine had been developed. Perhaps Astrology caught on among the intellectuals in part *because* it fit so well
into this pre-existing framework. This integration both clarified the
existing concepts, and raised new and exciting questions. To understand how Astrology fit in, and to increase our own ability to properly
manipulate astrological symbols, we have to understand these pre-existing systems. This means that we must study the theory behind
Hippocratic medicine, as well as the theory of the four elements. The
material presented includes the *major* theoretical justifications that were
given for the workings of astrology from the Hellenistic Period onward.

Despite what we have led ourselves to believe, a cursory reading
of Hippocrates is not redolent with astrological truths. Very little of the
immediate Hippocratic corpus has any direct astrological reference at
all. Of course, this is hardly surprising, because the typical dating period for the Hippocratic corpus is circa 400 B.C.E., which came before
the period of Grecian astrological interest.[2] What references there are
to fixed stars show that they were used as chronocators, or time markers.[3] This being the case, where did pre-modern medicine get its reputation for having astrological ideas so thoroughly integrated?

Before we can answer this question, we need to understand what
Hippocratic medicine was. It was first and foremost, observational,
but not empirical.[4] Its observational nature places medicine as a fore-

runner to the Aristotelian tradition, pre-dating Aristotle by a century. Broadly speaking, Aristotelianism is based on observation of nature, while Platonism is based on reasoning from first, or at least, generally agreed upon principles. W.H.S. Jones illustrates this difference by contrasting our modern idea of a *hypothesis*, or testable idea, with Plato's use of the Greek term from which our word originated. He says that the Greek "hypothesis" was a postulate, a starting point for debate or discussion: the lowest common denominator to which all sides could agree in the beginning.[5]

The great emphasis in Hippocratic medicine was on diet and regimen. This is where the astrological brain kicks in, if only by analogy. The ideal of Hippocrates (not to mention most Greek philosophers!) was to lead a balanced life. If the body is balanced, then disease is less likely to take hold. This philosophical position is still held by many people. It is, for example, the guiding light behind virtually *any* form of preventative medicine, from taking vitamins and anti-oxidants, to practicing vegetarianism, or initiating various "life-style" changes.

Hippocrates listed several factors which are important to ascertaining the proper regimen, which essentially consisted of food, drink, and exercise, including:

    (1) The season of the year: "In winter eat as much as possible and drink as little as possible, and food should be bread, with all meats roasted; during this season take as few vegetables as possible, for so will the body be most dry and hot."[6]

    (2) The age of the person: "Young people also do well to adopt a softer and moister regimen, for this age is dry, and young bodies are firm. Older people should have a drier diet for the greater part of the time..."[7]

    (3) The gender: "Women should use a regimen of a rather dry character, for food that is dry is more adapted to the softness of their flesh..."[8]

    (4) The constitution: "Those with physiques that are fleshy, soft and red, find it beneficial to adopt a rather dry regimen for the greater part of the year. For the nature of these physiques is moist."[9]

We finally get something we can sink our teeth into, because Astrology eventually became the preferred mode for distinguishing the constitution from its components, or humors.

The four primary qualities that comprise the temperament are hot, cold, wet, and dry. In food, this is represented by cooked (hot), raw (cold), soft food (wet), or hard food (dry). Each of these qualities actually represents a cluster of concepts, and their opposites. For example, the qualities hot and cold do not represent extremes of a temperature continuum, as we would define them. They represent *qualities* of energy, where *hot* represents high energy or physical heat, and *cold* represents low energy or physical cold. But these qualities are opposites in a critically different way than the way we normally envision them. Take temperature. We moderns would see "cold" as being the "absence" of heat.[10] From a purely chemical perspective, molecules in a hotter gas vibrate more rapidly on average than molecules in a colder gas. Mixing the gases will produce an intermediate result. In other words, in our thinking the "cold" portion is completely canceled out by a portion of the "hot" component. But this is not how it works! People are, in fact, more than capable of expressing opposite qualities without one canceling the other! In psychological testing there is often an index of consistency, which is actually a measure of to what extent an individual will give the same answer to the same question. If such an index is deemed necessary, it becomes clear exactly how capable we are of expressing "incompatible" ideas and emotions! Opposites do *not* cancel each other out!

Thus, a person may have hot and cold qualities *simultaneously*. In fact, to be in balance would be to manifest equal quantities of each, not to have a "zero-sum state" in which "hot" cancels "cold," perhaps producing lukewarm.

The balanced state should not be lukewarm. Rather, it is the ability to be high energy (hot), or completely at rest (cold) as the moment and the circumstances require. Being merely hot is to approach all circumstances as a Type A personality: everything is a challenge to be conquered. To approach things from a cold perspective is to be motionless: to wait for the problem to go away or resolve itself without having to do anything. The force of the wave of circumstances smashed up against the rock of inaction. This is the difference between doing *anything* and doing *nothing*.

The balanced state is what every form of Eastern martial arts training attempts to convey. It is the conscious manifestation of *chi* or *ki*, the state of potential action or inaction in any and every moment, because the mind and body are both at rest with the circumstances. The balanced person can adopt either strategy as the particular moment warrants. The "hot" or "cold" approach becomes merely a position, an *asana* or form, rather than a way of life. To balance is to transcend.

The difference between the concept of "opposite" as representing two states of extreme quality—or alternately one state as the absence of the other—is critical to our understanding of some basic astrological concepts, because this is where our notion of the aspect "opposition" originates. Plutarch (46–circa 114 C.E.) discussed the ramifications of these two different approaches in considerable detail in his work, *On the Principle of Cold*. Here he attempted to assign cold to one of the four elements, with Air, Water and Earth all contenders. (He ultimately reaches no conclusion.) However, he listed some of the key differences as follows:

- If hot and cold are not independent qualities, then cold is simply the negation of heat. Negative qualities are "inert and unproductive"[11] Thus, if cold produces alterations in bodies that become cold, then cold cannot be inert. He then mentioned that cold bodies often become condensed or viscous, which clearly *are* changes in property.

- A negative opposite state cannot be a function of degrees. The example he gave is silence. Silence is the absence of sound. One does not discuss "slightly" silent, or "mostly" silent. If the room is not completely silent, then it is not silent at all.

- If the two opposites can be perceived simultaneously, one cannot be the negation of the other, because silence is annihilated by any sound. We do not perceive a mixture of sound and silence in a given moment.

- The state of absence is simple, while its opposite is complex. There are many kinds of sounds, but only one silence.

- If there are four elements, then there must be four qualities, not two and their negations.

In thought, dryness is the position that this moment is unique, that reality can be "objectively" known. "Wet" thinking takes the position that separate concepts are interconnected. At this point, the fashion is to call dry thinking left-brained, and wet thinking right-brained. While this may not be literally true, there is certainly a symbolic truth. Dry thinking is object-oriented; while wet thinking is spatially oriented. Alternately, dry thinking is algebraic, while wet thinking is geometric. The basic difference between dry and wet is the difference between solid and liquid. This difference was considered from the beginning to be of critical importance: a liquid has no shape of its own, but assumes the shape of its container. A solid is rigid. Thus, dry thinking is rigid, while wet thinking is fluid, formless. The square peg in a round hole is the epitome of the danger of extreme dry thinking. Confronted with an inappropriate "shape," the dry thinker has no solution: the pieces are incompatible and there is no way to bring them together. Submergence and drowning is the epitome of the danger of extreme wet thinking. There is nothing for the wet thinker to grasp onto for support. Yet one other way to contrast the two is to say that the epitome of dry thinking is clarity; the epitome of wet thinking is ambiguity. And yes! The very process of attempting to explain the concept is dry!

Rob Hand has produced two questions which, in a modern context, allow us to classify the elemental qualities quickly and easily. Is it high or low energy? If high, it's hot. If low, it's cold. Does it create bonds or break them? Alternately, does it enhance distinctions or blur them? If it creates bonds or blurs distinctions, it's wet. If it breaks bonds or enhances distinctions, it's dry.

Applying these questions to Uranus, we get: high energy, breaks bonds. Therefore, Uranus is hot and dry, hence of a fire nature. With Neptune, we get low energy, and a blurring of boundaries or distinctions. Therefore, Neptune is cold and wet, hence of a water nature. Pluto can be both/and, so it does not have a clear elemental nature.[12]

The natures of the planets are traditionally given as follows.[13]

Saturn	Cold & Dry
Jupiter	Hot & Moist
Mars	Hot & Dry
Sun	Hot & Dry
Venus	Hot & Moist[14]
Mercury	Maybe yes, maybe no
Moon	Cold & Moist

One other point, which is at first a little puzzling. The Qualities Hot and Cold were considered Active, while the Qualities Wet and Dry were considered passive. That is because the Qualities Hot and Cold were said to act, while the Qualities Wet and Dry were said to be acted upon. In modern parlance, the Hot-Cold continuum has been couched in terms of energy or kinetics; the Dry-Wet continuum in terms of matter. Energy is active, while matter is passive.

When did these concepts of the qualities originate? To answer this question, we need to go back to the origins of Greek philosophy, which fall in the 6th Century B.C.E. Prior to this time, and that means the period of Homer and Hesiod, philosophy as we would recognize it did not exist. Thales, Pythagorus, and Heraclitus began an inquiry into the nature of the world—its origins, its functions, its workings—that has continued ever since. And this inquiry has, in turn, spawned other inquiries, including modern science, which used to be called natural philosophy.

Philosophy provided a set of explanations for how things worked that transcended the earlier mythological approach. How things worked included their origin, and initial attempts to speculate on this question entailed asking, "What is the ultimate quality of reality?" Thales picked water. ("The Earth was without Form and Void?" Sounds wet to me!) Anaximenes picked air or spirit, and Heraclitus, fire. What they chose reflected in part on their concept of reality: fire, for example, represented energy and flux. It was Empedocles who introduced the four "roots," which we now refer to as the elements, using Plato's terminology. He also included two driving forces: love and strife, attraction and repulsion. We should add that, at this time in Greek thought, the planets were conceived as being meteors, or terrestrial vapors: hardly a position conducive to devoting much attention to these mere "emanations."[14]

This theory of Empedocles was ready-made for two later developments: the concept of atomism developed by Democritus from Leucippus, and the grafting of Babylonian astrology into a Greek philosophical matrix, a point explicitly made by Bouché-Leclercq.[15]

It was the idea of atoms that introduced the concept of an unchanging unit of matter. The elements or forms were *not* originally conceived of as bits of matter in the atomic sense, but rather as *processes*. Atomism transformed the elements into matter, with Earth being the most dense, and Fire the least dense. Even to the atomists, the concept of dynamics was extremely important in the development of Greek philosophical ideas. Unfortunately, it has often been replaced in modern reading by terms which suggest a static, or material state instead.[16]

Later, Plato developed the theory of forms: that all dogs share a form of "dogness," and that their adherence to the form "dogness" is what makes them dogs. Aristotle, who was originally Plato's pupil, rejected the form as the primary vehicle: each dog is unique, but they share certain qualities that lead us to call them dogs.[17] This position of Aristotle's has been represented superficially as empiricism, but it is only empirical in the sense that it may be based on observation, not empirical in the sense of the scientific method.

Because Aristotle took change as a given, and because cyclic models of change had become commonplace in Greek thought, Aristotle introduced a twist into Empedocles' conception of the four roots. No longer are they immutable, because change is universal. One element can change into another through the shift of *one* of its qualities, but through a cyclic process:

Fire	hot & dry	becomes moist
Air	hot & moist	becomes cold
Water	cold & moist	becomes dry
Earth	cold & dry	becomes hot

Notice that this pairing combines one active "element," Hot or Cold, with one passive "element," Wet or Dry. Thus, we continue the interplay of energy and matter, with the transitions between elements occurring when we shift from energy to matter and back to energy. Einstein lives! Aristotle explicitly excluded elemental shifts in which *both* qualities changed, such as a shift from Hot & Dry to Cold & Wet.

This cyclic process was anticipated, but not specifically discussed, in Hippocrates. Thus, we have Hippocrates' discussion of appropriate foods and regimen for different seasons:

Spring	Warm & Wet	increase drink, softer food	more sleep
Summer	Hot & Dry	lots of drink, wet food	slow walking
Fall	Dry & Cold	lessen drink, harder food	less sleep
Winter	Cold & Wet	little drink, dry food	rapid walking

There is also a cyclic process in human development, thus:[18]

Children	Hot & Moist
Young Men	Hot & Dry
Mature Men	Dry & Cold
Old Men	Moist & Cold

Now it is obvious that the sequence for the ages of man is exactly the same in terms of root qualities as that for the seasons. While this point was not explicitly made by Hippocrates, it was no doubt noticed and later incorporated into the astrological world view.

I would also caution on the use of this particular table because it is *clearly* a male-biased system. In our current life-cycle, menopause occurs during the mature woman phase, and it is *anything* but cold and dry! In earlier days, it *might* have been possible to argue that menopause represented the transition to the old woman, but is still no explanation of hot flashes and night sweats!

These concepts are all well and good: but the question is, how do they work? Here, we must first examine how the Greek philosophical theory was applied to astrology. Rob Hand has pointed out that there were two primary methods of defining the astrological elements in terms of the four qualities, and that these in turn were based on previous theorizing about whether the elements were immutable, or changeable. The model for change was the seasons: they are *cyclic*, not *progressive*. Scholars have noted[19] that the Greek philosophical system was static: change could occur, but it was the repetition of the seasons, as well as the turn of the wheel of fortune.

In the Aristotelian system, each element (and season) possessed two qualities: *being*, and *becoming*, unlike Empedocles, who envisioned them as static. Thus, we have:

Spring	Wet, becoming Hot
Summer	Hot, becoming Dry
Fall	Dry, becoming Cold
Winter	Cold, becoming Wet

It is only a short step to add the elements to the table, thus:

Air	Wet, becoming Hot
Fire	Hot, becoming Dry
Earth	Dry, becoming Cold
Water	Cold, becoming Wet

Let's add another column to this chart and see it in the context in which it developed, and was known:

Spring	Air	Wet, becoming Hot
Summer	Fire	Hot, becoming Dry
Fall	Earth	Dry, becoming Cold
Winter	Water	Cold, becoming Wet

Hand has commented that this cycle of the seasons can be viewed physiologically as well: anabolic, or building, processes encompass Winter and Spring, while catabolic, or destructive, processes occur in Summer and Fall.[20] Winter? For those of you without a good grounding in the secret life of plants, the growth cycle of most temperate plants begins in *Winter*, not Spring. One of the truly amazing sights is to go for a walk in the woods in February in the 40° North latitudes, where one may observe skunk cabbage growing like crazy amidst patches of snow! Skunk cabbage has a rather unique metabolic shunt which allows it to produce sizable quantities of heat, thus giving it a jump-start on the season. But this is merely the extreme. Growth starts *before* the light and temperature conditions are ideal. Metabolic activity is the basis behind the running of the sap that we so highly appreciate in the form of maple syrup. This growth phase is anabolic, in two phases. In the first and early stage, growth occurs with a net *decrease* in weight, because stored fats and sugars are used to produce new tissue. The later phase, generally post-Spring, is marked by continued tissue growth, now with a net increase in weight. This anabolic phase corresponds to the Wet phase of the cycle, the period of maximum metabolism. The Dry phase begins in Summer, and the metabolic rate declines, to reach its nadir in early Winter.

This botanical analogy also points out something that was rather obvious to the Greeks, but has become lost upon us. We date our Seasons to the beginning of each of the Tropical Cardinal signs. These points do in fact represent important geocentric solar points: The Aries Ingress marks the transition from the Sun having Southern Declination to Northern; the Cancer Ingress is the point of maximal solar Northern Declination (not to mention the longest period of daylight); the Libra Ingress is the transition from Northern Declination to Southern; and the Capricorn Ingress is the point of maximal Southern declination. However, it is at the Cross-Quarter Points—15° of the Fixed Signs— that we observe the *biological* transition of the Seasons. Thus, the metabolic changes associated with Spring begin around Groundhog Day (Candalmas), the Spring growth spurt is essentially complete by Beltane, the heat of Summer dries much vegetation by Lammas, and the leaves and fruits have turned or dropped by Halloween (Samhain).

To the extent that there is a seasonal component built into our theory of the (astrological) elements, then the elements, as we are elucidating them, can *only* apply to the Tropical Zodiac, not the Sidereal one. The Sidereal Zodiac has no intrinsic seasonal component, while the Tropical zodiac is explicitly defined *in terms of the season of the year.* Given the importance that the Greeks ascribed to the elements in Astrology, it is obvious why Greek Astrology *became* Tropically-based, once the difference between the two zodiacs became known and understood.

The Stoic system, by contrast, applied only one quality to each element, thus:

Fire	Hot
Earth	Dry
Air	Cold
Water	Wet

The Stoic system was used astrologically as the description for the elemental nature of the astrological signs by those Stoic astrologers, such as Vettius Valens, but without fully recognizing the ramifications of the difference in elemental attribution.[21] However, this was *not* the case in Ptolemy. The earliest known example at this point is from Vettius Valens, who was definitely Stoic.[22] This different sequencing creates different results, depending on the system, and we lack any evidence that, until now, *anyone* has discussed the ramifications of the two systems for astrological practice.

Before we can approach this question, we first need to understand the basis for the Stoics' system. First, we have to recall that the two active qualities are hot and cold, while wet and dry are passive. As Sambursky points out, the Stoics redefined the elements by assigning only one quality per element. However, they maintained the characterization of Fire and Air as being the active elements. This meant that they had to be ruled by Hot and Cold, so Fire was assigned to hot, and Air to cold. This maintained the quality, and astrologically it maintained the integrity of the masculine (active) and feminine (passive) signs. However, it wreaked havoc with seasonal considerations. Now it is the Fall that is cold, and the Winter dry. Neither is a convincing case in a Mediterranean climate, where the Winter is the rainy season, overlapping into Spring.

It also wrecked havoc with one other Aristotelian characterization: gender. Thus, we see in al-Biruni, who was citing the Aristotelian system: "When therefore you know the active virtues of a sign whether heat or cold, and the passive virtues, whether dryness or moisture, it will not be concealed from you what particular element of the world and what particular humour of the body each sign resembles.... All the hot signs are male and the cold female."[23]

However, the Stoics placed the highest priority on their understanding of active versus passive. Thus, it was held that the active processes had binding capacity, while the passive substances could only be bound; i.e., they had no intrinsic binding capability by themselves. They could only be acted upon. For the most part, the Stoics did not succeed in convincing others to adopt their system, at least with regard to the elements. Other Stoic ideas, such as the *pneuma*, were more successful. The Aristotelian system was too entrenched—and too useful—in medicine and other applied areas. The Stoic system of elemental qualities created more problems than it solved. It was quietly dropped.

The system of the qualities ultimately applied to more areas in astrology than simply medical. The compass directions have bedeviled horary astrologers far more than natal ones. Lost object horaries are often much more difficult to delineate than other kinds of horaries. Compass directions are part of the problem.

There were two schools of thought about compass directions: either they derived from the seasonality of the Signs, or from the Angular Sign location of a "natural" chart. These are shown in the following table.

Here we see two different approaches to the directions. If we begin with East, then the two lists begin by agreeing: the Cardinal Sign associated with the East is Aries, the first sign of Spring. In the Fall, the equinoctial sign also aligns in both sets: Libra represents the West in

Time Line for Principal Philosophers Discussed

	~-2100	Divination from star placements practiced in Mesopotamia
	~-1800	Star name lists known to be compiled in Mesopotamia
	~-1646	The Great Omen Series in Mesopotamia
	-747	Dated observations of eclipses begin in Mesopotamia
Thales	b. ~-624	Correctly predicts eclipse for May 28, 585 BC
Anaximander	b. ~-610	Introduced sundial to Greece from Egypt; 4 qualities
Pythagoras	b. ~-580	Numbers have sacred relationships.
Heraclitus	b. ~-540	Fire is principle element
Empedocles	b. -490	Developed theory of the four immutable "substances"
Leucippus	b. ~-490	Introduces idea of the atom, picked up by Democritus
Hippocrates	b. ~-460	Utilized the four humors in diet
Meton	b. ~-440	19 year Metonic nodal cycle
Plato	b -427	coined the term "element"; *Timaeus*
	-410	Early horoscope constructed for 13 Jan in Mesopotamia
Eudoxus	b. ~-400	First unambiguous Greek use of the zodiac
Aristotle	b. -384	elements change when they combine; 2 qualities per element
Alexander	-336	Succeeds Phillip of Macedon & begins Eastern conquests
Aristarchus	b. ~-310	proposes heliocentric system
Aratus	~-270	"Publication" of *Phaenomena*: to poetry of constellations
Ctesbius	b. ~-250	Improves water clock to best accuracy for next 2,000 years
Hipparchus	b. ~-190	Developed precession, compiled fixed stars
Dorotheus	b. ~5-30?	*Carmen Astrologicum*
Dioscorides	b. ~20	*De materia medica*: the major source on drugs
Ptolemy	b. ~100	*Tetrabiblos* and more
Galen	b. ~130	compiles Western system of medicine

Schools of Philosophy

Aristotelianism	dates from Aristotle; circa 360 B.C.E. Retained atomism; elements could change into each other; atoms were material. His school was called the Peripatetics.
Atomism	5th Century B.C.E. Leucippus & Democritus. Physical matter is comprised of atoms, which are of infinite shapes and sizes.
Dialectics	method of teaching by question & answer; developed by Socrates, 5th Century B.C.E.
Gnosticism	The world as we know it was a mistake, created by the Demiurge. We contain sparks of the divine light, granted us by Sophia
Neoplatonism	Founded by Plotinus; flourished second to fifth Centuries C.E. Revived Plato's geometrical conception of the elements, along with a strong dose of mysticism
Platonism	Founded by Plato, 5th Century B.C.E. Ultimate reality consists of unchangeable Forms; earthly entities are unreal, and partake of the nature of the Forms or Ideals
Presocratics	Theorists of nature who lived before Socrates, principally Pythagoras, Anaximander, and Thales
Pythagoreans	Followers of Pythagoras. Flourished 4th Century B.C.E. Reality is based on Number. Number has divine nature
Skepticism	No certain knowledge can be obtained by man. Democritus.
Stoics	Founded by Zeno, 3rd Century B.C.E. The logic of the Universe cannot be changed. Thus, the chief duty is to conform to destiny. The soul is material. All physics is based on the continuum.

both systems. Of course, the Fixed and Mutable signs do not agree. In the case of North and South; Winter and Summer, we have a disagreement. Lilly gives Capricorn the South and Cancer the North.[24] The use of North for Cancer makes sense, because it is derived from the Declination of the Sun: in Summer in the Northern Hemisphere, the Sun has Northern declination Then Lilly derives the actual compass direction for the fixed and mutable signs by using a combination of the Triplicity and seasonal declination. Thus, Leo, being a Fire sign, is East with a Northern component, being of the Summer. Sagittarius is East, with a Southern component, since the Sun in Sagittarius has Southern declination.

	By Element al-Biruni,[26] Schoener, Lilly	By Season al-Biruni, Schoener, Morinus
North	Water Triplicity	Winter Signs (cold & wet)
South	Earth Triplicity	Summer Signs (hot & dry)
East	Fire Triplicity	Spring Signs (hot & wet)
West	Air Triplicity	Fall signs (cold & dry)

Thus far, Lilly is still following Ptolemy. However, the second system, the seasonal one, was based on qualities of the season. In this system, the Winter signs were given the Northern direction, because in Winter the Northern winds predominate, while in Summer the Southern winds predominated. Both systems maintain their own consistent logic, and even though Lilly favored the elemental system, he was familiar with the other system was well. Lilly may in some respects be somewhat insular, as least as far as 17th Century developments were concerned.[25] Still, Lilly was perfectly aware of the Aristotelian characterization of the Triplicities. He said, "They [the signs] are againe divided in division of the Elements, for some Signes in nature are Fiery, Hot and Dry, *viz* ♈ ♌ ♐, and these three Signes constitute the *Fiery Triplicity*...."[26] What Lilly and the other authors failed to mention was the inherent incompatibility of the two systems.

I strongly suspect that the lack of understanding of seasonality by Lilly's time was not the fault of Astrology, but a case of diluted teaching of Aristotle: what we may now designate *Aristotle Lite*. By the 17th Century, after the rediscovery of Plato, and following the shifts engendered by the Reformation, the study of Aristotle was reduced. Consequently, the major source for the theoretical underpinnings of this system was gradually disappearing from the curriculum, so it is hardly surprising if the later astrologers didn't understand the concepts.

Lilly's contemporary, Morinus, discussed the Aristotelian elements quite thoroughly in his major treatise on astrology.[27] Like his scholastic predecessors, Morinus presented his work by arguing from first principles. In practice, this means that there is virtually no astrology in the first eight "books" (actually chapters). In the ninth, in which he considers the four elements, he essentially follows the historical precedence by discussing the qualities of the elements in Section I before going into the astrology of the elements in Section II. Thus, it is clear that in Lilly's day, the full Aristotelian system was accessible *if one truly chose to look.*

But what do we make of these two systems of compass directions? Clearly, the Aristotelian elements and seasons disagree with each other. This inconsistency could develop in *any* usage of the qualities as the basis for the rulership of some entity, compass directions, or otherwise. This inconsistency in turn resulted in the need to integrate two sets of conditions: the seasonal one, and the elemental one. This was also accompanied by the adoption of the system of humors, originally developed by Hippocrates' time, into astrological usage at a later date. Thus, we have the humors:

Sanguine	hot & moist
Choleric	hot & dry
Melancholic	dry & cold
Phlegmatic	wet & cold

The humors were an extremely important concept in medical astrology, and their usage also encompassed what we may label protopsychology. The humors represented the four primary bodily fluids, whose balance was considered essential to health, and whose imbalance produced disease. Thus, we may fill out our table:

Season	Humoral Fluid	Humoral Type	
Spring	Blood	Sanguine	Wet, becoming Hot
Summer	Yellow Bile	Choleric	Hot, becoming Dry
Fall	Black Bile	Melancholic	Dry, becoming Cold
Winter	Phlegm	Phlegmatic	Cold, becoming Wet

In Hippocrates, we learn that "... humours vary in strength according to season and district; summer, for instance, produces [yellow] bile; spring, blood, and so on in each case."[28] Thus, diseases could be characterized by season because each season naturally tended to an excess of one humor. Similarly, weather which was unseasonal would produce a temporary imbalance of the humor characteristic of the "out-of-season" season (*e.g.,* "wintery" weather in Spring would result in an temporary excess of phlegm, the Winter humoral fluid), which could in turn bring on a disease.

Later, we get the characterization of temperament types or complexion. First, let's consider the organs principally associated with the humoral fluids:

Humoral Fluid	Humoral Type	Principal Organ	Qualities
Blood	Sanguine	Veins	Wet, becoming Hot
Yellow Bile	Choleric	Gall Bladder	Hot, becoming Dry
Black Bile	Melancholic	Spleen	Dry, becoming Cold
Phlegm	Plegmatic	Brain	Cold, becoming Wet

The humoral fluids formed the rest of the body. They were, so to speak, the elements of the body. Food taken in through the stomach is transferred to the liver where it is converted to the four humoral fluids, which then form the rest of the body. We have already seen that an imbalance in humoral fluids is characteristic of the diseased state.

The other function of the humors was in the characterization of temperament or complexion, the pre-scientific form of psycho-spiritual explanation of character. To quote Siraisi,

> Humoral theory is probably the single most striking example of the habitual preference in ancient, medieval, and Renaissance medicine for materialist explanations of mental and emotional states. In late antiquity and the Middle Ages, Christian, Muslim, and Jewish critics all took Galen to task for psychological materialism; they believed that the theory of temperament or complexion implied that material causes (the elements) determined the nature of the human soul and moral qualities, and they objected on philosophical or religious grounds. But complexion was often thought of as a balance of qualities rather than of substances and as only notionally perceptible to sense. From a purely psychological standpoint rather than from religious or philosophical points of view, the ascription of a role in shaping personality to specific bodily fluids is an even stronger assertion of materialism.[29]

So just what were these psychological types? Feeling a little hazy in your definition of sanguine and phlegmatic? We may add this to our table:

Air	Sanguine	Wet, becoming Hot	Sweet taste, plump, buoyant, enthusiastic
Fire	Choleric	Hot, becoming Dry	Bitter taste, irascible, impulsive, angry
Earth	Melancholic	Dry, becoming Cold	Fresh taste, sad, serious, nervous
Water	Phlegmatic	Cold, becoming Wet	Salty taste, corpulent, indolent, lethargic

Now, clearly these temperaments were conceived by sanguine types, because it certainly looks like sanguine is "good!" Before we get too turned off by this obvious case of sanguine chauvinism (is everyone else humouristically challenged?!) let us remember that the major purpose of this system was to diagnose disease.

This brings us to the great debate: allopathic versus homeopathic. The allopathic approach is to apply a dose of an antagonistic substance to cure a condition, while the homeopathic position is to apply a *small* dosage of a *like* substance in order to cure a condition. The Hippocratic–Galenic tradition preferred allopathic:

> Galen of course thought that a dry medicine was good for a moist disease, and that a compound medicine, by mixing a very cold with a slightly cold drug in varying proportions a medicine of any desired degree of coldness might be obtained.[30]

It is to Galen, by the way, that we trace the strong astrological integration in medicine. Galen wrote specifically on astrology in *Prognostication of Disease by Astrology*,[31] which included a detailed discussion of critical days in disease—a concept that dated to at least Hippocrates—with a discussion of the influence of the planets.

If we want to use the information on the temperaments, we next have to know how to calculate them—and the options are almost endless! Essentially all systems consist of variations in tallying up planets, house cusps, and points (such as Fortuna or the North Node) by element, then translating each element into its two components, then tabulating the four qualities to come up with an overall temperament type. The variations concern *which* bodies to use, and whether the points used should be weighted.

For example, we have Henry Coley:

> I. Consider what Sign possesseth the Horoscope (or Ascends at Birth) and Judge according to the Nature of that Sign, as if *Gemini* Ascend an Aireal Sign, the Native is Sanguine; if *Cancer* a Watry Sign, Phlegmatique; if *Leo* a Fiery Sign, Cholerique;

if *Virgo* an Earthy Sign, Melancholy, &c. If two Signs are concerned in the Ascendant, mix their significations.

II. You are also to consider the Lord of the Ascendant, the Planet or Planets therein, or in Aspect (partile) thereunto.

III. The *Moon*, and those planets she is in Aspect with.

IV. The Lord of the Geniture, and Sign the *Sun* is in (*viz.* the Quarter of the Year). {Author's note: notice that this one criterion uses the *seasonal* qualities rather than the strictly astrological ones.}

V. Lastly, Consider the qualities of the several Significators, and Collect their Testimonies, *viz.* Hot, Moist, Cold, Dry; and Judge according to the Major Testimonies [*The qualities of the Signs, and Planets, you will find in the first part.*]

If Heat, and Moisture Predominate, the Native is Sanguine; if Cold and Moisture, Phlegmatique; If Heat, and Dryness, Cholerique; if Cold, and Dryness, Melancholy. [*Note that if one Planet be* Almuten *of the Geniture, and Lord of the Horoscope, allow him a threefold Vertue in the Complexion of the Native, or the Moon in the Ascendant, you are to double her Testimonies.*][32]

But wait! We have a modern system that derives from precisely this system! It is found in cosmobiology, of all places! Reinhold Ebertin, in his work on health, reviewed the classical literature on the temperament types, both by Sign Element and Season. In fact, the description of the four temperaments on pages 148-151 are the best so far printed in a modern context. Ebertin modeled his system on Christiansen-Carnap's Cosmopsychological types. These are given below.[33]

Aries, Leo, Sagittarius	Tense extrovert
Taurus, Virgo, (Scorpio), Capricorn	Tense introvert
Gemini, Libra, Aquarius	Relaxed extrovert
Cancer, Pisces	Relaxed introvert

The sole exception in this table is Scorpio: "Scorpio has been placed within brackets and put with signs belonging to the Tense Introvert type in Table 15, since we do not know how it can possibly be equated with the Relaxed Introvert signs Cancer and Pisces—it lacks their tenderness and composure."

Ebertin's further discussion of these four types is directly applicable to use with the four classical temperament types, and is highly recommended. We are left, however, with Ebertin's reluctance to see anything soft about Scorpio, especially since Edith Wangeman followed this up by assigning Aquarius to the Tense category.

The system of points that Ebertin assigned were as follows:

3 points	Ascendant, MC, Sun, Moon
2 points	Mercury, Venus, Mars
1 point	Jupiter, Saturn Uranus, Neptune, Pluto, North Node

I am extremely reluctant to break patterns of symmetry. But are Ebertin and Wangeman right? I think the answer (at least to Ebertin's assignment) lies in the issue of the Seasons. This concept that is somewhat integrated into our understanding of the signs, but yet a concept that is little credited with having any particularly useful information to convey.

Until now, with the exception of the Ebertin discussion above, we have restricted ourselves to discussing the Four Elements as such. Let's now add the signs into the picture:

Air	Libra, Aquarius, Gemini	Sanguine	Wet, becoming Hot
Fire	Aries, Leo, Sagittarius	Choleric	Hot, becoming Dry
Earth	Capricorn, Taurus, Virgo	Melancholic	Dry, becoming Cold
Water	Cancer, Scorpio, Pisces	Phlegmatic	Cold, becoming Wet

In the above table, I have maintained the astrological convention of listing the signs by Quadruplicity: Cardinal, Fixed and Mutable. But let's take a different approach. In this table, there are only three signs in each hemisphere that are "pure:" that is, they have the same qualities based on element and season. Thus, in the Northern Hemisphere, we have Gemini, Leo and Pisces; in the Southern Hemisphere, Taurus, Cancer and Libra.

Sign	Element	Elemental Qualities	Seasonal: North	Seasonal: South
Aries	Fire	Hot & Dry	Hot & Wet	Cold & Dry
Taurus	Earth	Cold & Dry	Hot & Wet	Cold & Dry
Gemini	Air	Hot & Wet	Hot & Wet	Cold & Dry
Cancer	Water	Cold & Wet	Hot & Dry	Cold & Wet
Leo	Fire	Hot & Dry	Hot & Dry	Cold & Wet
Virgo	Earth	Cold & Dry	Hot & Dry	Cold & Wet
Libra	Air	Hot & Wet	Cold & Dry	Hot & Wet
Scorpio	Water	Cold & Wet	Cold & Dry	Hot & Wet
Sagittarius	Fire	Hot & Dry	Cold & Dry	Hot & Wet
Capricorn	Earth	Cold & Dry	Cold & Wet	Hot & Dry
Aquarius	Air	Hot & Wet	Cold & Wet	Hot & Dry
Pisces	Water	Cold & Wet	Cold & Wet	Hot & Dry

Notice that if Season really *is* the significant factor that the Greeks believed it to be, we have a real hypothesis to test about the difference between Northern and Southern Hemisphere expression of the signs. It is not the *Element* that changes, but the *Season*. Perhaps some of our Aussie and Kiwi astro-buddies can help us by observing whether they detect differences in the expression of the signs Down Under, versus in the Northern Hemisphere. Notice also the solution to the Ebertin issue: Scorpio in the Northern Hemisphere belongs to the Fall, which is Cold and Dry, *precisely* the assignment of Tense Extrovert by season that Ebertin assigned!

There is already some interesting confirmation for the importance of the seasonal component. Beverly Fodor has found a correlation between the assignment of people to Jung's four psychological types and the season of birth. This in turn is strong evidence for the seasonal nature of the qualities. At any rate, if we examine this table further, some of the "difficulties" with the elemental assignations become clearer. Let's consider these by Element.

The Fire Signs: In the Northern Hemisphere, Sagittarius is the lowest energy of the three (the reverse is true in the Southern Hemisphere), because Sagittarius has a cold component, while the other two don't. Aries, on the other hand, is wetter than the other two signs. What does this mean? Remember that one of the fundamental characteristics of wet thinking is that it is either amorphous, or tolerant of ambiguity. Among other things, *this makes Aries less dogmatic than either Leo or Sagittarius.* Leo and Sagittarius are both interested in category distinctions, so both are much more status-conscious than Aries. In the Southern Hemisphere, this should reverse, making Aries more dogmatic than Leo and Sagittarius.

The Air Signs: The social butterfly quality of Gemini fits exactly with the nature of hot and wet: an enthusiastic (hot) person floating from person to person (wet). Libra, on the other hand, has a *real* balancing act, having *all four qualities* to express. Aquarius is "colder" than we expect for an air sign, being Wintery. Any questions?

The Earth Signs: Taurus is "warmer" than we expect, and "wetter," making Taurus a much more social sign than we would expect for Earth. Isn't it interesting that the two Venus-ruled signs each have components of all four qualities? Does the magnetism of Venus require that one be capable of being all things to all people? Virgo is also warmer, which is to say higher energy. It takes a lot of energy to be perfect! (Just kidding–maybe!) Capricorn, on the other hand, is wetter. What does this mean? Capricorn has the reputation for bringing order (dry) to others (wet).

The Water Signs: Cancer (in the Northern Hemisphere) is the third sign that has all the qualities represented, illustrating perhaps the lunar quality of changeability. Pisces is the ultimate water, the ultimate ocean. Scorpio, on the other hand, has the mixture of wet and dry, the same relative components as Capricorn. (And look how many people lump Scorpios and Capricorns together, especially in negative ways). Wet and dry: to create connections, or to break them? Both possibilities exist here. This is, in one sense, a dangerous combination. If we think of the concept of emotionally "cold-blooded," and then add to that the ability to make or break a situation, you have the ingredients for ruthlessness.

If we move back up the ladder to the Four Elements and Four Qualities, let us recall the basic lesson of this Chapter. The Qualities and Elements had essentially been worked out in Greek philosophy before Astrology really came onto the Greek stage. Astrology found a ready-made theoretical framework: a model for personality and biology that deepened Astrology, and gave medical practitioners a system for measuring qualities which in turn provided a key to understanding and treating illness. A symbiosis was created between medicine and astrology, one that was broken when medicine rejected the Humoral Paradigm in the 17th Century. Astrology has yet to face up fully to this break, and to either heal it, or pass beyond it.

In Chapter 5 we will examine how the elements became embedded into one of the most important components of a classical delineation: the essential dignities.

Endnotes

1   *op. cit., Hippocrates IV*, Aphorisms 1.

2   *op. cit.*, Potter (1), page xi.

3   *e.g.*, "At or just before the dog-star, purging is troublesome," from *Hippocrates IV*, Aphorisms 4-V. The reference is to the time of year, not the quality of Sirius. Tester's statement that "The earliest clear references to Babylonian astrology in Greek are in the Hippocratic medical work *On Diets* of about 400 B.C.E." (page 15) in fact makes sense only when one recalls that astrology and astronomy were not distinguished until about 700 C.E. Jones (1, p 68) noted that Spring was generally associated with the acronychal rising of Arcturus in February, Summer with the heliacal rising of the Pleiades, Autumn with the heliacal rising of Arcturus, and Winter with the setting of the Pleiades.

4   W.H.S. Jones (1), page 6, referring to this, made the statement, "...by the end of the fifth century, philosophy had discarded medicine, although to its great loss medicine did not discard philosophy."

5   *Ibid.*, page 7.

6   *Hippocrates IV*, page 45.

7   *Ibid.*, page 47.

8   *Ibid.*, page 53.

9   *Ibid.*, page 47.

10   In fact, our modern idea has a Greek origin as well. Aristotle, writing in *On Coming-to- be and Passing Away*, changed the original concept of the separate qualities, as he explored the deeper meaning of hot - "active" and cold - "passive." He said "... for the more the differences of material signify 'a this,' the more it is a real

thing, whereas the more they signify a privation, the more unreal it is. For example, 'hot' is a positive predication and a 'form,' while 'cold' is privation, and Earth and Fire are distinguished from one another by these differences." (page 195). This is most definitely *not* the position of Hippocrates, who was less concerned with the intellectual ramifications of "active" and "passive," and more concerned with diet and regimen.

[11] *op. cit.*, p 231.

[12] Rob Hand. 1994. The Four Qualities and the Four Elements. Lecture given at NCGR Conference, "Back to the Future," Aug 1994 in Princeton, NJ.

[13] We shall present a further refinement of this table in Chapter 6.

[14] *op. cit.*, Bouché-Leclercq, pp 8-10.

[15] *Ibid.*, pp 11-13.

[16] Note, for example, that Galen's work is translated as *On the Natural Faculties*. The alternate translation given in Brick for "Faculty" is "Powers," which is actually much closer to the original meaning. "Powers" shows the dynamism that Galen intended much more clearly.

[17] *op. cit.*, Lindberg, pp. 48-49

[18] *op. cit., Hippocrates IV*, Regimen, I. XXXIII.

[19] for example, Boorstein.

[20] On this and many other points where references to Rob Hand's work is concerned, giving an exact reference is sometimes difficult. Rob's principal work at this stage is in the editorial production of all the Project Hindsight publications. He has not yet obtained the leisure to write systematically on these subjects, and we don't *want* him to have this leisure yet, because that would mean that the translation phase would have stopped! In addition, because Rob and I speak together at several conferences per year, plus serving together on the Board of Directors of the National Council for Geocosmic Research, we engage in an ongoing dialog about many of these matters, and most of it is not in print. Therefore, I apologize to the reader for not always being able to point to a specific source, and I apologize to Rob in case I have unwittingly codified a remark that he has subsequently transmuted in his own thinking.

[21] This point was made outside of astrology by Sambursky (1959), page 3. However, what is fascinating is that in Sambursky's survey on the Stoics, there is no indication that they themselves actually worked with their one quality - one element system exclusively, because later practitioners maintained Aristotle's classification system in its totality.

[22] While this may shift in the future, Robert Schmidt has reported that the earliest instance he can find in the astrological literature of an attribution of air as being cold (a Stoic attribution) dates to Valens. Reported during Hand's lecture "Astrology: The Four Qualities and the Four Elements" at the NCGR "Back to the Future" Conference, August 1994, Princeton, NJ.

[23] al-Biruni, p 211.

[24] Lilly, *CA*, page 204.

[25] Discussing Lilly's contributions is problematic, not the least because of his subsequent vital importance to horary astrologers. One may speculate that his Puritan religious scruples may have prevented him from becoming too conversant with the alchemists. This latter point is significant because the alchemists, and the alchemically oriented astrologers, developed the theory of elements to a much greater degree than astrology did alone.

[26] Lilly, *CA*, page 87.

[27] *Op. cit.*, XI, Chapter 7.

[28] *Hippocrates IV*, page 89.

[29] Siraisi, p 106.

[30] Thorndike, Volume I, page 140.

[31] *Ibid.*, pp 178-179.

[32] Coley, pp 534-535, square brackets [ ] contain Coley's comments; { } are mine.

[33] Ebertin, page 152.

—— Chapter Four ——
Historical Context:
From the Fall of Rome to the End of the Renaissance

"Do you want to have a powerful memory for what is good? Then take care to learn the reason behind what has to be learnt. For reason is the indissoluble bond between truth and memory. This is perhaps why our Plato said that what has been well understood can never be entirely forgotten."
Marsilio Ficino[1]

In the last two Chapters, I discussed some concepts from Babylonian and Greek astrology, showing how our geocentric frame of reference affected the nature of the kinds of sky observations that were possible, and the nature of the phenomena that were considered remarkable. The Greeks added a method of characterizing the individual based on seasonal and other systems.

In this chapter I will take up some of the technological considerations necessary for the promulgation of astrological technique, and give some background into the kinds of methodologies practiced by Classical astrologers.

When Astrology re-entered the West about five centuries after the Fall of Rome, there were two lines of transmission of astrological knowledge. Both involved the Arabs. In the first guise, the Arabs saved Greek literature from the trash heap by preserving it while Europe slept the sleep of the illiterate. Secondly, the Arabs elaborated on the Greek system that they learned. This elaboration included the integration of Vedic astrological material, including calculational methods and lunar mansions.

While Vedic methods provided the Arabs with new insights, the largest shadow cast from Greek astrological literature was the shadow cast by Ptolemy. As we have seen, Claudius Ptolemy wrote several works in the 2nd Century A.D., including the *Tetrabiblos*. It was ultimately translated into Latin under the name *Quadripartitum*. Ptolemy's work had such a profound impact that most of the rest of the Greek material was unjustly ignored. Ptolemy was influential in two ways. The *Quadripartitum* was required reading for all Western scholars. And Ptolemy's methods were studied by the Arabs, then passed back to the West through their techniques. There was also the addition of the *Centiloquium*, or hundred aphorisms, attributed to Ptolemy, but almost certainly by a later author.

Ptolemy's mundane work involved eclipses and lunations. He attributed countries to broad latitudinal bands that were then given to particular signs. It was part of a larger system called *climata* that pretty much everybody these days ignores. What is perhaps ironic is that our modern system of using founding charts of cities and countries was known: but mainly ignored. Plutarch (approximately 46–119 B.C.E.) in his work *Parallel Lives* described the work of the astrologer Tarrutius, who was asked to come up with a chart for Romulus, the founder of Rome. According to Thorndike, "He further estimated that Rome was founded by [Romulus] on the ninth day of the month Phamuthi between the second and third hour. "For," adds Plutarch, "they think that the fortunes of cities are also controlled by the hour of their genesis."[2] This technique was mostly ignored for centuries, finally emerging from obscurity through the 17th Century work of Andreas Goldmayer of Nürnberg.

As we proceed into the so-called Dark Ages, the Medieval Arabs and Jews became the keepers of the flame. Their knowledge was brought back to Europe especially through the Moorish invasion of Spain in 1237 A.D. Some works were known earlier, such as the translation of the astronomical tables of al-Khawārizmī by the Briton Adelard of Bath in or around 1126. The "Arabs" employed major conjunctions in their mundane work and brought in concepts like the Lunar Mansions. They introduced the *Hyleg* and related points. The use of Arabic Astrology was controversial because of its theological overtones: in other words, to the Christian world, Arabs were heathens!

Let us also set the stage by considering the technology available to Astrology as it existed: because astrological technology affects astrological practice. Clocks, when available, were accurate only to within about 10 minutes per day. In other words, the closest a clock with a Foliot balance (the standard mechanism through the mid–1600s), could come to approximating local mean time was within 10 minutes per day. A clock not reset for two days could lose or gain 20 minutes! This kind of technology, which was used in all the town cathedrals of Europe as well as in city clocks, just did not have the kind of accuracy that we have today. Neither did timing candles, first introduced in England in 870. These were calibrated to burn at a particular rate—if there was no draft, of course! Today we argue over seconds of arc and rounding errors of one minute, but some of our ancestors would have been ecstatic to get within one degree.

In Greek and Roman times, the clocks of record were either sundials or water clocks. Sundials could be quite accurate, but were obviously only of use on sunny days. Water clocks were principally adapted to the measure of short periods of time. One of their common uses was the restriction of the length of lawyers' speeches!

So, even if a clock was available, the time was not necessarily accurate. When this level of inaccuracy is built into your time-keeping system, it will affect your astrology. It was not common for people, even those with a fair degree of wealth, to have a timed birth chart. Because of the difficulties with timed charts, rectification was common and necessary.

Horary methods were often used in preference to natal because of the difficulty with timed charts. There is no unequivocal reference to horary in Ptolemy, but Dorotheus of Sidon, working in the first Century A.D. (i.e., before Ptolemy), wrote about horary.

Ephemerides were based on tables prepared from the Arabic period on. Among the earliest tables were those of al-Khawārizmī Later the Alphonsine Tables, Toledan Tables, Rudolphine Tables, and Eichstadian Tables (used by Lilly) were recomputed for various different locations, such as London or Pisa.[3] Vincent Wing, a student of Lilly, produced more accurate tables in the 1650s. None of these were as accurate as our modern tables: aspects such as Mars-Saturn conjunctions, or planetary stations, could be off by days.[4]

Longitude cannot be accurately measured in the absence of accurate timing devices. Now you might be aware, from a seafaring standpoint, that Prince Henry the Navigator of Portugal was offering a prize for an accurate way to compute longitude at sea. Relative longitudes were known on land. Ptolemy in his *Geography* had discussed the issues involved with projecting the spherical Earth onto flat maps. He had worked out the projection for longitude and latitude, so that all maps could be correlated with each other. This ptolemaic work (in Greek) was brought from Constantinople to Florence in 1400.[5] Shortly, copies were translated into Latin and became generally available.

Navigation required the magnetic compass for locating position, a development that occurred in China by 1000 C.E., although its use in

China was more common for *Feng Shui* than for navigation. The compass was not mentioned in European writings until the 12th Century. The compass pointed to North. No matter how useful this was, there was just the suspicion that this was an instrument of Satan, even as late as Columbus' time.

Even if the navigators could determine their direction, distance was a problem. An accurate measure for the circumference of the Earth was not known, and the circumference (or diameter) is necessary in order to compute the distance equivalent of a degree of either longitude or latitude. This problem was solved on a crude empirical basis by Vespucci: the bottleneck was that any measurement of distance traveled required accurate time pieces which were simply not available. In astrology, house cusps could be calculated to modern accuracy, if the time given is taken as accurate.

As we progress through to the Renaissance, certain technical improvements become evident. Calculations improved as algebra and trigonometry advanced. The calculation of Directions changed as the astronomy and mathematics improved. Logarithms (1619) improved calculational facility. And for the average Astrologer, the improved math meant better ephemerides and tables. With the invention of printing, the tables and ephemerides became more accessible, almanacs including ephemerides became best sellers, and books of genitures became popular references. Interestingly, in both Italy and Germany, astrological and other prophecies of doom became the major best sellers during the first century of printing![6]

Astrology was not merely omnipresent because of astrological practitioners. Everywhere the educated person looked, Astrology or astrological symbolism could be seen. Town clocks often showed the Sun sign, Moon sign, and Ascendant sign as well as the hour and minute. Astrological symbolism was found in art. Astrological anecdotes were to be found in literature and philosophy, whether *The Canterbury Tales*, Aquinas, or the Classical literature. This was a period when most people believed in divination. Until about the 1530s, divination was completely accepted in all sectors, high and low, scholarly and popular. How much different it would to be to practice Astrology in a culture where the ability to divine the future was taken as natural!

To begin our Medieval survey: Johannes(?) Campanus (1232?–1296) of Novara (in Lombardy) was Chaplain to Popes Urban IV, Nicholas IV, and Boniface VIII. Although given a great deal of lip service, his *Theorica planetarum* was never published in his lifetime. (It is more available today, and in English no less!) Campanus' name has come down to us because a house system is named after him. While he did write down the equations for the house system that bears his name, he did not originate it. (This is also true for other house systems: the Regiomontanus system existed long before Regiomontanus, for example.) Campanus also published on Euclid's *Elements*, the calendar, the astrolabe, planetary tables, general astrology, and medicine. His planetary work simplified the number of epicycles necessary to calculate planetary positions.[7]

In the next century we encounter John of Eschenden. Writing in 1345, he predicted the Black Plague of 1348 from the Eclipse of 1345, which occurred just two days before the conjunction of Mars and Saturn. The Mars-Saturn conjunction was second in popularity only to the Jupiter-Saturn conjunction for mundane prediction. But of course, the Mars-Saturn was usually bad by definition, so predicting the plague off the Mars-Saturn would only come naturally! Eshendon only practiced mundane because he was not disposed toward other branches of Astrology. This begins to introduce a theme.

Writing a bit later in the same century, we find the great Medieval critic of Astrology, Oresme (died 1382). His major work was the *Livre de Diviancions* (1361). This was noteworthy from a literary standpoint because Oresme chose to write in French, not Latin, in order to appeal to the masses. Like Eschenden, he criticized electional, horary, and natal; but retained astro-meteorology, mundane, & medical. He dedicated the work to Charles V (The Wise; 1364–1380) of France; yet Charles may have had as many as six Astrologers in his service: Pierre de Valois, Gervais Chrestien, André de Sully, Pèlerin de Prusse, Domenico de Chirvasso, Yves de Saint-Branchier and Thomas de Pisan!

Table One. A brief(?) Chronology.

476	End of the Western Roman Empire
	Proclus (d. 485) becomes head of Platonic Academy at Athens
529	Justinian closes the School of Philosophy in Athens
537	Perhaps *The* Arthur of Britain killed in Battle of Camlan
625	Mohammed begins dictating the *Koran*
730	The Venerable Bede's *Historia ecclesiastica gentis Anglorum*
760	*Book of Kells* written
762–815	Productive period of Masha'Allah
771–814	Reign of Charlemagne. Became Holy Roman Emperor in 800.
810	Muhammed ibn Musa al Chwarazmi coins the word "algebra"
circa 850	Al-Kindi; author of *On the Stellar Rays*
846	Arabs sack Rome
987–996	Reign of Hugh Capet, founder of French Capetian Dynasty
1000	*Beowulf*
1040	Duncan murdered by Macbeth. Macbeth reigns until 1057.
1050	Astrolabes arrive in Europe

1054	Permanent separation of Eastern and Western Christian Churches
1066	Conquest of England by William of Normandy
1080	Toledan tables
1092–1167	Abraham Ibn Ezra
1170	Thomas à Becket murdered
1260–1327	Meister Eckhart
1273	Thomas Aquinus: *Summa theologica*
circa 1282	Guido Bonatti's *Liber Astronomiae*
1309–1377	Babylonian Captivity of the Papacy
1314	Jacques de Molay, Knights Templar Grand Master, burned at stake
1337	Beginning of Hundred Year's War
1348–1350	The Black Death
1378–1417	The Great Schism
1382	John Wycliff translates *Vulgate* (Latin Bible) into English
1387	Chaucer's *Canterbury Tales*
1409	Council of Pisa, called to end Great Schism
1415	Battle of Agincourt (Henry V)
1429	Joan of Arc raises the siege of Orleans
1431	Joan of Arc burned at the stake
1440	Platonic Academy founded in Florence
1453	Fall of Constantinople
	First Gutenberg Bible printed
1455–1485	Wars of the Roses
1473	Sistine Chapel built
1486–1535	Heinrich Cornelius Agrippa
1489	Ficino's *Liber de Vita*
1492	Columbus discovers the Bahamas; Isabelle expels the Jews from Spain
1493–1541	Paracelsus
1498	Savanarola burned at the stake
1501–1576	Jerome Cardan
1503–1566	Nostradamus
1509–1547	Reign of Henry VIII
1517	Luther nails up his Theses
1519–1556	Reign of Charles V, Holy Roman Emperor
1520	Jesuit Order founded.
	Luther excommunicated.
	Act of Supremacy passed by Henry VIII
1531–1535	Pizarro conquers Peru.
1536	Johann Schoener's *Tabulae Astronomicae*
1545–1563	Council of Trent reforms Catholic Church
1547	Jerome Cardan's *Libelli Quinque*
	Nostradamus' first predictions published
1558	Claude Dariot's *L'Introduction au jugement des Astres*
1558–1603	reign of Elizabeth I

1571–1630	Johannes Kepler
1572	St. Batholomew's Day massacre
1582	Gregorian calendar introduced
1588	Drake destroys Spanish Armada
1590	First Shakespearean plays
1601	Kepler becomes astronomer/astrologer for Emperor Rudolf II
1602–1681	William Lilly
1619	Harvey announces his discovery of blood circulation
1625–1649	Reign of Charles I
1647	William Lilly's *Christian Astrology*
1648	Treaty of Westphalia
1661	Morin's *Astrologica Gallica*

We also have a female astrologer of this period: Tiphaine (Épiphanie) Raguenel, who acquired quite a reputation. She was the wife of Bertrand du Guesclin, a soldier famous in the service of the Duke of Brittany and Constable of France under Charles V. Guesclin was not limited in his astrological circle to his wife. Simon de Phares mentioned Yves de Saint-Branchier, an astrologer to Bertrand Du Guesclin, who specialized in "that part of electional astrology for picking and choosing the appropriate date to go to war against one's enemies, or to postpone it."[8] This, of course, was also a theme worked over by other astrologers such as Guido Bonatti. Among other things, part of the game was to provoke the enemy at a time when the Malefics were impacting the nativities of the enemy leaders.

The major news event of this portion of the later Middle Ages was The Plague. The magnitude of the problem was not anticipated by Astrologers, but they were called upon to render Judgment on its explanation. Jacques Angeli in his *Treatise on Comets* discussed the aspects for 1385. There was a "triple conjunction" (meaning a series of double conjunctions within a short period of time) of Jupiter-Saturn (26° Gemini on 11 April O.S.), Mars-Saturn (4° Cancer on 11 June O.S.), and Mars-Jupiter (12° Cancer on 28 June O.S.). This was following the comet of 1382. The Triple Conjunction of all the then-known superiors was considered a major event. The presence of Mars near Jupiter and Saturn at the time of a Jupiter-Saturn conjunction made that conjunction—the major big one—even bigger in magnitude. The idea of a triple conjunction was considered a major event, so the presence of the comet during that period of time was considered even more so. But that was the official explanation.

In about 1478, an astrological history of the kings of France was published that focused on Jupiter-Saturn configurations. The two major dynastic changes were attributed to these major conjunctions. The

Capetian dynasty began in 987 with a Jupiter-Saturn conjunction in 988 at 29° Sagittarius, the last of the series of Jupiter-Saturn conjunctions in the Fire element. The Valois dynasty began in 1328 with Philip VI, following the Jupiter-Saturn conjunction of 1325 at 17° Gemini, in the middle of a mixed series of Jupiter-Saturn conjunctions between the Air and Water elements.

In Germany, the Imperial Astrologer to Frederick III was Johannes Lichtenberger. He issued a prediction based on the Grand Conjunction of 25 November 1484 that followed a solar eclipse in Leo that in the next twenty years, there would be a false prophet, and a lesser prophet, a master at the art of interpreting the Scriptures. Luther saw himself as the lesser prophet, and wrote a preface to Lichtenberger. (Luther's own involvement in astrology may have been negligible, but his colleague and successor Philip Melanchthon was very engaged. As a result, we have recorded times for several critical events in the early history of Lutheranism.) The Catholic hierarchy saw Luther as the false prophet. That issue aside, Lichtenberger lifted many of his predictions from Paul of Middelburg, whom we will encounter again shortly.

In 1492, Columbus discovered the Bahamas, with the help of a copy of Regiomontanus' ephemerides. Lest we think that he brought it along only for navigational reasons, we may consider the following story from several years later. Columbus knew enough about Astrology to ask Governor Orando of Santo Domingo to protect his ships in port, because Columbus believed that an aspect between Mercury and Jupiter presaged a tempest. Orando did not take the warning seriously, and lost twenty vessels to a tropical storm.

And speaking of explorers, "In 1519, Magellan planned to circumnavigate the globe with five vessels. He asked the Astrologer Ruy Faleiro to become a party to it. Faleiro did not want to join the voyage. He had seen in the horary chart that the astrologer/astronomer in charge of the expedition would lose his life. The astronomer Andrea de San Martino who accompanied Magellan was massacred with him by the Philippine natives."[9]

Simon de Phares (1440–1495) was in the service of John, Duke of Bourbon. After receiving a visit from Charles VIII, he was banned from practicing in Lyons. Simon moved to Paris, where his case against the Archbishop of Lyons was taken up by the Parlement of Paris in 1491. The faculty selected eleven of Simon's books to be burned (mostly written by those nasty Infidels, the Arabs), and in 1494 the Parlement turned Simon over to the Inquisition, though this was probably a political move, inspired by their desire to show their autonomy from The Crown. Apparently pardoned by Charles VIII, he published *A Collection of the Most Celebrated Astrologers* in 1498.

Shortly thereafter, Pope Alexander VI made the Astrologer Paul of Middelburg a bishop, in which capacity he participated not only in the Lateran Council of 1512–1517, but also in calendar reform. (Paul had successfully predicted the career and downfall of Savonarola as a false prophet in Florence, and was credited by Thomas Montis with predicting the advent of an outbreak of syphilis from the Jupiter-Saturn conjunction of 1484.)

As we proceed through our astrological survey, we cannot neglect the times. The same Charles VIII who was trying to protect Simon de Phares was also invading Italy in his spare time, beginning in 1494. The meddling of the French and the Germans in Italian affairs throughout the Renaissance threw the Italians into cultural shock. Partly, this manifested through an upsurge in interest in divination and prediction. Italy became frenzied ground for all occult practices, including Astrology, that claimed to predict the future. This included a large number of cheap, popular books of prophesy, written in Italian verse, not Latin. These works were often attributed to physician/astrologers, religious saints, or holy people. Interestingly, those that wished to introduce a certain level of snob appeal often included the word *iuditio* (judicial) in the title, thereby invoking the imprimatur of Astrology. The shoddiness of the product was such that, given the novelty of the printing press at this time (it had just come into use in 1453), we could literally label this one of the first instances of "pulp" literature. The overwhelming nature of public interest probably contributed to the subsequent rapid decline of these practices when the other shoe dropped in the next century.

As we continue our survey, the big issue in the early 1500s was the massive number of conjunctions in Pisces in 1524. Was this a Biblical size flood, or merely a wet year? At least 56 commentaries on this period exist from prior to that year, beginning in 1499 with the publication of the *Ephemerides* of Johann Stöffler of Justingen (1452–1531). (Thorndike erroneously listed the first reference as being from 1503). To quote Niccoli:

> "Johann Stöffler ... predicted that, due to multiple planetary conjunctions that year in the sign of Pisces, a large number of catastrophes would take place in 1524. As has been observed, the quarrel soon took a nonprofessional turn and involved not only astrologers but also physicians, theologians, and philosophers, all of whom would of course have encountered astrology during the course of their university studies."[10]

Niccoli discussed the massive effects that this debate—both scholarly and popular—had on people in general. She mentioned one point worth considering: in Italy, the words for "flood" and "deluge" were often interchanged. This may seem trivial, but the amount of deforestation that had occurred from 1450 to 1550 produced an unusual amount of flooding during this period. She also emphasized that Stöffler had not restricted his prediction to floods: that was added later as the discussion focused on the meaning of Pisces. Later on, more was added about flooding, the extreme being Tommaso Giannotti, the personal Astrologer to Count Guido Rangoni, himself an astrological fanatic. Giannotti claimed that the configuration of 1524 in Pisces exactly matched the configuration for Noah's flood, except that in Noah's case, it was in Aquarius. Unlike many scholars, Thorndike admitted that it was a wet year.[11] However, he commented:

> Four main features may be discerned in the literature connected with the conjunction of 1524: first, the perennial tendency to predict great ills from such conjunctions; second, a more recent tendency to decry the stress laid by Arabic astrologers upon such conjunctions and to revert to the Ptolemaic emphasis upon eclipses; third, the separate question of the possibility of a second deluge..., with its moral and theological as well as astrological and meteorological interest; fourth, a number of personal controversies and literary duels between persons who were often rival astrologers than defender and opponent of the art. For although the question of a flood might seem to give theologians or other opponents of astrology an opening for attacks on the art, it was rather disagreement among the astrologers themselves that especially marked the outburst of writings on the subject.[12]

Thorndike felt that the most significant result from his survey of the literature for the conjunction of 1524 was the extent of the disagreement among the astrologers, as well as the extent to which they engaged in self-criticism. The theologians supported astrological prediction completely. Furthermore, Arabic methods seemed more important than those of Ptolemy.[13] Did this period result in a devaluation of the major conjunctions, coupled with a return to the Ptolemaic tendency to use eclipses and lunations in mundane? Table 2 is a non-statistical list that I made simply by tallying up references as I ran across them, mostly in Thorndike, of which astrologer preferred which technique.

It does seem that there were more prominent astrologers of the day who were using grand conjunctions than those using eclipses. So this became one of the issues that was re-evaluated following the 1524 debacle because this was one of the most extreme examples of conjunction, at least in living memory.

Thorndike restricted his discussion of this astrological configuration to meteorology. Niccoli also cited references that one of the major foci of discussions was theological. This conjunction fell just after Luther diced things up with his split from the Catholic Church in 1517. Therefore, the theological discussion revolved around whether these conjunctions meant that Luther was a Prophet (after all, Pisces ruled Christianity as well). Whether the writer was Catholic or Protestant, there was no question about there being a deluge at this time! Perhaps this is why there was so little retribution toward Astrologers when 1524 finished without a flood the size of Noah's.

While Thorndike did not detect problems for Astrology and Astrologers as a result of the predictions related to 1524, this may have been optimistic. Niccoli related that one of the principal reactions of the populace in Italy as the presumptive flood date in February 1524 approached, was a carnival-like satirical atmosphere, mocking both Astrologers and the representatives of papal authority who hired them. Anti-astrology satire became a way to protest against the nobility, and to promote democracy. There were also rumblings of Savonarola's tract against Astrology. Thus, although Paul of Middelburg may have predicted his downfall, Savonarola may have had the last laugh.

Table 2. Astrologers Publishing on Eclipses & Grand Conjunctions 1400–1500.

Eclipses	Grand Conjunctions	
Nicole des Plains	Thomas Brown	Johann Lichtenberger
Pietro de Monte Alcino	Jean de Marende	Jean Collemain
Giovanni de Fundis	Pierre d'Ailly	Jérôme Torrella
Arnould des Marais	Jean de Bruges	Conrad Heingarter
Jean de Glogau	Nicola Carlo	Matteo Moreti
Baldino de Baldinis	Gilles de Charpeaux	Joseph Gruenpeck
Johann Lichtenberger	Antonio de Camera	Jacques Loste
	Aegidius de Wissekerke	

The year 1524 did not pass without event, however. In Germany, there was a major Peasants' Revolt that Luther condemned. However, Luther inadvertently exacerbated the situation, because Lutheranism was, after all, an expression of a State Church apart from Rome, hence inspirational to German patriots. Germany at this time was ruled by the Spanish Habsburg Emperor Charles V, and resentment of this foreigner contributed to the revolt. As we have seen, Astrology was not unrepresented in the Lutheran rebellion. Philip Melanchthon, Luther's lieutenant, was heavily involved in astrology, and Johannes Schoener was a personal friend.

On the other side of the Holy Roman Empire, Charles V was invading portions of France. And the Swiss Cantons were dividing up and fighting each other over Catholicism versus Calvinism and Zwingalism.

There were also problems brewing on other fronts. The Sorbonne had an oath requiring all faculty members to always consider the Faith as primary above philosophical or other "truths." In other words, if theological doctrine conflicted with any other idea or theory, doctrine must always be accepted. The opposition of the Sorbonne to astrology (for theologically purist reasons) meant that the teaching of all mathematical disciplines in Paris was much more primitive than in other places. The only practitioners of mathematical arts were not Parisian natives. This was commented upon by Philip Melanchthon (1549) and others.

Among the other notable Astrologers of this period was Henry Cornelius Agrippa (1486–1535). He was one of the most famous philosophers of the Occult in general. He served as Astrologer to Francis I of France, but was fired for predicting unfavorable events. He, like Cardan and many others, contributed to the Doctrine of Signatures, the idea that things which reassembled each other were linked. In Astrology, the major use for this idea is in assigning *natural* rulerships, i.e., rulerships of things, such as birch trees or malachite.

Nostradamus (Michel de Notre Dame, 1503–1566) was certainly the most famous French Astrologer. He served (as a physician, of course) Henry II, Catherine de' Médicis, and Charles IX. We should note that his prophesies may have been more accurate than his contemporaries. But he did not invent the art, the style, or the method. Prophesy was an accepted part of life.

Jerome Cardan (1501–1576) was a physician, astrologer, mathematician, chiromancer, gambler, and generally irascible person. As a physician—and certainly one of the foremost of his day—he had the misfortune to be born just slightly too early to have benefited from the advances of Vesalius and Harvey. As a result, his medical methods fell rapidly into obscurity. Cardan also ran afoul of the Inquisition, but the causes were complex. It was not his use of Astrology *per se* that was problematic. It was his publication of the chart of Jesus Christ, along with some less than discreet comments about the Dominicans, that got him arrested and imprisoned in 1570 for heresy. Of course, it did not hurt that the new pope, Pius V, was not only a zealot but a former Dominican! It is also noteworthy from our perspective that Cardan stepped back from some of the natal techniques in use during his time. This was specifically because he felt that his chart showed that he should have died in his forties though he lived to his seventies. Also he had not foreseen his own son's execution from the boy's chart. This tracks rather well with the most serious modern criticism of Classical European techniques: the focus on times and methods of death.

And what of the great thinkers of the day? One of the major currents of the day was Humanism. Foremost among the Humanists was Erasmus, whose *Praise of Folly* was one of the most scathing critiques of the day. Humanism was a refuge for thinking Catholics in the midst of the Protestant upheaval. One of Erasmus' more noteworthy colleagues was Sir Thomas More. Thorndike had this to say:

> Erasmus often ridiculed superstition in his writings but did not always maintain a like attitude in practice. He wrote Mosellanus in 1519 that the bitter dissension at the University of Louvain between the adherents of the old and new learning must be either due to a conspiracy or to fate. 'I have consulted a number of astrologers,' he continued, 'men illustrious in their profession. They refer the cause of the evil to last year's eclipse. This occurred, unless I am mistaken, in Aries. Aries moreover pertains to the head. Furthermore Mercury is vitiated of the influence of Saturn. Hence this evil most potently affects those who are under Mercury, among whom they number the inhabitants of Louvain.' Erasmus thus seems to have consulted the astrologers in all seriousness, although he also thought he detected a conspiracy.[14]

And then there was Copernicus. Published in full in 1543, *De revolutionibus* was eagerly awaited by many. Copernicus was loathe to publish in full, mainly because of the icy reception he had received to his preliminary work. It is interesting that its publication was preceded by extensive correspondence. One of the publicists was Rheticus, whose *Narratio prima* (1539) took up the astrological implications of the theory! To Rheticus, the heliocentric theory freed the planets from the "fixed" sphere of the stars, which meant that there was now a way to deal with longer ages through cycles! And it was mainly through the offices of astrologers that the work was finally published.

Collin Wilson quoted Luther as saying of Copernicus: "People give ear to an upstart astrologer who strove to show that the earth revolves, and not the heavens..."[15] It was truly more difficult for the Heliocentric system to run the theological gamut than the astrological one. Galileo, in replying to one of his disciples, P. Dini, stated that heliocentricism made no difference to Astrology.

Copernicus had written personal notes to himself in his copy of Ptolemy's *Quadripartitum* and he also owned works of the Arabic astrologer Albohazen Haly. His astrological speculations concerning the heliocentric system followed concepts attributed to Hermes Trismegistis.

While we think of Copernicus as firing the major blow—the one that crushed the Ptolemaic world view—his was not the major astronomical innovation of the 16th Century which impinged on astrology. That distinction went to the Nova of 1572, the "new star." This had deep philosophical as well as theological implications. These included: first, that the heavens were not eternal and incorruptible; and second, that God's creative work had not ceased on the seventh day. The learned community of the 16th century knew the work of the Greek Hipparchus, and thus, the heliocentric theory. *Nothing* prepared them for change in the *Primum mobile*. Tycho Brahe not only observed *De nova stella*, he speculated on whether it should be treated astrologically like a comet. Then it disappeared from view in 1574. Tycho speculated that while it was composed of celestial material, it was less perfect than the fixed stars, and this accounted for its short life span among them. Could the theologians breathe a sigh of relief? The appearance of a bright comet in 1577 brought speculation back to more comfortable topics. The main theory of comets remained Aristotle's: that they were terrestrial exhalations or vapors. The open question was whether they caused the calamities, or were a sign of the calamities. Tycho discussed one astrological aspect: at the time, not only were comets used for divination (that is, the appearance of the comet could be interpreted astrologically), but the converse was also true. Particular astrological conditions might *result* in the appearance of a comet. Tycho challenged the later hypothesis.

The later part of the 16th Century was marked by attempts to systematize and improve the art. One example of "clean-up" was the discussion of "critical days." Critical days were used in medical astrology to predict the course of illness, and had been discussed as early as Hippocrates (5th Century B.C.E.). They had been discussed in detail by Galen on the basis of a medicinal month of 26 days, 22 hours.

An influential introductory manual to horary and electional Astrology was written by Claude Dariot (1530 or 1533–1594), a French physician of the Calvinist persuasion as well as a student of Paracelsus. His book was originally published in Latin, and then rapidly translated into French and English. The English version was a major source for William Lilly in the next century.

And speaking of England, which we hardly have, there was comparatively little astrological activity in England during the first part of the Renaissance, because Astrology was not taught in the universities. As we have noted, there were Astrologers Royal. Things got much more interesting in the second half of the 16th Century, with the activities of Leonard Digges and John Dee.

It is worth emphasizing that then, as now, the Astrologer of the day was generally not exclusively an Astrologer. Astrology was generally combined with medicine as a career. While it was not unheard of, most of the prominent Astrologers were employed as something else, with Astrology being a significant adjunct to one's other professional work.

Meanwhile, back at the Catholic Reformation, Pope Paul IV in 1559 added those books of judicial astrology which predicted future events to the *Index*, *i.e.*, those works banned by the Catholic Church. The works of four astrologers were specifically condemned. The Spanish *Index* of 1559 added Cardan's commentary of the *Quadripartitum*. Cardan was arrested by the Inquisition in 1570–1571, about half the time being spent under house arrest. Sixtus V issued a bull against judicial astrology in 1586. Astrology used for navigation, agriculture, or medicine was specifically exempted. Astrological activity, both through the university faculties and the publication of annual predictions, declined markedly in Italy as a result. However, its enforcement was lax in Spain, and even more lenient in France.

It is interesting that the critics of astrology, who became more numerous as the 16th Century progressed, mainly objected to one of three things: (1) the implications of astrology as far as free will was concerned, (2) bad predictions published by astrologers, and (3) the very idea that the future could be predicted. The decline of Astrology corresponded to the decline of prophesy in general as the political situation in Italy became, if not more stable, at least less pestilential. We see every indication of a prophesy fad which ran from about 1480 to 1530 in Italy, corresponding to increased political chaos. Astrology got caught up in the fad as part of its intellectual justification, but then got tarred by its brush when the fad subsided. Astrology took the blame for much of the excess carried on in its name. The remaining blame went to women, a traditional scapegoat.

It is evident that during this period of decline, at least on the Continent, the blows against Astrology were not coming from the scientific community, as we are now misled to believe. It is also interesting that weather prediction and medical astrology were often exempted from criticism. This is almost the same situation that we encountered two centuries earlier, as part of the theological worry of the time that other forms of Astrology impinged too much on free will, and thus, redemption or damnation. Thus, we may conclude that it was primarily for *theological* reasons that Astrology declined on the continent of Europe.

We finally come to one of the things that is unfortunately necessary to understand about the astrology of this period: the need for modern translation of the *English* texts. While 17th Century English *looks* like modern English, it is really midway between modern English and Shakespearean English. This means that unless you understand French you don't always get the right meaning because you pick the wrong cognate. For instance, when Lilly or other 17th century sources use the word "judge," the word they mean is "predict," which is much clearer in the French.

One of the other unusual things we can find from perusing Lilly is the use of a constellational zodiac. In *An easy and familiar method whereby to judge the effects of the Eclipses, Either of the Sun or the Moon*, which was published in 1652, Lilly used a constellational zodiac. It was not a sidereal zodiac because he used uneven divisions of the constellations: that is basically the difference. The first section of the work was a rehash of Ptolemy's predictive method for eclipses. The second part is a cookbook section that explains how to delineate an eclipse in each of the twelve signs, as well as in each of the 36 decanates.

Lilly's younger contemporaries included Nicholas Culpeper, who wrote the most famous herbal to date, which is still in print over three centuries later. Culpeper also wrote on the diagnosis of illness. Lilly's semi-official successor and adopted son was Henry Coley, a urine caster. In addition to writing one of the clearer 17th Century expositions on astrology called *Clavis Astrologiae*, he also shared translation duties with Lilly in "Englishing" Bonatti's aphorisms, while Lilly translated about one quarter of the aphorisms of Cardan. England was well-represented by astrological physicians, with works by Richard Saunders, William Salmon, and Joseph Blagrave.

William Ramesey compiled the most significant English treatise on electional: *Astrologia Restaurata; or Astrology Restored* (1653), which also contained material about other aspects of astrology as well.

On the Continent at this time were two remarkable astrologers. Placido Titi (1603 –1668), just one year younger than Lilly, became an ascetic monk, and began a personal "Back to Ptolemy" movement. In the process, he invented a new house system which he believed expressed Ptolemy more accurately than the Regiomontanus system, the most popular in his time. He explained this system in *Tabulae Primi Mobilis*, first published in 1657.

And herein lies the tale, which I partially told in a previous work.[16] By the 17th Century, Europe had polarized into two camps: Catholic and Protestant. In addition, Latin, the former standard language for all intellectual work, was being replaced by the vernacular. Now we know that Lilly and many of his contemporaries still knew Latin. However, the major effect on Lilly's generation was the trauma known as the

English Civil War. England had survived Bloody Mary and an abortive attempt at returning to Catholicism. In the meantime, the Puritans and the Scottish Presbyterians had risen to criticize the Church of England in not going far enough in ecclesiastical reform. The conflict shook the country and toppled a king, and Lilly was right there, reading charts to determine the veracity of war news, and charting the onset of military campaigns and battles.

Given this surfeit of "interesting times" (in the sense of the Chinese curse), it is hardly surprising that many English turned away from the Continent. By the 17th Century, Catholic and Protestant sources on the Continent were at least reading each other. In England, the hostility to things "Papist" was still especially strong. This appears to have truncated the flow of other sources into England. Thus, we have the interesting paradox that Lilly was, on the one hand, quite conversant in Arabic sources, yet he was relatively isolated from the Continental astrology of his time. Lilly's bourgeois education meant that he was also unaware of the advent of Platonic philosophy which was first injected by Ficino.

It was left to the next generation of astrologers, who included John Gadbury (1627–1692), John Partridge (1644–1715), John Bishop, and Richard Edlin, to look South again. This meant that they were also confronted with a major new French force in Astrology, Jean-Baptiste Morin.

Morin (1583–1650), or Morinus in Latin, was another physician, in this case, with royal connections. His work of thirty years, the *Astrologia Gallica*, was published posthumously in 1661. Morin was both a systematizer and a simplifier. Perhaps taking a page from his friend Descartes, he attempted to place Astrology on a more intellectually defensible footing. He engaged in the typical Medieval practice of arguing from first principles, and began his work with God. As he neared the astrological material in Book 9, he presented a full discussion of the elements. He simplified the Essential Dignities by dropping Term and Face (see Chapter Five for information about these dignities). He shifted the interpretation of planetary meaning toward the modern synthesis by emphasizing aspect patterns and house placement (as opposed to house rulership, which was the principle classical consideration). While Lilly was blissfully ignorant of this rationalizing attempt by Morin, his successors were helped by one of Lilly's contemporaries, a partisan of the opposite side of the English Civil War, Sir George Wharton. While Lilly was a Puritan Roundhead, Wharton was a Catholic Loyalist Cavalier. While the Cavaliers were not *necessarily* Catholic, they were certainly more sympathetic to that position than many of the extremist Roundheads. Thus, it is hardly surprising that Wharton became the first translator of Morin. We have already seen how Wharton and Lilly crossed swords in print. The other side of the coin is that Wharton saved Gadbury from a charge of treason.

Morin's work was known and cited by John Bishop and John Partridge in their books. Further, Partridge introduced Placidian house cusps into the English astrological world. The result, as I indicated in *Essential Dignities*, was the popular adoption of the Placidus House System. When Raphael I popularized Astrology again in the 19th Century, after close to a century of little publishing activity, it was Partridge that he chose as the "greatest" English Astrologer. It was Raphael's adoption of the Placidean House System from Partridge which resulted in its popularity today.

Morin was to Continental Astrology what Partridge was to British. In 1902 Henri Selva published *La Theorie des Determinations Astrologiques de Morin de Villefranche conduisant une méthode rationelle pur l'Interpretation du Thême Astrologique*, in which he brought back Morin's methods. These were picked up immediately in France by authors such as Juveno and Paul Choisnard, and the encyclopedist Henri Gouchon. Morin's methods continue to be taught in France today. In addition, Morin's techniques were introduced to the German-speaking world by Fritz Schwickert ("Sinbad") and Adolf Weiss through their monumental five volume 1925–1927 edition of *Baumsteine der Astrologie*. The first volume of this work was translated into English in 1972, with a direct translation of the 21st Book of Morin appearing in English in 1974. The English translation never became popular. However, in 1939 Adolf Weiss moved to South America, and translated a portion of *Baumsteine* into Spanish, and that volume, *Astrologia Racional* remains the cornerstone of serious Astrology in the Spanish-speaking world. The other reference cementing French and Spanish Astrology is that the standard reference work in both languages, Henri Gouchon's *Dictionnaire astrologique*.

But I digress... From roughly 800–1650, astrology was everywhere, and the basic controversies of the period were technical ones, as well as the theological question of fate versus free will. Any controversies were *not* waged over whether natal, electional, and horary were valid, but whether they were *sinful*. Medical, mundane and weather forecasting were not questioned. Other ancillary interests included the making of astrological talismans, an area that overlapped with magic and alchemy. This later phenomenon, because of its linkage to magic, was often the cause for Church sanction against a practitioner. It also was one of the obvious points of intersection with alchemy, which was usually viewed with considerable suspicion by the Church, but practiced widely by the more hermetically inclined.

The religious backlash against Astrology occurred in the Catholic retrenchment following the advent of Lutheranism and Calvinism. The intrinsic fatalism implied by astrological prediction was anathema to the concept of free will. Free will was necessary in turn for true repentance and salvation. So major branches of astrology were summarily banned. Accordingly, it disappears from the universities in Italy, Spain, and France as a result of papal decree and not as a result of critique by scientists. For example, Louis XIV banned astrological calendars and almanacs in 1682, and not as a result of "scientific" pressure!

In Germany, at the beginning of the 18th Century, the President of the Academy of Berlin was still making astrological forecasts as part of his Observatory duties, and treatises on the affects of astrology on weather and human character were appearing into the 1720s.[17] The problem here was that, as academic support tailed off, the brand of astrology remaining was the popular Madame Zelda variety that we still endure. Obviously, that was not exactly going to reestablish the prestige of astrology!

I think you can make a far better case for the ultimate decline of Astrology at the end of the Renaissance as being religious repression rather than scientific. If you actually follow the literature of the day, one of the great English rejoinders to the critics of astrology was Sir Christopher Heyden's *A Defense of Judicial Astrology* (1610). He was mainly responding to the fate/free will issue as posited by John Chamber in his *Treatise against Judicial Astrology* (1601). This was essentially the same critique that had been leveled at astrologers several centuries prior. That was still the critical debate that was going on during the period astrology began to decline.

Virtually all the founders of the Royal Society in England were practicing alchemists, astrologers, or other of the fellow travelers. However, they decided to divorce their occult interests from the scientific ones they would pursue through the Royal Society. The following generations forgot the distinction, and occult interest was obliterated entirely.

Endnotes

[1] Letter 105, Volume 1, page 129.

[2] Thorndike, Volume 1, page 209. Actually, the practice is much older. Cramer refers to the consultation by Seleucus Nicanor (321-281 B.C.E.) with the Chaldean astrologers about electing a time for the founding of Seleuceia. The story goes that the Chaldeans, not wishing to see Seleuceia eclipsing Babylon in importance, deliberately chose the wrong time. However, the workmen started work early, thereby giving the city the "right" time - and the city Babylon was indeed eclipsed! (Page 11).

[3] Raymond Mercier's contribution in C. Burnett's book explains the pedigrees of these various tables, and the details of their origin and calculation.

[4] This irony is reflected in a clash between William Lilly and George Wharton that is preserved in *Christian Astrology*. In the horary that begins on page 219, "If I should purchase Master B. his houses?" Lilly suddenly departs from his delineation by interjecting, "yet was I no Taylor or Scrivener, as *Wharton* affirmes, or indeed any profession at all; nor was my Master a Taylor, or my Wife a Scriveners Widdow." What? The reference was to an attack by Wharton: "Whereby you see that *Lilly* is as bad a Taylor, as he is Astronomer, that could mend his Clothes no better; the truth is, he was not born to be a Workman." Why this interchange? This all concerned Wharton's charge that Lilly was sloppy in his Almanac in the calculation of the House cusps for the Mars-Saturn conjunction. In examining the two consecutive Mars-Saturn conjunctions given by Wharton, for 1646 and 1648, I found Wharton's house cusps to agree to modern calculation to within a minute or two on each cusp. However, the 1646 conjunction was 13 hours off, while the 1648 one was off by 12 hours and 2° of the ecliptic! Two degrees can change the Essential Dignities known as Term and the Face of the planets, and thus the Almutens (see Chapter 5), so this is *not* a trivial difference.

[5] op. cit., Boorstin.

[6] op. cit., Barnes and Niccoli.

[7] Epicycles were a series of circles which were used to describe planetary movement. Because of the influence of the Pythagoreans, it was believed that Planets, being perfect, could only move in circles, the perfect figure. We know today that planetary orbits are elliptical; the expression of these ellipses as circles made computation difficult at best. The mathematics of planetary movement was much more challenging in the Middle Ages: besides, in the absence of calculational aids, the calculation of planetary positions by the use of multiple circles for each planet was imposing at best.

[8] translation Lehman.

[9] Knappish, page 205, Lehman translation.

[10] Niccoli, page 140.

[11] Thorndike *V*:231.

[12] *Ibid. V*: page 180.

[13] *Ibid. V*: page 233.

[14] Thorndike *V*: pp 176-177.

[15] Wilson, page 146.

[16] Lehman (1).

[17] *op. cit.*, Knappish, pp 243-244.

—— Chapter 4 ½ ——
Historical Interlude:
The Cyclic New Ages

For man has in his nature a desire to seek the ends; and he
often finds preliminaries tedious and refuses to engage in
them. Know, however, that if an end could be achieved with-
out the preliminaries that precede it, the latter would not be
preliminaries, but pure distractions and futilities.
Maimonides, *Guide to the Perplexed*[1]

The New Age isn't new. We are arguably in at least the Fifth Wave of it. This Interlude is not necessary to the understanding of the rest of this book. However, because the New Age phenomenon has often woven astrological threads into its web, many astrologers will find this information to be an interesting counterpoint.

First, I'm going to let the cat out of the bag. The first modern New Age began in the 18th Century. It was a "fellow traveler"[2] with the Romantic Period in literature. Let's first explore the prerequisites for a New Age, then go back and pick up our thread from the Middle Ages and follow it through time.

As we will see, leftist New Age Periods are strongly sympathetic to Astrology, while conservative New Age Periods are antagonistic. Accordingly, we can follow the trail for what happened to Astrology in the 18th Century in part by shifting where we look for the trail.

What constitutes a "New Age?" A New Age is actually a discrete intellectual period, one which repeats at somewhat irregular intervals. It is a curious amalgam that only appears within societies dominated by a monotheistic religion. Its components include:

    1. A flirtation with Paganism, or at least another religious tradi-
       tion. The moral turpitudes of one's fellow co-religionists be-
       come a source of righteous indignation. The institution, not
       particular practitioners, are blamed for this phenomenon. Early

root religions, whether Neoplatonic, Gnostic, Druid, Wiccan, or simply matriarchal, are "rediscovered," often in a form which only resembles the original in tentative ways.

2. Rediscovery of Eastern religions. Hinduism, Buddhism, Jainism, Islam, or Shintoism are seen as better paths to enlightenment or realization than the Western Tradition. Forget about the fact that many practitioners of these religions are just as dissolute!

3. The revival of magic and divinatory practices. The hunger for meaning must be fulfilled, and it's much easier to lay Tarot spreads than to spend 15 years sitting *Zazen*, or to engage in the process of self-evolution presented by the alchemical path. The forms of magic, astrology, and alchemy are eagerly sought, but often the real content is lacking because practitioners want a quick fix.

4. The invention of lineages. In the midst of the genuine transmission of techniques from generation to generation, pseudo-credentials are invented, often utilizing the same power points from New Age to New Age, like the Great Temple of Luxor.

5. Belief in the esoteric unity of all religions in the case of leftist New Ages. The worship of the Stars as divine is often believed to be a nearly universal primitive religious state. As religion becomes more complex, the shift is to show that all true mystical experience is nonsectarian. Rightist New Ages believe in the damnation of all other religions.

6. A leftist New Age springs from the mouth of political radicalism, and then becomes a place of refuge in the ensuing period of conservatism. A rightist New Age is the expression of political conservatism translated into religious righteousness.

There are a number of different periods that match these criteria. Before a New Age could occur, several other pre-requisites are necessary:

1. The dominant religion had to develop to a certain level of decadence. A New Age movement is inconceivable in a period in which a high level of piety is observed by a large portion of the institutional hierarchy.

2. Enough historical and/or cross-cultural information needs to be available for possible adherents to a different tradition to have something to work with in order to create their idealized version of the "new" religion.

3. A certain level of education is needed in order for the potential converts to have access to the new material at all.

4. A certain level of political and/or economic stability is necessary. When conditions are *truly* bad, either repressive measures or apocalyptic prophecy are the likely results. A New Age requires a level of leisure to produce.
5. A new technology or twist helps. Whether the advent of mesmerism or delta-wave training cassettes, it is helpful to have an explanation for why this "new" knowledge is becoming available now.
6. A "new" old manuscript or two is helpful, whether it is really new or not. Otherwise, a good conspiracy theory will do just fine.
7. An apocalyptic message is frequent, but not absolutely necessary. Either the World will end in our lifetime, or shortly thereafter. Such a significant change in consciousness is about to happen that the new people might just as well be considered a new species.

The Middle Ages had plenty of heresies and at least one New Age. The New Age in question was Jewish: the period of the development of the Kabbalah in the 13th Century. What was significant about this development of Crown Theology was that it represented a fundamentally different way of viewing God. Interestingly, the "new" old manuscript in this case is the *Zohar*, thought to have been written by the 13th Century Spaniard Moses de Leon.[3] This more mystical approach removed Yahweh even further from the sense of personal God that he represented to earlier Jews. It placed the mystic in a position to experience, through meditation and other exercises, communion with God's glory, if not God Him- (Her- or It-)self.

It would be a mistake to call all mysticism New Age, or all New Age practitioners mystics. It probably *would* be correct to assert that most New Age people are open to mysticism, because it is generally the essence of New Age to be open to the more emotional aspects of the religious experience. In the case of Kabbalah the earlier period of development mentioned above probably constitutes a true New Age, while the later period in 15th Century Spain does not. The reason for the later exclusion is that the second period was unquestionably mystical, but the Jewish community by this time was experiencing fierce anti-Semitism, and thus was not stable enough for a true New Age period. It is worth reflecting that in times of community duress and upheaval, mystical approaches to the divine are often extremely popular, presumably because the real world is too hideous to contemplate. However, the uncertainty of the world out there during these periods tends to produce a literature strong on consolation and prophesy (which includes finger-pointing: see *Isaiah* and *Lamentations* for early examples), and weak on community building.

Islam also had its New Age in almost the same time period, through the flowering of Sufi mysticism. Sufism was known in Islam within a century of the Prophet's death. In this period, a form of piety developed that was based on asceticism and strict adherence to the *Koran*.[4] While this period resulted in massive conversion to Islam in great part because of the success of their military conquests, asceticism was an individual matter. Although many of these ascetics were revered as true holy men and women, the fact remained that Islamic asceticism, like Christian asceticism, does not appeal to the masses when times are good. (In bad times, asceticism may be practiced because there is no economic choice, and then it might as well be pious as well as necessary!)

By the 13th Century, Islam was well established, times were good, and a great flowering of Sufism could occur. One of the great exponents of this Age was the poet Rumi, whose doctrine of love remains inspiring to many people beyond the borders of Islam and Sufism.[5] This Islamic New Age seemingly lacked the apocalyptic spirit so indicative of the Christian New Ages. By locating the site of ecstatic awareness in each individual, the Sufis were not dependent upon what went on in the outside world.

Until this same period Western Christianity was insufficiently developed to produce much beyond the usual heresies. These heresies generally involved either Gnostic themes, or questions concerning the nature of the Trinity. The Eastern Church cleverly avoided these issues by declaring the nature of the Trinity to be a Great Mystery. In the West, Inquiring minds wanted to Know. Christianity had still not reached its peak in terms of the understanding of the esoteric experience, and the exploration of the mortification of the body for the purification of the soul. These developments awaited the full flowering of the mendicant orders and mystical geniuses like Meister Eckehart (1260? - 1327).

It was *after* the flowering of Christian mysticism that we see the beginning of New Age periods in Christianity. The first period probably occurred in the 13th Century as well. During this time, we see the likes of Eckehart building on the previous mysticism of Augustine, Hildegard von Bingen (1098-1179) and Joachim of Fiore (1135? - 1201), and the flowering of the Beguines and the Beghards, not to mention the Waldenses. Prior to this time, individuals such as Hildegard spoke and wrote ecstatically, but as long as they retained obedience to Mother Church and Father Hierarchy, they were tolerated, even extolled. Both Hildegard and Eckehart were members of holy orders.

What developed in the 13th Century was twofold. First, the Beguines and Beghards represented mass movements highly critical to the wealth of the Church. Secondly, Joachim had taught that there were three Ages of Man. The first, the Age of God the Father, ended with the birth of Jesus. The second, ruled by the Son, would end in 1260, while the third, ruled by the Holy Ghost, would bring utopia to Earth before the Final Coming.[6] It was further prophesied that the Advent of the Age of the Holy Spirit would be preceded by a time of troubles and corruption, which would be cleansed before the New Order appeared.

Please notice that it was not mysticism *itself* that brought on the New Age. Rather, mystical or ecstatic experience became one of the *expectations* of the New Age practitioners.

Then we have the next wave in the generation of Luther (1483-1546). Martin Luther began his path by criticizing the Church, without the intent of creating a new one. Once the blow was struck, a number of other denominations appeared. Politically, it is clear why Protestantism succeeded. It allowed kings and princes to secede from the temporal and financial power of the Church. However, the initial appearance of this secession was not what we now imagine. The Princes of the day were *not* interested in freedom of conscience. They were interested in universal membership in a Church whose hierarchy ended with the sovereign. This is the key to understanding all the religious massacres that took place in the following century. Even if it was possible to imagine a church hierarchy without the Pope, it was impossible to separate an individual from his(!) community and church. The church and the community were *completely* intertwined. Thus, to adhere to a different religion was tantamount to treason. It took more than a century of bloodbaths to (mostly) settle the issue of religious tolerance, at least to the point of transcending the treason issue—except for the Jews, of course! And this level of uneasy tolerance was necessary for development of alternate religious pathways, including, ultimately, secularism.

Luther himself believed that the world was in its last days. Luther was a man at least as obsessed by the devil as by God.[7] His apocalypticism was at least in part responsible for his brash, angry style. It was the final trumpet call before Doom!

As we saw in Chapter Four, France invaded Italy, beginning in 1494, resulting in a flood of apocalyptic literature to explain the catastrophe.[8] At almost the same time Luther was challenging the hierarchy, the de' Medicis in Florence were casting wide the gates to Classical Learning through their Platonic Academy, the translations of Marsilio Ficino, and through their patronage of the arts. We shall examine Ficino in some detail in Chapter Twelve, but for now, suffice it to say that

Ficino and the rest of the Humanist movement brought back a significant portion of the Greco-Roman corpus of literature. This, in turn, presented religious as well as other alternatives.

It was left for the Enlightenment to return to the New Age. In the 18th Century, Astrology was declining or at least going underground— *precisely* when new archeological and cultural knowledge was flooding the European Continent. By this time, in the wake of scientism, Deism had become a popular intellectual position. Imagine the impact of the early information on Hinduism and Buddhism that was coming back through the Dutch and British East India Companies! Meanwhile, the sons of England who had escaped military service in America were flocking to Italy on their Grand Tours and discovering the very decadence that had so offended Luther 250 years before. The difference being, of course, that when you're rich, secular, and young, decadence can be very appealing! Part of this decadence came from, of all things, archeological digs. They were digging up pagan erotic art! Here was all this nudity, not to mention enlarged penises, and yet the quality of execution was superb! This was *Art*, not pornography. And what did this say for the paucity of the Christian imagination?

Meanwhile, artifacts acquired by traders in the East were making their way to the West, often with only fragmentary information about their context. Thus, this generation of French *philosophes* and English gentry began to formulate the myth of the World Religion. Symbols like the bull and the egg were interpreted as having the same meaning worldwide, and examples seemed to be turning up everywhere.[9] And during this period of time, Thomas Taylor was creating English translations of the Neoplatonists, thereby making this material accessible to the English audience.[10]

By now, the brew has sex, creation, mystery, titillation, paganism... how about some astrology mixed in? It was only a few short steps to add the stars as objects of veneration, then mix in a solar cult, and *Voilà!* The New Age has appeared! And yes, there were Rosicrucians!

What happened to the rest of the 18th Century? Toward the end of the 17th Century there was all this activity: Morin's and Placido's revisions, Saunders' and Culpeper's medical, Lilly's and Coley's horary, and Ramesey's electional. The answer appears to be that the 18th Century *may* not have been as different from the 17th Century as it might have appeared. Patrick Curry has documented portions of this period in 18th Century England. There is *no* question that the 18th Century represented a decline in the fortunes of astrology. How could it compare with the notoriety of Lilly's prediction of the Fire of London, or the broadsides during the English Civil War? But decline is not synonymous with disappearance. There was certainly enough left for Goethe (1749-1832) to study it passionately, and write quite competently on it when he chose.[11]

Throughout the 18th Century, almanacs containing astrological placements continued to be published and purchased, especially *Old Moore's Almanack*, begun originally by Francis Moore in 1699. Robert Zoller has unearthed evidence for a flourishing industry of dockside astrology in the Colonies: variants on the "Ship at Sea" horary, or electional astrology for when a ship should sail.[12] Presumably, the same activity was taking place at European ports, whether Southhampton, or Rotterdam.

We have at least two English astrological authors from the 18th Century: Ebinezer Sibly (1751-1799) and John Worsdale (1766-1826).

Sibley's astrology occasionally makes one wince because he was not a brilliant student of the Art. He was a physician, and a dabbler in a number of the occult arts. He is known today mainly as the author of a derived chart for the United States. The importance of this chart has been unduly emphasized. It was thought, since he was a contemporary of the American Revolution, he might somehow be privy to information about its actual time of inception. There is no evidence that he was. He simply derived the time by directing a standard mundane chart for the period.

Sibly's work was first published in 1790, and had gone through eleven editions before the posthumous one in 1817. I have examined several editions and found no differences between them. Now, clearly, *some people* had to be buying this work, which was equivalent in size to Morinus' tome, to go through twelve editions! It may also not be irrelevant that Raphael I included much the same mixture of Astrology and the occult arts that Sibly produced. Of course, this dating of this New Age to roughly the 1780s puts Sibly right in the middle, but his path seems separate. According to Godwin, Sibly's background was from Calvinism to Swedenborgian Christianity. Thus, while it may well have been New Agers who were buying his work, Sibly was more of a conventional astrologer with an interest in herbalism as befitted his medical background. Then, as now, not all Astrology was New Age.

John Worsdale was the younger of the two, and he had strong words to say about his senior. Writing in the 1820s, before his death, he said:

> ... yet all those who are Students in this department of Astronomy, ought to know that there are several works, which if adhered to, will constantly mislead them in all their operations and judgment. The Authors of the works I allude to, are Gadbury, Coley, Parker, White and Sibly. These pirates have dishonoured this predictive science by the fallacious innovations, and notorious

prevarications which pollute their pages; they have multiplied the most flagrant errors in directional motion and judgment, which ought to have been deposited in the confines of oblivion, for it is plain ... that they were deficient in Astronomical calculations....

The Works of Mr. William Lilly on Horary questions, and on the subsequent mutations of the World, are interesting and of considerable importance to all genuine students in this celestial science, and though the Author was unacquainted with the true method of directional motion in Nativities, and the correct division of the Heavens by duplicate horary times, yet he certainly was the greatest professor of the Mundane, and Horary departments of this science, that ever wrote in the English language.... The works of Mr. John Partridge, and Mr. William Lilly, are of more value than all the others that have been published in this Kingdom; but if the industrious Students are disposed to purchase the works of other Authors, which are altogether a confused heap of rubbish, they are at liberty to do so, as Booksellers may always be found, who will be very ready and willing to supply their customers with works on Nativities, at enormous prices, if the deluded purchasers think it proper to dispose of their cash for articles that are of no use, or value whatsoever.[13]

Ah, sarcasm, a truly declining art form! Worsdale's earliest work on natal was published in 1796. Much of Worsdale's objection to Sibly was Sibly's occult dabblings. Worsdale was pure astrologer with more than a bit of scientific bent, much like Zadkiel or Paul Choisnard in later generations. Worsdale's astrology gave a typical Medieval reading to the chart, complete with emphasis on predicting the year of death!

In addition, we find the first astrological magazine appearing in London in 1791 through the offices of William Gilbert, a talisman-maker. The *Conjurer's Magazine* contained a mixture of magical and occult arts of a more extreme nature than Sibly's rather tame occultism. As early as this time, we see the curious juxtaposition of interest in all fields of the occult: Natural Magic, Kabbalah, Hermetic Astrology, and "scientific" astrology. Sound familiar?

This Enlightenment New Age owed a great deal to the change in philosophical currents which had occurred in the 18th Century. Jean-Jacques Rousseau (1712-1778) provided a source of inspiration to Neo-pagans and Romantics alike. He invented the Noble Savage. Here was the radical position that Natural Man was innocent, not plagued by original sin. Gone were the hierarchies of Civilization.[14] The simple life of poverty was better. Rousseau borrowed liberally from accounts pouring in from the New World about the bravery and morality of the

Native Americans. These were often in contrast to the behavior of the Europeans who presumed to convert them to The One True Church, whichever one it happened to be. Here was the confrontation of Christian society with Something Completely Different and it took a great deal of hubris to believe that Christianity was turning out morally superior types. (Of course many settlers, such as the Puritans, were capable of a great deal of hubris!)

This contrast of civilization and tribal living provided a profound moral justification for any social movement that moved away from conventional Christianity. Furthermore, to the degree that the Noble Savages of the Americas could be projected back into the European past, this moral questioning broke down the myth that Progress is inevitable and good. Now, it became possible to look *backward* for inspiration. The focus was not on the earlier church fathers, but upon whole systems of thought which had been left behind. Earlier philosophies and religions could be valued more highly for having less of the dust of civilization clinging to the seams. That this echoed the ancient Greek belief in the (departed) Golden Age is all the more ironic!

This, in fact, is one of the ironies of a New Age period: while trumpeting New, these periods are actually immersed in a retrospective influx of ideas from a romanticized Past. These ideas were captured in the fiction and poetry of Romantic authors such as Scott, Keats, Shelley, and Byron. In general, the Romantics were favorable to astrology.

So how long did this New Age last? Despite our modern belief that such movements tend to follow fashions or fads, the Enlightenment New Age ran from about 1780-1835. This is hardly a fad! From an astrological standpoint, *Old Moore's Almanac* had a print order for 393,750 copies in 1803! *Vox Stellarum* reached a peak in 1839, with 560,000 copies, but *Vox* was not publishing astrological predictions. It was recycling past predictions on a random basis.[15]

It is clear that the New Age philosophy is sufficiently compelling that, once converted to it, the adherent tends to stick with it for life. The decline in the 1830s and into the 1840s was less because people stopped "believing" in it. There was simply little "public" activity going on.

The Spiritualist New Age began 31 March 1848 in Hydesville, NY, with the advent of "Modern Spiritualism" as the Fox sisters responded to rapping sounds heard in their cottage. This period marked the popularization of the technology of the séance as a method of communicating with the dead. In France, the technology was called the "celestial telegraph," a method for invoking communication with the dead via somnambulists. The other technology which was exploited in this phase was the scrying crystal. This Spiritualist Wave was consolidated in 1875 with the founding of the Theosophical Society.

We can understand a little more about this Wave by examining a chart for the time of the response of the Fox sisters to the rapping sounds. We see in this chart a striking stellium of 5th House Pisces planets, beginning with a very satisfying Moon-Neptune conjunction! This 5th House focus clearly illustrates the extent to which the Spiritualist "technologies" became a parlor game or entertainment. Jupiter exalted in Cancer in the 9th House does show a genuine spiritual interest and desire. The tight trine of Venus and Jupiter (and Cancer on the M.C.) shows the exceptional involvement of women in this wave, the first time that women attained such a prominent position in New Age circles. (The Enlightenment Wave was typically male-dominated.) With Mars in Gemini also in the 9th House, we might anticipate quarreling and fragmentation over differences in ideas. That Mars was also square Saturn suggests some hostility to authority. Venus ruled the 8th House: Venus conjunct Mercury thus becomes communication with the Dead!

And what of the interregnum in the 1830s and 1840s? There was a secret society called the "Orphic Circle" which ultimately merges into the forming of the Hermetic Order of the Golden Dawn in 1888.[16] As we have already seen, almanacs continued to sell well during this period. Thus, the period between New Ages was not so much marked by decline as by private study by adherents, with occasional savage public attacks. Some of Zadkiel's work, such as his *Grammar of Astrology* (1834), came out during this period. W.J. Simmonite began publishing an astrometeorological calendar in 1839. When the Spiritualist Wave emerged into the public eye, some of the emphasis had shifted. Some new players were added, but much of the *status quo* remained the same. In Germany, astrology was studied openly. Gustav Theodor Fechner could write on the connections between astral influence and a "superior omnipresent conscience."[17]

This interregnum in New Ages marked a shift in the Second Rightist New Age in America. Rightist New Ages? The first Rightist New Age in America was the coming of the Pilgrims! The Puritans who came to this country had "purified" their religion through the crucible of Calvinism. It had one critical element which, interestingly, Calvin himself had considered trivial: the belief in Predestination. Thus, salvation was for the "Elect."[18] Consider the criteria for a New Age:

1. A flirtation with another religious tradition. The Puritans were indignant about the Church of England, which they considered corrupt in its "papist" tendencies.

2. Rediscovery of Eastern religions. The Eastern religion in this case was a rabid strain of Old Testament Judaism which they applied with a vengeance. Ever notice all the "Jeremiahs" and other Old Testament names that these people gave their children? Unfortunately, this appreciation for the Old Testament didn't lead to an appreciation for the Jews!

3. The revival of magic and divinatory practices. Remember the Salem witch trials? In our modern parlance the Puritans "projected" their fears about witchcraft into mass hysteria which may simply have been nothing more than food poisoning by the ergot fungus in bread.

4. The invention of lineages. The Fundamentalist New Ages only cared for those lineages given in the *Old Testament*. All of a sudden, children were given unpronounceable names like Jeremiah and Jebediah.

5. Rightist New Ages believe in the damnation of all other religions. How could God elect any but the truly God-fearing members of *my* church?!

6. A rightist New Age is the expression of political conservatism translated into religious righteousness. Political conservatism in this case springs from the belief that the world is about to end anyway, so why worry about institutions?

The second Fundamentalist New Age occurred around 1800 with the preaching of James McGready. It is billed by its protagonists as the second "Great Awakening." It began in the South. In 1829 Charles Grandison Finney came to New York to institute the northern revival. Finney was responsible for inventing much of the style and sermon content that would still be recognized in gospel preachers today.

As the Civil War approached, this Second Fundamentalist New Age splintered over slavery. But 1859 marked a critical occurrence: the publication of Charles Darwin's *Origin of Species*. This work was to bedevil Fundamentalists for years because it was a direct frontal assault on their precious belief in biblical literalism. This was also being challenged by primarily German biblical exegetes, who were demonstrating that the Gospels could not possibly have been written by their purported authors.

After the Civil War, Fundamentalism saw its next wave through the preaching and work of Dwight Lyman Moody. In about 1867 he became an advocate of dispensationalist premillennialism. Say what? This idea holds that Christ will return to rescue the Faithful. They will be caught up bodily in the "rapture" prior to the End of the World, which presumably will be soon. Moody was the originator of the style of "family entertainment" which mixed music and other show biz with gospel preaching and conversion. Moody's work was carried on by the former pro baseball player, Billy Sunday, who packed in the crowds. His peak year was 1917. Billy Graham's crusades would mark the next wave of Fundamentalist New Age.[19]

As we can see, the leftist New Ages are positive toward astrology, while the Fundamentalist versions are negative. And as we can also see, both kinds of New Ages can be occurring simultaneously.

But let us return to the Spiritualist New Age which began in 1848. The next major wave of astrological publications—such as Zadkiel's abridgment of Lilly and Christopher Cooke's A Plea for Urania—resumed in 1850. However, the people involved, like Zadkiel, were active in the earlier Enlightenment Wave. This Spiritualist New Age was heavily overshadowed by the Theosophical Society and various Masonic and Pseudo-Masonic groups.

In Astrology, several trends emerged. First, we see the beginnings of a genuine style of metaphysical astrology that resulted from the astrological involvement of occult types such as Bailey and Weston. In the past, metaphysicians used astrological symbols in their rituals, and to understand the workings of their art. Thus, the astrological theory of the elements was integrated into alchemy as part of the procedure for learning the art, as well as for picking appropriate times and substances for their work.

Now, however, astrology was *modified* to reflect certain metaphysical concepts. For example, the occultists invented a number of hypothetical planets, in part because that was in vogue in astronomy,[20] but also because of the perception that some metaphysical issues had not been addressed by the known planets. Thus, we have the beginnings of the so-called esoteric rulerships and the seven rays.

The next trend was the continuance and flowering of "scientific" astrology. John Worsdale had spoken in favor of a more scientifically-based astrology. But what did that mean? At first, it primarily meant astrology for its own sake with as few occult trappings as possible. However, as the 19th Century progressed, so did the development of statistical methods. Scientific astrology began to have a statistical component. Paul Choisnard was one of the early practitioners of this in France. Of course, we have since seen the flowering of the statistical method as applied by the Gauquelins and others.

We may observe that while the Fundamentalist types were very put off by "science" and specifically evolution, leftist New Age types embraced it. Biological evolution was such a wonderful model for spiritual evolution.

The third trend was the integration of psychology into astrology. In part helped by the scientific respectability of psychology (at least, relatively speaking), this trend had two significant components. It represented the first major advance in the study and understanding of character since the breakdown of the Hippocratic medical model in the 17th Century. With the weakening in understanding of the qualities, almost no astrologer understood the elements anymore. Without the elements it was impossible to delineate character. Much of that system was medical anyway, which meant that nonmedical practitioners tended to get a bit queasy about it.

The second component of psychological astrology was of far less value to the development of astrology as a whole. The purpose of a psychiatric or psychological analysis program was to evoke a change in the patient—whether through drugs, or insight—allowing the patient to adapt better to his or her environment, or at least to feel happier. The purpose of an astrological consultation heretofore was to address particular issues in the client's life, and to judge accordingly. Judgment—which is to say prediction—is a dubious concept within a psychological framework, because it implies that the client lacks free will. A therapist is supposed to be "non*judgmental*" above all! If astrology was to survive this relationship with psychology, it could only do so by changing its focus away from judgment in the form of predictions to character description.

This trend towards nonpredictive character description was also being approached from another direction. Patrick Curry has traced the emergence of Alan Leo's non-predictive style of astrology in the wake of fear of arrest and prosecution. Leo was associated with the Theosophical Society, and also came up against the fate/free will issue from this spiritual position: just how much freedom does the (evolved) person have? If astrology can predict, then the answer is surely, not much!

The fourth trend in this period which accelerated from the Enlightenment New Age was the rediscovery of astrological history. From an astrological perspective, this trend may be diagnostic of New Age periods in general. We have previously noted that each New Age period has mined the past for real or imagined religious practices. However, Astrology has always remained somewhat apart from the New Age process. While particular adherents to New Age institutions may also be astrologers, not all Astrology practiced in a New Age period is in fact New Age-oriented. However, the same kind of mind that would be attracted to past religious ideals is probably also going to look favorably on past astrological practices.

Thus, the Enlightenment New Age period was marked by the translation of Ptolemy's *Tetrabiblos* into English by Mansah Sibly and J. Browne (1786), James Wilson (1820) and J. M. Ashmand (1822). It was also translated into German *for the first time* by J. Wilhelm Andreas Pfaff and G.H. Schubert (1823). We have already seen that the Spiritualist Wave opened with Zadkiel's abridgment of Lilly's *Christian Astrology*. A combined translation of the aphorisms of Guido Bonatti, along with Jerome Cardan's aphorisms, was re-released in 1886. Luke Broughton, the first great United States astrologer, published a magazine during the US Civil War and successfully predicted Lincoln's assassination. He practiced a form of back-to-Ptolemy delineation which included the full essential dignities. In France, the 1880s saw the writing of Eliphas Lévi, and Papus' review *L'initiation*. It was in that review that François Charles Barlet published the work which intrigued Henri Selva enough to virtually bring back Morin in its entirety into French astrology. From there, Schwickert and Weiss transmitted Morin's methods to German, Spanish and English language readers.

The Spiritualist New Age ended, as so much did (including the then-current Fundamentalist New Age, the Age of Billy Sunday), in the maelstrom of the First World War. However, the trends set in motion in Astrology continued between the World Wars, until the advent of the Technological New Age in the Sixties.

And what shall we use as the chart for the current New Age? How about the time when "The Moon is in the 7th House, and Jupiter aligns with Mars?" A chart is given for the opening of the Broadway musical *Hair*, which rumor has it is an elected chart. This would make sense, both because the lyrics certainly are given in the chart, and also because this would certainly be appropriate for a New Age event! It is certainly intriguing that the Jupiter from the Spiritualist New Age is conjunct the 9th House cusp of the current New Age! In the Spiritualist New Age, the first major theme was communication with the Dead, now in this New Age, there has been a shift toward belief in reincarnation, a belief heretofore mainly common in Oriental religion. I am struck by the conjunction of the Part of Fortune and the South Node, given the modern astrological tendency to equate the South Node with past lives. To judge from the book titles that have gone Best Seller, past lives are *definitely* profitable in this New Age!

With the Moon ruling the 9th House, we definitely want to *feel* our way through our spiritual practice, and with the Moon in Gemini, we surely want to talk about the experience! With Jupiter in the 10th House, along with Pluto, we clearly have some people who want to be perceived as Spiritual Masters. Since that Jupiter is in Leo, there is an issue of individual responsibility for enlightenment. Jupiter is square

Spiritualism Beginning	19:00:00 LMT	Mar. 31, 1848
Rochester NY	43°N 10'00"	77°W 37'00"
Regiomontanus	7:37:56 S.T.	J.D. = 2396118.5073
Natal Chart	R.A.M.S. = 0:37:56	Obl. = 23°27'33"
Tropical	No Ayanamsha	Geocentric Ecliptic

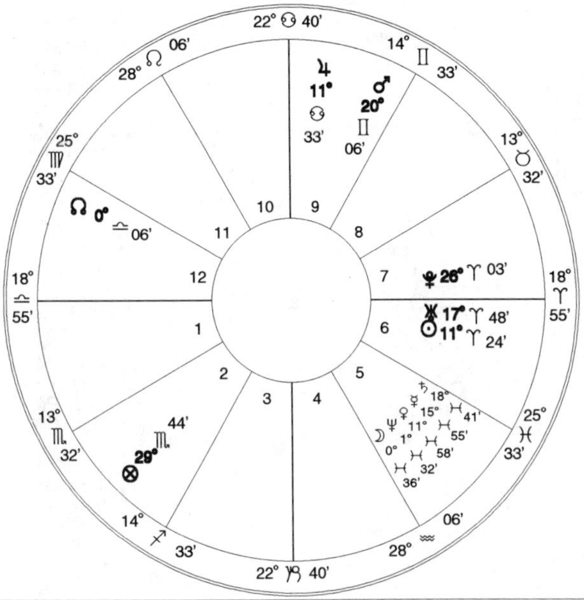

Almutens of Houses
1. ♀ ♄
2. ♂
3. ♃
4. ♂
5. ♄
6. ♂
7. ☉ ♂
8. ☽
9. ☿
10. ☽
11. ☉
12. ☿

Day Hours
♀ 5:43 AM
☿ 6:47 AM
☽ 7:50 AM
♄ 8:54 AM
♃ 9:57 AM
♂ 11:01 AM
☉ 0:05 PM
♀ 1:08 PM
☿ 2:12 PM
☽ 3:15 PM
♄ 4:19 PM
♃ 5:22 PM

Night Hours
♂ 6:26 PM
☉ 7:22 PM
♀ 8:18 PM
☿ 9:15 PM
☽ 10:11 PM
♄ 11:07 PM
♃ 0:04 AM
♂ 1:00 AM
☉ 1:56 AM
♀ 2:53 AM
☿ 3:49 AM
☽ 4:45 AM

Day of ♀
Hour of ♂

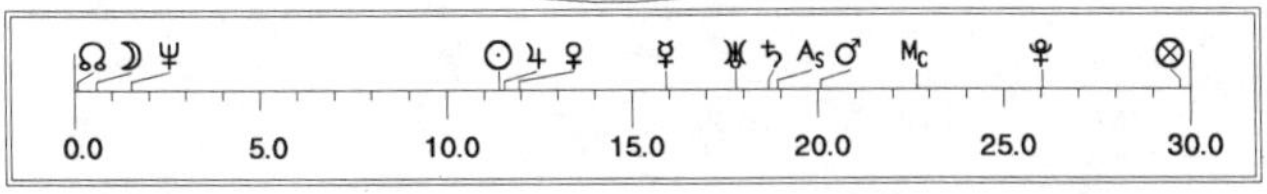

Table of Essential Dignities

Points	Ruler	Exalt.	Trip.	Terms	Face	Detr.	Fall	Score	Solar	Quality of Degree
☉	♂	☉ +	♃	♀	☉ +	♀	♄	+ 5	Ori.	Masc., Dark
☽	♃ m	♀	♂	♀	♄	☿	☿	+ 5	Ori.	Masc., Dark
☿	♃	♀	♂ m	☿ +	♃ m	☿ -	☿ -	- 3	Ori.	Fem., Dark
♀	♃	♀ +	♂	♃	♃	☿	☿	+ 4	Ori.	Fem., Light
♂	☿	☊	☿ m	♀	☉	♃	--	+ 3	Occ.	Fem., Light
♃	☽ m	♃ +	♂	♃ +	☿ m	♄	♂	+12	Ori.	Fem., Light, Deep, Lame
♄	♃	♀	♂	☿	♃	☿	☿	- 5p	Ori.	Fem., Light
♅	♂	☉	♃	☿	☉	☿	♄	--	Occ. Comb.	Fem., Light
♆	♃	♀	♂	♀	♄	♀	☿	--	Ori.	Masc., Dark
♇	♂	☉	♃	♄	♀	♀	♄	--	Occ. Beams	Masc., Light
☊	♀	♄	☿	♄	☽	♂	☉	--	Ori.	Masc., Light, Deep
☋	♂	☉	♃	♃	♂	♀	♄	--	Ori. Beams	Masc., Dark
As	♀	♄	☿	♃	♄	♂	☉	--	--	Masc., Dark
Mc	☽	♃	♂	♀	☽	♄	♂	--	--	Masc., Light, Deep
⊗	♂	--	♂	♄	♀	♀	☽		Occ.	Masc., Dark

Pl.	Antiscia
☉	18°♍36'
☽	29°♎24'
☿	14°♎05'
♀	18°♎02'
♂	9°♋54'
♃	18°♊27'
♄	11°♎19'
♅	12°♍12'
♆	28°♎28'
♇	3°♍57'
☊	29°♓54'
As	11°♓04'
Mc	7°♊20'
⊗	0°♒16'

J. Lee Lehman, Ph.D. - P.O. Box 501107 - Malabar FL 32950 - (407) 728-2277 Fax -2244

OLDTIME1

(C) 1992 Astrolabe, Inc.

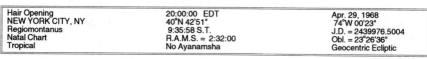

Hair Opening	20:00:00 EDT	Apr. 29, 1968
NEW YORK CITY, NY	40°N 42'51"	74°W 00'23"
Regiomontanus	9:35:58 S.T.	J.D. = 2439976.5004
Natal Chart	R.A.M.S. = 2:32:00	Obl. = 23°26'36"
Tropical	No Ayanamsha	Geocentric Ecliptic

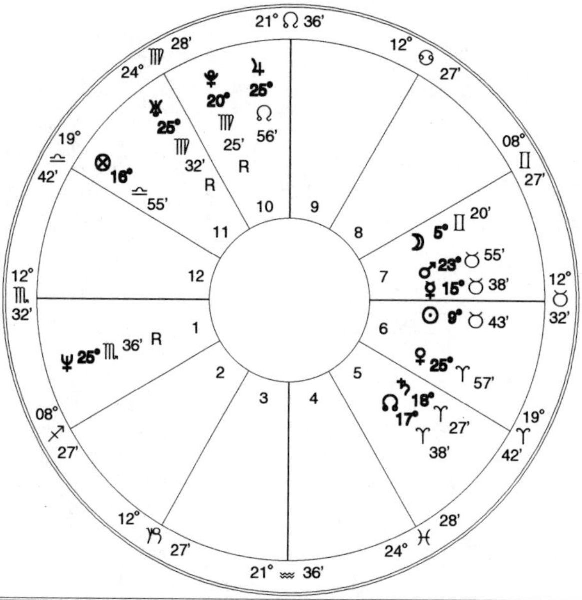

Almutens of Houses
1. ♂
2. ♃
3. ♂ ♄
4. ♄
5. ♂
6. ☉ ♂
7. ☽
8. ♀
9. ♃
10. ☉ ♃
11. ☿
12. ☿ ♄

Day Hours
☽ 5:57 AM
♄ 7:07 AM
♃ 8:16 AM
♂ 9:25 AM
☉ 10:35 AM
♀ 11:44 AM
☿ 0:54 PM
☽ 2:03 PM
♄ 3:13 PM
♃ 4:22 PM
♂ 5:31 PM
☉ 6:41 PM
Night Hours
♀ 7:50 PM
☿ 8:41 PM
☽ 9:31 PM
♄ 10:22 PM
♃ 11:12 PM
♂ 0:03 AM
☉ 0:53 AM
♀ 1:43 AM
☿ 2:34 AM
☽ 3:24 AM
♄ 4:15 AM
♃ 5:05 AM
Day of ☽
Hour of ♀

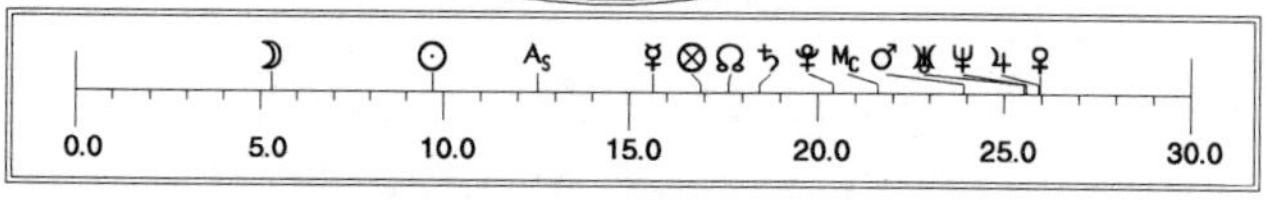

Table of Essential Dignities

Points	Ruler	Exalt.	Trip.	Terms	Face	Detr.	Fall	Score	Solar	Quality of Degree
☉	♀	☽	☽	☿	☿	♂	--	- 5p	Ori.	Masc., Void, Lame
☽	☿	☊	☿ m	☿	♃	♃	--	+ 3	Occ.	Masc., Dark
☿	♀	☽	☽ m	♃	☽	♂	--	+ 3	Occ. Comb.	Fem., Void
♀	♂ m	☉	♃	♂	♀ +	♀ -	♄	+ 1	Ori. Beams	Masc., Light
♂	♀ m	☽	☽	♄	♄	♂ -	--	+ 0	Occ. Beams	Fem., Light, Deep
♃	☉	--	♃ +	♂	♂	♄	--	+ 3	Ori.	Masc., Light
♄	♂	☉	♃	☿	☉	♀	♄ -	- 9p	Ori.	Fem., Light, Fort.
♅	☿	☿	☽	♂	☿	♃	♀	--	Ori.	Masc., Void
♆	♂	--	♂	☿	♀	♀	☽	--	Occ.	Masc., Void
♇	☿	☿	☽	♄	☿	♃	♀	--	Ori.	Masc., Smokey, Deep
☊	♂	☉	♃	☿	☉	♀	♄	--	Ori.	Fem., Light
☋	♀	♄	☿	♃	♄	♂	☉	--	Ori.	Masc., Light
As	♂	--	♂	♃	☉	♀	☽	--	--	Fem., Void
Mc	☉	--	♃	♃	♂	♄	--	--	--	Fem., Void, Deep
⊗	♀	♄	☿	♃	♄	♂	☉		Ori.	Masc., Light

Pl.	Antiscia
☉	20°♌17'
☽	24°♋40'
☿	14°♌22'
♀	4°♍03'
♂	6°♌05'
♃	4°♉04'
♄	11°♍33'
♅	4°♈28'
♆	4°♒25'
♇	9°♈35'
☊	12°♍22'
As	17°♒28'
Mc	8°♉23'
⊗	13°♓05'

J. Lee Lehman, Ph.D. - P.O. Box 501107 - Malabar FL 32950 - (407) 728-2277 Fax -2244

OLDTIME1

(C) 1992 Astrolabe, Inc.

Mars, ruler of the Ascendant (see Chapter Five for an explanation of why I didn't just mention Pluto). The square aspect represents a tension between the Spiritual Hierophant (Jupiter) and the individual seeker (ruler of the 1st House). With that Jupiter also square Neptune, there is a danger of self deception: the master may not truly be a master. With Neptune in Scorpio, we get to face head-on the issue of sexuality in spirituality, and so we get to witness the parade of spiritual masters being caught clutching their female disciples.

And there, before I engage in an unfortunate exercise of foot-in-mouth, we shall end our discussion of history. In the next chapter, we shall begin our study of classical techniques in earnest.

Sources for Data Used:

Spiritualist New Age: Margaret Fox (1833-1893) provided a certificate detailing the events to E. E. Lewis in 1848; this was reprinted in Edwin S. Gausted, Ed. 1963. *A Documentary History of Religion in America to the Civil War.* Second Edition. William B. Eerdmans Publishing Co.: Grand Rapids, MI.

Hair Opening: *NY Times*, April 30, 1968.

Endnotes

[1] Translated by S. Pines. Chicago, 1963. Cited on pages 164-165 in Colette Sirat. 1985. *A History of Jewish Philosophy in the Middle Ages.* Cambridge University Press: Editions de la Maison des Sciences de l'Homme, Paris.

[2] For those who don't recall the McCarthy Era in 1950s America, the term "fellow traveler" was being applied to socialists and other leftist persons who, while not Communist themselves, walked many of the same pathways, and could be considered to have Communist "leanings."

[3] Perle Epstein. 1988. *Kabbalah. The Way of the Jewish Mystic.* Shambhala: Boston, pages 54-55.

[4] For example, see John Alden Williams, ed. 1962. *Islam.* George Braziller: New York.

[5] For a good rendition of his life and works, see Annemarie Schimmel. 1992. *I am Wind You are Fire.* Shambhala: Boston.

[6] See Will Durant. 1950. *The Age of Faith.* Simon & Schuster: New York, pages 808-811.

[7] See Oberman, Heiko A. 1982, 1989. *Luther: Man between God and the Devil.* Translated by Eileen Walliser-Schwarzbart. Yale University Press: New Haven.

[8] See Ottavia Niccoli. 1987, 1990. *Prophecy and People in Renaissance Italy.* Princeton University Press: Princeton.

[9] A full discussion of this period can be found in Godwin, Chapter One.

[10] Not everything was looking up, however. In 1778, metaphysical works were ordered removed by the Royal Library of Darmstadt (Knappish, p 245). Diderot treated astrology with contempt in his *Encyclopédie.* So much for Enlightenment!

[11] He began his 1811 *Dichtung und Wahrheit* with a commentary on his own chart.

[12] Personal communication.

[13] Wordsdale, pp. iv-vii.

[14] *op. cit.,* Paglia, pp. 230-231.

[15] Howe, p 22.

[16] *op. cit.,* Godwin, p 205.

[17] Knappish, p 250.

[18] The concept of the "Elect" was part and parcel of the idea of predestination. If everything was predestined, then those people who would be "saved," the Elected, were known "in the beginning" to God. Exceptional vigor went into determining how to tell the Elected from the Damned. It would have been so much easier if God had deigned to have these people born with a scarlet "E" on their foreheads!

[19] For a history of the Fundamentalist waves, see William Martin. 1978. *A Prophet with Honor*. William Morrow & Co.: New York. Of course, the interpretation of the cycles or waves is my own, not the author's.

[20] In the late 19th Century, all orbital anomalies of known planets were assumed to result from undiscovered planets.

—— Chapter Five ——
Essential Dignities

I particularly want to warn all astrological students against accepting the pernicious ideas which are being put forward in a certain quarter regarding the rulership of the signs, and of the various parts of the human body, and inventing new and imaginary planets to assume rulership over the signs, etc.

While admitting that there may be some grounds for giving ♅ the rule over ♒, and ♆ over ♓, the acceptance of such rank heresies as ♃ ruling over ♒, Jason over ♐, ♆ over ♎, the Asteroids over ♓, and other impossible and improbable theories, is to deny one of the fundamental canons of Astrology.

– E. H. Bailey[1]

What can I say about essential dignities after writing a book about it? In 1989, my book, *Essential Dignities* was published: the first ever to address only that topic. At that time, the modern classical wave had barely begun. I had only a couple of years experience in delineating these concepts. Since then, the number of classical sources has grown. Yet most of the material presented at that time is still valid. Rather than attempting to write the Second Edition in the space of a chapter, and rather than attempting to reinvent the wheel, I will assume that those of you who are interested in this topic either have or will have that book. What I propose to do here is to expand upon several concepts that I covered only lightly, and to put the use of essential dignities into some perspective, based on more extensive experience.

Specifically, the topics I wish to discuss here include some information about variants in rulerships, peregrine planets, and Almutens. A concept related to essential dignity, mutual reception, will be discussed in Chapter 11.

Once upon a time there were five Essential Dignities. In the last two centuries, three of them have often been ignored, but here we shall present them in their entirety. Essential dignity and debility are both based on the zodiacal placement of a planet or point, such as the Lunar Nodes, the Part of Fortune, the Ascendant, or the M.C. The essential dignities and debilities are given in Tables One through Four. Point values are assigned to each dignity or debility, and their use will be considered presently.

Table One is the most familiar. However, the reader who learned Astrology with many modern sources will notice that Uranus, Neptune and Pluto are not represented in this Table, not even as so-called co-rulers. There are good historical reasons for this and you will find them in *Essential Dignities*, Chapters One and Four. In brief, the "modern" rulerships were assigned *after* the true concept of "rulership" was lost. In the modern sense, "rulership" is associated with analogy or likeness: Aries is believed to be "like" Mars or the 1st House. In the true

Table One. Essential Dignities and debilities: whole sign types. Point values given per Lilly.

Sign	Domicile (+5)	Exaltation (+4)	Detriment (-5)	Fall (-4)
♈	♂	☉	♀	♄
♉	♀	☽	♂	
♊	☿	☊	♃	☋
♋	☽	♃	♄	♂
♌	☉		♄	
♍	☿	☿	♃	♀
♎	♀	♄	♂	☉
♏	♂		♀	☽
♐	♃	☋	☿	☊
♑	♄	♂	☽	♃
♒	♄		☉	
♓	♃	♀	☿	☿

traditional sense, rulership meant *strength*. Comparing modern "rulerships" with classical ones is clearly a case of apples and oranges. The modern touchstone is affinity: which sign is most *like* Uranus. This would all be well and good, except that both concepts are called by the same name. If we referred to the modern versions as "affinity rulers," then there would be no conflict.

Planets in Domicile,[2] or sign Rulership, are strong. They are captains of their own fate, so to speak. They set their own agenda. Planets in Exaltation are more in the position of honored guests. Things are done for them, on their behalf. Whatever is done to or for them is supposed to be for their benefit. Exalted planets do not control their own agenda.

Table Two shows the Triplicity rulers. The Triplicity rulers are not as simple as the Lilly table that I had presented in my book. Lilly listed two Triplicity rulers for each sign, according to whether the chart was a day chart or a night chart. In the case of the Water Signs, the Triplicity ruler was Mars, whether the chart is day or night.

This somewhat simplified approach resulted from Lilly's distillation of Ptolemy. Ptolemy and the rest of the Greeks listed *three* Triplicity rulers per sign: a day ruler, a night ruler, and a mixed ruler. Additionally, there were two variants of this three-way listing: one from Ptolemy and one from Dorotheus, and both versions were transmitted to us. Lilly's simplification is justifiable based on a reading of Ptolemy, however. In Ptolemy's discussion of the Trigons or Triangles, short shrift was given to the mixed ruler of the three Trigons other than the case of Water; and Mars was mentioned as the primary ruler for Water. Thus, Lilly's Mars-ruled water Triplicity could be understood to represent the spirit, if not the letter, of Ptolemy. Ptolemy's use of the third or mixed ruler - other than in the case of Water - was principally in describing the effects on weather.

Planets in Triplicity are generally considered lucky. Good things happen not because you necessarily excel at them, but because you stumble upon a good result. This is when the Wheel of Fortune stops on your color. The Triplicities were derived from the Sign and Exaltation rulerships.[3] During the Medieval period, the Triplicity ruler was often used in preference to the Sign and Exaltation rulers, presumably because this derivation made it simpler to use one ruler than possibly three.

There were a couple of other uses for the three Triplicity rulers in the Medieval period. First, they could be used to represent different variants on a theme. In horary, one may ask about a new job while being currently employed. The modern approach would be to step houses: if the job is given by the 10th House, then the second job would

Table Two. Triplicities as given by Ptolemy and William Lilly. Point value is +3 for chosen type.

Sign	Ptolemy: Day	Ptolemy: Night	Ptolemy: Mixed	Lilly: Day	Lilly: Night
♈ ♌ ♐	☉	♃	♂	☉	♃
♉ ♍ ♑	♀	☽	♄	♀	☽
♊ ♎ ♒	♄	☿	♃	♄	☿
♋ ♏ ♊	♀	☽	♂	♂	♂

Table Three. Chaldean (Ptolemaic) and Egyptian terms. Point value is +2 for chosen type.

Chaldean Terms

♈	0 ♃ 6	6 ♀ 14	14 ☿ 21	21 ♂ 26	26 ♄ 30
♉	0 ♀ 8	8 ☿ 15	15 ♃ 22	22 ♄ 26	26 ♂ 30
♊	0 ☿ 7	7 ♃ 14	14 ♀ 21	21 ♄ 25*	25 ♂ 30*
♋	0 ♂ 6	6 ♃ 13*	13 ☿ 20	20 ♀ 27*	27 ♄ 30
♌	0 ♄ 6*	6 ☿ 13*	13 ♀ 19*	19 ♃ 25*	25 ♂ 30
♍	0 ☿ 7	7 ♀ 13	13 ♃ 18	18 ♄ 24*	24 ♂ 30*
♎	0 ♄ 6	6 ♀ 11*	11 ♃ 19	19 ☿ 24*	24 ♂ 30
♏	0 ♂ 6	6 ♃ 14*	14 ♀ 21*	21 ☿ 27*	27 ♄ 30
♐	0 ♃ 8	8 ♀ 14	14 ☿ 19	19 ♄ 25	25 ♂ 30
♑	0 ♀ 6*	6 ☿ 12*	12 ♃ 19*	19 ♂ 25*	25 ♄ 30*
♒	0 ♄ 6*	6 ☿ 12*	12 ♀ 20*	20 ♃ 25*	25 ♂ 30*
♓	0 ♀ 8	8 ♃ 14	14 ☿ 20	20 ♂ 26	26 ♄ 30

Egyptian Terms

♈	0 ♃ 6	6 ♀ 12	12 ☿ 20	20 ♂ 25	25 ♄ 30
♉	0 ♀ 8	8 ☿ 14	14 ♃ 22	22 ♄ 27	27 ♂ 30
♊	0 ☿ 6	6 ♃ 12	12 ♀ 17	17 ♂ 24*	24 ♄ 30*
♋	0 ♂ 7	7 ♃ 13*	13 ☿ 19	19 ♃ 26*	26 ♄ 30
♌	0 ♃ 6*	6 ♀ 11*	11 ♄ 18*	18 ☿ 24*	24 ♂ 30
♍	0 ☿ 7	7 ♀ 17	17 ♃ 21	21 ♂ 28*	28 ♄ 30*
♎	0 ♄ 6	6 ☿ 14*	14 ♃ 21	21 ♀ 28*	28 ♂ 30
♏	0 ♂ 7	7 ♀ 11*	11 ☿ 19*	19 ♃ 24*	24 ♄ 30
♐	0 ♃ 12	12 ♀ 17	17 ☿ 21	21 ♄ 26	26 ♂ 30
♑	0 ☿ 7*	7 ♃ 14*	14 ♀ 22*	22 ♄ 26*	26 ♂ 30*
♒	0 ☿ 7*	7 ♀ 13*	13 ♃ 20*	20 ♂ 25*	25 ♄ 30*
♓	0 ♀ 12	12 ♃ 16	16 ☿ 19	19 ♂ 28	28 ♄ 30

Table Four. The Faces (Chaldean decanates). Point value given by Lilly was +1.

Sign	0 - 10	10 - 20	20 - 30
♈	♂	☉	♀
♉	☿	☽	♄
♊	♃	♂	☉
♋	♀	☿	☽
♌	♄	♃	♂
♍	☉	♀	☿
♎	☽	♄	♃
♏	♂	☉	♀
♐	☿	☽	♄
♑	♃	♂	☉
♒	♀	☿	☽
♓	♄	♃	♂

be given by the 12th House, the third job by the 2nd House, etc. This stepping system is Vedic in origin. The Western classical approach might be to use the Day Triplicity ruler (if the question was asked during the day) for the present job, the Night Triplicity ruler for the next job, and so forth.[4]

The second common use for the three Triplicity rulers is to divide the life into approximate thirds (a neat trick, since the exact length of life is a theoretical construct as long as the Native is living), and to use the three Triplicity rulers as rulers of each third of life. How does this work? Take the 2nd House: personal wealth. If the first Triplicity ruler is the most dignified, then the Native would be weathiest in the first third of life, basically when the Native is growing up. If the third Triplicity ruler is in bad shape, then the Native would be in poverty, or at least not great shape, in old age.

The Terms are probably the most difficult of the essential dignities to understand, because their origin seems the most arcane. The simple fact is that we may never know what they really are, but only that they were derived empirically. The question is, empirically from what? Was it a case of the Babylonian astrologers sitting down in their teams of observers and tabulating when particular kinds of questions were asked, and what degrees the planets occupied then? Or were the Terms a translation of something else? Tester thought that they were derived from heliacal rising times.[5] We don't know.

What we do know is that Ptolemy listed two Term tables, those that we now call the Chaldean (Lilly called this set Ptolemaic) and the Egyptian. The two tables were variously adopted by astrologers, although there did seem to be an eventual Catholic-Protestant split, with the Catholic contingent under the "leadership" of Placidus favoring the Egyptian Terms and the Placidian House System, and the Protestant group (including Lilly) favoring the Chaldean Terms and the Regiomontanus House System. I presented some research in *Essential Dignities* that favored the use of the Chaldean ones.[6] Since then, I've worked extensively with the Chaldean Terms in horary, and feel quite comfortable with them. However, I suspect that it may be possible that, like different house systems, the two Term tables are actually showing different "slices of life."

The basis for assigning Terms seemingly was to reward those planets with greater numbers of essential dignities (Sign, Exaltation and Triplicity) in a sign, and to assign benefics more degrees than malefics. The planet which is the ruler by Sign, Exaltation, or Triplicity tends to get the first term position most frequently. This falls off dramatically after the first position. As one may note from the tables, Mars or Saturn gets the final position. This no doubt is the origin of the rule-of-thumb assigning the final degrees of any sign as having malefic qualities.

Planets in their own Terms denote the participation of the Native or planet in the business of that planet, but not from a position of power, wealth, or fortune. They are the blue-collar workers in the business of that planet. The issue of that planet is important, but the outcome is uncertain.

In horary, the Terms are used differently. Here they are used to describe the person in question. For example, the Term ruler of the Ascendant is used to physically describe the Querent, or person asking the question. If the Ascendant ruler is in the Terms of Saturn, then the Querent may be sober, older, serious, deformed, pale, or a day laborer; any of these being qualities of Saturn.

The final essential dignity is the Face. The derivation of the Faces is extremely clear, but the justification is opaque. The division of the 360° circle into units of 10° was developed by the Egyptians and then adopted by everybody else. These 10° sections in fact represented asterisms, components of constellations, and were time markers on the way to being able to measure planetary positions to smaller units: degrees, and finally, minutes. The order of the Faces is simple: begin with zero Aries. The first 10° of Aries is assigned to Mars, the ruler of Aries. From there, each face ruler in sequence is the so-called Chaldean order: Mars → Sun → Venus → Mercury → Moon → Saturn → Jupiter → Mars, and so on through the signs. Reading down any column in the faces gives the order of the planetary ruler in the days of the week: the Sun for Sunday, the Moon for Monday, etc.

While the Faces are mostly ignored in modern method, this was not true through the Renaissance. Ramesey gave a listing of an eclipse in each face individually and its qualities.[7] Lilly in his eclipse book considered Solar and Lunar Eclipses in each face position. Wing used the Faces in weather forecasting, a practice which extended at least back to the Middle Ages. The Face represents worry or concern about the planet in question: it is somewhat tenuous that the Face should even be considered dignified. The classical descriptions of planets in their Faces is not especially complementary either. Ramesey called a planet in its own Face "at the last shift, or as we say, *at the last gasp* not knowing how to bestow himself, nor what course to take."[8] Others used words like fear.

For further clarification, I have reproduced Table Five from *Essential Dignities*, in order to give something of the flavor of the five different dignities.

Table Five. Key words associated with the five essential dignities.

Ruler	Exaltation	Triplicity	Term	Face
power	persuasion	lucky	competency	fear
owner	guest	self-made	clone	climber
success	recognition	fortunate	adequate	danger
prosperity	comfort	well-off	settled	anxiety
strength	pride	harmony	facsimile	denial
productive	majestic	favorable	mimics	concern
authority	grace	auspicious	acceptance	loathing

Before we begin to consider specific applications of the theory of essential dignities, one other concept should be discussed. In astrological method prior to Lilly (and Lilly also did it, although he tended not to discuss it[9]) there were two methods of obtaining the ruler of a planet, house cusp, or other placement, such as the Part of Fortune. The simple method, which is the one that survived to the 20th Century, was simply to assign the sign or domicile ruler of the zodiacal position in question. The more complex method—which was clearly favored from the Medieval period through 1600—was to calculate the *Almuten* or *Dominator/Dominatrix* of the zodiacal position. In order to calculate the Almuten, the exact degree of the cusp or position is needed, plus whether it is a day or night chart. For example, one may calculate the Almuten for an Ascendant of 15 ♎ 30 in a night chart as follows:

Sign (domicile) ruler: ♀ 5 points
Exaltation ruler: ♄ 4 points
Triplicity ruler (night): ☿ 3 points
Term ruler (Ptolemaic): ♃ 2 points
Face ruler: ♄ 1 point

Both Venus and Saturn get five points total, so they are Co-Almutens of the degree.

To simplify this process, I have devised Tables 6 and 7. They show the Almuten for each degree of the zodiac, given day or night.

Now we get to the word *peregrine*. Unfortunately, since the Modern Era (post 1800) peregrine has come to mean something other than what it originally did. For centuries, if not millennia, the definition of peregrine was: a planet which lacks all essential dignity. It was sometimes further specified that the planet not be in mutual reception by

Table 6. Almuten rulers by degree: DAY.

	♈	♉	♊	♋	♌	♍	♎	♏	♐	♑	♒	♓
0	☉	♀	☿	☽♂	☉	☿	♄	♂	♃	♄♀	♄	♀
1	☉	♀	☿	☽♂	☉	☿	♄	♂	♃	♄♀	♄	♀
2	☉	♀	☿	☽♂	☉	☿	♄	♂	♃	♄♀	♄	♀
3	☉	♀	☿	☽♂	☉	☿	♄	♂	♃	♄♀	♄	♀
4	☉	♀	☿	☽♂	☉	☿	♄	♂	♃	♄♀	♄	♀
5	☉	♀	☿	☽♂	☉	☿	♄	♂	♃	♄♀	♄	♀
6	☉	♀	☿	♃	☉	☿	♀♄	♂	♃	♄	♄	♀
7	☉	♀	☿	♃	☉	☿	♀♄	♂	♃	♄	♄	♀
8	☉	♀	☿	♃	☉	☿	♀♄	♂	♃	♄	♄	♃
9	☉	♀	☿	♃	☉	☿	♀♄	♂	♃	♄	♄	♃
10	☉	♀	☿	♃	☉	☿	♄	♂	♃	♂♄	♄	♃
11	☉	♀	☿	♃	☉	☿	♄	♂	♃	♂♄	♄	♃
12	☉	♀	☿	♃	☉	☿	♄	♂	♃	♂♄	♄	♃
13	☉	♀	☿	☽	☉	☿	♄	♂	♃	♂♄	♄	♃
14	☉	♀	☿	☽	☉	☿	♄	♂	♃	♂♄	♄	♃
15	☉	♀	☿	☽	☉	☿	♄	♂	♃	♂♄	♄	♃
16	☉	♀	☿	☽	☉	☿	♄	♂	♃	♂♄	♄	♃
17	☉	♀	☿	☽	☉	☿	♄	♂	♃	♂♄	♄	♃
18	☉	♀	☿	☽	☉	☿	♄	♂	♃	♂♄	♄	♃
19	☉	♀	☿	☽	☉	☿	♄	♂	♃	♂	♄	♃
20	☉	♀	☿	☽	☉	☿	♄	♂	♃	♂	♄	♂
21	☉♂	♀	☿♄	☽	☉	☿	♄	♂	♃	♂	♄	♂
22	☉♂	♀	☿♄	☽	☉	☿	♄	♂	♃	♂	♄	♂
23	☉♂	♀	☿♄	☽	☉	☿	♄	♂	♃	♂	♄	♂
24	☉♂	♀	☿♄	☽	☉	☿	♄	♂	♃	♂	♄	♂
25	☉♂	♀	☿	☽	☉	☿	♄	♂	♃	♄	♄	♂
26	☉	♀	☿	☽	☉	☿	♄	♂	♃	♄	♄	♃
27	☉	♀	☿	☽	☉	☿	♄	♂	♃	♄	♄	♃
28	☉	♀	☿	☽	☉	☿	♄	♂	♃	♄	♄	♃
29	☉	♀	☿	☽	☉	☿	♄	♂	♃	♄	♄	♃

Table 7. Almuten rulers by degree: NIGHT.

	♈	♉	♊	♋	♌	♍	♎	♏	♐	♑	♒	♓
0	♂	♀☽	☿	☽♂	☉	☿	♄	♂	♃	♄	♄	♀
1	♂	♀☽	☿	☽♂	☉	☿	♄	♂	♃	♄	♄	♀
2	♂	♀☽	☿	☽♂	☉	☿	♄	♂	♃	♄	♄	♀
3	♂	♀☽	☿	☽♂	☉	☿	♄	♂	♃	♄	♄	♀
4	♂	♀☽	☿	☽♂	☉	☿	♄	♂	♃	♄	♄	♀
5	♂	♀☽	☿	☽♂	☉	☿	♄	♂	♃	♄	♄	♀
6	♂	♀☽	☿	♃	☉	☿	♀	♂	♃	♄	♃	♀
7	♂	♀☽	☿	♃	☉	☿	♀	♂	♃	♄	♄	♀
8	♂	☽	☿	♃	☉	☿	♀	♂	♃	♄	♄	♃
9	♂	☽	☿	♃	☉	☿	♀	♂	♃	♄	♄	♃
10	♂☉	☽	☿	♃	☉	☿	♀	♂	♃	♂♄	♄	♃
11	♂☉	☽	☿	♃	☉	☿	♀♄	♂	♃	♂♄	♄	♃
12	♂☉	☽	☿	♃	☉	☿	♀♄	♂	♃	♂♄	♄	♃
13	♂☉	☽	☿	☽	☉	☿	♀♄	♂	♃	♂♄	♄	♃
14	♂☉	☽	☿	☽	☉	☿	♀♄	♂	♃	♂♄	♄	♃
15	♂☉	☽	☿	☽	☉	☿	♀♄	♂	♃	♂♄	♄	♃
16	♂☉	☽	☿	☽	☉	☿	♀♄	♂	♃	♂♄	♄	♃
17	♂☉	☽	☿	☽	☉	☿	♀♄	♂	♃	♂♄	♄	♃
18	♂☉	☽	☿	☽	☉	☿	♀♄	♂	♃	♂♄	♄	♃
19	♂☉	☽	☿	☽	♃	☿	♀☿♄	♂	♃	♂	♄	♃
20	♂	☽	☿	☽	☉♃	☿	☿♀	♂	♃	♂	♄	♂
21	♂	☽	☿	☽	☉♃	☿	☿♀	♂	♃	♂	♄	♂
22	♂	☽	☿	☽	☉♃	☿	☿♀	♂	♃	♂	♄	♂
23	♂	☽	☿	☽	☉♃	☿	☿♀	♂	♃	♂	♄	♂
24	♂	☽	☿	☽	☉♃	☿	♀	♂	♃	♂	♄	♂
25	♂	☽	☿	☽	☉	☿	♀	♂	♃	♄	♄	♂
26	♂	☽	☿	☽	☉	☿	♀	♂	♃	♄	♄	♃
27	♂	☽	☿	☽	☉	☿	♀	♂	♃	♄	♄	♃
28	♂	☽	☿	☽	☉	☿	♀	♂	♃	♄	♄	♃
29	♂	☽	☿	☽	☉	☿	♀	♂	♃	♄	♄	♃

sign or exaltation. A peregrine planet cannot have any dignities. You might ask why only Sign and Exaltation. I don't know! While this point is not explicitly discussed, it *does* appear that for a long time, the Terms and Faces, if not the Triplicity, were considered significantly weaker.[10] There *is* some indication that occasionally minor dignities were used, but only if there were multiple minor dignities to consider.

Let's attempt to consolidate and clarify these concepts by examining some charts.

Nicholas II

Nicholas II was the last Russian Czar. He and his family were assassinated during the Communist takeover. Nicholas' grandfather, Alexander II, had been a reformer, but he was murdered by a bomb. Alexander II's son, Alexander III (1845-1894), cancelled many of his father's reforms, and in turn, died quite suddenly at a relatively young age, without having trained Czarevitch Nicholas to take over.

Nicholas' Virgo Ascendant was ruled by Mercury, which is conjunct the Midheaven, one of the ancient signatures of royalty. His Mercury was in Gemini, strong in its own rulership. Nicholas' chart has two planets in their own Signs: Mercury and Mars. This basically means that he was able to pretty much think and act as he chose. Between them, Mercury and Mars rule or are Almutens of the 1st, 2nd, 4th, and 5th Houses. So they rule his health (1st), wealth (2nd), inheritance (4th),[11] and his children (5th).

One of his major biographers contends that Nicholas was born in the wrong place: he was temperamentally suited to being the kind of Constitutional Monarch found in England.[12] In fact, he bore an uncanny physical resemblance to his cousin, George V of England, who was three years Nicholas' senior. As a private man, his character was exemplary. He was—typical for the time—fluent in several languages, a must for any member of the European Royal family tree that descended from Queen Victoria of England. Apart from the language facility, Nicholas may have been bright, but he was not one of the great intellectual lights of his day. Thus, the Mercury may be showing in the context of language, but certainly *not* deep thought. Further, as a military strategist, he was downright lousy. So how do we interpret his dignified Mars?

Dignity is not the same as talent. All the dignity guaranteed was at best that his mind was sound, and that he was able to exercise it. He did. Look what happened! *Because* he was Czar, he was able to do what he wanted. A peon with the same dignities would probably *have* to have more talent, because otherwise, how could he or she possibly be able to have that level of independence?

We are tempted, of course, to characterize Mercury in Gemini as a quick mind, or at least a quick study. We would expect therefore, that Nicholas would have been quick on the uptake when new material was presented to him. Yet, we discover that "Nicholas... learned by rote...."[13] How could this be? Educators characterize the difference between the modern Japanese-style education program and the American-style one as the difference between rote memorization and context learning.

The theory is that people who are trained by rote memorization fit into their working environments very well. They are disciplined. The more anarchic American style fosters independent or creative thinking. Notice that neither style is "smarter" or "better." However, one style may be more suited to the particular circumstances.

Let's instead begin by saying that Nicholas had a *strong* mind. "In many respects, his education was excellent. He had an unusual memory and had done well in history. He spoke French and German, and his English was so good that he could have fooled an Oxford professor into mistaking him for an Englishman. He rode beautifully, danced gracefully and was an excellent shot."[14] Strong mind? Clearly. But notice that his Mercury was opposite Saturn. Saturn? Saturn is the perennial Father, in Nicholas' case, Alexander III. Saturn in the 4th House, the House of the Father in Classical Astrology, only furthers the argument that this is the proper interpretation for Saturn. "In 1890 Alexander III still was only forty-five years old. Expecting that he would continue to occupy the throne for another twenty or thirty years, he dawdled about giving his son the experience to succeed him. Nicholas happily accepted the playboy role to which he had tacitly been assigned..."[15]

While Mercury was the most dignified planet in Nicholas' chart, his Saturn was peregrine. To the outside world, Alexander III was a bear of a man, autocratic and firm-willed. Yet he really had no idea how to raise his son. How Alexander III appeared to the world is *not* shown in Nicholas' chart; Nicholas's chart shows how Alexander appeared to his son. The ruler of the 4th House, Mars, is the second most dignified planet in Nicholas' chart. Alexander did give Nicholas everything he could. Nicholas' chart shows *no* evidence of the all too frequent circumstance of kings and crown princes despising each other.

But to return to Mars: every planet in Nicholas' chart *except* Mercury is ultimately disposed by Mars. Let's diagram the dispositor relationships.

$$\odot \ -> \ \varphi -> \ \mathbb{D} \ \ \text{4} \ \ -> \ \ \sigma$$
$$(\varrho) \qquad \quad (\mathbb{H}) \qquad (\Psi)$$

ϱ disposes itself.

Nicholas is therefore said to have two *Final Dispositors*. The final dispositor(s) in a chart is/are any planets which ultimately dispose only themselves. This arrangement implies that Nicholas put practically all his eggs into the military basket—all his eggs but his mind. (A terrible thing to lose, a mind!)

So what can we say about Nicholas' Mars? Mars is strong in Aries. We shall have more to say later about Mars rising before the Sun. However, for now, Mars gets what it wants through the 4th and, partly, the 5th House. The Sun is Almuten of the 9th House. With the Sun only having dignity by mutual reception, Mars is the stronger of the two.

A word about calculating points for Almuten or other purposes. The print-outs used in this book are produced by Astrolabe's Print Wheels program. While the format given shows all the essential dignities as given here, the "Score" column is not calculated the way that I do it. The reason is that Rob Hand chose to include points from mutual receptions as part of the total score, something I had played with initially, and shortly rejected. For example, if you examine the Table of Essential Dignities for Nicholas, the Sun and the Moon are in mutual reception by Exaltation, which is marked on the table with an "m" in the "Exalt." column. The exaltation is given +4 points. Otherwise, neither the Sun nor the Moon has any dignity, so I would score each one as being peregrine for -5 points. (Notice on the Mercury line that dignity is designated by a "+" in the appropriate column.) Accordingly, when I discuss planets, my characterization of peregrine will often apply to planets that are shown in the print-out as possessing dignity points.

In classical usage, if one has a choice of which planet to use, the Sign Ruler of the House, or the Almuten of the House, the planet which has the greater dignity will predominate. This is especially true in Horary. In Nativities, both planets will eventually work, with one preferred over the other. I believe the difference between the effect in Horary and Natal is that the Horary reading involves only one question. In the lifetime represented by the typical Nativity, there is much more time for multiple sub-plots, so eventually all the sub-plots will manifest.

Nicholas' situation is a good example of this phenomenon. With Mars strong and in, as well as ruling, the 9th House, Nicholas should have been good at war with foreign powers. When he served as a regular officer while his father was still alive, he was popular with the other officers. He did a good enough job at the process of *being* a soldier. However, the officers of Czarist Russia for the most part were sons of the nobility who were distinguished only by their lineages, not by their competency.

However, the Almuten of the 9th House is the Sun, which is located in the 9th House, albeit conjunct the M.C. Nicholas' Sun had dignity only by mutual reception, which, as we will see, means he is only strong when he has good help. The quality of his help depends on the condition of his Moon, the planet in mutual reception to his Sun. Like the Sun, his Moon only has dignity by the mutual reception. So the only help Nicholas gets is from the women in his life, generically his mother and wife.

Thus, Nicholas' judgement about foreign affairs (9th House) were colored, on the one hand, by the Army (Mars ruling the 9th House in the chart of a sovereign will surely show the importance of the military in foreign policy), and on the other, by his wife, or the general public, the other usual lunar reading. With the Moon in Aries, this "advice" from spouse or public is liable to be changeable and short-term, and of no particular distinction. With the Sun in Taurus, Nicholas could be very stubborn once he made a decision, and thus unlikely to cut his losses when he made a mistake.

Since we have already considered the Elements and their Qualities, we can begin to examine complexion or character using what we have learned. I propose to do it via three different procedures using the same points: the qualities of the Lights, planets through Saturn, and the Ascendant, Midheaven, and Part of Fortune. I am going to keep this simple and avoid weighting anything.

		Triplicity	Seasonal	Traditional
☉	Taurus	cold & dry	hot & wet	hot & wet
☽	Aries	hot & dry	hot & wet	cold & wet
☿	Gemini	hot & wet	hot & wet	dry
♀	Cancer	cold & wet	hot & dry	wet
♂	Aries	hot & dry	hot & wet	hot & dry
♃	Aries	hot & dry	hot & wet	hot & wet
♄	Sagittarius	hot & dry	cold & dry	dry
Asc	Virgo	cold & dry	hot & dry	cold & dry
M.C.	Taurus	cold & dry	hot & wet	cold & dry
⊗	Cancer	cold & wet	hot & dry	cold & wet

Nicholas had an even mixture of hot and cold by Triplicity, but a preponderance of dry. That means that his temperament varied between melancholic and choleric. This example shows a very important point. All people are not purely one type! The quality of dry that Aristotle emphasized[16] was: "Moist is that which, though easily adaptable to form, cannot be confined within limits of its own, while dry is that which is most easily confined within its own limits but is not easily adaptable in form." A person who has dry predominating has difficulty changing in order to fit the *external* circumstances, but a high degree of will about self-discipline. Thus, Nicholas was slow to grasp the changing political circumstances in Russia, slow to grasp the need for democratic reform, slow to grasp the folly of military involvement in World War I. But he demonstrated great discipline with regard to his personal life, regulating his schedule with precision, writing in his journal eve*ry day*, eating meals at the same time of day. A predominately wet person may seem to change constantly with changes in style or shifts in the political winds, while actually remaining internally unaffected by all the apparent external change.

Contrast this with Nicholas's temperament description from the seasonal qualities of his planets. The seasonal component shows a strong sanguine type: hot and wet. This is the type which looks best on paper: a cheerful person, high energy but not too agressive. Nicholas would appear to vacillate, to lack strong dogmatic opinions, to be affected by the positions of others. A sanguine person appears upbeat, and is pleasant for other people to be around.

The Traditional type, which I shall explain in Chapter 6, gives an even distribution of the qualities. Only the traditional calculation gives circumstances in which a particular planet can have *one* quality instead of two.

The difference we are proposing between "dry" and "wet" change is that a wet person changes on the surface - wetness, is, after all a *surface* (literally!) phenomenon: the ability, even the necessity, to make surface changes, while the essence remains unchanged. Why? Consider the liquid. You can pour water from a pitcher to a glass, and the water poured assumes the shape of the glass, having previously assumed the shape of the pitcher. The water has "changed" shape almost effortlessly. That is its nature. But has anything *really* changed? No-- this amorphous nature is simply the definition of a liquid. For a solid to change shapes, it must be physically broken up or damaged. Dry change is fairly impervious to the winds of external events and pressures, but after the serious effort of breaking the solid up, the change is fundamental—and permanent.

The empathy and emotional involvement of the wet person impedes real change, because so much is going on at the surface. Today's emotional storms will be followed by tomorrow's tempest, and the wind direction could well shift! The most extreme example of this is the hurricane: potentially dangerous winds, a circular flow of energy, and at the center, a disquieting calm. On the other hand, the same objectivity that is the hallmark of the dry mind can sometimes batter the fortifications down, resulting in permanent change, because this time, the wind doesn't shift.

So was Nicholas rigid or amorphous: dry or wet? On the whole, he appeared wet. He *did* vacillate. He *was* far too susceptible to others' opinions. Yet there *was* a dry component to his character. However, look at which parts of his chart show dryness in the seasonal system: Saturn, the Ascendant and the Part of Fortune. He had the *personal* (1st House) self-discipline (Saturn) of dryness.

Notice that the use of seasonal qualities mirrors the modern application of hemisphere emphasis. Seasons are Quadrants associated with the Cardinal points, not defined with respect to the particular chart's angles. Nicholas's chart in modern parlance would be described as bucket: a bowl configuration (all planets within 180° of each other), except for one, operating as the handle of a bucket. A bucket is nothing but a hemisphere defined in terms of the planet placements, not the angles. A splash pattern will produce a fairly even quality distribution by season, while a wedge will generally have a strong seasonal component, and the hourglass configuration (two groups of planets roughly opposite each other) will also tend to cancel out seasonally like the splash.

We have already considered Nicholas' Saturn in relation to his father, but Saturn also rules the 5th House of children in his chart. With Saturn peregrine, Nicholas was at least as much at a loss for what to do for his children as his father had been with him. Thus the sins of the fathers... or perhaps, the mothers, since his son had hemophilia!

By the way, we can immediately confront one of the differences between a classical delineation and a modern one. There is no "problem" if there is no planet in a house: in other words, "empty houses" were not ever mentioned in classical work, because the concept was simply meaningless. One of the prime differences between a classical reading and a modern one is that a classical reading will interpret a house *at least as strongly* through the planet(s) *ruling the cusp of the house* as through planets being *in* the house.

Mary Godwin Wollstonecraft Shelley

Mary Godwin Shelley's birth was recorded by her then-famous father, William Godwin, in his diary. Mary's mother, Mary

Wollstonecraft, an ardent feminist, died of infection shortly after the birth. Mary was raised by her father for the first four years, until he remarried. In certain respects, Shelley repeated her mother's adventures. Feminism was difficult when sexual liaison almost certainly led to pregnancy: the biology of the sexes was too unequal. Mary eventually ended up in a liaison with Percy Bysshe Shelley. They married soon after Shelley's then current wife committed suicide; the circumstances were so distressing that the couple was ostracized. Two children of their union died, and Shelley drowned when Mary was only 24. Mary attempted to live quietly from then on. Unfortunately, the last personal "friend" to remain alive engaged in a vicious personal attack, and Mary's reputation suffered enormously as she was relegated to a spectral appendage of The Master, Shelley.

As we examine her chart, we are immediately struck by the Virgo stellium in the 4th House, and Cancer Rising. The modernist would immediately be tempted to wax eloquent on Mary as a nurturing homebody, wrapped up in providing a comfortable environment for herself and others. Actually, this is someone who would be reluctant to go out in public, or to make a public display. Virgo is not exactly known for histrionics. There is little question that, with this combination, Godwin Shelley would be reluctant to engage in public display. However, the Moon in Sagittarius certainly suggests a bit more spark! Let us examine her chart more closely. An expression that was applied to her was "fire under snow."[17] How appropriate for the combination!

First, let us not forget that Pluto was conjunct her M.C. We have already noted that in classical delineation, Dad is the 4th House, so Mom is the 10th House. Mary Wollstonecraft was literally destroyed by Mary Godwin's birth, so the symbolism is sure enough! Mary's Father is given by the Sun, ruler of the 4th House. With Sun in the 4th House, Dad literally worked at home, as a writer. The conjunction of the Sun to Uranus is telling, since Godwin was known (and later reviled) for his radical writings, and continued support for the French Revolution, even in the face of the Reign of Terror which followed the initial excitement of liberation.

Mary had one stunningly dignified planet, Mercury, and one stunningly debilitated planet, Saturn. Mercury in Virgo has a serious head start, since Mercury is exalted in Virgo, as well has having sign rulership there. Mercury ruled the 5th House, and was co-Almuten of the 9th. With the square between Mercury and the Moon, Godwin Shelley was caught between her thoughts and her emotions. In her case, the conflict was creative, not merely procreative. It was also political, but that was her familial gift.

Godwin Shelley's Saturn was in Detriment. When a planet is in Detriment, you are three steps back at the starting line. With the Fall you are only two steps back! In addition, Saturn is peregrine. (Not all peregrine planets are in Detriment or Fall, nor is a planet in Detriment or Fall automatically peregrine.) Saturn was the sign ruler of *four* houses ——the entire Southwest quadrant of her chart! Among other things, Saturn is natural ruler of poverty and material want, and this was precisely the problem Godwin Shelley had after her husband drowned— the need to support herself and her remaining two year old son. Her husband, given by the 7th House, ruled by Saturn, was useless to her in this regard. *She* got to be her own Saturn, and with all the seriousness of a person with Saturn in the 1st House, set about putting her life in order, by becoming a self-supporting female author, an almost impossible aspiration for the day. But with hard work (naturally!) she achieved it. And further, she managed to achieve it while keeping alive the flame of Romanticism as it developed in that literary period: the primacy of *all* emotional intensity, the willingness to plunge into the very heights and depths of life, to be the hero who endures travail on the way to the eventual grail.

So a *Virgo* is in the vanguard of a Movement that celebrated the experience of emotion?? Well, yes! First of all, Mercury in Virgo was going to give her exceptional writing power. Further, she was unusual for having her Mercury far enough away from the Sun so that it was neither combust, nor under beams, conditions we shall take up in Chapter 6. Her Mercury and Venus were in contra-antiscial relationship to each other, a condition we shall return to in Chapter 9. However, for now, the contra-antiscial relationship can be considered to be analogous to a strong aspect, so that gave Godwin Shelley considerable ability to express (Mercury) her passions (Venus).

	Triplicity	Seasonal	Traditional
☉	cold & dry	hot & dry	hot & dry
☽	hot & dry	cold & dry	hot & dry
☿	cold & dry	hot & dry	dry
♀	hot & wet	cold & dry	wet
♂	cold & dry	hot & dry	hot & dry
♃	hot & dry	hot & wet	wet
♄	cold & wet	hot & dry	cold & wet
Asc	cold & wet	hot & dry	cold & wet
M.C.	hot & wet	cold & wet	hot & wet
⊗	cold & wet	cold & wet	cold & wet

We should, perhaps, briefly consider her lover/husband, Percy Bysshe Shelley.[18] Shelley was a Leo with a Sun-Venus-Uranus conjunction in the 5th House, with the Sun ruling the 5th. Shelley was a strong advocate of free love. Of course! With Sun-Uranus-Venus, what kind of an attention span did he have? With this conjunction in the 5th, and ruling the 5th, where was it going to play out? And with the Sun dignified in Leo, and Venus peregrine, who was the "winner" in this behavior? Any questions?!

The other stunning conjunction in his chart was Mars-Jupiter-Neptune in Libra. Jupiter ruled Shelley's 8th House, and had dignity only by face, while Mars was in Detriment, but in his own Terms. Shelley died (8th House) by drowning (Neptune) in a storm (Mars) in a boat which was designed for speed (Mars), but which was extremely susceptible to taking on water. That Mars-Jupiter-Neptune in Libra was tightly trine Pluto, in the sign of the Water Bearer.

For the most part, we shall leave the synastry between them for another work. However, we may note that Percy's Sun in Leo was compatible with Mary's Moon in Sagittarius, his Moon in Pisces with her Cancer Rising, and his Taurus Rising with her Virgo. Other planets lined up rather strongly by aspect, so the bond between them was certainly understandable.

Let us also consider her complexional balance. She was completely balanced in Triplicity between wet and dry, with a small preponderance of cold. This meant that she would express mainly the melancholic and phlegmatic temperaments. *She* was not the one to be seen charging in where Angels fear to tread.

In examining her temperament from a seasonal perspective, we find instead a very dry person, with a closer balance between hot and cold. This balance of hot and cold indicates, as we have seen, the ability to move between reckless and conservative. She was, in fact, an enigma to her contemporaries. Her "lifestyle" was radical for the time -- getting involved with a married man, then marrying him just after his first wife committed suicide, not to mention authoring *Frankenstein*. People expected to meet a virago; instead, they met an unassuming, "feminine" woman.

But dry? Dry is the self discipline we met in Nicholas. By all accounts, Mary was *extremely* self disciplined, and her father had schooled her in Stoic philosophy, perhaps the perfect perspective for the dry type. By all accounts, it was Mary who imposed the discipline on Percy's writing, teaching him to devote regular periods to writing on a daily basis. In editing his poetry posthumously, she was taking his vision and *crystallizing* it: surely a dry discipline! Could we say that Mary's dry temperament contained Percy's wet? We have also seen in Nicholas' case that the dry personality is much less susceptible to pressures from the outside world, because it is not easily changed. For much of Mary's life, social pressure was extraordinarily virulent against her. While she suffered for this, it did not seem to faze her very much. And she *never* seemed to consider social approbation as a factor in any decision that she made.

She did find a creative way to express her cold placements: the Moon, Venus, M.C., and Fortuna. Firstly, both the Moon and Venus are cold in nature, so being seasonally cold is a comfortable state for them anyway. The Moon ruled her 1st, 2nd and 12th Houses. Aristotle said of hot and cold: "for 'hot' is that which associates things of the same kind (for to 'dissociate,' which, they say, is an action of Fire, is to associate things of the same class, since the result is to destroy things which are foreign), but cold is that which brings together and associates alike both things that are of the same kind and things which are not of the same class."[19] A "cold" person can juggle multiple different types of people in her life, while a "hot" person is more likely to prefer to be surrounded by people who are much more alike (as in: more like himself/herself). A "cold" person can learn from, and empathize with, a multitude of types and situations, because the cold person's response to provocation is to wait it out. Accordingly, a cold person is much better equipped to be an observer of others. A "hot" person is not unsympathetic, but is much more at a loss to understand people who are in some way fundamentally "different." Thus, in the areas of her life where it counted, Mary's "coldness" allowed her to appreciate diversity, characterize it on paper, and generally to benefit from it.

However, Mary's strong hot placements - the Sun, Mars, and Jupiter were all hot seasonally - also showed that she *did* like to associate with people like herself. She enjoyed the company of writers. After Percy's death, she did experiment with living with another woman who shared many similar circumstances.

From a seasonal perspective, only Mary's Saturn is out of quality: hot, rather than cold. (It is an interesting thing that the planets' intrinsic wetness and dryness was not considered as important as hotness/coldness; again, the predilection for the "active" nature of hot and cold.) This means that *all* of her planets except Saturn had recourse to function in a fashion similar to their own nature. In other words, Mary's "tools" were pretty well adapted to their own jobs. Planets in their own qualities are like having camouflage: they don't stick out like a sore thumb. Other people don't tend to notice them because they act like they are expected to act. From the standpoint of the Native, a planet in its own nature has a shorter learning curve associated with it. It is *much* easier to learn to use a Venus in Pisces than Venus in Leo! This is yet one more way that Godwin Shelley confounded her contemporaries: here was this bright, competent woman who *looked* the part of the mindless wonder that the men considered the ideal of Womanhood.

In the traditional system, Mary's mixture is somewhat wet, about even between hot and cold. I don't get the impression that this fits from her biographer. Mary's life was filled with the kind of tragedy that could completely cripple a less disciplined mind: she consistently showed herself capable of her best writing as a catharsis for mourning. This hardly strikes me as a "wet" strategy.

Godwin Shelley is a good example for contemplating the meaning of opposites. Do opposites annihilate each other in the modern sense (matter plus anti-matter produce energy while ceasing to be "material"), or simply mix to produce competing temperaments because neither component can be destroyed? I believe that, from a psychological perspective, the mixture hypothesis is the best. Mary described herself as "sanguine" in temperament. "Sanguine" is hot and wet, which is *not* her predominant type. However, Mary was trained by her father in stoicism, and she was taught to *value* a sanguine temperament. To a certain extent, she could believe that she was manifesting one. She could manifest the forward looking positivism of the sanguine type, but she was too clear (dry) in her thinking to enjoy the pleasant muzzy-headedness of the wet component of the true sanguine.

Percy was balanced between hot and cold in Triplicity, with a small predominance of dry. Thus, the two of them shared the phlegmatic temperament type, while Shelley also manifested to choleric. By season, Percy was also very dry, with a mix of hot and cold. Shelley alternated between fits of enthuisiasm and periods of relative quiet. As a couple, they adopted regular work habits which duplicated those that Mary developed as a child.

Since Mary and Percy both had significant hot and cold components, one immediately can understand that their relationship could metaphorically run "hot and cold." Obviously, any possible combination of the two is possible, from the doubly hot combination of initial passion, to one who wants it and the other who doesn't, to mutual coldness. According to their journals, this is *precisely* the way it worked: there were times when they were very clearly wrapped up in each other, times when one was in the mood, and times when they had both withdrawn from each other, the latter generally corresponding to Percy's infidelity periods.

We have occasionally referred to the various planets as ruling professions (Mercury ruling writers; Mars the military), or ruling conditions (Saturn ruling older people; Mercury youths). We have been treading around a concept that often becomes confused into the discussion of sign rulers: **natural rulers**. Now, what is a natural ruler? Astrologers throughout the millennia have tended to ascribe nouns to planets, signs and houses. So that for example, you can say that Saturn rules the element lead, or that Mercury rules quicksilver, or the element Mercury, or you can say that the Moon rules women, or that Aries rules England. These are natural rulerships.

Thus far, I have made no attempt to ascribe *sign rulership* to the Outer Planets. However, there is no necessary reason to exclude Uranus, Neptune and Pluto from *natural rulerships*. If it were a question that involved electricity, most classical horary astrologers would be perfectly happy to use Uranus. There is a little horary debate about whether it is better to use Uranus or Neptune for airplane travel and air flight, because flight astrology specialists disagree. There is some indication from the study of crashes that suggests Neptune to be a better Significator of airplanes and aviation. And, after all, an airplane in flight is truly a Ship at Sea!

	Triplicity	Seasonal	Traditional
☉	cold & wet	cold & dry	cold & dry
☽	cold & dry	hot & wet	hot & dry
☿	cold & wet	cold & dry	hot
♀	hot & wet	cold & dry	hot & wet
♂	hot & dry	cold & dry	dry
♃	hot & dry	cold & dry	wet
♄	cold & dry	hot & dry	cold & wet
Asc	hot & dry	hot & dry	hot & dry
M.C.	hot & dry	hot & wet	hot & dry
⊗	hot & wet	cold & wet	hot & wet

I would certainly, in a question about rape, look at Pluto... no question about it. If the question were drugs or oil, Neptune should be considered. On the other hand it's also instructive to find out what the classical ruler was if it is something that existed in earlier days. How does one find the classical ruler? *The Book of Rulerships!*

It is instructive, for example, in the case of petroleum or oil. The traditional natural ruler is the Moon, so if you want to go back and look at Bhopal, or a number of the accidents where we talk about gas or chemical leaks, you will find the Moon as prominently as you see Neptune. If it were a question of deception or forgetfulness, obviously you would want to look at Neptune. However, if it is a question about whether a statement is truthful, you would also want to look at the ruler of the 3rd House!

Prince Charles

Let's repeat the exercise for complexion type for Charles as well. In seasonal type he is cold and dry. Remember, it is the dry quality that possesses the ascerbic wit. The sanguine type is popular because he or she is the glad-hander, an obvious people person of an upbeat type. The choleric type is hot-headed. Charles is *not* hot-headed! He is very cool, even in a tense situation, such as being shot at by crazy fanatics. Being cool *is* being cold. And it's very hard to seem charming when you're basically dry. Witty, maybe, but not charming! Princess Diana's chart is also cold and dry by season, but only slightly. Given that she outdoes Charles on all the popularity polls, the moral may be that it pays to be cool, but not cold!

By Triplicity we see a weak hot and dry, or choleric type. I describe this as weak because there is a numerical majority in the two categories hot and dry, but it is not overwhelming. As a choleric type, Charles is athletic, competitive, ambitious, and eager - but within bounds. He is much more comfortable around people who share his basic views (hot). He is theoretically capable of change (often fixed signs are no more than theoretically capable of change!), but impervious to outside pressure in that direction (dry). Accordingly, he is incapable of adjusting his behavior to meet expected societal norms, and is likewise incapable of understanding the objections of others to his opinions. Now this does not mean that he cannot "train" to be King: he can. What this means is that he finds it difficult to adjust simply because others think he should. If his persona doesn't "play" with the press, he is not likely to change it.

By the traditional system, Prince Charles is hot, with a fairly even mixture of wet and dry. Again, this doesn't seem entirely convincing.

We can begin to conclude from these examples that the seasonal component to the complexional type appears to be more useful in delineation than the Triplicity one. My experience leads me to place about 2/3 reliance on the seasonal system and about 1/3 on the Triplicity system. As we will see, the Traditional method has components of each, but some other ideas are also embedded in it. The Medieval emphasis on Triplicity as the premier rulership type may need some re-casting, with the idea that the Triplicity patterns have the further usefulness of being a system of rulership. But let us explore this in a little more detail. If we re-examine Table Two, let us consider instead the *quali-*

ties of the planets comprising the Triplicity rulerships. In the first row, the Fiery Triplicity, we have the Sun, Jupiter and Mars. Now both the Sun and Mars are hot & dry, which is what the Triplicity is, but Jupiter is Hot and Wet. In the case of Earth, only Saturn is Cold and Dry. In the case of Air, only Jupiter is Hot and Wet. Finally, in the case of Water, only the Moon is Cold and Wet. Thus, it is clear that the Qualities that have been assigned to the Triplicities were not the basis for assigning the ruling planets!

I think it is also useful to examine the Triplicity qualities, especially where they double conflict with the seasonal emphasis. For instance, in Charles' case, the two planets with this double shift are the Moon and Venus! We can also compare Charles' chart to Mary Shelley's, as far as the seasonal correspondence between planet and quality. The two seasonally hot planets are the Moon and Saturn, both naturally cold. Each of these does end up with the right wet/dry component: the Moon - wet; Saturn - dry. The rest of Charles' planets are in cold seasons, so the Sun, Mars, and Jupiter are likewise out of quality. All three are in the dry season, so at least there is some correspondence to the planet's natural qualities. Only Venus is properly cold. This implies that Charles sticks out like a sore thumb (or maybe like big ears?) because he is put in positions where he has to act "against" his nature.

This particular type of analysis looks a lot like part of the considerations against Judgment in Horary. One of the considerations is whether the planetary hour ruler agrees with the ruler of the Ascendant by nature or Triplicity.[20]

With Charles' Leo Rising, the Sun shows a lot about how Charles will be seen. Charles' Sun is in Scorpio, which is not a great start as far as public acclaim: he is a private man thrust into a very public position. He has a reputation for courage and for seriousness. His Sun is peregrine, which suggests that he wanders (peregrinates), not always coming to the point. The Sun's Face is Venus. Charles has the bad luck to have a wife more popular than he is. The women in his life - the Moon and Venus - both possess strong dignity, while the male components - Sun and Mars primarily - are both peregrine. The biggest dignity of all is the Moon, his Mother!

The Moon is placed *very* strongly in the 10th House, which is not only the House of the Mother, but also the House of Monarchy: the Head of State. And that is exactly what his mother is! The Sun and Mars are Almutens of the 10th. Now eventually Charles (the Sun) may get a crack at being king himself, but for much of his life his mother (the Moon) is already *placed* there! The Moon at 0° Taurus has a lot of real estate to go through before leaving this, one of her favorite, signs.

Let's consider another House. The Co-Almutens of the 2nd House are Sun and Jupiter. Charles' Sun is peregrine. He doesn't have direct control of his fortune, since he is #2 in the family corporation. But the quality of the fortune is *big*, from the nicely dignified Jupiter in Sagittarius. But-- Jupiter is at 29°, a malefic degree by all accounts. (All of the signs have a term ruler of Saturn or Mars for the 29th degree: surely this does not help its reputation!) Another way of looking at this is that Jupiter is about to leave sign. Circumstances are about to change, and Jupiter is in Fall in Capricorn!

One standard classical way of reading the affairs of a house over time is to use the multiple sign rulers in a particular House. Charles' 2nd House is rather small: roughly 40 % of it is under the sign Leo, and roughly 60 % under Virgo. This would mean that the second (somewhat more than) half of life's finances would be given by Mercury. Charles' Mercury is peregrine, in aspect to Saturn in Virgo in the 2nd House (oh boy!) and opposed by the Moon. This suggests that Charles' finaces do *not* improve in the second part of life (which he is presumably already in). Further, it suggests that an action by his Mother (Moon opposing his Mercury of finances) will have a detrimental effect of his finances (Mercury-Saturn). This has already occurred. Elizabeth has declared that the House of Windsor pays taxes. Elizabeth is still listed as the world's wealthiest woman, but this knocked her down some on total assets!

One interesting twist to examining the dignities is to focus on one dignity in particular. Since fear is an especially potent motivator, let's look at his Faces. The planet which most dominates Charles' Face column is Saturn. His own Saturn is peregrine. So he sits and waits in the wings. This cannot be entirely pleasant.

Thus, we see that the major use of dignities and their derivatives is to gauge the strength of the planets concerned. The stronger the dignities of a planet, the easier it is for that planet to accomplish what it "wants." Precisely what those desires may be are determined by the sign placement of the planet, its house placement, and its aspects. A planet in Debility is strong, just as a planet in Dignity is. The difference is that the planet in Debility will tend to turn the normal functioning of that planet upside down to get what it wants.

Dignity does not imply genius or talent, except possibly in the sense of "street smarts," those qualities which help to accomplish a goal, but aren't that useful at setting the goal in the first place. Dignity implies power. It is up to the individual to choose the Light or the Dark Side of the Force. In the next Chapter, we shall learn how to add the Accidental Dignities into this picture to create even more detail.

Sources for Data Used

Prince Charles: Data provided by Judith Gee; op. cit. Rodden, Lois M. 1980. *The American Book of Charts*. Astro Computing Services: San Diego, CA.

Nicholas II: Palace records assumed. Cited in *Fowler's*.

Mary Godwin Shelley: Time given from Father's diary. Cited in Sunstein. From Blackwell Database: Astrolabe: Brewster, MA.

Endnotes

1   British Journal of Astrology, June 1931: *24*(9): 170.

2   Ever wonder about this curious nomenclature? We talk about planets being in their "own House" or "Domicile" when we mean their own sign. The origin of this concept is Greek. In the Greek system, whole sign Houses were used: starting with the *sign* of the Ascendant, the 1st House would begin at the beginning of the sign and run until the end of the sign. In this whole sign system, by definition, a planet in its own House was also in its own sign.

3   For illustrative purposes, consider the Fire signs. The Sun is the Day ruler because the Sun rules Leo, one of the Fire Signs. Jupiter rules Sagittarius, another Fire sign. Mars, the thrid Triplicity ruler, rules Aries. In the case of the Earth signs, Venus rules Taurus, the Moon is exalted in Taurus, and Saturn rules Capricorn. For the Air signs, Saturn is exalted in Libra, Mercury rules Gemini, and Jupiter has no relationship. For the Water signs, Venus is exlated in Pisces, the Moon rules Cancer, and Mars rules Scorpio. Thus, all the rulerships *except* Jupiter as mixed ruler of Air are derived from either the rulership or exaltation.

4   There is one other common classical method to handle questions of this sort. Most of the time, there are at least two signs within a single House. Thus, the sign on the 10th House would give the current job, the second sign in the House would give the next job. Stepping more than once or twice in a horary is not likely to work anyway, because it starts getting too theoretical.

5   *Op. cit.*, pp 76-76.

6   There is an error in the Term table on the inside front cover of *Essential Dignities* in the sign of Pisces: the numbers in *this* chapter are correct: Mercury's terms in Pisces run from 14° to 20°.

7   *Op. cit.*, pp 315-318.

8   *Op. cit.*, page 67.

9   We have already seen Lilly's student Coley use Almutens in his definition of the method for calculating the complexion of the Native: see Chapter 3.

10   For example, Saunders referred to major dignity and minor dignity, with Sign, Exaltation and Triplicity being major.

11   In classical usage, the 4th House rules the patrimony, which is the inheritance of land and property. The 8th House inheritance is the more liquid assets.

12   Massie, p ix.

13   Massie, p 31.

14   *Ibid.*, p. 17.

15   *Ibid.*, p 18.

16   Aristotle, pp 271-273.

17   Sunstein, p 5.

18   His data is 4 August 1792, 22:06:57 UT, Horsham, England, 51N04, 0W21. Source: a letter from his father to the family solicitor; from the Blackwell Database, published by Astrolabe.

19   Aristotle, p.271.

[20]   Gadbury, page 237: "Some Astrologers hold the Question to be Radical, when the Lord of the Ascendant, and the Lord of the Hour, are of one nature and Triplicity; which is easily known: suppose Leo ascend the Horoscope at the Querent's Interrogation, and Mars happen to be Lord of the Hour; here the Question will be found Radical, because the Sun, who is Lord of the Horoscope, and Mars, are of one Nature, *viz.* Hot and Dry; Or if at the same time, Jupiter fortune be Lord of the hour, the Question will then be admitted Radical, because Jupiter is of the same Triplicity with the Sun understand the same with the rest."

—— Chapter Six ——
Accidental Dignities

The real trouble with this world of ours is not that it is an unreasonable world, nor even that it is a reasonable one. The commonest kind of trouble is that it is nearly reasonable, but not quite. Life is not an illogicality; yet it is a trap for logicians. It looks a little more mathematical and regular than it is; its exactitude is obvious, but its inexactitude is hidden; its wildness lies in wait.

G. K. Chesterton[1]

In the last Chapter, we have considered the Essential Dignities. Now we move on to the Accidental Dignities. First, we begin by defining the difference.

Essential dignities are a result of the tropical zodiacal degree placement of a body or position. *Accidental dignities* occur by the propitious placement of that body or position within the horoscope. Let us consider a list of Accidental Dignities in Table One, which I will present from Lilly.

The accidental dignities and debilities can be divided into several generic types:
- House placement (i.e., angular, succedent, cadent)
- Motion (swift, slow, direct, retrograde)
- Oriental and Occidental
- Moon increasing or decreasing in Light
- Closeness to the Sun
- Aspects to malefic and benefic planets
- Conjunctions with fixed stars.

Table One. Accidental Dignities & debilities. Source: Lilly, *Christian Astrology*, p 115.

Accidental Dignities		Accidental Debilities	
In the M.C. or Ascendant	5	In the 12th House	-5
In the 7th, 4th & 11th Houses	4	In the 8th & 6th House	-2
In the 2nd & 5th Houses	3	Retrograde	-5
In the 9th House	2	Slow in Motion	-2
In the 3rd House	1	♄ ♃ ♂ Occidental	-2
Direct (except ☉ & ☽)	4	♀ ☿ Oriental	-2
Swift in Motion	2	☽ decreasing in light	-2
♄ ♃ ♂ Oriental	2	Combust of the ☉	-5
♀ ☿ Occidental	2	Under the ☉ Beams	-4
☽ increasing in light, or Occidental	2	Partile ♂ with ♄ or ♂	-5
Free from combustion & ☉ Beams	5	Partile ♂ with ☋	-4
Cazimi	5	Besieged of ♄ or ♂	-5
Partile ♂ with ♃ or ♀	5	Partile ☍ with ♄ or ♂	-4
Partile ♂ with ☊	4	Partile □ with ♄ or ♂	-3
Partile △ with ♃ or ♀	4	In ♂ or within 5° of Caput	
Partile ✶ with ♃ or ♀	3	Algol	-5
In ♂ with *Cor Leonis*	6		
In ♂ with Spica	5		

We can begin to understand the logic of this system if we examine each of the categories separately. However, one point before we proceed: the Outer Planets, and any other bodies that we choose to include (such as asteroids), may have *accidental* dignity even if they don't have *essential* dignity. You may note from Table One that some of the accidental dignities are concerned with whether the body is Inferior or Superior. All of the Outer Planets (including the modern ones, Uranus, Neptune, and Pluto) are superior. In the case of the asteroids that are Apollo bodies (i.e., have orbits that go from the asteroid belt to within the orbit of Mercury), the orbit is part Superior, part Inferior. Are we to classify these bodies—such as Icarus, Apollo, or Toro—as part Inferior, part Superior? It remains to be seen.

However, the other classification—whether a body is intrinsically benefic or malefic—is a bit more problematic. Venus and Jupiter were considered benefics, while Mars and Saturn are considered malefics. The Sun and Moon were not classified at all; Mercury was of mixed qualities. What shall we say for Uranus? Or Neptune? Or Pluto? Until we can classify them in a satisfactory manner, those *particular* accidental dignities which apply to benefics and malefics cannot apply, although other accidental dignities can be used.[2]

House placement

From very early in the development of the twelve house system, different houses were valued differently. Primary importance was given to the angular houses. Sources as early as Dorotheus placed the Ascendant and M.C. as the angles of greatest importance.[3] The precise order of importance of the houses was not agreed upon: for example, Manilius gave the I.C. greater importance than the Ascendant.[4]

Lilly's order is fairly easy to rationalize, however. First, he gave top priority to the Ascendant and Midheaven, which does follow accepted practice. Then, he gave the next level of importance to the Descendant and I.C., as well as to the 11th House. So how did the 11th House creep in here? Despite being succedent, the 11th House was the house of good fortune back into Hellenistic astrology, so its priority in Lilly's list is understandable.

Just as the Greek sources agreed on the primacy of the angles, so they agreed that the 12th House was the *worst* placement. On this, Dorotheus and Manilius agree completely. The 8th and the 6th Houses likewise had lousy reputations, since the 8th House represented Death, and the 6th House, illness. The other two succedent houses got the next level of "good" points in Lilly's system. Finally, we have what's left of the cadent houses. There is no question that the 9th House had a better reputation than the 3rd House. In fact, Dorotheus ranked the 2nd and 3rd Houses as being "not good" places.

Motion (swift, slow, direct, retrograde)

We have already noted in Chapter Two that observation of retrograde periods, and accordingly, planetary speed, goes back to the Babylonians. Later, Dorotheus stated that retrograde planets show "difficulty [and] misfortune."[5] We may recall the list of meanings of retrograde planets that we gave in Chapter Two. Retrograde planets:

- bring confusion[6]
- auger discord and contradiction[7]
- bring delay[8]
- can bring results suddenly[9]
- can bring return of a lost object[10]
- can bring a surprise outcome.[11]

Specific lists for the other portions of the speed cycle are harder to come by. Thus, Lilly gave one relevant aphorism: "A Retrograde Planet, or one in his first station [i.e., stationary going retrograde], Significator in the Question, denotes ill in the Question, discord and much contradiction."[12] Lilly's source was probably Bonatti, who spelled the situation out in more detail when he said:

The 25th Consideration is, Whether the Planet that is Significator be Retrograde, or Stationary to Retrogradation; for then it signifies mischief and damage; yet being Stationary, is not so bad, as being Retrograde. For the last notes the mischief to be, as it were, present and in being. But being Stationary notes that 'tis past and over.

The 26th Consideration is, Whether the Significator be in his Second Station, that is towards Direction: for that signifies also hindrances and evil, which already hath been and is past, yet some say that this Second Station is as good as direction: but this is only a way of speaking, as when one hath been sick and begins to grow well, we say he is recovered and sound, which is not simply true, but somewhat near it; for the First Station is not so bad as Retrogradation, so the Second Station is not so good as direction.[13]

John Partridge "Englished" the aphorisms of Bethem and presented them in his own work, *The Vade Mecum*. Two of them are similar to Bonatti: "5. If [the Significator is] Stationary to Retrogradation, he is a sound man receding from health; yet there is hope of recovery remaining. 6. If Stationary, he is as a Sick man amending."[14]

Thus, we see the sequence:

Direct = best,
Stationary Retrograde = getting worse,
Retrograde = worst,
Stationary Direct = getting better.

Oriental and Occidental

We have already seen a generic definition of oriental and occidental in Chapter 2. Oriental in general means rising before the Sun. Occidental in general means setting after the Sun. It basically defines when a planet will be visible: morning (oriental) or evening (occidental).

It is considered better for a superior planet to be oriental and for an inferior planet to be occidental. Why? Let's consider Inferior planets first. Recall from Chapter 2 that, geocentrically, Inferior planets appear to oscillate around the Sun. Therefore, if we use the Sun as the Ascendant in an Equal House system (Solar Houses), Venus and Mercury can only occupy the 11th, 12th, 1st or 2nd Houses. If Mercury or Venus is in the 11th or 12th, in this system, then said Inferior planet is oriental; if it is in the 1st or 2nd, the planet is occidental. If we examine the chart for the Sunrise prior to Nicholas II's birth, which is presented here in equal houses, we observe Mercury in the 1st House and Venus in the 2nd House. Both are Occidental: they rise after the Sun. If we examine the Sunset chart before Mary Shelley's birth, we see Mercury and Venus in the 7th House, both are setting *after* the Sun, so they are also Occidental.

If Mercury or Venus is *visible* in the morning (Oriental), then said planet is slowing down. Slowing down is "bad." Being slower of motion is "bad." Therefore, being oriental is "bad," so Venus or Mercury Phosphorus (at Dawn) is worse than Venus or Mercury Hesperus (at dusk).

When a Superior Planet is oriental, the Sun is moving away from conjunction with that body. Say what? Let's consider an example. If we take Mary Shelley's chart, we see that Mars is just 6° behind the Sun. We have already seen in Chapter 2 that superior planets disappear from the evening sky when they approach the conjunction to the Sun. When the Sun separates from them enough so that they are visible again (superior planets move slower than the Sun), they will now appear in the morning sky: that is, they will be oriental. The Sun is moving away from Mars, and so Mars is "moving" out of the range of combustion, or the Sun's beams (see below). This is considered good, although in Mary's case, Mars was still Combust. And this is what an oriental Mars, or other superior planet, is: a planet that has escaped combustion!

There are two kinds of positions that a superior planet can occupy: in the night sky, or in the morning sky. In the morning sky, the planet could rise before the Sun (as Shelley's Mars, or Nicholas II's Mars). That planet is in the Eastern part of the sky when the Sun rises. However, a planet may also be in the Western portion of the sky in the late night just before dawn, and hence, on its way to setting. Mary Shelley's Jupiter was in this state. If we draw an imaginary line in her chart from 7 Virgo to 7 Pisces, and orient her Sun as the Ascendant (Solar Houses again), we see that Jupiter would be in the 7th or 8th House. If we rotate our imaginary axis again so that 7 Virgo is the Descendant, Jupiter would be in the 1st or 2nd House of this chart. Jupiter would be visible in the pre-dawn sky in the West. Jupiter would *not* be visible at sunset, but would rise a couple hours later, and be visible throughout most of the night. So is Jupiter Oriental or Occidental? The answer depends on which definition you use, and herein lies the confusion about Oriental and Occidental Superior planets. (There is no such confusion about Inferior ones.)

The first coordinate system is defined as follows: start with the Sun. Any planet from 0° to 180° *measured by diurnal motion* is Oriental.[15] In Mary Shelley's case, we begin with her Sun at 7° Virgo. Diurnal motion is *backwards* through the signs. Jupiter at 19° Aries is less than 180° from the Sun, so Jupiter is Oriental by this system. But does this make sense? Jupiter here would be visible most of the night, yet be considered Oriental simply because it was still visible at dawn?

The other coordinate system was defined by Ptolemy. Again, let us define our system by using the Solar House System: the Sun as the Ascendant. Now, any planet that is *either* in the Quadrant from the Ascendant to the M.C., or in the Quadrant from the Descendant to the I.C. is Oriental. Occidental planets occupy the Quadrants from the M.C. to the Descendant, or from the I.C. to the Ascendant.[16] Back to Mary Shelley. We put 7° Virgo as the Ascendant. Now her Jupiter occupies the Quadrant from the M.C. to the Descendant: Jupiter is Occidental. This system gives the position in a more satisfying manner according to whether the planet in question is visible for most of the night, or not. It is this second system that we will use henceforth.

Ptolemy also made a germane comment concerning the nature of the action of an oriental or occidental planet: occidental planets are "slower to take action." Now clearly, Superior planets, having more ponderous orbits, are slower to take action anyway—except possibly Mars. Mercury and Venus are, if anything, too quick. Thus, Mercury and Venus benefit from being "slowed down" in action, while Superior planets are benefited by being hurried along, relatively speaking, by orientality.

One other tradition was maintained concerning whether the planets were oriental or occidental. The qualities (hot or cold, wet or dry) were believed to shift according to whether the planet was Oriental or Occidental. Table Two is taken from Gadbury.[17] Lilly said the following:

> See to what Planet the Significator commits his disposition, and if Orientall or Occidentall; if it be to Saturn, Jupiter or Mars, and they Orientall, the matter is sooner performed; later, if Occidentall, doe the contrary in Venus and Mercury.[18]

This was a rule that was applied more commonly before the 17th Century. In fact, it is part of the basis for the complectional (or complexional; take your pick) system that I referred to in the last chapter as "traditional." By Lilly and Gadbury's time, the qualities were mainly used medically anyway. In the table, we contrast two systems of the qualities of planets: the earlier system of the German John Garcaeus Junior (1530-1575), and the later system of Gadbury.

Table Two. Qualities of the Planets depending on Orientality & Occidentality. From Garcaeus and Gadbury.[19]

	Gadbury	Gadbury	Garcaeus	Garcaeus
	Oriental	Occidental	Oriental	Occidental
♄	cold & wet	cold & dry	cold & wet	dry
♃	hot & wet	hot & wet	hot & wet	wet
♂	hot & dry	hot & dry	hot & dry	dry
♀	hot & wet	cold & wet	hot & wet	wet
☿	hot & dry	hot & wet	hot	dry

In the Garcaeus system, occidental planets have only one quality, and Mercury has only one quality in any case. This system has an implicit Stoic point of view, because the Stoic system is the *only* one which allowed for single qualities. Those systems based on Aristotelian elements always had two components: one of being, one of becoming.

This system of Garcaeus was used in describing the complectional character of the five planets: the orientality or occidentality of the planet determined its complexional nature *regardless of sign*. We shall encounter the rest of this complectional system shortly.

Closeness to the Sun

We should remember, as Firmicus reminds us, that the category of planetary location relative to the Sun is actually Oriental - hidden - Occidental.[20] It is the "hidden" category that we examine next. There are three categories of nearness:

- *Cazimi*, or in the heart of the Sun, which means a conjunction with an orb of less than about 17' of arc.[21]
- *Combust*, or conjunct the Sun from 17' to about 8° of arc. Different sources vary slightly on the number of degrees. Lilly restricted combustion to occurring within the same sign, but this was not a typical restriction, and considering that the origin of the concept was a question of visibility, it is one that doesn't make any astronomical sense.[22]
- *Under the Sun's Beams*, conjunct the Sun from about 8° to about 17° of arc. The reason this category exists is that the planet in question *can* be seen if the viewing conditions are good. The actual ability to see a planet that is near to the Sun is basically determined by a combination of the brightness of the planet in question (e.g., Mercury is harder to see than Venus,

because it is not as bright), and the atmospheric conditions. Thus, we should label this category as referring to sometimes visible.

A planet near the Sun was thought to be "burned up," having no power of its own. However, to truly understand this concept, we have to re-integrate an idea that was common in Hellenistic Astrology, but then got lost somewhere along the way.

The Babylonians viewed the situation simply: a planet which was invisible, or which had impaired visibility, could not function to its greatest potential: it was impaired. That is essentially the interpretation which survived. However, the Greeks took a different view. The Sun and the Moon—the two luminaries—were considered to be as royalty. Now how would it look for royalty to wander around solo, without attendants? Bad... very bad! Thus, the Greeks developed the idea of attendants, literally spear-bearers. (Shall we update this to "Secret Service" or "bodyguards?" I don't think so!) Antiochus of Athens (2nd Century C.E.) gave a rather indefinite orb (at least three signs, possibly up to the opposition for spear bearing).[23] Ptolemy limited attending planets to within one sign of the luminary in question.[24] Attending planets had to have something in common with the Luminary. Morning (Oriental) diurnal planets[25] are better with the Sun; evening (Occidental) nocturnal planets[26] with the Moon. Since the Sun and the Moon are natural rulers of the Native's parents, unattended luminaries means that the Native was born to low station in life. We might posit a somewhat different range for attendance: 48°, the maximum elongation of Venus. Thus, Antigonus, in discussing the nativity of the Emperor Hadrian, commented that Hadrian's Moon with Mars and Venus in Occidental attendance, both in dignity; and his Sun, attended by diurnally placed Mercury and Saturn; both bode well in explaining how he became emperor.[27] Antigonus singled out Jupiter especially, Jupiter attending the Sun, and being conjunct the Ascendant (29° Capricorn). This issue of attendance was considered sufficiently important that Antigonus stated that it was this circumstance of having *all five* planets attending both lights that was so propitious about Hadrian's chart, especially as the whole configuration was centered on the Ascendant, (any other angle would do). Such an angular configuration would, by itself, be indicative of "kings ruling over many nations."[28]

So here we have a conundrum: on the one hand, Lilly can refer to the combustion as the worst of all debilities,[29] on the other, an unattended Sun bodes ill for the father! Combustion is definitely a mixed blessing, as Firmicus also indicated. Firmicus noted that when the Sun was with the chart ruler, the Sun gave enhanced responsibility to the chart ruler, but also enhanced pride.[30] And pride goeth before a fall? What do we do with all this?

Mary Godwin Shelley had Mars combust. Her father was an eminent writer, a Mercury-ruled profession (Sun in Virgo). But Mars? Shelley's Mars was peregrine, so her father, William Godwin, had perennial money problems. And despite a good deal of contemporary fame, Godwin's popularity dropped noticeably during his lifetime to the point that he was a virtual unknown shortly after his death.

As for Shelley's Moon (mother), the Moon was unattended, peregrine, and conjunct the Descendant, the Portals of Death.

Maybe Mercury and Uranus are also attendant upon the Sun, with Uranus being likewise combust, but Mercury just outside of beams. However, both are Occidental, which probably means that they should be considered primarily combust, not attending. Godwin's writings (Mercury) were on politics, and he *was* a radical leftist for his time, a supporter of the French Revolution and of human rights, which certainly made him Uranian! Mercury within the circle of attendants may show the number of writers who clustered around Godwin. Many of these writers, however, were there for a handout.

Looking at this whole situation from Godwin Shelley's perspective (after all, it is her chart, not her father's!) the Sun rules the 4th House of patrimony. Because of her father's money problems, Godwin Shelley ended up supporting him. His estate had nothing for her. What she got from him was his Stoic approach to life, the intellectual advantages of his library and learning, and his literary friends.

If we consider her Mars and Uranus primarily as combust planets, and not as attendants of the Sun, the pattern shifts away from her father and onto her. There is no question that Shelley's life was revolutionary for her time. She evidently had few regrets, and often was completely oblivious to the extent that her lifestyle shocked others - a rather typical response of a Uranus type.[31] While Shelley was not especially personally combative in the martial sense, she inherited from her father the point of honor that it is better to tell the truth in all circumstances. Thus, her only approaches were to either give her unjaded opinion, or to keep completely silent. To a society that was used to the niceties of the white lie, this no doubt was shocking.

Let's review some of the ideas about what a combust planet does in the chart. Combust planets:

- keep matters from coming to light; this can be used in electional astrology to start an enterprise where secrecy is valued[32]
- bring illness and death if the combust planet is the Significator in a question of life[33]
- bring ill consequence to the combust Significator[34]

- obscure matters when under the Sun's beams.[35]

Get the impression that combustion wasn't so great? On the other hand, a planet Cazimi, or in the heart of the Sun, *was* supposed to be great. Unfortunately, I haven't seen this in practice. There are few classical examples to really ponder, but it seems from my experience to matter greatly whether the cazimi planet has essential dignity. This also seems to make a considerable difference with respect to combust planets. Dignified combust planets *definitely* act better than ones without essential dignity.

The Moon increasing or decreasing in Light

We begin our discussion of the Moon with the phase that almost everyone uses at the beginning: the New Moon. Since we have just finished a discussion of combustion, we should note that the actual New Moon–the exact conjunction–would correspond to a Moon cazimi, which should be momentarily advantageous, in a sea of combustion. As Lilly said, "In all Questions, know there's not so great an affliction to the Moon, as when she is in conjunction with the Sun; the ill aspects of the Infortunes doth much afflict her, but none so powerfull as her own Combustion."[36]

As the Moon separates from conjunction, she is waxing, or increasing in light. Dorotheus gives one intriguing example of the use of the phases of the Moon: for determining the price in transactions that involve buying and selling.[37] From the time that the Moon emerges from the Sun's beams until the first square, the item purchased will be neither underpriced, nor overpriced. From the first square to the Full Moon, then the seller benefits, as would the plaintiff in bringing a lawsuit. From opposition to second square, the buyer benefits from a lower price. From the second square to the next New Moon, neither side is favored.

A more conventional presentation of the phases is given by Gadbury, who retained the tradition that there is a shift in quality of the Moon, depending on her phase.[38] This is summarized in Table Three.

Table Three. Qualities of the Moon according to her phase. From Gadbury & Garcaeus.

New Mood to 1st Square	Hot & Wet
1st Square to Full Moon	Hot & dry
Full Moon to last Square	Cold & dry
Last Square to next New Moon	Cold & wet

Remember our old friend, the seasonal sequence of qualities from Chapter 3? Of course you do! This sequence of qualities is *exactly* the sequence for Spring - Summer - Fall - Winter. The derivation of Rudhyar's modern lunation cycle is obvious. This table is the source of the complectional definition of the Moon in our "traditional" system: the phase of the Moon is considered more significant than the sign of the Moon.

At any rate, during the waxing portion of the cycle, the Moon is metaphorically hotter, which means more active, or productive. It is interesting that we see Dorotheus's cycle of commodity prices in a different light through this table: when the Moon is in a wet phase, the price is fair. When the Moon is wet, there is a true connection between buyer and seller. The advantage shifts to one party during the two dry phases of the cycle, when the connection between the two is either severed, or minimized.

Aspects to malefic and benefic planets

First, in case it isn't clear: Saturn is the greater malefic; Mars the lesser. Jupiter is the greater benefic; Venus the lesser. This particular class of accidental dignity or debility needs hardly any explanation, because it is very close to modern usage, to the extent that modern astrologers can keep from tripping over the word "malefic." A phase of temporary insanity has descended over part of the astrological world, leaving some practitioners under the odd belief that there are no problems, only opportunities.

In any case, a conjunction, sextile, or trine between the planet in question and a benefic planet (or the North Node, which is also considered benefic) is considered good. A conjunction, square or opposition to a malefic planet is considered bad. It only remains to define the word *partile*. A partile aspect is one in the *same* degree. Now this is a very important distinction: I did not say "within one degree." An aspect between one planet at 15° 01' Scorpio and another at 15° 59' Leo is a partile square, while another between 15° 01' Scorpio and 14° 59' Pisces is a *plaktic* trine, not partile. As an aside, in horary, when the rule for perfection, or a positive outcome, involves an approaching ptolemaic aspect, a separating partile aspect will still give perfection.

Conjunctions to fixed stars

Lilly's list of accidental dignities and debilities only includes three fixed stars: Regulus (*Cor Leonis*), Spica, and Algol.[39] In fact, the appropriate list is highly dependent on the question at hand. For example, in any question of blindness, *any* fixed star which has something to do with blindness is relevant to the interpretation, and could just as well be assigned a dignity or debility.[40] Similarly, there are stars associated with shipwrecks, other kinds of disasters, war, fires, floods... all the really *fun* things! Lilly gave a 5° orb for Algol, which may be way too much: probably 2° is more like it.[41]

There are actually two coordinate systems in use for examining the effects of the fixed stars. The problem is latitude, because many of the stars used are nowhere near the Ecliptic. Consequently, a "conjunction" based solely on ecliptic longitude would not appear to be a conjunction at all if observed in the sky. When Lilly, or the rest of the Renaissance astrologers, used the fixed stars, it was through tables based on ecliptic longitude. The original system, that of the Babylonians, relied on direct observation, and had emphasized what star was rising or setting, hence their coordinate system was based on what we now call oblique ascension. Fortunately, both systems can be studied through some modern computer programs, so we may expect to get a clearer picture about the nuances of the two systems over the next few years.[42]

Some Example Applications

Since we have now discussed the components of the accidental dignities system, let us return to our example charts and apply them, and then finally consider the question of the relative importance of the accidental versus the essential dignities, or perhaps more correctly: what is the difference between the two?

This is where we can also consider the combination of temperament components in our "traditional" column. Let me review this calculational system specifically:

- For the Sun, use the seasonal qualities of the Sign
- For the Moon, use the phase qualities
- For the planets, use the qualities assigned by orientality or occidentality
- For the Angles, the Part of Fortune (and the Node, if you like), use the Triplicity qualities of the sign.

Is this a mixed bag, or what?

Nicholas II

We can begin with the house placements of Nicholas' planets. He had Mercury, Uranus, Venus, and Saturn in the angular houses, the most dignified placements. The Moon, Jupiter and Neptune are placed in the 8th House, which is high on the debility scale. Also, with his Sun within 5° of the M.C., his Sun can be considered angular as well.[43]

Planets in angular houses tend to get the most attention: from ourselves, and from others. We have already seen how Mercury in Gemini gave Nicholas the power to express himself: as Czar, his communicated wish was his command. We have also seen how this strong Mercury may have conferred some language ability, but it is not the guarantor of genius. Angular Mercury is even more promint than its essential dignity suggests.

His Mercury was opposite equally angular Saturn, but in this case, Saturn was peregrine. That peregrine Saturn represented in part his father's vacillation and uncertainty about how to raise him. However, Saturn is also the quintessential authority figure, and so it shows, among other things, the Native's vacillation about authority, which is even more aggravated with Saturn retrograde. Nicholas *was* an absolute monarch, but it was not a position that he relished, except occasionally. Now the I.C. is the least public of the angles,[44] but in Nicholas' case, it was critical. With Saturn there, in the house that rules patrimony, his inheritance from his father, namely Russia itself, was at best a mixed blessing, a diverse place that lacked cohesion and unified purpose. And this opposition between the students and merchant class (Mercury) and authority (Saturn) was certainly to gain prominence during his reign. Uranus was likewise angular, and hence, more important. However, Uranus was also Occidental (not good).

Now about the 8th House: We know the 8th is "bad" because it rules, among other things, death. So here we have Jupiter, the ruler of the 7th, the spouse, in the 8th, of death. Further, the 8th House Moon is "attended" by Jupiter and Neptune, both planets which have some native ecclesiastical connection. And Rasputin? A holy man in the tradition of Russia's holy crazy-wise men, which I think makes him far more Neptunian.

In order to examine Nicholas' planets by orientality/occidentality, let's first list them, and then classify them according to whether this is the way they are supposed to be. This is shown in Table Four.

Table Four. Occidental and Oriental planets of Nicholas II. Those with dignity by placement are marked with an asterisk.

Oriental	Occidental
Jupiter*	Mercury*
Moon	Uranus
Neptune (*)	Venus*
Mars	Saturn
Pluto (*)	

I have marked Neptune and Pluto as having dignity by being oriental, because this is the placement one would expect, since they are superior planets. Whether this terminology is meaningful remains to be seen with usage, since oriental and occidental refer to appearance, which is not a general function of these outer planets.

Conspicuously lacking in oriental and occidental dignity are the two malefics, Saturn and Mars. Now we may recall that if the planets are oriental or angular they are quick starters, if they are occidental or succedent, they are slower to react.[45] With Mars cadent but oriental, and Saturn angular but occidental, we have the best of both worlds, the ability to react slowly or quickly. However, the absence of dignity on the part of Saturn would tend to put reaction time in the category, "too little, too late."

Mars, which tends to be belligerent anyway, is a little slowed down by being cadent. While not considered dignified by nature of its Orientality, I would have to consider this to be desirable. Why? Mars is a malefic, and specifically, it is the malefic that creates problems by being rash and impetuous. Therefore, any placement that would slow down Mars, or in any way apply the brakes would be advantageous. This is, by the way, one of the reasons it is important to understand the nature of the accidental dignities, and not to apply them without thinking about it.

We also can observe, in a modern context, that Nicholas' Mars was in a Gauquelin sector: the cadent houses, and the late part of the angular ones (late diurnally, meaning the section right around the angle in question) are the ones which show the higher tenancy in the charts of successful people of that type. Mars in a Gauquelin sector is the placement for successful athletes. Now obviously, no future Czar of Russia was going to have the opportunity to try out for track and field! But, like others of his class, Nicholas rode, and evidently he rode well.

We have already observed that Nicholas' Mercury was opposite Saturn. An aspect with Saturn is another form of accidental debility. This Mercury was also combust, but as we have observed, that also makes Mercury one of the Sun's attendants, although possibly not, since Mercury is occidental. Now what to believe: attendant, or combust? Were this a horary, I would unequivocally say, combust, at least as far as an interpretation of Mercury as Significator of an issue. However, in a natal chart, the answer is closer to mixed!

Another way to interpret this idea is as follows. Mercury is a weak attendant to the Sun, although Occidental planets are not as good attendants to the Sun as Oriental ones. The Sun gains a good counselor, because Mercury is dignified, not only by essential dignity, but by being Occidental and angular. Mercury in Gemini or Virgo combust has comparatively little debility: possibly, a small speech impediment, possibly a little difficulty in verbalizing thoughts which come too quickly for words. But the intellect (such as it is) is fully at the disposal of the Sun, and hence, the life force. The Sun in either Gemini or Virgo (or in Nicholas' case, Taurus) is peregrine. But this dignified attendant in the form of Mercury adds to the prestige of the Sun through such a useful mouthpiece. What does Mercury get out of the deal? Pride... intellectual pride!

We could hypothesize the same effect in a different chart with Venus as the Sun's attendant, if Venus were in either Libra or Taurus. However, Mercury is neither a diurnal nor a nocturnal planet. Venus is a nocturnal planet, so it would probably only be correct to consider Venus as a possible attendant in the chart for a night birth. In comparing Venus to Mercury as an attendant, the native is served less by intellectual skill or wit, as by charm, or simply magnetism. A quick sort through my files revealed Hitler (Venus under beams [USB]), Aleister Crowley (combust), Karl Marx (USB), and Oliver Cromwell (USB); all born at night. Let's examine Crowley's chart in more detail, so we may understand this phenomenon more clearly.

Aleister Crowley

We know Crowley was an active member of the Golden Dawn in England, the author of a Tarot deck that is still in use, and a ghost writer for Evangeline Adams. First, his qualities are shown below.

Crowley has the most "unbalanced" distribution we have examined yet by Triplicity, with a clear preponderance of hot and wet, which gives the sanguine temperament. Notice that, of the ten planets and positions used in this calculation, only three (Sun, Venus, and Saturn) are actually in air signs. The rest of the count is created by combining fiery angles with watery Moon, Mercury and Jupiter.

Crowley	Triplicity	Season	Traditional
☉	hot & wet	cold & dry	cold & dry
☽	cold & wet	cold & wet	hot & dry
☿	cold & wet	cold & dry	dry
♀	hot & wet	cold & dry	wet
♂	cold & dry	cold & wet	dry
♃	cold & wet	cold & dry	wet
♄	hot & wet	cold & wet	cold & wet
Asc	hot & dry	hot & dry	hot & dry
M.C	hot & dry	hot & wet	hot & dry
⊗	hot & wet	cold & wet	hot & wet

By season, Crowley's distribution is also lop-sided, but in this case, it is very cold, with an even distribution of wet and dry. To my mind, this fits far better with the image I have of him. Crowley *was* a very cool customer! By the traditional method, Crowley is hot and dry.

Crowley had three planets strong by essential dignity: Venus in Libra, Mars in Capricorn, and Saturn in Aquarius. This is perhaps the time to mention an important aphorism in horary which also applies to natal: that malefic planets in dignity are less malefic in action than when they lack dignity.[46] On the other hand, with both malefics in Saturn's signs, Crowley was certainly one of the more charismatic manifestations of the Dark Side of the Force! Saturn ruled his 8th House, while Mars ruled his 5th, so perhaps we can begin to understand something about sexuality as a memorable theme in his spiritual quest. With the Moon in the 9th House in Pisces, the spiritual interest was definitely there. His Moon was disposed by Jupiter, one of the Sun's "weak" attendants (since all of the potential attendants are Occidental).

So here is Crowley, with a Sun in Fall, but Venus dignified in weak attendance. Which is better (or worse): a dignified Sun with less than dignified attendants, or dignified attendants with a less than dignified Sun? Let's contrast Crowley with the opposite condition, personified in this case by Catherine de Medici.

Catherine de Medici

Again, let's begin with Catherine's qualities:

	Triplicity	Season	Traditional
☉	hot & dry	hot & wet	hot & wet
☽	hot & wet	hot & wet	hot & wet
☿	cold & wet	cold & wet	hot
♀	hot & dry	hot & wet	wet
♂	cold & wet	hot & dry	dry
♃	cold & wet	cold & dry	hot & wet
♄	cold & dry	cold & wet	cold & wet
Asc	hot & dry	hot & wet	hot & dry
M.C	cold & wet	cold & wet	cold & wet
⊗	hot & wet	cold & wet	hot & wet

Catherine was equally balanced between hot and cold by Triplicity, with a slight preponderance of wet. By season, she was strongly wet, with a mixture of hot and cold. By the traditional method she was sanguine, hot and wet. No question: she was wet in all systems. One of the more heinous events that Catherine presided over was the St. Bartholomew's Day Massacre, which was in part a political solution in France to warring factions at the highest levels of government. Factions, and their attending conspiracies, are a hallmark of the wet temperament applied to politics: wet people see and make connections. While we may laud the sanguine type for the wet "people-orientation," that same wet quality applied in a more malicious context sees spies and plots everywhere. And given sufficient resources (which Catherine had) the wet person will make sure that her spies are there in abundance so her plots will succeed! Catherine was, if nothing else, a zealous practitioner of *realpolitik*. One particular aspect of the wet temperament is that wet is more susceptible to conspiracy theory. Catherine was certainly more than uncommonly alert, and the politics of France at this time supported her suspicions.[47]

Catherine had Sun in Aries with Venus in Aries: the Sun exalted, Venus in Detriment, but barely dignified by Face. So: who fared better? Well... Crowley didn't become king, but then, he was hardly born to it. Catherine's abrasive demeanor certainly did *not* serve as a role model for subservient womanhood. Her Sun provided the powerhouse, and her attendant Venus was definitely not in great shape. Thus, Venus basically suffered the fate of a combust planet: attendant in form only. In Crowley's case, it was the dignified Venus that enhanced his (solar) prestige.

While we're at it, we can remark on the high count of angular planets in Catherine's chart, as well as in Crowley's. Catherine's Saturn and Pluto in the 10th House with Saturn ruling the 10th, does nicely illustrate the nature of her reign: the mailed glove. Crowley has Neptune and Pluto in the 10th, with the Sun and Mars as co-Almutens of the M.C. In his case, we have the hero's journey (Sun and Mars) with a spiritual (Neptune and Pluto) slant: or perhaps only snake oil! Unfortunately, it was a debilitiated hero's journey, with the Sun in the exact degree of Fall.

We are left with the conclusion that combust planets in the natal chart can either act as attendants, or as combust, or both. The key to determining the *modus operandi* is to examine the essential dignities of the planets involved.

We may now return to the last two types of accidental dignities: aspects to benefics or malefics, and fixed stars. We have already remarked on Nicholas' Mercury-Saturn opposition. The good news on the ledger was the conjunction between Nicholas' Moon and Jupiter, although it was separating. However, since Jupiter had dignity only by term, the conjunction wasn't that helpful.

Finally, Nicholas' Sun was within 5° of Algol. Bad... very bad. Algol was the *losing-your- head* star. Nicholas, however, was a victim of modern technology, not just ancient star lore!

Mary Godwin Shelley

Let's repeat the portion of the exercise that we have not already performed for Mary Shelley. First, her oriental and occidental placements are summarized in Table Five.

Table Five. Occidental and Oriental planets of Mary Godwin Shelley. Those with dignity by placement are marked with an asterisk.

Oriental	*Occidental*
Mars*	Uranus
Saturn*	Mercury*
Pluto (*)	Venus*
Moon	Neptune
	Jupiter

Now it may not be intuitively obvious that her Moon is Oriental. If there is any doubt about a placement, the simplest thing to do is calculate a sunrise or sunset chart for the day - whichever is closer in time - and then put the *natal* placements in that wheel. (In other words, use the actual position of the Moon, not the sunrise or sunset position.) This gives you the correct alignment of house cusps. In Shelley's case, 7° Virgo on the Descendant gives 21° Sagittarius on the M.C., which puts the Moon in the Oriental Quadrant. Notice that whether you do a sunrise or a sunset chart, the oriental quadrants are the same: from the Ascendant to the M.C., and from the Descendant to the I.C.

Both of Mary's Inferior planets are accidentally dignified by virtue of occidentality. They are essentially dignified anyway, so this merely adds to their strength. Mary's two malefics also gain accidental dignity, which simply makes their essential debility that much more of a problem. Mars is a natural ruler of the romantic male in a woman's chart (along with the Sun), and Saturn is Daddy. Both were certainly important in her life, but did they really help her, or did she do more to help them? She supported her father financially, and established her late husband's fame by publishing the definitive version of his works, not to mention editing same to the point of clarity. But were they monsters in her life? No! Except, of course, those pieces of their personae that ended up as part of Frankenstein's monster!

Mary had Venus square Saturn, a benefic sqaring a malefic. Need we point out the archetypical meaning of radical daughter confronting conservative Daddy? Daughter won, but not without cost!

Prince Charles

Prince Charles' oriental and occidental planets are shown in Table Six. Charles, unlike Mary Shelley, has Inferior Planets essentially debilitated, which cannot help his quintessential case of foot-in-mouth disease. These bodies will act in haste, relatively speaking, which means he will tend to speak too much, or inappropriately. On the other hand, with Mars occidental, there is more of a brake on his temper.

And speaking of foot-in-mouth... unlike our last two examples, here we have a case where attending planet Mercury is peregrine, and the Sun is peregrine. And finally we see some Oriental attendants, which is what they are supposed to be, if attending the Sun. However, Venus is definitely a nocturnal planet, Neptune probably should be classified as such, and Mercury is mixed, so again we have a weak case for attendance. If we take Mercury literally as his attendant, since Mercury at least is mixed, how good is the advice he is getting? Not very! And the quality is definitely not enhanced through Mercury's conjunction to the South Node. Or alternatively, if it is good, it is not being put to him in a way that he can either understand it, or act on it. The same analogy with Nicholas provides a slightly different slant, but the same outcome: in Nicholas' case, he had advisors who understood a great deal, but, with his Sun in a different sign than his Mercury, it is doubtful that Nicholas could really take it in. Nicholas had good advice that he was unable to act upon; Charles is not getting the best advice, or he is getting it in a way that he cannot use it.

Table Six. Occidental and Oriental planets of Prince Charles. Those with dignity by placement are marked with an asterisk.

Oriental	Occidental
Mercury	Mars
Venus	Jupiter
Neptune (*)	Uranus
Saturn *	
Pluto (*)	
Moon	

Incidentally, if we examine this Hellenistic concept of attendants, especially as it applies to one's parents, we see in Charles' chart Mum (the Moon) dignified in Taurus in the 10th House. True enough for Elizabeth II. However, she is unattended, except for the North Node, which must be enough in this case! Dad, the Sun (switching to solar symbolism here), is peregrine, and Prince Phillip is *not* the one in charge. Of course, where to draw the line between Sun as Dad and Sun as self is another matter!

The one other dignity shown in Charles' chart is the out-of-sign trine between the Moon and Jupiter. However, the Moon is so strongly identified with his mother, that I don't know how much benefit Charles actually derives from this.

So what does it mean?

For several years, my Horary study group in San Francisco took advantage of a very nice DOS-based program written by Allen Edwall. In consultation with Carol Wiggers, Allen programmed the accidental dignity points into "Horary Helper," so that the user had the accidental points available without having to calculate them, a great aid to their usage! Consequently, for all the horaries we studied, we had both the essential and accidental dignity "points" for all the Significators in the chart.

If you go back and look at the list of accidental dignities and their point values, it will become obvious that the point values add up. For example, Nicholas II's Mercury gets 5 points for being in the M.C., 4 points for being direct, 2 points for being swift, 2 points for occidental, and -5 points for being combust. This totals 5+4+2+2-5 = 8 points, plus 5 points for being in Gemini, plus 2 points for being in Term, for a combined total of 15 points. Partly, I suspect, because the point values for the combined calculation were higher, my group was initially attracted to this value. The higher numbers generated by combining the various accidental possibilities appeared to produce more precision, because there were more possible values. I, however, being conservative, stuck to the essential dignities as the primary means of evaluating the Significators. After about three years, the group switched back to the essential dignities: the accidental ones were simply not giving the correct answer.

Does this make the accidental dignities useless? No. In the first place, horary is completely different from natal in one critical respect. Horary questions do not evolve into new possibilities - not if there is any chance of getting the answer right! The important horary consideration is whether the chart shows any action, and whether the players are strong enough to take advantage of the action.[48] People can and do change, and are affected by environmental influences in ways that one can hardly anticipate years in advance. In addition, in horary, the planets that are used in the delineation are defined by the nature of the question, and hence what rules what in the chart. In the natal chart, however, *all* planets will generally be active at some point in the life, and often many in roughly the same time period. Hence, the accidental dignities become more important as the chart is seen as a series of players, each vying for solo attention.

The essential dignities tell which planets have the power to affect results, or be affected in turn. The accidental dignities specify the stage on which those planets operate, the kinds of aid or interference the other planets will provide, and how effectively the power can be applied. They may also tell something of the Native's ability to maximize any opportunity which may be knocking. Accidental dignities are especially important in mundane: especially angularity, conjunctions with fixed stars, and closeness to the Sun. The difference may be summarized by stating that the accidental dignities can bring prominence, but essential dignities bring strength.

In the next chapter, we will take up another concept which underlies some of the considerations of both essential and accidental dignity: sect. We still don't know quite what to do with it, except to remark that sect may represent an independent system of dignity, or perhaps a matrix for the functioning of the entire chart.

Sources for Data Used:

Aleister Crowley: Data from Crowley with the time "11 p.m. to 12" given in *Confessions of Aleister Crowley*. Edited by Symonds and Grant (Hill and Wang, 1970). From Blackwell Database: Astrolabe: Brewster, MA.

Catherine de Medici: "... Barbault, in "TPA" gives the "version de theme de Junctin de Florence, l'astrologue de l'epoch" with the time of birth as 'au lever du jour'... For our compilation 10h.15m. after sunset (04:15:20 UT, 05:00:20 a.m. LMT) is used since this falls between dawn and sunrise and fits the criteria of "au lever du jour" (dawn or sunrise)." From Blackwell Database: Astrolabe: Brewster, MA.

Hadrian: 7 a.m. LMT (06:36 UT) in Halica, Spain derived from his horoscope in Neugebauer & Van Hoesen, pp. 80, 90, 91. From Blackwell Database: Astrolabe: Brewster, MA.

Endnotes

[1]   Chesterton, G. K. 1908. *Orthodoxy. The Romance of Faith*. Image, New York: page 81.

[2]   I discussed some of these issues with regard to rulerships in *Essential Dignities*, pages 101-107.

[3]   *op. cit.*, p. 164.

[4]   *op. cit.*, p. 151.

[5]   *op. cit.*, p. 165.

[6]   al-Biruni, page 60.

7   Lilly *CA*, page 299.
8   *Ibid.*, page 4
9   *Ibid*, pp 107, 198, 211, 406.
10   *Ibid.*, pp   211, 357.
11   *Ibid.*, page 211.
12   *Ibid.*, page 299.
13   Bonatti (Bonatus) (1676). 25th & 26th aphorisms.
14   Partridge, page 323.
15   Lilly, *CA*, p. 114. Lilly does not, unfortunately, specify his coordinate system completely, but simply refers to the planet being between conjunction and opposition to the Sun. However, if that planet is to also match the second condition of rising before (Oriental) or after (Occidental) the Sun, then the arc to opposition *must* be in the direction of diurnal motion.
16   Ptolemy (Robbins), p. 243.
17   *op. cit.*, p. 94.
18   Lilly, *CA*, page 300.
19   The information on Garcaeus' system was provided to me in manuscript form by Rob Hand, who is translating this work for Project Hindsight.
20   *op. cit.*, page 38.
21   Rob Hand has mentioned that he has found a reference in Bonatti (as yet unpublished) that specified that the latitude must also be in arc for the planet to be truly considered cazimi.
22   Lilly, *CA*, page 113.
23   *op. cit.*, p. 23. He also did not limit the terminology to attendance on the Luminaries.
24   *op. cit.*, pp 241-243.
25   The naturally diurnal planets (other than the Sun, of course) are Jupiter and Saturn.
26   The naturally nocturnal planets (other than the Moon) are Mars and Venus.
27   The data for Hadrian, for those who wish to study the chart further, is 24 January 76 C.E., 6:36 am UT, Halica (37N30, 6E00). Several points are germane to this present discussion. First, this is a nocturnal chart, and Antigonus listed the Sun as being an attendant of the Moon, although the Sun rises before the Moon. Both Mercury and Saturn have unequivocally risen. Saturn is 34° ahead of the Sun (Saturn 0° Capricorn; Sun 4° Aquarius). Mars is 23° behind the Moon, and is also out-of-sign compared to the Moon (Moon 27° Aquarius, Mars 20° Pisces). Thus, we can conclude that attendance was not based on being in the same sign.
28   Cited in Cramer, page 169.
29   Lilly, *CA*, page 301.
30   *op. cit.*, pp 142-143.
31   It is typical of a Uranian to be oblivious to a moment's revolutionary qualities, as everyone around the Uranian is reeling, just as it is typical of a Plutonian to deny obsessing over something that the Plutonian's associates agree unanimously can only be obsession! The major meaning of a combustion for the Native may be this obliviousness: the planet being invisible, it is out of sight, out of mind. Meanwhile, however, everyone else is painfully aware of it, because invisibility does not affect the Native's ability to express it, only to control or temper it!
32   Dorotheus, p 264. But note that in the Centriloqium of "Hermes Trismegistus, translated by Henry Coley, he states that it is better for secrecy if the Moon is coming *from* combustion, page 337.
33   Lilly, *CA*, pp 129-131, Coley, p 327.
34   Partridge, p. 51.
35   *Ibid.*, p. 344.
36   Lilly, *CA*, page 301.

37   *op. cit.*, p 322.

38   *op. cit.*, p. 94.

39   The positions of these stars in 1950 coordinates are: Regulus 29 Leo 33, Spica 23 Libra 34, and Algol 25 Taurus 53.

40   We should add here that, in addition to the traditional list of fixed stars associated with blindness, Diana K. Rosenberg has found that *any* star which represents an eye in a constellation can be considered a blindness star. The most important "eye" star is Aldebaran (9 Gemini 31 in 1950 coordinates). the eye of the bull.

41   See the Index that appears as Appendix B under the category "Fixed Stars" for a more complete list of names, and source listings for the meanings.

42   At this time, one computer program, Solar Fire 3.0, has a planetarium module which is very helpful for visualizing these systems. Solar Fire also allows the user to choose ecliptic longitude or oblique ascension (parans) for studying conjunctions.

43   Lilly, *CA*, p 391.

44   Manilius, page 147, but note the exact quotation: "[The I.C.] though situated] in the lowest position, bears the world poised on its eternal base; in outward aspect its influence is less, but is greater in utility."

45   Ptolemy, p. 241.

46   Dorotheus, p. 164-165, Bonatti, Aphorism #32.

47   In case you're wondering, Niccolo Macchiavelli was exactly balanced hot & cold, wet & dry, which certainly allowed him to advocate a position of maximum flexibility. My point about wet is that a person who is highly dry is going to give little or no credence to even the *possibility* of conspiracies because s/he cannot imagine anyone being able to work that closely together, a wet quality. A very wet person may be unable to believe that people *aren't* working together at all times, about all things.

48   For example, in a question of relationship, it is not only important to discern whether the parties are capable of coming together (this is known generically in horary as perfection), but also whether they will do so if inclined. This translates as follows: John may be attracted to Mary, but he may be too unsure of himself to get up the nerve to ask her out. Or, his mother may just have died, and all of his attention is going into sorting out her multi-billion dollar business empire...

── Chapter Seven ──
Everything You ever wanted to know about Sect...

Night and day, you are the one...
Cole Porter

We now come to the second *radically* different departure of classical astrology from the "modern" version: sect. We have already seen that the concept of strength which animates the classical concept of essential dignities is a complete break from the modern theory of analogy between planet (or asteroid) and sign. The discontinuity here is that in the modern synthesis, whether a chart is day or night is completely irrelevant. Let's begin by considering some of the ways that classical delineation differed, depending on whether the chart was diurnal or nocturnal.

- The Sun or the Moon became the primary Luminary, or **Sect Light**, depending on the time of day. This is actually *the* major difference between day and night charts, because most of the other differences are derived from this very point.
- Many of the lots, or Arabic parts, are calculated differently depending on the time of day.
- The condition of the other planets, except Mercury, differs. This system, which was transmitted in a somewhat dilute fashion as *Hayz*, is probably best understood as an alternate system of accidental dignity or debility.

We can begin this study by understanding that the planets were assigned to the day or night as shown in Table One.

Table One. Assignment of Day or Night Condition of the planets and
  Luminaries.

☉	Day
☽	Night
☿	Mixed
♀	Night
♂	Night
♃	Day
♄	Day

Within this system, there was a degree of diurnality or nocturnality.
The Sun and the Moon were the most extreme, followed by Jupiter and
Mars, then Saturn and Venus. The word *sect* is applied to diurnal or
nocturnal placement. Thus, we could also present the planets on a spectrum:

Moon	Most Nocturnal
Mars	
Venus	Least Norturnal
--	
Mercury	Diurnal or Nocturnal
--	
Saturn	Least Diurnal
Jupiter	
Sun	Most Diurnal

Beginning from these concepts, there are multiple ways to study
sect as it applies to a chart in general, and the planets specifically.
These ways are as follows:

- The chart itself is defined as diurnal or nocturnal according to
  the location of the Sun. If the Sun is above the horizon, in other
  words, in the 12th House through the 7th House, the chart is
  diurnal. If the Sun is below the horizon, in other words, in the
  6th through the 1st House, the chart is nocturnal. Diurnal planets are happier in a diurnal chart; nocturnal planets are happier
  in a nocturnal chart.
- A planet is diurnally or nocturnally placed depending on its
  house location. A planet is diurnally placed if it is in the 12th
  through the 7th House during the day, or in the 6th through the
  1st House during the night. A planet is nocturnally placed if it
  is above the horizon by night (houses 12 through 7), or below

the horizon by day (houses 6 through 1). Again, diurnal planets are happier when dirunally placed; nocturnal planets are happier when nocturnally placed. Rob Hand has stated that this appears to be the most important aspect of sect: whether a planet's own sect agrees with the sect of the chart.[1]

- A planet may be considered to be diurnal or nocturnal depending on whether it rises before or after the Sun. An oriental planet is diurnal; an occidental planet is nocturnal. This *may* be the preferred way to handle Mercury and Venus, because they can only differ from the Sun's sect if the Sun is relatively near the horizon, because both are constrained in their independence from the Sun's position. Unfortunately, orientality and occidentality in that sense have never been given an orb: one presumes that the planet in question has to be reasonably near the Sun for this rule to apply. For our purposes, we will consider that the planet in question has to be within 48° of the Sun to apply this rule, because that is the maximum elongation of Venus from the Sun: the same rule we applied in the last chapter for whether a planet could be considered an attendant of a Luminary.

- A planet is diurnally or nocturnally placed according to its zodiacal sign. Just as planets have an intrinsic sect, so do signs. All the Fire and Air signs (the "masculine" signs) are diurnal; all the Earth and Water ("feminine") signs are nocturnal.

The latter component of sect, the so-called diurnal and nocturnal nature of the signs, has been put into question by Hand, since he points out that sect is supposedly independent of sex, and that these two systems of polarity may actually be rival systems of polarity, in the same sense that Sign and Exaltation can be considered alternate systems of rulership.[2] The problem is this: with the way the system was described, diurnal signs are masculine and nocturnal signs are feminine. What's wrong with this picture? Let's summarize what Ptolemy says in Book I, Sections 6-7, about masculine and feminine, and diurnal and nocturnal planets. This is shown in Table Two.

Ptolemy stated that planets are feminine because they are moist; masculine planets are dry, and Mercury is mixed, being of neither type. However, diurnal planets are that way for being hot and "active;" while nocturnal planets are that way because they are moist and "passive." The malefics were deliberately assigned backward, in order to mitigate their worst qualities.

So here's the kicker: as long as masculine and feminine are defined as being different by dry and moist, then the attribution by sign breaks down, because Air signs are wet (and hence feminine), and Earth signs

Table 2. Ptolemy's planetary attributions of sect and sex.

	Sex	Sect
☉	Masculine	Diurnal
☽	Feminine	Nocturnal
☿	Mixed	Mixed
♀	Feminine	Nocturnal
♂	Masculine	Nocturnal
♃	Masculine	Diurnal
♄	Masculine	Diurnal

are dry (and hence masculine). If the differentiating factor is active and passive, then we have seen that this doesn't work either, because the spectrum hot/cold is active, while wet/dry is passive. Furthermore, if the sect nature of the planets is justified on the basis of diurnal planets being hot, while nocturnal ones are wet, then again we have a problem: Air signs are both Diurnal *and* Nocturnal, being both Hot and Wet, while Earth signs are *neither*, being Cold and Dry!

In reality, there is *no* difference between the masculine and feminine signs, and the diurnal and nocturnal ones. And in reality, the *only* sect attribution which stands out as being odd is Mars, because presumably the night is primarily cold and wet (since nights are wet and days are hot), and Mars is hot and dry. Saturn is cold and dry, and the day is hot and dry, so Saturn's attribution as a diurnal planet is at least mixed.

A planet is in *hayz* when it is in a chart of its own sect, placed according to sect, and in a sign of its own sect. Thus, only the Sun, Jupiter and Saturn can be in hayz in a day chart; only the Moon, Venus and Mars can be in hayz in a night chart; Mercury is *never* in hayz. If hayz is a form of accidental dignity, then the equivalent debility is Out of Sect, in which the chart, placement and sign are *all* out of sect. As Hand points out,[3] there were two systems in use for Mars. The presumably older system give Mars in hayz when it is in a nocturnal chart, above the horizon and, in a feminine (nocturnal) sign. However, the later system specifies a nocturnal chart, nocturnally placed, in a masculine (diurnal) sign, in recognition of Mars' innate quality as a hot and dry planet.

Let's begin to examine this system by taking up our examples.

Nicholas II

In Nicholas' case, Jupiter was in Hayz. Jupiter ruled his 7th and 8th, and had some dignity, namely, by Term. While this is not a lot of essential dignity, he did have a good marriage by all evidence.

Table 3. Nicholas II's planets. Chart is Diurnal. "Preference" denotes the planet's natural sect.

	Preference	Placement	Sign	Comment
☉	Day	(Diurnal)	Nocturnal	
☽	Night	Diurnal	Diurnal	Out of Sect
☿	Mixed	Nocturnal	Diurnal	Occidental is defined as nocturnal
♀	Night	Nocturnal	Nocturnal	Occidental is defined as nocturnal
♂	Night	Diurnal	Diurnal	Out of Sect?
♃	Day	Diurnal	Diurnal	*Hayz*
♄	Day	Nocturnal	Diurnal	

He had Moon and Mars (maybe) Out of Sect. The Moon ruled the 11th House, which in a monarch's chart is the Legislature, which was certainly *not* Nicholas' friend. As a literal interpretation of the 11th House, how about Rasputin as friend? Not a pretty picture! Nicholas in fact kept the Legislative branch as debilitated as possible for as long as possible. And we have also seen that Nicholas was not exactly lucky in war, the standard martial activity.

Mary Shelley

Mary Shelley's placements are shown in Table 4. Shelley had no planets in hayz, and the Sun is out of sect. Her Sun had essential dignity only by Face, which we have already seen indicates more about anxiety and fear than real strength. We would be safe in saying that the solar principle would not exactly be strong in her chart! So other than the obvious result of Percy Shelley's drowning, what does she do? She creates the perfect *anti*-hero in the form of Victor Frankenstein, of course! And in the process, she practically invented science fiction, a definite solar fiction, and pioneered in the gothic novel division.

Table 4. Mary Shelley's Placements. Night chart. "Preference" denotes the planet's natural sect.

	Preference	Placement	Sign	Comment
☉	Day	(Nocturnal)	Nocturnal	Out of Sect
☽	Night	Diurnal	Diurnal	
☿	Mixed	Nocturnal	Nocturnal	Occidental is defined as nocturnal
♀	Night	Nocturnal	Diurnal	Occidental is defined as nocturnal
♂	Night	Diurnal	Diurnal	
♃	Day	Nocturnal	Diurnal	
♄	Day	Diurnal	Nocturnal	

Prince Charles

Table 5. Diurnal and nocturnal placements for Prince Charles. Nocturnal chart.

	Preference	Placement	Sign	Comment
☉	Day	(Nocturnal)	Nocturnal	Out of Sect
☽	Night	Nocturnal	Nocturnal	*Hayz*
☿	Mixed	Diurnal	Nocturnal	Oriental is defined as diurnal
♀	Night	Diurnal	Diurnal	Oriental is defined as diurnal
♂	Night	Diurnal	Diurnal	
♃	Day	Diurnal	Diurnal	
♄	Day	Diurnal	Nocturnal	

Prince Charles' placements are shown in Table 5. His mother, the Queen, is once again shown by the Moon, which simply increases in dignity as we pile on the techniques, here adding dignity by Hayz. Meanwhile, poor Charles keeps looking less dignified: the Sun ruling his Ascendant is Out of Sect.

Aleister Crowley

Table 6 shows the placements for Aleister Crowley. All the planets except the Moon and Mercury are mixed in sect. Mercury is simply strongly nocturnal. The Moon is in hayz, and no planets are out of sect. Thus, sect only emphasizes the Moon, which otherwise *could* be considered peregrine, since its only essential dignity is a mutual reception by Triplicity. The Moon rules Crowley's 12th House, which, among other things, is the house of witchcraft.[4] Hmm... could this have *something* to do with the nature of his Tarot deck? The Moon is in the 9th House, a placement Rob Hand refers to as the "dominant" religion of a culture. (A religion out of favor is the 3rd House.) I'm not sure how we reconcile the Golden Dawn as being of the dominant religious type! Unless, perhaps, we consider dominance in our culture as not so much referring to Judeo-Christianity, as male dominant. Then perhaps...

Table 6. Diurnal and nocturnal placements for Aleister Crowley. Night chart.

	Preference	Placement	Sign	Comment
☉	Day	(Nocturnal)	Diurnal	
☽	Night	Nocturnal	Nocturnal	*Hayz*
☿	Mixed	Nocturnal	Nocturnal	Occidental is defined as nocturnal
♀	Night	Nocturnal	Diurnal	Occidental is defined as nocturnal
♂	Night	Diurnal	Nocturnal	
♃	Day	Diurnal	Nocturnal	
♄	Day	Nocturnal	Diurnal	

Catherine de Medici

Catherine de Medici's positions are given in Table 7.

All of Catherine's planets except Saturn are of mixed nature, so none of them stand out particularly in this system. Saturn is Out of Sect and strong in its own sign and in the 10th House. Thus, we have a Saturn of extremes, either strongly dignified, or strongly debilitated. This Saturn rules the 10th, 11th and 12th.[5] Among other things, Saturn rules religious dissent.[6] We have already commented upon Catherine's complicity in the massacre of the French Huguenots. But we should add that during her regency there were *six* wars of religion!

Table 7. Diurnal and nocturnal placements for Catherine de Medici. Night chart.

	Preference	Placement	Sign	Comment
☉	Day	(Nocturnal)	Diurnal	
☽	Night	Diurnal	Diurnal	
☿	Mixed	Diurnal	Nocturnal	Oriental is defined as diurnal
♀	Night	Nocturnal	Diurnal	Occidental is defined as nocturnal
♂	Night	Diurnal	Nocturnal	
♃	Day	Nocturnal	Diurnal	
♄	Day	Nocturnal	Nocturnal	Out of sect

So how bad is it to have a planet out of sect, or how good is it to have a planet in *Hayz*? By now, it should be obvious that there are many factors which make up a classical reading, and it is hard to sort them all out for a definite answer. However, I would like to consider this question somewhat by comparing two people in those two categories for Mars.

Muhammad Ali & George Foreman

Muhammad Ali, the boxing champion, has Mars in Taurus, which is its Detriment! I don't think any of us would quibble that boxing is a *very* martial sport! His Mars is also in hayz, and so we shall examine this further once we do a quick review on the rest of the components of his chart. First, his qualities:

	Triplicity	Seasonal	Traditional
☉	cold & dry	cold & wet	cold & wet
☽	hot & wet	cold & wet	hot & wet
☿	hot & wet	cold & wet	dry
♀	hot & wet	cold & wet	wet
♂	cold & dry	hot & wet	hot &dry
♃	hot & wet	hot & wet	hot & wet
♄	cold & dry	hot & wet	cold & wet
Asc	hot & dry	hot & dry	hot & dry
M.C	cold & dry	hot & wet	cold & dry
⊗	hot & dry	hot & dry	hot & dry

Ali is mildly hot and dry by Triplicity, which is to say choleric. The advantage to a boxer of dry rather than wet, is that you want to beat up your opponent, not empathize with him! On the other hand, too much dryness could make it difficult to anticipate your opponent's next move. Check out the difference by Season: here Ali is just about as wet as it is possible to be, and mainly hot, which makes the temperament type sanguine. I think that this may be a good statement of his involvement in Islam: a wet temperament would certainly be much more attracted to a religious teaching. Being sanguine, Ali would be naturally upbeat about things, so guilt is not going to be a good motivator. In other words, the evangelical Christian approach—we all are sinners— is not going to work well on a sanguine type. At that time—the Sixties—in that place—Black America —embracing Islam was a *positive* statement, frightening as it may have seemed to White America. Ali was saying something good about himself by becoming a Black Muslim. In the Traditional column, Ali is still hot, with an even mix of wet and dry.

Ali has no planets that are very highly dignified. The most dignified planet he has is Mercury, which is dignified by Triplicity. Well— nobody ever said his poetry was *that* good! His Mercury is conjunct the Moon, so he pretty much says what he thinks. His Moon, Mars, and Venus are peregrine. Ali's most elevated planet is Mars, conjunct the M.C. and square Pluto, which I'm sure contributed to him losing his temper at least once in his life!

Let's next examine which of his planets are oriental, and which occidental.

Table 8. Occidental and Oriental planets of Muhammad Ali. Those with dignity by placement are marked with an asterisk.

Oriental	Occidental
Mars*	Moon
Saturn*	Mercury*
Uranus (*)	Venus*
Jupiter*	Neptune
	Pluto

Ali's planets show quite a bit of accidental dignity by orientality and occidentality. *All* of his traditional planets rise when they are "supposed to." This is a very unusual configuration, and undoubtedly adds considerably to the strength of his chart! Prominence by orientality and occidentality? Through the "accident" of plenty of people willing to pay good money to see two grown men attempt to kill each other by ritualized means, Ali was able to gain prominence. Now this is not without skill—there is no question that Ali combined quickness and good reaction time with solid force. However, this is not exactly mainstream either, and sporting skills are ones that don't last the entire lifetime!

We can compare Ali's situation with George Foreman, who distinguished himself by re-winning the world title after his 40th birthday, certainly an incredible feat. Foreman also lacks any planet with more essential dignity than Triplicity. (It is interesting that both boxers have a sign rulership mutual reception with Saturn; we will take up this interesting circumstance in Chapter 11.) Mercury is Foreman's most dignified planet, with Triplicity and Term, and is separating from conjunction to Mars, natural ruler of boxing.

Foreman also has significant *accidental* dignity: in his case, dignity through angularity. Foreman has both the Moon and Saturn conjunct the M.C. and Ascendant respectively, and both from the cadent side, the Gauquelin sector side in modern parlance. Mercury rules his Ascendant, and it is square Saturn on his Ascendant, and he becomes the *oldest* heavyweight champion?! Foreman has exactly the same Triplicity temperament break-out as Ali: 6 Hot, 4 Cold; 6 Dry, 4 Wet.

	Triplicity	Seasonal	Traditional
☉	cold & dry	cold & wet	cold & wet
☽	hot & wet	hot & wet	cold & dry
☿	hot & wet	cold & wet	dry
♀	hot & dry	cold & dry	hot & wet
♂	hot & wet	cold & wet	dry
♃	cold & dry	cold & wet	hot & wet
♄	cold & dry	hot & dry	cold & wet
Asc	cold & dry	hot & dry	cold & dry
M.C	hot & wet	hot & wet	hot & wet
⊗	hot & dry	hot & wet	hot & dry

By contrast with Ali, Foreman was equally mixed between hot and cold, but again, Foreman showed a predominance of wet. As we have observed with Ali, the wet temperament may be quite suited to religious practice, but Foreman, with his greater cold component, is more "hot and cold" in his moods: in other words, he is less consistently upbeat. Thus, a Christian message is probably more appropriate, given the greater variability in his moods. In the Traditional system, Foreman has an absolutely even distribution of qualities.

Now back to Muhammad Ali. Ali's placements by sect are shown in Table 9.

Table 9. Diurnal and nocturnal placements for Muhammad Ali. Night chart.

	Preference	Placement	Sign	Comment
☉	Day	(Nocturnal)	Nocturnal	Out of sect as possible
☽	Night	Diurnal	Diurnal	Out of sect as possible
☿	Mixed	Nocturnal	Diurnal	Occidental is defined as nocturnal
♀	Night	Nocturnal	Diurnal	Occidental is defined as nocturnal
♂	Night	Nocturnal	Nocturnal	*Hayz* (maybe)
♃	Day	Nocturnal	Diurnal	
♄	Day	Nocturnal	Nocturnal	Out of sect

While Ali has Mars in Hayz (old style), both his lights are as out of sect as possible, given that the chart is a night chart. Ali's Saturn is also purely out of sect. So while Mars giveth, the Sun, Moon and Saturn taketh away. And how so? Well, with the conjunction of Mercury and the Moon, one of the casualties of Ali's success was his mind: the medical problems that he acquired, certainly as a result of repeated battering of his head. This conjunction is located in his 6th House: acute medical problems. Here we are tempted to note that Ali's Saturn-Uranus conjunction is also conjunct Algol, using our 5° orb for accidental debility.

Remember the Hadrian example from Chapter 6? Here we have the Sun attending the Moon, like Hadrian, at an angle. Venus is also attending, being a nocturnal Occidental planet. Given this arrangement just past the angle (the whole configuration straddles the angle, since Venus is involved), this suggests some indication of Ali's prominence or fame. But unlike Hadrian, it was not enough to make many nations bow down.

Accidental dignity means being in the right place at the right time. Essential dignity is the power to express a planet in the way that the planet finds easiest to do. However, the accidental dignities often have a bigger down-side than the essential ones do. Timing is quite capable of taking the Native further, faster. But this is the knack of maximizing the returns from the spin of the Wheel of Fortune. The problem is that it is too easy to get cocky. A person with essential dignities has much more to fall back upon in hard times.

So what was the cost to Foreman? Foreman learned to channel and understand his anger through getting involved in evangelical religion, and specifically, through working with children from economically challenged backgrounds. His chart has a focus on the 5th House, so he was able to pull himself out of himself through working with others, especially children. Of course, with Venus ruling the 9th House opposite Uranus, he certainly found an interesting way to fund his ministry! His goal in returning to the ring at age forty was to make sure that his charitable projects were properly funded.

Had Foreman *not* gotten a grip on his anger, how much good would his "accidental" success do? Probably not much. With Neptune in the 2nd House, and peregrine Venus ruling the 2nd, and peregrine Saturn Almuten of the 2nd, Foreman is not especially good with his own money. He himself has talked about how money ran through his fingers. Without his spiritual interests, the money would simply have dissipated.

If we examine Foreman's diurnal and nocturnal placements, Foreman shares a number of qualities with Ali. Like Ali, his Sun is as out-of-sect as possible. However, his Moon is of mixed sect. Like Ali, his Saturn is out-of-sect. Also like Ali, his Mars is in Hayz, but this time, it is in Hayz new-style: in a masculine, rather than a feminine sign.

Foreman has Jupiter as spear-bearer or attendant to the Sun and no attendant to the Moon. George didn't get nearly as much press as Ali!

Table 10. Diurnal and nocturnal placements for George Foreman. Night chart.

	Preference	Placement	Sign	Comment
☉	Day	(Nocturnal)	Nocturnal	Out of sect as possible
☽	Night	Nocturnal	Diurnal	
☿	Mixed	Nocturnal	Diurnal	Occidental is defined as nocturnal
♀	Night	Diurnal	Diurnal	Oriental is defined as diurnal
♂	Night	Nocturnal	Diurnal	*Hayz* (maybe)
♃	Day	Diurnal	Nocturnal	
♄	Day	Nocturnal	Nocturnal	Out of sect

One thing that we should be clear about when we study techniques that have a diurnal component: distributions are not what they seem because of various astronomical or statistical factors. For example, Mars in Hayz is less common than Mars out of sect. Why? For Mars to be in Hayz, Mars must be above the horizon while the Sun is below the horizon. Even though Mars is a superior planet, there is a distinct correlation of Sun and Mars diurnal placement. I have illustrated this point with Figures 1-5, which show the distribution of the Sun, Mercury, Venus, Mars and Jupiter in the Eastern and Western Hemispheres in a sample of cricket sports data.

Let me explain. Cricket matches almost always start before noon, unless there is a weather delay. Accordingly, the Sun is nearly always in the Eastern Hemisphere at the start of the game. If there is no correlation between the Sun's position and the planet in question, we would expect a distribution split between the two hemispheres. And this is what we see—for Jupiter. (Saturn produced the same pattern. I simply didn't illustrate it here.) Mercury and Venus are highly correlated with the Sun—Mercury more than Venus. (This means that the Mercury distribution is skewed further away from 50-50 than the Venus one.) This you would expect, because we have already studied how Inferior planets appear to oscillate around the Sun, so they can never be further away than the 48° elongation of Venus.

But now look at Mars! The Mars distribution is as extreme as Mercury! While this degree of extremity is not found in all samples, it is quite common to see a significant correlation of the Mars position with the Sun's (this has been called the Mars-Dawn effect). Therefore, Mars tends to share the same hemisphere as the Sun more often than not. Therefore, Mars has diurnal placement more often than not. Therefore, Mars is more likely to be out of sect by placement than in sect. We shall examine this dependency of Mars' placement on the Sun's later in this chapter when we examine the question of Hayz and Out of Sect placements in the Gauquelin professional data.

This point is critical, because these distributions can come up and bite us on the nose if we aren't careful. I would like to conclude this chapter by demonstrating this fact using some *very* well known data: the Gauquelin professions.

For many years, the Gauquelin professional data has represented one of the most powerful statistical arguments for an astrological effect. Not only has the Mars effect been replicated—sometimes grudgingly—by other researchers, but other professions have been added to the original ones studied by the Gauquelins.

Figure 1: The Sun ☉

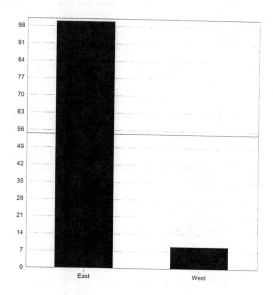

Figure 2: Mercury ☿

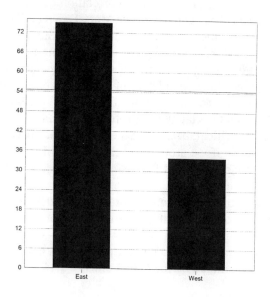

Figure 3: Venus ♀

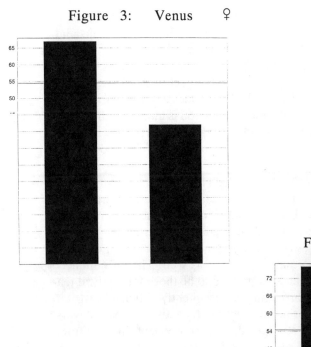

Figure 4: Mars ♂

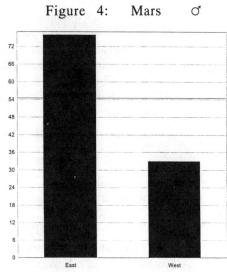

Figure 5: Jupiter ♃

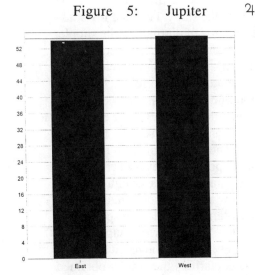

While many have hailed these results as a major confirmation of an astrological effect, questions have remained. The two most outstanding—from an astrological perspective—are these.

- While the Gauquelin "Plus Zones" are near the angles, they are not quite where astrologers would expect them to be. Astrologers would have expected the Plus Zones to be primarily in the angular houses: instead, the distribution is mainly in the cadent ones, which are reputed to be weak. This effect has been explained by John Addey as the combination of 3rd and 4th harmonic cycles.[7]

- The Gauquelins and other workers have observed that the plus zone effect breaks down in birth sets dominated by births since 1950. They have observed that since that time, the number of induced births has increased markedly. Induced births—whether caesarian or drug-accelerated—tend to occur during the day, and during the normal work week as well. The only induced births that take place at night tend to be those for medical reasons, such as hemorrhaging. Consequently, a typical distribution of births of, for instance, currently active football players, will show a much stronger diurnal component than a similar sample taken for players active around 1920. Francoise Gauquelin has worked extensively on a "nycthemeral curve," which is a characterization of the "normal" diurnal distribution of births prior to generally practiced induction.[8]

This study began as a result of a remark that Rob Hand made in one of his lectures. Rob speculated that it might be interesting to go back to the Gauquelin professional data and see if the results differ by day and by night. I decided to undertake the study. I created my study using the 12 Gauquelin sectors. The question of diurnal is quite simple. A diurnal chart is one which has the Sun in Gauquelin Sectors 1–6 (houses 12 through 7). A nocturnal chart has the Sun in sectors 7–12 (houses 6 through 1). Therefore, I separated the data for each profession into two groups by selecting the Sun placement. As a control, I created sets by selecting for the Sun in either odd sectors or even sectors. This control would show the variation between sectors, but minimize the diurnal effect. The results are shown as Figures 6–13.

The results for Mars were quite surprising. In every set, the day births show a peak of Mars diurnally placed, and a trough of Mars nocturnally placed. The night births show a peak of nocturnally placed Mars and a trough of diurnally placed Mars. The odd-even sector controls show little variation between the two subsets, which supports the contention that the variation observed here really is the result of a diurnal-nocturnal *astronomical* effect. This clarifies the results obtained by F. Gauquelin in her study of diurnal placement, since she did not separate the subsets of day and night births.

The professional data is not untouched by the dreaded specter of induced births. In fact, all of the professional data sets I studied had diurnal - nocturnal ratios of nearly 50:50. This effect was discussed to a certain extent at the time that the skeptics were attempting to fail in their replication of the Gauquelin sports champion results. It was referred to at the time as the "Mars-dawn" effect: the observation that the placement of Mars is not completely independent of the position of the Sun.[9] Of course, the skeptics were interested in showing that the Plus Zone effect was *totally* a result of the Mars-dawn effect: in this they were not successful.

This work does not challenge the Gauquelin Plus Zone results in any way. However, it does become obvious that the angularity effect is not the only factor which needs to be characterized in a sample. The magnitude of this effect is shown in Table 11, which compares the Chi-square values for the angularity effect (i.e., the Gauquelin Plus Zones) and the diurnal effect reported here. Clearly, the magnitude of the diurnal effect is too large to be ignored. However, it is fortunate that the effect almost disappears in a sample with a day:night ratio of 50:50.

The results reported here for Mars are not the same for the other planets. Two samples are shown in Figures 14 - 17. There seems to be little effect of Saturn placements—diurnal or nocturnal. In the case of the Moon and writers, while the distribution is not quite as flat as for Saturn, there is not much of interest going on with respect to Sect. I have reported on the effect of Sect on the other planets in more detail elsewhere.[10]

Table 11. Chi-square values for the diurnal effect (houses 12 through 7 *vs.* houses 6 through 1) and the control group (odd houses *vs.* even houses).

Profession	Diurnal Chi-square	Control Chi-square
Sport Champions	172.465	5.537
Military	246.225	8.598
Painters/Musicians	232.716	5.135
Politicians/Actors	259.867	8.032

If we return to Figure 9, which shows the distribution of Mars in the sports champions by day and night, we may study the difference in distribution with that of the other Mars placements such as the military one shown in Figure 8. The distribution in Figure 8 is fairly symmetrical, as are the other Mars distributions by profession. By contrast, the champions born in the day show a definite peak in Mars in the diurnal sectors (remember Gauquelin sectors are counted in reverse order from Houses), while champions born at night show a definite peak in Mars with a diurnal placement as well, because the diurnal placement *at night* is houses 6 through 1, or Gauquelin sectors 7 through 12. Thus, Mars in successful sports champions is *definitely* acting like a diurnal planet. Now is this because it is better to have Mars debilitated because of the challenge, or because Mars really works better diurnally? Only time will tell.

This exercise clearly illustrates that it would be ill-advised in the future to ignore Sect as an issue in the study of *any* statistical matter in astrology that utilizes a diurnally-based effect, such as house placement. In a sense, it matters little whether this effect is astronomical (i.e., a function of the orbit of Mars) or astrological (a function of the interpretation of the placement of Mars). The ancients who posited the difference between diurnal and nocturnal Mars did not distinguish these two separate causative principles. Accordingly, we don't need to do so either.

But what does it mean? And how important is it?

What the little exercise above suggests is that there really *is* something to this diurnal/ nocturnal stuff. But what? In examining the increasing corpus of Greek astrological works that have become available to us, we see that Sect and issues of Sect are considered extremely important. Yet most authors from Bonatti onward have defined *Hayz*, and then either never mention the concept again, or indicate that it's not at all important. For example, Bonatti's 40th Aphorism is:

> To consider if an Infortune, whether he be Significator or not, be Peregrine; that is, not in any of his Dignities, for then his malice is increased; but when in his Dignities it somewhat abates it; that is in his House, Exaltation, or Terms; but in his Triplicity or Face very little, and in Hayz least of all.[11]

This quotation is quite revealing on two points. First *Hayz* is considered here with the *Essential* Dignities, not the Accidental ones. There does seem to be some evidence to suggest that these matters of Sect were considered an intermediate category between essential and accidental dignity. But clearly, Bonatti was certainly lukewarm about the effectiveness of *Hayz*. Dariot,[12] Lilly,[13] Gadbury,[14] and Ramesey[15] all define *Hayz* correctly, although using an Arabic definition which substitutes "Masculine" sign for "Diurnal" sign, and "Feminine" sign for "Nocturnal" sign. Having defined it, they don't ever mention it subsequently. Partridge doesn't even bother to define it, because he says that nobody uses it.[16]

So: were the astrologers of the Medieval and Renaissance wrong? Was there something that they missed completely? Or was the Greek method of Sect interpretation simply not as useful as it was made out to be?

Since the Gauquelin professional data was so useful in showing that the diurnal/nocturnal condition cannot be ignored, I decided to go the distance to study the difference in the professions between planets in Hayz and planets Out of Sect. Here's the theory. We have already established that sports champions who were born at night have a different Mars distribution than those who are born during the day, and that this effect is not merely the result of the difference between *any* population split into day births and night births. Therefore, what we would next explore is whether this difference is because more champions have Mars *Hayz*, or fewer have Mars out of sect: or even the reverse. And in turn, we could ask the same question for other professions with demonstrated diurnal planetary effects, such as actors and Jupiter, the Moon and writers, scientists and Saturn, and so forth. As an aside, the results for all the professions should illustrate in yet one more way the degree of the so-called Mars-Dawn effect.

The professional data is just about even between day and night births. The Moon, Jupiter and Saturn show almost even frequencies in comparing *Hayz* with out-of-sect. This shows that there is little relationship between solar position and planetary placement. However, for Venus there is a *fivefold* difference between the number of cases of Venus in *Hayz* versus Venus out-of- sect. We have already seen that this is because Venus is a nocturnal planet. To be out-of-sect, it would have to be in the opposite hemisphere from the Sun, which is fairly uncommon. This confirms our usage of oriental an occidental placement, as giving a more even result!

To read this table, examine the rows for each planet, looking for values that deviate considerably from the average value. These are marked with an asterisk (*). Then see what is happening in the opposite case by Sect. First, let's look at the professions themselves. The three "hard" professions are to the left: sports, science, and the military. We are using the analogy with "hard" and "soft" sciences here: the "hard" professions involve fairly rigid and objective criteria for success. The next four columns are the "fine arts" professions, where success is from producing a more subjective result. Finally, we have politics. The sleaze profession?

I mention this because only Jupiter Out-of-Sect is producing any interesting effect at all within the hard professions. This suggests that

Table 12. Summary of Hayz and Out-of-Sect placements for the eight
Gauquelin Professions. In this table, Venus is defined by placement in the same way as the superior planets. Values given are
percentage of the profession that meet the crtieria. Average column is the sum of all professions. Under Mars, (*) means that
Hayz is defined with in sect being feminine signs and out-of-
sect masculine signs; while (†) means that Hayz is defined with
in sect being masculine signs and out-of-sect feminine signs.

	Sports	Science	Military	Painters	Writers	Journal.	Music.	Politic.	Average
☽ Hayz	12.6	12.5	13.0	13.1	13.4	11.6*	13.9	13.2	12.7
☽ OOS	11.9	13.4	11.9	12.4	13.4	13.5	12.2	14.3*	12.8
♀ Hayz	4.0	4.6	4.2	4.5	4.4	4.4	4.0	5.0	4.4
♀ OOS	20.0	20.0	20.8	19.9	17.8*	18.8	19.4	18.4	19.7
♂ Hayz*	9.6	9.9	9.3	7.5*	8.4	9.9	9.9	8.9	9.2
♂ OOS*	16.1	15.9	15.0	14.7	15.1	15.1	15.4	16.3	15.6
♂ Hayz†	10.3	9.8	9.4	9.4	9.9	8.9*	9.8	9.4	9.7
♂ OOS†	15.6	16.8	16.7	17.2*	16.3	16.1	14.9*	14.5*	16.2
♃ Hayz	13.0	12.5*	15.3*	14.3	12.4*	14.3	12.8	14.1	13.5
♃ OOS	11.5	11.6	12.4	10.7*	10.7*	13.9*	12.4	12.9	11.9
♄ Hayz	11.9	12.3	12.0	12.0	12.1	9.8*	11.1	12.1	12.1
♄ OOS	11.4	12.7	12.0	10.9*	13.8*	12.4	11.6	12.1	12.2

the quality of dignity by *Hayz* or debility by out-of-sect is not associated with the kind of tough-knocks qualities necessary to be successful
in these "hard" professions. This in turn suggests that the *Hayz* complex is somewhat subtle in manifestation, which means, among other
things, that the effect is going to be harder to see.

Notice in turn how the painters, writers, and journalists (as well as
the politicians) have more hits. Notice also that the writers and journalists differ in their characterization: we may be seeing one of the
components that explains why one writer becomes a journalist, and
another does not. In particular, the journalists have Saturn more frequently in *Hayz*, while the writers more frequently have Saturn Out-
of-Sect, suggesting perhaps a greater amount of discipline (or maybe
just boredom!) in the practice of journalism compared to writing in
general. Unfortunately, painters, writers and journalists would not normally be associated with Saturn. Or the military with Jupiter, except

perhaps as an indicator of charisma, which may be a component of the successful military type.

While we are left with the conclusion that there is something here, that "something" appears to be somewhat evanescent. Another term, mentioned by al-Biruni, is *Halb*. A *Halb* planet is a diurnal planet above the horizon by day, or below the horizon at night. In other words, a *Halb* planet is one where the diurnal or nocturnal placement matches the nature of the planet. To explore these matters further, we can re-compute Table 12 using the combination of chart sect plus *Halb*. This is shown in Table 13.

Table 13. Summary of Chart Sect-*Halb* and Out-of-Chart Sect-*Halb* placements for the eight Gauquelin Professions. (For example, Mars would be in *Halb* in this table if Mars were in a nocturnal chart, above the horizon, which is nocturnally placed.) In this table, Venus is defined by placement in the smae way as the superior planets. Values given are percentage of the profession that meet the criteria. average column is the sum of all professions.

	Sports	Science	Military	Painters	Writers	Journal.	Music.	Politic.	Average
☽ Halb	24.6	25.5	24.6	24.8	27.8*	25.0	24.9	25.8	25.4
☽ OOH	24.9	24.4	25.2	25.3	24.4	24.0	25.1	25.4	24.7
♀ Halb	7.6	8.7	7.5	7.7	9.2*	7.9	7.3	10.3*	8.2
♀ OOH	41.2	41.4	42.4	41.4	39.6*	40.0	41.1	41.4	41.3
♂ Halb	19.9	19.7	18.7	17.0*	18.3	18.8	19.8	18.2	18.9
♂ OOH	31.8	32.7	31.6	31.9	31.4	31.3	27.9*	30.8	31.9
♃ Halb	25.0*	26.4	28.6*	26.5	25.2*	27.7	25.8	28.2	26.8
♃ OOH	24.2	22.8	24.5	21.1*	23.4	25.0	23.1	25.6*	23.5
♄ Halb	24.1	25.9	25.1	23.6	25.2	22.2*	23.3	23.4	24.7
♄ OOH	23.4	24.8	23.8	22.5*	25.3*	23.4	24.0	23.2	24.0

First of all, the two tables are quite similar in outcome to each other. By itself, this is already an indication that the extra component in *Hayz* is not effecting the outcome profoundly: this means that *Hayz* may really *be* overkill, and that Chart Sect-*Halb* is sufficient for our purposes. Second, we have added an intriguing relationship of Venus Chart Sect-*Halb* and Out- of-*Halb* for the writers: the writers are showing an excess of Venus in Chart Sect-*Halb* (as are the politicians), while the writers are also showing a deficit of Out-of-*Halb* placements. This is *exactly* the kind of pattern which makes sense astrologically, and probably makes this kind of study worth extending.

Let's return to our four types of Sect rulership and see how our conclusions stack up with the classification scheme.

- The chart itself is defined as diurnal or nocturnal according to the location of the Sun. Diurnal planets are happier in a diurnal chart; nocturnal planets are happier in a nocturnal chart. We have seen that this factor is strong, whether astronomical or astrological in origin, and of course, this is also the basis for other techniques, such as the calculation of the Lots, and the Triplicity ruler of a chart.

- A planet is diurnally or nocturnally placed depending on its house location. Combined with the chart Sect, these two factors comprise the *Halb* condition, and we see above some evidence that this effect is worth pursuing. Again, diurnal planets are more comfortable when diurnally placed; nocturnal planets are more comfortable when nocturnally placed.

- A planet may be considered to be diurnal or nocturnal depending on whether it rises before of after the Sun. An oriental planet is diurnal; an occidental planet is nocturnal. We have already concluded that this is the right way to handle Mercury and Venus.

- A planet is diurnally or nocturnally placed according to its zodiacal sign. This placement doesn't seem to work out strongly or at all. If there is any effect, it is *extremely* subtle. The attribution of sect to signs should score as a *very* distant last place. In any case *Halb*, which coincidentally is German for "half," may be more significant than the whole *Hayz*.

In the next chapter, we will take up another sector of the sect puzzle when we study the Lots or Parts, specifically, the Part of Fortune.

Sources for Data Used:

Muhammad Ali: from birth certificate. The same birth day and time is given in Jose Torres' biography *Sting Like a Bee*. (Abelard-Schuman, 1970, p.83). From Blackwell Database: Astrolabe: Brewster, MA.

George Foreman: from birth certificate. From Blackwell Database: Astrolabe: Brewster, MA.

Fig. 6. Gauquelin Painters & Musicians: Mars (day/night)

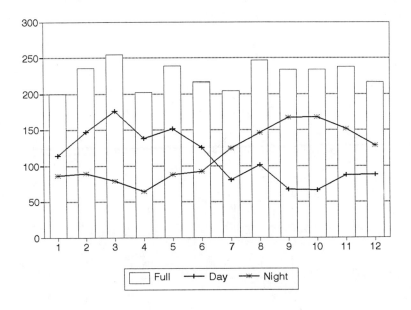

Fig. 7. Gauquelin Politicians & Actors: Mars (day/night)

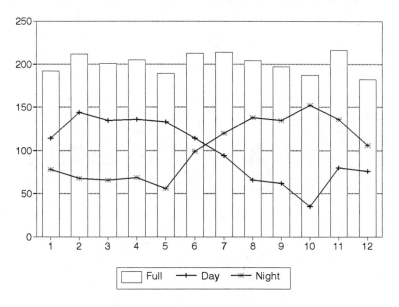

Fig. 8. Gauquelin Military: Mars (day/night)

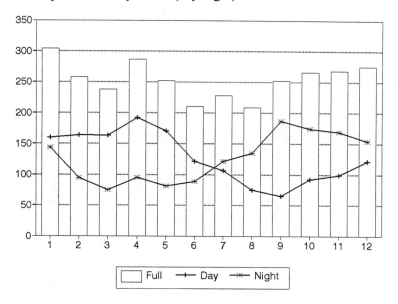

Fig. 9. Gauquelin Champions: Mars (day/night)

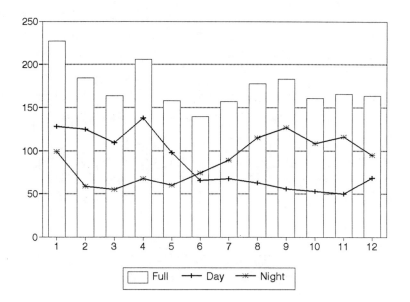

Fig. 10. Gauquelin Painters & Musicians: Mars (odd/even)

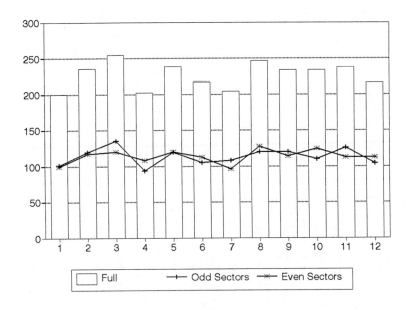

Fig. 11. Gauquelin Politicians & Actors: Mars (odd/even)

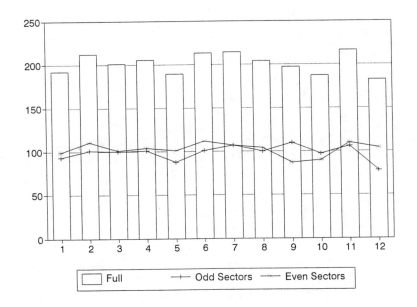

Fig. 12. Gauquelin Military: Mars (odd/even)

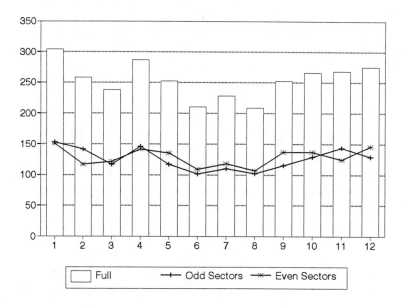

Fig. 13. Gauquelin Champions: Mars (odd/even)

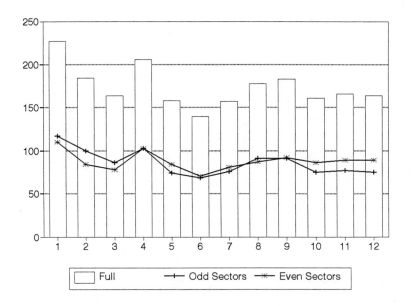

Fig. 14. Gauquelin Writers: Moon (day/night)

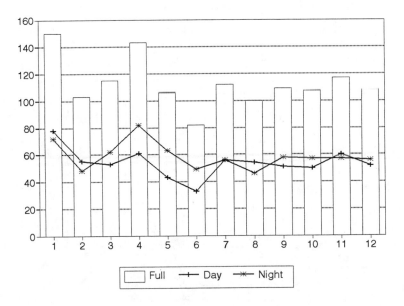

Fig. 15. Gauquelin Writers: Moon (odd/even)

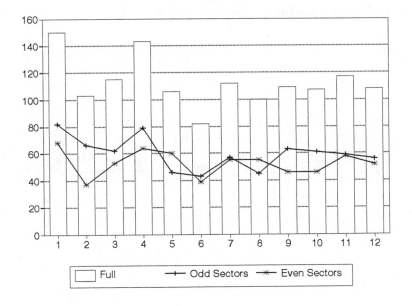

Fig. 16. Gauquelin Scientists: Saturn (day/night)

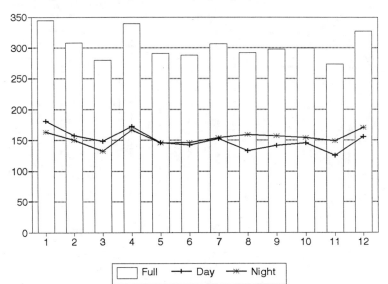

Fig. 17. Gauquelin Scientists: Saturn (odd/even)

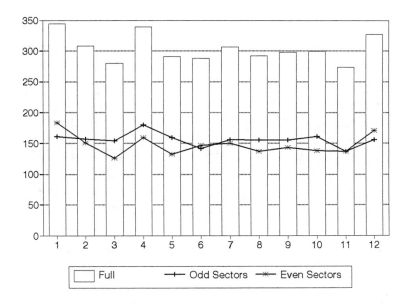

Endnotes

1   *Op. cit.*, page 6.

2   *Op. cit.*, page 3.

3   *Op. cit.*, page 7.

4   Lilly, *CA*, page 56.

5   While Mars is Almuten of the 11th House, Mars is in Fall in Cancer, while in dignity by Triplicity; thus, Mars has a net negative Dignity. With Saturn the sign ruler of the 11th House considerably more dignified than the Almuten of the 11th, we would tend to prefer the sign ruler to the Almuten.

6   Gadbury, p. 67, Edlin, p.25.

7   John Addey. 1976. *Harmonics in Astrology*. Cambridge Circle, Ltd.: Green Bay, WI.

8   Francoise Gauquelin. 1985. The nycthemeral expectancy. Astro-Psych. Prob. **3** (1): 20- 23.
Ibid. 1987. When the time of birth is not the natural one. Astro-Psych. Prob. **5** (2): 30- 35.

9   Dennis Rawlins. 1981. sTARBABY. Fate *34*: 67-98.

10   J. Lee Lehman. 1994. The Mars Diurnal Effect: Gauquelin Sectors meet Classical Method. Astrology Quarterly *64*(2): 3-25.

11   Bonatti, *The Astrologer's Guide*.

12   Dariot, page 37.

13   Lilly, page 113.

14   Gadbury, page 45.

15   Ramesey, page 111.

16   Partridge, page 22.

───── CHAPTER EIGHT ─────
THE PART OF FORTUNE

The Part of Fortune is something that astrologers usually learn about fairly early in their studies: it is a point derived from the positions of the Sun, Moon and Ascendant. Most astrologers also learn that it is classified as one (the best known) of the so-called Arabic parts: points similarly derived from summing or subtracting planetary positions and house cusps. This is partially true.

The Part of Fortune and its mirror image, the Part of Spirit, extend their history way back before the flowering of Arabic astrology in the Middle Ages, and may pre-date, if not the concept of houses, at least the common usage of houses. These parts are responsible for a system of "houses" which for a number of centuries were used more commonly than the houses we use today.

Figure 1. Methods of calculating the Part of Fortune.

Modern:	
Fortuna, Day & Night	= Ascendant + ☽ - ☉
Spirit, Day & Night	= Ascendant + ☉ - ☽
Ancient:	
Fortuna, Day	= Ascendant + ☽ - ☉
Fortuna, Night	= Ascendant + ☉ - ☽
Spirit, Night	= Ascendant + ☽ - ☉
Spirit, Day	= Ascendant + ☉ - ☽

First, let's define our terminology. Modern astrology calculates the part of Fortune (Fortuna) by taking the Ascendant position, adding the lunar position, and subtracting the Sun's position. The part of Spirit is calculated by again taking the Ascendant, then instead adding the Sun's position, subtracting that of the Moon (see Figure 1). This is not the ancient system. In the ancient system, the calculations for Fortune and Spirit were reversed for night charts: the nighttime Fortuna was our modern part of Spirit, while the nighttime part of Spirit was our modern part of Fortune. This is discussed by G. P. Goold:

> In ancient times, and through the Seventeenth Century, it was standard practice to reverse the positions of the Part of Fortune and the Part of Daemon (Spirit).

The use of the daytime/nighttime reversal was common through the seventeenth Century, while our modern system was firmly entrenched through the simplifications introduced by Raphael I in the early nineteenth Century. These simplifications were, for the large part, arbitrary, showing mainly Raphael's lack of understanding of ancient geocentric astronomy and astrology:

> The circumstances regulating the fortune of wealth are to be judged of from that part alone which is expressly denominated the Part of Fortune; the position of which is, in all cases, whether arising in the day or in the night, always as far removed from the ascendant as the Sun is distant from the Moon.[1]

There are certain features about this interplay of the parts of Fortune and Spirit which may not be initially obvious. One such characteristic is shown in Test One. If the angular separation of the Sun and the Moon are held constant, for a given degree of the Ascendant, no matter where in the zodiac this separation occurs, the part of Fortune will always fall in the same place. In this test, The Ascendant is given as 0 Aries in order to simplify calculations. The top line shows the Moon as also at 0 Aries, the Sun at 0 Cancer (in numerical equivalent, 0 Cancer is 90°, or one-quarter of the 360° circle). In order to subtract the solar position, another 360° has to be added. When this is done, the result is 270°, which is 0 Capricorn in zodiacal coordinates. As long as the Moon is 90° behind the Sun in ecliptic longitude, and the Ascendant is zero Aries, the part of Fortune will be zero Capricorn regardless of the actual ecliptic positions of the Sun and Moon. This same relationship holds for any angular separation; the closing square is but one example. It is necessary, however, that in the comparison that dexter and sinister aspects not be mixed: we often consider the opening and closing aspect as synonymous, but they are not.

Test 1. If we hold the Ascendant fixed at 0 Aries, and the angular separation fixed, what happens to Fortuna in differing signs of the Sun and Moon?

Moon		Sun		Fortuna	
360°	Zodiacal	360°	Zodiacal	360°	Zodiacal
0°	0 ♈	90°	0 ♋	270°	0 ♑
30°	0 ♉	120°	0 ♌	270°	0 ♑
60°	0 ♊	150°	0 ♍	270°	0 ♑
90°	0 ♋	180°	0 ♎	270°	0 ♑
120°	0 ♌	210°	0 ♏	270°	0 ♑
150°	0 ♍	240°	0 ♐	270°	0 ♑
180°	0 ♎	270°	0 ♑	270°	0 ♑
210°	0 ♏	300°	0 ♒	270°	0 ♑
240°	0 ♐	330°	0 ♓	270°	0 ♑
270°	0 ♑	0°	0 ♈	270°	0 ♑
300°	0 ♒	30°	0 ♉	270°	0 ♑
330°	0 ♓	60°	0 ♊	270°	0 ♑

The relationship between the positions of the parts of Fortune and Spirit is double the angular separation between the Sun and Moon, as shown in Figure 2. This graph—which was created by entering values for every 10° of separation between the Sun and the Moon, shows that the two parts are conjunct if the Sun and the Moon are conjunct or opposite each other. If the angular separation between the Sun and Moon is 20° (say at 0 Leo and 20 Leo), then the two parts will be 40° apart. Further, the parts of Fortune and Spirit have the Ascendant as their midpoint.

The part of Fortune itself basically shows the phase relationship between its three components. This point has been most clearly elucidated by Rudhyar:

The Part of Fortune synthesizes the three factors with which we must deal, if we are to get a clear and complete grasp of the cycle of soli-lunar relationship; sun, moon, and earth-locality...

If now we consider the Part of Fortune from the point of view of action, we can define it as the *focal point for the expression of the power generated by the soli-lunar relationship.* This power manifests... in various ways—as sex, as love, as personal magnetism, as radiant health; in short, as any and all kinds of personal expression which pertains to the level of human activity where the dualism of 'life' reigns supreme. And because it is also at this level that we can discover the root of what men call 'happiness,' the connection between the Part of Fortune and the individual's capacity for happiness—and the special nature of this happiness—becomes explainable.[2]

Figure 2. Relationship between Fortuna and Spirit
based on Sun-Moon Angle

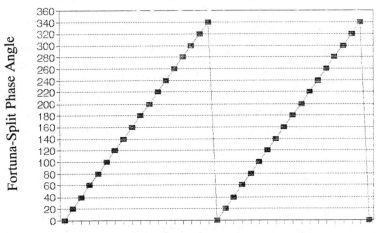

Degree Separation of Sun and Moon

Another way to consider this relationship between the Sun, the Moon and the Part of Fortune is as follows.

If you were born at a New Moon, the Part of Fortune is conjunct the Ascendant. If you were born at a Full Moon, the Part of Fortune is conjunct the Descendant.

If you were born during the day, and you were born with the Moon increasing in Light, that is, moving from the conjunction to the opposition, then your Part of Fortune will be in the lower hemisphere of the chart. The closer you were born to the New Moon, the closer it will be to the Ascendant. If you were born between the Full Moon and the next New Moon, then your Part of Fortune will be in the upper hemisphere of the chart. In either case, as the Moon moves away from the Sun at the

New Moon, the movement of the Part of Fortune is in the order of the signs, or counter-clockwise, around the chart.

If you were born at night, and you were born with the Moon increasing in Light, that is, moving from the conjunction to the opposition, then your Part of Fortune will be in the upper hemisphere of the chart. The closer you were born to the New Moon, the closer it will be to the Ascendant. If you were born between the Full Moon and the next New Moon, then your Part of Fortune will be in the lower hemisphere of the chart. In either case, as the Moon moves away from the Sun at the New Moon, the movement of the Part of Fortune is against the order of the signs, or clockwise, around the chart.

When we examine how the Part of Fortune was used, we see some things out-of-use, some things still in use. The Part of Fortune briefly represents a boon: we shall see some of its uses as we proceed, but it was essentially a point of good luck. It is a benefic point.

There were two uses to the Part of Fortune, however, and only one involved the meaning of Fortuna directly. The second use of Fortuna was as the starting point for the Circle of Athla. The Circle of Athla was a system of "houses" or "lots" (henceforth referred to as lots to avoid confusion with our current meaning of houses) calculated based on the part of Fortune as the "Ascendant." The designation "lot" for these "houses" is because of the then-current designation of the Parts of Fortune and Spirit as the Lots of Fortune and Daemon. The twelve lots are then created by sequentially adding thirty degrees to Fortuna: the system is analogous to Ascendant-based equal houses. There are two possible way to construct these "lots." The way which would reflect Greek thinking would be to use "full sign" lots (i.e., the 1st Lot starts at 0° of the sign in which the Part of Fortune occurs). The second method, which would be more characteristic of later Arabic or medieval thinking, would begin from the degree position of the Part of Fortune itself. Further work will be necessary to clarify this point.[3]

The name *athla* comes from the same root as our word "athlete." It means a prize in an athletic competition, although its usage evolved to include other kinds of prizes as well. Nigel M. Kennell has uncovered a reference to *athla empsucha* (literally, "living prizes," whether animals or slaves) being awarded to teachers in competitive displays (*epideixeis*) in the first century BCE.[4] Thus, the meaning of "circle of athla" is "circle of prizes" or "circle of rewards." It is also clear that other "circles" could be set up using the other principal lots, such as the lot of Spirit,

Lot of the Mother, Lot of Father, Lot of Brothers (translate: siblings), or the Lot of Basis. Any of these alternate charts would then be used to read about the relevent affairs: wealth, spirit (which these days we would use to include psychological factors), the condition and circumstances of the mother, father, or siblings. Thus, we see that this system allowed for a much more detailed delineation of particular factors than provided by a house and its house cusp alone.[5] As Rob Hand has pointed out, the Greek word *horoskopai*, the original of our English "horoscope," should actually be understood as the point which marks the 1st House or Lot in *any* house or lot system, not merely the conventional houses as we know them.[6]

There have been few references to lots in modern times. (Classical is defined here in the apotheosis of traditional techniques reached in the seventeenth Century.) David C. Plant mentioned them briefly in an article on the Arabic parts.[7] One of the best explications of the lots in English is by Goold. In the Project Hindsight material, the most references to this system are in the works of Vettius Valens.

Otherwise, the best source on the importance of the lots in actual practice is the work by Neugebauer and van Hoesen, *Greek Horoscopes* and the Valens material being translated by Project Hindsight. *Greek Horoscopes* translates the available examples of actual chart readings given by Greek-speaking astrologers in the first five centuries A.D.

The study of *Greek Horoscopes* requires more careful scrutiny than many astrological works, precisely because of the use of houses interchangeably for either modern-type houses or lots. However, if one persists and calculates placements in both systems when an Ascendant is given, it becomes clear that the overwhelming number of references to the placement of planets in either houses or lots were placements in lots.

Unfortunately, sometimes the lots were interpreted differently from the houses, and occasionally not. The one major exception was Manilius, but this is a somewhat disturbing source, because so far, no other confirming source has been found. Further, there is no evidence that Manilius actually *practiced* astrology: his poem is more of a *tour de force* stylistically than thematically. A summary of the meanings of the lots according to Manilius is given in Table 2. While I have experimented with these meanings, most of the time I revert to our more conventional house definitions, because they appear to give a much more accurate delineation.

Table 2. Manilius' meanings of the Lots.[8]

1.	Res familians	Fortune, in the usual sense of the word
2.	Militia peregrinatio	Military service and (foreign) trips
3.	Officia publica	Civil affairs
4.	Opera forensia	The profession of law or advocacy
5.	Conjugia; socii; hospites	Marriage & other affectionate associations
6.	Opes; salus	Riches acquired
7.	Pericula	Perils or dangers
8.	Nobilitas; fama; gratis	Nobility or reputation
9.	Nate infantum	Education of children
10.	Actus Dominica imperia	Action, authority
11.	Valetudo morbi; medicatio	Health & sickness
12.	Volorum effectus	Realization or hope

The reflection point of the Part of Fortune is the Part of Spirit. It is not opposite Fortuna, but a reflection of it: an alternate theme, if you will, to the common path of increase represented by Fortuna. Remember, Fortune and Spirit are in symmetrical positions with respect to the Ascendant–Descendant axis. If you are examining a chart that does not have a Part of Spirit calculated, it is often easier to find the distance between Fortuna and the Ascendant or Descendant, and then project that number of degrees to the opposite side of the Ascendant or Descendant, respectively, to find the Part of Spirit.

The Greeks used an additional lot, calculated in the form of the angular difference I discussed in Figure 1 between the Part of Fortune and the Part of Spirit (Daemon in Greek):

> Lot of Basis... add to the Horoscopos the distance from the Lot of Fortune to the Lot of Daemon if the nativity falls in the day, otherwise the opposite direction is to be taken.[9]

As for the meaning of the Lot of Basis, while we have one from Antiochus of Athens, I am concerned about the degree of secondary derivation (a part calculated from other parts) used in its definition. However, for those who wish to experiment with this Lot, Antiochus said:

The Lot of Basis... is established as a contributing cause of life and breath; for the Basis itself is the giver of breath of the *Horoskopos*, and signifies bodily matters and sojourns abroad.[10]

We have evidence that the part of Fortune was used two ways. The first, described above, was as an alternate system of houses. The second was directly as a placement, as described by Firmicus Maternus, when the Part of Fortune was delineated using whether its dispositor, or its Term dispositor, was angular, in a good or a bad house, in dignity, or whether the dispositor(s) aspects Fortuna itself.[11] It was considered fortunate for the dispositor of the *Sect Light* (the Sun in a day birth, the Moon in a night birth) to be aspecting the Part of Fortune. It's better still if said dispositor aspects both the sect light and the Part of Fortune itself. Better yet if Fortuna is on an angle, and aspected by the Moon.

8. But if there is not one ruler of the sign of the Part of Fortune and of its terms and of the terms of the Sun and Moon, the one which has the greatest power should be the most important in the forecast; if this one is benefic and in favorable signs, in his exaltation or in his own house, or on first angles and in aspect to the Part of Fortune, a great and noble chart is indicated.

Firmicus said that the most powerful planet can only be considered such if that planet is angular. If it is not angular, then the person will never achieve greatness. We may thus conclude that the ancient interpretation of the part of Fortune was as a point which could either be used for predicting the functioning of planets through their lot positions, or for distinguishing between especially notable charts and the more common type.

There is, of course, one other use we should mention, especially since it is one of the relatively few techniques to survive intact: the use of the part of Fortune in horary astrology. For this, we may turn to Henry Coley:

18. The Part of Fortune well placed in a good House of the figure promises Gain to the Querent by persons or matters signified by that House and the Lord thereof, but if Debilitated expect the contrary.[12]

Partridge treated Fortuna extensively, in horary, natal, directions, and mundane. To quote him on horary :

46. In every Question, consider the part of Fortune; for if that be well dignified, the Querent gains by Things or Men signified by that House it is in; but if ill dignified, let him expect loss from such, the same may be said of Jupiter and Venus.[13]

Examples of uses were mentioned extensively by Lilly, Partridge, Gadbury, and many others. Two examples we may cite come from Bonatti:

> 85. Whether the part of Fortune fall in a good or bad place of the Figure; that is in an Angle, or in a Succedent or in a Cadent House; and how the same is aspected, and by whom, a Fortune or an Infortune? and whether it be in reception of that Planet by whom it was aspected? For questions may sometimes seem good, but the part of Fortune happening in an untoward Place, weakens it much and renders it less profitable so as to deceive the Querent's hopes. And on the contrary a question may seem ill yet the part of Fortune happening luckily, joined with a good planet that receives it, etc., lessens the evil, and not so much happens to the Querent as the Figure otherwise seems to threaten.

> 124. to regard in Nativities and Questions, the Significators of the Querent's and Native's estate and also of his preferment, calling or profession; which thou may'st take to be the Lord of the 10th, or of the Ascendant, if the other shall not be fit to signify the same; ... if there be in either of the said Angles any of the aforesaid helping and fortunate Fixed Stars with the part of Fortune or any of the Planets, he will far surpass his forefathers in dignity. And if such Fixed Stars shall be of the 1st Magnitude and sole Significators, the Native or Querent shall be raised to vast honors and riches, almost inestimable; which if beheld by the Lord of the Ascendant, then his fame and honor lies in his own person; if by the Lord of the 2nd, in his riches; if by the Lord of the 10th in his offices, command, or empire;.... But this shall not endure long, for they seldom go beyond 27 or 30 years....for they shall die an ignoble filthy death, or if they escape it, the same shall happen to their next successor.

Like the planets, there were accidental dignities and debilities associated with the Part of Fortune. (Accidental dignities or debilities are those which have to do with the placement of the part or body *relative* to other bodies or houses, although in the case of a part, it may also refer to sign placement. Table 3 shows the dignities of the Part of Fortune as given by Coley.[14]

Table 3. A Table of Fortitudes and Debilities of Fortuna, with their associated point values, according to Henry Coley.

Fortitudes		Debilities	
In ♉ or ♓	+5	In ♏, ♑, ♒	-5
In ♎, ♐, ♌, ♋	+4	In ♈	0
In ♊	+3		
In ♍	+2		
In the Asc or M.C.	+5	In the 12th or 6th House	-5
In the 7th, 4th or 11th House	+4	In the 8th House	-4
In the 2nd or 5th House	+3		
In the 9th House	+2		
In the 3rd House	+1		
☌ ♃ or ♀	+5	☌ ♄ or ♂	-5
△ ♃ or ♀	+4	☍ ♄ or ♂	-4
✶ ♃ or ♀	+3	□ ♄ or ♂	-3
		Terms of ♄ or ♂	-2
☌ ☊	+3	☌ ☋	-3
☌ Regulus	+6	☌ Caput Algol	-4
☌ Spica	+5		
Not Combust	+5	Combust	-5

Partridge discussed the Part of Fortune in transits:

> In manners and things relating to riches, the Transits of the part of Fortune, the second House and his Lord are most to be observed; but for Honour, the *M.C.* and his Lord, the Sun and his Dispositor, but for Health or Sickness, the Ascendant the Sun and Moon.[15]

So much for theory. Let's examine our usual suspect charts to explore these classical concepts. One exercise I might suggest to the reader: I shall be reading the Part of Fortune using the day-night shift. To make up your own mind about the value of the day-night switch, I encourage you to consider the daytime Fortuna in the night charts given, and see what your results may be. But first, let's add a new chart, and go through our usual preliminaries with it.

Case Study. Union Carbide & Bhopal

Diana Rosenberg and Arlene Nimark wrote an excellent summary detailing the events leading to the Bhopal disaster.[16] We present here two charts: the incorporation of Union Carbide, and the time the gas leak was discovered, which was when the first workers became sick, which is unfortunately the nature of early warning at such a chemical plant.

In the incorporation, the Ascendant ruler is Saturn, placed in the seventh House and widely conjunct Neptune. Union Carbide's business is chemicals; the conjunction between chart ruler and Neptune is thus appropriate.

In classical references, Partridge gave chemistry[17] and chemists[18] to Mars. Chemistry is just the politically correct modern offshoot of alchemy, with the spiritual dimension dropped, and an empirical process added. Dariot,[19] Lilly,[20] Ramesey[21] and Gadbury[22] all agree with the attribution, and assign Mars as ruling alchemy. If we use Mars for "Better Living through Chemistry" (to quote a Competitor's ad campaign), we find Mars on the 8th House cusp and ruling the 10th House, perhaps representing "Better dying through Chemistry?" Mars is conjunct the Royal Star Regulus: when things go wrong, they go wrong in a big way! (The Fall of Kings, as they used to say.) Death through chemistry impacts the corporate status. This is far more descriptive (and exact!) than any attempt to extract this from either the wide Sun-Neptune square, or the wide Saturn-Neptune conjunction.

Table 4. Qualities for Union Carbide incorporation.

	Triplicity	Seasonal	Traditional
☉	cold & wet	cold & dry	cold & dry
☽	hot & wet	hot & wet	cold & dry
☿	cold & wet	cold & dry	hot
♀	hot & dry	cold & dry	wet
♂	hot & dry	hot & dry	hot &dry
♃	hot & wet	hot & wet	wet
♄	hot & dry	hot & dry	cold & wet
Asc	cold & dry	cold & wet	cold & dry
M.C	cold & wet	cold & dry	cold & wet
⊗	hot & dry	hot & dry	hot & dry

The elemental qualities for Union Carbide's incorporation are shown in Table 4. Union Carbide has a Triplicity balance of wet and dry, with a slight edge for hot. That a chemical company should have an approximately even mix of wet and dry makes sense. If the business is making chemicals, for every chemical bond "made" (wet) , other bonds are broken (dry). Since most of our modern chemical reactions require energy to create the new compounds, a hot chart is of some advantage. However, the seasonal qualities tell us something more fundamental about the corporate philosophy: here there is a balance of hot and cold, but an abundance of dry. A dry corporation is not going to show great social responsibility, because it does not see itself as being that intimately connected with its environment, a wet quality. A dry organization will see only its immediate linkages: raw materials and personnel, and not quality of life issues. In the Traditional calculation, the company is predominately cold.

Union Carbide's sect placements are shown in Table 5. Mars is out of sect, and Saturn is in Hayz. We have already seen that Mars is a natural ruler of chemistry, and hence quite important to Union Carbide's success as a company (unless it ever diversifies out of chemicals, of course). Furthermore, Mars is at 29°, accidentally debilitated in the late degrees of a sign, although this being Regulus, the net affect is positive, and further essentially dignified by Term and Face. And Mars is co-Almuten of the Ascendant.

While Saturn may be in *Hayz*, Saturn is also in Detriment in Leo. Saturn is further accidentally dignified by angularity, being in the 7th House. Saturn, the chart ruler by sign, is thus quite accidentally dignified, but essentially debilitated, being peregrine as well as in Detriment. How do we interpret this?

A planet with a great deal of accidental dignity is likely to come to prominence, often by being in the right place at the right time. However, with essential debility, that planet will act in a way counter to the normal meaning of that planet. Saturn's essence is sober responsibility and conservatism. Saturn in Leo will tend toward personal glorification over responsibility to others, and recklessness in inappropriate situations. Translated into a corporate context, this means that Union Carbide will tend to think less of the welfare of its workers, the environment, or the general public, the three areas of social responsibility, and more of its immediate corporate interest, which presumably is profit. Thus, we have a company willing to put its workers or the public at risk, combined with a tendency to take risks unnecessarily. Rosenberg and Nimark documented an earlier example of risk-taking by Union Carbide that had results chillingly like Bhopal, so we can see that we are not dealing with just one isolated incident.

Table 5. Union Carbide incorporation. Chart is Diurnal. "Preference"
denotes the planet's natural sect.

	Preference	Placement	Sign	Comment
☉	Day	(Diurnal)	Nocturnal	
☽	Night	Nocturnal	Diurnal	
☿	Mixed	Diurnal	Nocturnal	Oriental is defined as diurnal
♀	Night	Nocturnal	Diurnal	Occidental is defined as nocturnal
♂	Night	Diurnal	Diurnal	Out of Sect
♃	Day	Nocturnal	Diurnal	
♄	Day	Diurnal	Diurnal	Hayz

Since we are doing the Part of Fortune, let us see what we may see.
Fortuna is disposed by the Sun, which is peregrine. Union Carbide has
to make its own breaks. Saturn is applying to Fortuna by conjunction,
and Uranus by opposition. What does this mean? The Part of Fortune
cannot make aspects, only receive them. This means that the statement
only applies to the Radix chart itself, because Fortuna can be directed,
or progressed. Lilly said, "If you acquire the time, *viz. About what part
of his life, or when the Native may expect Wealth, or the goods of Fortune?* though it's best discovered by the *Significators* and Fortuna directed to Beneficiall *Promittors,...*"[23] And again, on the same page:
"Fortuna being directed to the good or evil aspects of the *Fortunes* or
Infortunes shewes the encrease or diminution of Riches:..."

The fact that the Part of Fortune cannot make aspects merely puts it
in the same category as the angles: a perfection cannot occur by moving
an Angle forward in zodiacal degree to meet an aspect with a planet in a
later degree. In other words, it is like walking or driving: you approach
a building; the building does not approach you. The application by Saturn is probably not especially germane, at least as far as the interpretation of the natal chart is concerned, because the time frame is pretty
long. However, the opposition of Uranus is of immediate concern because of our understanding of the Circle of Athla. The 7th Lot represents danger. With Uranus partile (exactly) opposite Fortuna, Union
Carbide is intrinsically susceptible to danger by accidents: it is, so to
speak, accident prone.

Table 6. Qualities for Bhopal gas leak.

	Triplicity	Seasonal	Traditional
☉	hot & dry	cold & dry	cold & dry
☽	hot & dry	hot & wet	hot & dry
☿	cold & dry	cold & wet	dry
♀	cold & dry	cold & wet	wet
♂	hot & wet	cold & wet	dry
♃	cold & dry	cold & wet	wet
♄	cold & wet	cold & dry	cold & wet
Asc	cold & dry	hot & dry	cold & dry
M.C	hot & wet	hot & wet	hot & wet
⊗	cold & dry	hot & wet	cold & dry

Now let's study the chart for the Bhopal incident itself. The qualities at the time of Bhopal are given in Table 6. While there is a slight Triplicity dominance of cold over hot, the really striking condition is dry, which is heavily dominant. Dry is coming apart at the seams! A gas leak is nothing other than a substance escaping from its normal course. While it is the "wet" quality of Air that allows it to escape (remember, wet is defined as not being confined to a shape, but rather, assuming the shape of its container), the dry quality here is manifested as a crack in the container! Dry is rough, and if we remember that boulders are "drier" than sand or clay, we begin to appreciate the symbolism for a broken pipe becoming drier! Truly dry substances do not make good containers! Of course, in the seasonal qualities, we see the reverse: the wet count is high, again with hot & cold fairly balanced. In the Traditional system, the overall quality is cold and dry, which certainly doesn't sound like a leak to me. One interesting point about the Traditional system: the Occidental phase of the planets only has one quality associated with it, and the quality associated is classified as *passive*, being either wet or dry. The implication of this system is that Orientally-challenged charts lack the same level of energy that the higher-charged Oriental planets possess. Interesting. To return to our comparisons, however, between the three systems of qualities, we see a conflict.

In reading the charts for disasters, the three placements which consistently show the nature of the problem are Mars, Saturn, and the South Node. In this chart, the South Node and Saturn are conjunct in the 3rd

House in a seasonally *dry* sign, so we see the problem specifically that was outlined in the Triplicity breakout above.

The sect placements for the Bhopal disaster are given in Table 7. Every planet in this chart is of mixed sect except Venus, which is in Hayz. Venus, however, Almuten of the 7th House (the public) is Peregrine. The public was *not* in position of strength, especially since the sign ruler of the 7th House, Jupiter, had dignity only by Term.

We have already seen that the incorporation chart for Union Carbide contained a potentially dangerous configuration with Uranus opposite Fortuna. Here we see *Pluto* opposite the Part of Fortune. Remember the 7th Lot? *Danger?* Fortuna was co-disposed by the Moon and Venus. Venus may have been in *Hayz*, but she was also peregrine, as was the Moon. Neither planet provides any strength to Fortuna, and this was a *very* expensive mistake. The peregrine Moon was in the 8th House of death.

The only planet with any essential dignity was Jupiter. As many of us have observed, Jupiter is often "good" only by exaggerating whatever situation arises. *Q.E.D.*

Table 7. Bhopal Gas Leak. Chart is Nocturnal. "Preference" denotes the planet's natural sect.

	Preference	Placement	Sign	Comment
☉	Day	(Nocturnal)	Diurnal	
☽	Night	Nocturnal	Diurnal	
☿	Mixed	Nocturnal	Nocturnal	Occidental is defined as nocturnal
♀	Night	Nocturnal	Nocturnal	Occidental = nocturnal. *Hayz.*
♂	Night	Diurnal	Diurnal	
♃	Day	Diurnal	Nocturnal	
♄	Day	Diurnal	Nocturnal	

When the Bhopal plant opened, the Moon at 11 Sagittarius was opposite Union Carbide's corporate Moon. The manufacturing plant's Sun is on the Solstice Point of Union Carbide's Sun. The gas leak occurred on December 2, 1984, with the transiting Sun opposite Union Carbide's Moon. Earlier that year there had been an Eclipse whose shadow fell over the Eastern U.S.A., site of Union Carbide's headquarters. The longitude of that Eclipse was at 9° Gemini, conjunct Union

Carbide's Moon and Jupiter. The Eclipse immediately prior to the Bhopal gas leak was on November 22, 1984. The Ascendant at Bhopal for that Eclipse was conjunct the M.C. of the Union Carbide incorporation chart.

We can further explore the situation with Union Carbide by using a different chart: the chart for the first time that its stock was traded. This will show more of the perception of the company from the standpoint of its stockholders. The 1st Trade Qualities are shown in Table 8.

This trade chart is somewhat hot and *definitely* wet by Triplicity. What could this mean in a stock? Union Carbide's First Trade is ruled by Mercury, with the Ascendant at 0° no less! One would expect that a Mercury-ruled chart with a high wet quality would mean a company that is quite susceptible to rumors as far as the strength of its share price, especially as that Mercury is in Pisces. Mercury is in Detriment and Fall there, which is likely to make Pisces less factual and information-based, and more gossip, rumor, and hopeful or wishful thinking. Add to this the conjunction of Mercury with Uranus, and you have the potential for real unreliable data transmission! The chart is *very* cold and *very* wet by season as well. The quality of a cold stock should be a tendency toward a "wait-and-see" attitude: a hot stock would presumably be more volatile than a cold one. And here is the conflict with the Traditional system, which gives a strong hot reading, which would produce volatility.

Table 8. Qualities of Union Carbide 1st Trade.

	Triplicity	Seasonal	Traditional
☉	cold & wet	cold & wet	cold & wet
☽	hot & wet	cold & dry	cold & dry
☿	cold & wet	cold & wet	dry
♀	hot & wet	cold & wet	hot & wet
♂	cold & dry	cold & wet	hot & dry
♃	hot & wet	cold & wet	hot & wet
♄	cold & wet	cold & dry	dry
Asc	hot & wet	hot & wet	hot & wet
M.C	hot & wet	cold & wet	hot & wet
⊗	hot & dry	cold & dry	hot & dry

Sect relationships for the 1st Trade chart are shown in Table 9. Venus is out of sect, while Jupiter is in *Hayz*. Venus is peregrine anyway, and is sign ruler of the 6th, and Dominatrix (Almuten) of the 11th House. This looks rather like a malefic Venus: the oriental placement of Venus is definitely the malefic placement, and here Venus is conjunct the M.C., so this is a Venus definitely capable of making trouble for the stock. The conjunction of the two benefics here is not so great, because both are peregrine, and thus less likely to perform *consistently*. When we are looking at peregrine activity over the life of a person, or in this case a stock, the wandering quality inherent to peregrine can simply result in an unpredictable or inconsistent approach to those areas of life ruled by the planet. So Venus provides yet one more promise of volatility.

Table 9. Union Carbide 1st Trade. Chart is Diurnal. "Preference" denotes the planet's natural sect.

	Preference	Placement	Sign	Comment
☉	Day	(Diurnal)	Nocturnal	
☽	Night	Nocturnal	Diurnal	
☿	Mixed	Nocturnal	Nocturnal	Occidental is defined as nocturnal
♀	Night	Diurnal	Diurnal	Oriental = diurnal. Out of Sect.
♂	Night	Diurnal	Nocturnal	
♃	Day	Diurnal	Diurnal	*Hayz*
♄	Day	Nocturnal	Nocturnal	

The Bhopal chart had a very tight Mercury-Neptune conjunction that was just past the Part of Spirit at 28 Sagittarius. When we consider the transit of Bhopal (Gas Leak Discovered) to the 1st Trade chart, notice that transiting Venus is conjunct the 1st Trade South Node, surely not a good sign! Furthermore, transiting Saturn is approaching a Saturn return, but specifically square the 1st Trade Neptune. Saturn rules the M.C. and 9th Houses of the 1st Trade: the company image (10th) and the company on foreign soil (9th). Notice further that the transiting South Node of Bhopal is smack on the 1st Trade Saturn.

What is interesting here is that the transit of Bhopal shows much more activity with the 1st Trade Chart than with the corporate chart. Of course, one expects that a stock, being naturally more volatile than its parent company, probably *would* be a better short-term indicator of activity. Clearly, we know in retrospect that Bhopal did *not* destroy Union Carbide, nor even seriously damage it long-term. It was the short-term effect that was dramatic. As far as the stock was concerned, there was a relatively minor downward tick that didn't last very long. Remember the seasonal "cold" quality to the First Trade: a possible damper on volatility?

Now let's consider the Part of Fortune. The Part of Fortune is disposed by Jupiter, which we have already seen is not strong. Further, Mercury is in a partile separating square from Fortuna, so we see yet again the theme of rumor-mongering and its effect on share price. The other major aspect to Fortuna is the approaching trine from Neptune. Need I say more?

Other Example Charts

Next, we can return to the example charts that we have been using so far.

Czar Nicholas II

Nicholas's Fortuna was at 20° Cancer in his 11th House. Fortuna is disposed primarily by the Moon. The Moon, as we have already seen, is peregrine. This does not suggest a man who will end up with a net accumulation of assets!

Let us examine this chart through the Circle of Athla. Fortuna is at 20° Cancer.

Using Manilius' Lots: The Dispositor of Fortuna is the Moon, conjunct Jupiter and Neptune in the IX lot of children. The IX Lot is ruled by Jupiter. Jupiter has some dignity: this shows a man very involved with his children, which is accurate. But does he derive fortune (remember, this is Athla) from these children? No.

Using Valens' Hellenistic Lots: The children are the V Lot, ruled by Mars in Aries, strong but violent, with Saturn retrograde in the V Lot showing misfortune. Manilius would put the V Lot as marriage, and his marriage was *not* unfortunate in any way.

The South Node is in the VIII Lot of Death (Hellenistic) and Saturn rules it: Saturn also rules the VII Lot of Danger (Manilius) or Marriage (Hellenistic). Using the Hellenistic interpretation of the XII Lot as self-undoing, here we have Venus: self-undoing through a woman. There is no question that Czarina Alexandra and her attempts through Rasputin to "cure" the Czarevitch of his hemophilia did much to undermine Nicholas' reign.

Of course, we could use other circles to examine the children, and we can also separate the boys from the girls. Valens gave the Lot of Sons as Ascendant + Mercury - Jupiter.[24] In Nicholas' case, this placement is 14 Scorpio 47, ruled by Mars. If we use this lot to form its own Circle, than Saturn falls in the first Lot of the Son, already a danger flag. The son's health is the 6th Lot from the 1st, which gives 14° Aries: Neptune is sitting right there.

The Lot of Children is calculated as Ascendant + Saturn - Jupiter by day; Ascendant + Jupiter - Saturn by night. This Lot falls at 5 Taurus 58. Pluto in the 1st Lot from this part also does not look good for the children in general. The 6th Lot is ruled by Venus, which is not in as bad shape as the health lot for the son.

Nicholas' XI Locus was Taurus, with Pluto within 3°. Next question? Accomplishment by destruction?

Mary Shelley

Mary has the same configuration between her Fortuna and Uranus as Union Carbide: fortunately, she wasn't a chemical company! Her Fortuna was disposed by Jupiter, which has dignity by Triplicity, so occasionally she would have good luck in this department. However, with Uranus at the Lot of Danger (the VII Lot), there would be sudden or unexpected changes in her fortune, quite likely as a result of accidents. How about a husband who stood to inherit if he lived, but drowned instead, thus cutting off this fortune for another generation?

One particular Locus or Lot has been highlighted by the Project Hindsight material: the XI Lot, which Robert Schmidt is translating as the "house of acquisition."[25] Neugebauer and Van Hoesen translated the same term as the Lot of Accomplishment.[26] In Shelley's case, her XI Locus would be Capricorn, and so Saturn ruled. She did not make her money by saturnian means, but she did accumulate it *slowly*. With her Saturn detrimented in Cancer it was not substantial, and she had to earn every penny!

Let's back up to look at the XI Locus for the other three charts we have already examined. The XI Locus for Union Carbide is Gemini. Mercury is disposed by Mars, which we have already seen is our guiding planet for chemicals. For the gas leak, the XI Locus is 5° Pisces, a degree with Venus as Almuten. Venus is peregrine, separating from Jupiter, the sign ruler of Pisces, and itself in net negative state because of being in Term (+2) and Fall (-4). Thus, neither ruler is in good shape, suggesting loss rather than gain.

Let's also examine a couple of her other Lots. The Lot of the Father is Ascendant + Sun - Saturn by Night; Ascendant + Saturn - Sun by Day. Since Mary was a Night birth, her Lot of the Father was 0 Virgo 49, conjunct her Mars, and in her 4th House. Her father's finances are given by the 2nd Lot from the Lot of the Father: ruled by Venus, he got his money from women: his wife and his daughter. The

Lot of Marriage of Women is Ascendant + Saturn - Venus by either day or night: Shelley's is at 8 Aries 39, square Saturn, quincunx Sun, and quincunx Neptune. Enough said?

Prince Charles

Prince Charles' Fortuna is ruled by Saturn, which is peregrine in his chart. If we do equal loci off Fortuna, then Saturn is in his VII Locus of danger. This would not be true with whole sign loci, because Saturn is in the next sign (Virgo) from the VII Locus cusp (Leo). If it is the case, it becomes stronger evidence that Charles' fortune will suffer a net decline by the end of his life. (At this point, as Prince of Wales, he is not in direct control of it in any case.) However, if Saturn is not in the VII Locus by whole sign, Pluto is! Either way, this doesn't look good for the heir to the House of Windsor.

Charles' XI Locus of Accomplishment is Sagittarius, with Jupiter conjunct the Locus cusp if degrees are applied. The dispositor of the cusp, Jupiter, is the strongest planet by dignity in his chart. This should indicate that he gets a substantial fortune, which he should by inheritance. However, with that Jupiter about to leave its own sign, and opposite Uranus, we have to wonder if we aren't seeing the end of the monarchy, or at least a substantial change after Charles.

Aleister Crowley

Aleister Crowley's Fortuna was disposed by Venus (Exaltation +4, Term +2, compared to Jupiter +5). Venus was strong by sign, but combust. Venus is in the VIII Locus in the Circle of Athla, which represents either success or reputation. Crowley certainly made a reputation for himself! Separating from a partile sextile to Fortuna was Neptune, which just *may* be relevant to an understanding of Crowley.

Crowley's Locus of Accomplishment is ruled by Saturn, which is dignified in Aquarius, though retrograde. Said Saturn is in his XII Locus, which is realization or hope in Manilius' system.

Crowley did *not* become fabulously wealthy with these aspects, but then he wasn't born into the House of Windsor either. He did achieve fame, however.

Catherine de Medici

Catherine de Medici had the Part of Fortune conjunct Neptune, which may be good, in a machiavellian kind of way! Her Fortuna, like Crowley's, was disposed by a dignified Saturn. Not only was Saturn the most dignified planet in her chart, it was in the 10th House. The only problem with that Saturn was that it was square her Sun. Beyond hinting at danger to men in her life (like her husband, who died in a tournament), the Sun-Saturn square may illuminate one of the other conflicts in her chart, which is also shown by Fortuna in the 12th House. Catherine was not the designated ruler of France. She wielded her power as Regent, supposedly acting for the benefit of her son. That this was merely a formality goes without saying. That she increased her fortune through bribery and under-the-table dealings is almost a foregone conclusion. But that was standard behavior for the monarchs of her day.

The XI Locus of her Circle of Athla was Sagittarius. Jupiter has dignity by Term, and is conjunct the 7th House cusp. Catherine did not begin as a monarch, but married one, namely the King of France. With Jupiter *Rex* having dignity by Term, as well as being retrograde, hubby was not exactly the model king. Venus, ruler of the 7th House is in Aries in Detriment, so hubby was basically just your average macho jock, who happened to come with a scepter and crown! With Sun conjunct Venus in the 1st House, I don't doubt that Catherine came to care about him, if not love him. (Remember, dynastic matches did not require much more than periodic nonrevulsion to proceed.) Hubby's essential ineffectiveness was further confirmed by the V Locus, with Gemini on the cusp. Mercury is the least dignified planet in her chart! Now, who said that getting yourself killed in a tournament is *bright*?

George Foreman

George Foreman's Fortuna is in Aries, not bad for a fighter! Mars disposes it, and Mars is peregrine. Fortuna is fortified by a trine from Venus, which is opposite Uranus. The trine from a benefic is good, but Venus herself is peregrine, so it's not good for much. That Venus is conjunct the IX Locus in his Circle of Athla: the IX Locus has to do with children, and we may recall that Foreman has been very active in community services for children. But the sextile from Uranus suggests that fortune is erratic, which has certainly been true. Foreman's XI Locus is Aquarius, ruled by Saturn, which is conjunct his Ascendant. Again, Saturn is peregrine, making him work harder than many for what he does get. World Heavyweight Champion at 40? Just a little bit of work!

Muhammad Ali

Muhammad Ali has Fortuna conjunct Pluto, and square Mars. Now we know Pluto can bring windfalls - we just never know whether the windfall is on the plus or the minus side of the ledger. Ali's Sun, Mercury, and Venus are all in his VII Locus of danger. With Mars square Pluto natally, we already know that Ali has the potential for rage and revenge! With Mars at his X Locus of action and authority, Ali was effectively able to harness this energy to his own (financial) advantage. It is intriguing that Foreman has Fortuna in Aries, while Ali has Fortuna square Mars.

Thus, we can see that the Circle of Athla gives us additional information about success and financial reward that is otherwise less obvious in the chart. Because it is based on equal signs or houses from Fortuna, it has the further advantage of being easy to calculate without recourse to calculator or computer. Perhaps we should recultivate it!

In the next chapter, we shall take up quincunxes, semi-sextiles, and solstice points.

Source for Data

Union Carbide and Bhopal: Diana K. Rosenberg and Arlene Nimark. 1986. Union Carbide and 'The Mills of God.'" N.C.G.R. Journal *4*(2): 11-16.

1st Trade Chart for Union Carbide: Bill Meridian. 1995. *Planetary Stock Trading*. Cycles Research Publications: New York.

Endnotes

[1]   *Op. cit.,* pages 348-349.For a fuller discussion of Raphael's simplifications, see my book *Essential Dignities*, Chapters 1 and 4.

[2]   Rudhyar, pp 65-66.

[3]   This question of full sign versus degree is a fairly consistent thematic "disagreement" between Hellenistic and later Arabic sources. For example, Ptolemy discusses aspects and antiscia by sign, while since the Arabs, we would restrict this to degrees, and orbs of degrees. There is little question that the earliest house system consisted of full sign houses, with the 1st House beginning at 0° of the sign that contained the Ascendant.

[4]   From an Internet post to ANCIEN-L%ULKYVM.BITNET on July 11, 1995.

[5]   When it comes to multiple siblings, or other similar multiplicities of the affairs of a house, the tendency to alternate houses (second brother is the 5th, 3rd the 7th, 4th the 9th) is taken from Vedic astrology. The Western tradition on this would be to either take the second sign ruler of the house, of to go through the sequence of Triplcity rulers.

[6]   See Rob Hand's Introduction, page iii in Valens, Book II, Part 1.

[7]   Plant, David C. 1990. Classical origins of the Arabian parts. Astrological Journal *32*(4): 250-254.

[8]   Bouché-Leclercq, pp 297-298.

[9]   *Greek Horoscopes*, page 9.

[10] *Op. cit.*, page 33.

[11] *Op. cit.*, pages 135-137.

[12] *Op. cit.*, page 75.

[13] *Op. cit.*, page 341.

[14] *Op. cit.*, 1st Edition, page 36.

[15] *Op. cit.*, page 229.

[16] Rosenberg, Diana and Arlene Nimark. 1986. Union Carbide and 'The Mills of God.'" N.C.G.R. Journal *4*(2): 11-16.

[17] *Op. cit.*, page 109.

[18] *Op. cit.*, page 13.

[19] *Op. cit.*, page 21.

[20] Lilly, *CA*, page 67.

[21] *Op. cit.*, page 54.

[22] *Op. cit.*, page 68.

[23] Lilly, *CA*, page 563.

[24] All formulas given here are taken from Rob Hand's compilation of Greek Lots and Arabic Parts that he used in the programming of Chart Wheels 3.

[25] For example, Valens *Anthology*, Book 2, Part 1, page 34.

[26] *Op. cit.*, pages 81, 84, and 85.

——Chapter Nine ——
When a Quincunx is not Inconjunct

> But no friendliness towards one another has been granted to
> adjacent signs: sympathy between them is blunted because
> the sight of each other is denied them. Their attentions are
> bestowed on distant signs which they can see. Again they are
> signs of opposite sex, linked male to female right round the
> circle, and each in turn is forever beset by its neighbors.
>
> Sixth signs, as well, are not reckoned as capable of any influ-
> ence...
>
> Manilius[1]

When is a Quincunx (or Semi-sextile) not inconjunct? This question may seem to be a contradiction in terms because most modern
astrologers would consider the two terms to be synonymous. The purpose of this chapter is threefold. The first is to show that, in fact, these
two terms are not synonymous. The second is to clarify the usage of
Quincunx (150°) and Semi-sextile (30°). The third is to discuss the
component of classical analysis which completely changes our modern conception of Inconjunct, namely antiscia (solstice points).

Contemporary common usage dictates that the term "inconjunct"
could refer to either the Quincunx or the Semi-sextile. Let's consider a
modern interpretation. The Quincunx and Semi-sextile are considered
to be aspects produced by dividing the zodiacal circle of 360° by twelve.
Because both aspects are produced by the twelvefold division of the
zodiac, they are considered related. However, modern astrologers have
often been hard-pressed to distinguish between the two. To quote Sue
Tompkins:

"Signs in Quincunx do not confront each other as with the opposition or get in each other's way as with the square; they are coming from

completely different places and heading in different directions, and they don't even see each other, rather like two planes on unrelated flight paths. To become conscious of our Quincunxes seems to take even more effort than to become aware of the other types of conflict in our charts....

> Whereas a square or opposition might be descriptive of major conflict to be resolved and thus by extension, major drama to be enacted in the life, the Quincunx is more descriptive of some kind of additional irritation and stress.[2]

Tompkins says the following about semi-sextiles:

> Charles Carter says he believes this aspect to be of 'negligible importance unless it is implicated in a larger formation', and I must say, I am inclined to share this view. Like quincunxes, semi-sextiles often support and confirm other information already in the chart, and this can often be seen particularly in progressions.[3]

It is fascinating the Tompkins' book on aspects (like so many other modern books) follows the structure of defining the types of aspects briefly, then devotes the rest of the book to generic aspects between planetary pairs. It is as if there were nothing to say about the specific aspects except within the context of two particular planets! No wonder so many astrologers believe that there is no difference between any two kinds of aspects, that the only significant issue is whether there is any aspect, or no aspect. This idea has reached its summit in Cosmobiology, in which all hard aspects are treated alike, and all soft aspects are ignored.

A major element in the modern interpretation of Quincunxes has been the idea of the so-called sixth House and eighth House Quincunxes. The idea is that sixth House Quincunxes are less problematic than eighth House ones. The author generally then discusses the combinations like Aries-Virgo and Aries-Scorpio where this works, and not Leo-Capricorn and Leo-Pisces, where it doesn't! I believe that this concept developed because it is partially right. The problem is that its proponents didn't have enough information to go far enough to make the concept useful. The 6th house-8th house Quincunx idea is yet one more instance of carrying the equation of Mars = Aries = first House too far.

The component missing from the modern interpretation of Quincunxes and Semi-sextiles is simply this: there *are* two kinds of both aspects, but the two kinds are not defined by 6th house or 8th house types. They are defined by whether or not the two signs *behold* each other. Lilly then described those signs as follows:

These are called Signes inconjunct, or such as if a Planet be in one of them, he cannot have any aspect to another in the sign underneath: as one in Aries can have no to another in Taurus or Scorpio, or one in Taurus to one in Aries, Gemini, Libra or Sagittarius, so understand the rest.[4]

Shall we go about understanding the rest? What Lilly did not state explicitly was that there are three different ways that two signs can behold each other:

- the signs are related by Ptolemaic aspect (conjunction, sextile, square, trine or opposition);
- they are related by Antiscia, also called Solstice points;
- they are related by Contra-antiscia, the point opposite the Antiscia.

Solstice points? Back to Ptolemy. In Book I of *Tetrabiblos,* Ptolemy defined the aspects first, strictly by sign: in other words, Taurus was trine to Virgo. Next he discussed "commanding" and "obeying" signs. The specific definition as given in the Robbins translation is:

> ...the names 'commanding' and 'obeying' are applied to the divisions of the zodiac which are disposed at an equal distance from the same equinoctial sign, whichever it may be, because they ascend in equal periods of time and are on equal parallels. Of these the ones in the summer hemisphere are called 'commanding' and those in the winter hemisphere 'obedient,' because the sun makes the day longer than the night when he is in the summer hemisphere, and shorter in the winter.

This is a crucial passage, one that has been misread by scholars, with interesting consequences for astrologers, so I also present the Ashmand translation:

> Any two signs configured with each other at an equal distance from the same, or from either equinoctial point, are termed commanding and obeying, because the ascensional and descensional times of the one are equal to those of the other, and both describe equal parallels.

> The signs in the same summer semicircle are commanding; those in the winter semicircle, obeying; for, when the Sun is present in the former, he makes the day longer than the night; and, when in the latter, he produces the contrary effect.

What did Ptolemy mean by "the divisions of the zodiac which are disposed at an equal distance from the same equinoctial sign, whichever it may be, because they ascend in equal periods of time and are on equal parallels" (Robbins) or "Any two signs configured with each other at an equal distance from the same, or from either equinoctial point" (Ashmand)? The key is given in the Robbins edition as "ascend[ing] in equal periods of time." Unfortunately the Greek scholar Bouché-Leclercq listed the wrong pair combinations. Robbins cited Bouché-Leclercq's signs; thus, anyone who read the footnotes in Robbins would get the wrong impression about this concept. This may be because the zodiac of Ptolemy's time - though tropical - did not have the Spring Equinox at 0° Aries, but somewhat later in Aries. This resulted in a skewing of the signs involved.

Scholarly questions aside, what in blazes was Ptolemy talking about? To answer this question, we must remember that the development of the early techniques was so tightly intertwined with astronomical observation that there was no distinction in meaning between "astronomy" and "astrology."

What Ptolemy meant when he said "equal distance from the same equinoctial sign," is: 29° Pisces and 1° Aries are at "equal distance" from the same Equinoctial point, in this case 0° Aries. This is the definition of what is *now* called the Contra-antiscion. Wilson called this the parallel, along with its converse - the solstice point or antiscion - which we will consider shortly. In this example, Pisces is the obeying sign (Winter hemisphere) while Aries is the commanding sign (Summer hemisphere.)

The primary ancient definition of the Spring Equinox (in the Northern Hemisphere below the Arctic Circle) is that the Day and the Night are of equal duration. There is another equally important element, one we mostly ignore. In the Northern Hemisphere the Sun rises in the East-Northeast from the Spring until the Fall, and rises in the East-Southeast from the Fall until the Spring. Declination is the term for the celestial equivalent of Earth East-West longitude. Thus, the Spring Equinox represents the shift in the Sun's rising position from Southern Declination to Northern Declination. The Fall Equinox represents the shift in the Sun's rising position from Northern Declination to Southern Declination. The signs of Northern Declination sunrise (Aries through Virgo) are the Summer or Northern Hemisphere signs. The signs of Southern Declination sunrise (Libra through Pisces) are the Winter or Southern Hemisphere signs.

Now let's examine the contra-antiscia. The day length the day before the Spring Equinox (29° Pisces) is slightly shorter than the night. Remember, at the Equinox, days and nights are defined as being of equal length. After the Equinox (1° Aries) the day length is slightly longer than the night. The ratio of day length is converse between these two Contra-antiscion points. These points are also divided by declination. 1° Aries has Northern Declination, i.e., the Sun rises slightly North of East; 29° Pisces has Southern Declination and rises slightly South of East. Next, consider Solstice Points, also known as Antiscia. Ptolemy called the antiscia "Signs which Behold each other and Signs of Equal Power." This is the specific quotation from the Robbins translation:

"Again, they say that the parts which are equally removed from the same tropical sign, whichever it may be, are of equal power, because when the sun comes into either of them the days are equal to the days, the nights to the nights, and the lengths of their own hours are the same. These are also said to 'behold' one another both for the reasons stated and because each of the pair rises from the same part of the horizon and sets in the same part."

Here we may define 29° Gemini to be equal in distance to 0° Cancer as 1° Cancer. The day is longest (by definition) when the Sun is at 0° Cancer; thus, 29° Gemini and 1° Cancer represent days of equal length, nights of equal length. (Remember, folks: these definitions do not extend to 16 decimal places. When I say equal, I mean within the observational capacity of the ancient Greeks!) Both 29° Gemini and 1° Cancer have Northern declination; they are commanding (Summer) signs; they are of equal power.

Various pairs of Signs are related to each other by antiscion as shown in Table 1.

Table 1. Antiscial & contra-antiscial signs.

Antiscial signs	Contra-antiscial signs
♈ ♍	♈ ♓
♉ ♌	♉ ♒
♊ ♋	♊ ♑
♎ ♓	♎ ♍
♏ ♒	♏ ♌
♐ ♑	♐ ♋

If we examine these pairings further, we may discern certain relationships. First, the antiscial signs, or solstice point signs, are *always* on the same "side" of either the Spring or Fall Equinox. Thus, both Aries and Virgo are between the Spring Equinox and the Fall Equinox. The sign pairs are the same whether this is the Northern or Southern Hemisphere, although which Ingress constitutes "Spring" is different. These are combinations of two commanding signs or two obeying signs, so these are combinations of "signs of equal powers."

In the case of the contra-antiscial signs, by definition the two signs occupy different sides of the solstitial axes . For example, Aquarius is between the Libra Ingress and the Aries Ingress. Taurus is between the

Aries Ingress and the Libra one. These are combinations of obeying sign (the Winter side of the axis) with commanding sign (the Summer side of the axis). We leave for our Southern Hemisphere friends to work out whether the definition of which group of signs constitutes "commanding," and which "obeying," differs between Northern and Southern Hemisphere.

Any combination of signs which is *not* in ptolemaic aspect, antiscial, or contra-antiscial relationship to each other is Inconjunct. An easy method to discover which kind of Quincunx or Semi-sextile you are examining is to determine whether the Quincunx or Semi-sextile in question involves one fixed sign. If the 150° aspect or the 30° aspect does, then you are looking at a true inconjunct. This is because the Antiscia and the Contra-antiscia of the fixed signs are square to each other by Sign, while the Cardinal and Mutable signs are always antiscial or contra-antiscial to each other. The involvement of a fixed sign spells *inconjunct*.

Now that we've caught up to Lilly, please note his wording. He stated that signs not "beholding" are "inconjunct:" these two words are reciprocals of each other. Now if you study Table 1, you will notice that *every* two signs not beholding each other are related to each other by being separated by either 30° or 150°: they are all Quincunx or Semi-sextile each other by sign. However, you may also notice that not all signs separated by 30° or 150° are on this list. Rob Hand has observed that the Latin word applied to nonbeholding Quincunxes and Semi-sextiles was *remotus*, which can be translated as aversion.

This is the reason that Astrologers mistakenly divided Quincunxes into sixth House and eighth House versions. The correct classification is those which *behold* and those which do not. Using Lilly's terminology we can also state it as those which are *inconjunct* and those which are not. Since the modern tendency is to begin talking about *any* sign concept by using Aries, it just so happens that the Aries-Virgo are beholding, and Aries-Scorpio are not.

Planets beholding do not act like Planets inconjunct. Therefore, not all Quincunxes and Semi-sextiles are created equal: some are inconjunct and some are not. The ones that are beholding should be interpreted differently.

Tompkins' remark that Quincunxes "don't even see each other" is remarkable given that the Ptolemaic concept we are discussing here is *beholding*! Beholding Quincunxes and Semi-sextiles *do see each other* even though they share the same problem that all Quincunxes and Semi-sextiles have. Furthermore, the two signs only differ in some qualities: male/female, diurnal/nocturnal, element, Quadruplicity, and not *necessarily* the qualities hot/cold, moist/dry. Inconjunct planets which share *no* qualities *cannot* reach an accommodation on the basis of any perceived similarity. But beholding planets have the advantage of being able to see the other point of view; thus, accommodation is easier. Furthermore, if the combination of signs shares a temperamental quality, accommodation is eased. These combinations are shown in Figures 1 and 2, for the quincunx pairs and the semi-sextiles. We can see that those combinations of signs where the elements are Fire and Earth share the quality of dry, and the Air and Water combinations share the quality of dry. *All* of the antiscial pairs share one of these two qualities. However, *none* of the contra-antiscial combinations do. This already allows us to propose that antiscial combinations are easier to work with than contra-antiscial ones because it is easier to find components of commonality.

Quincunx Affinities

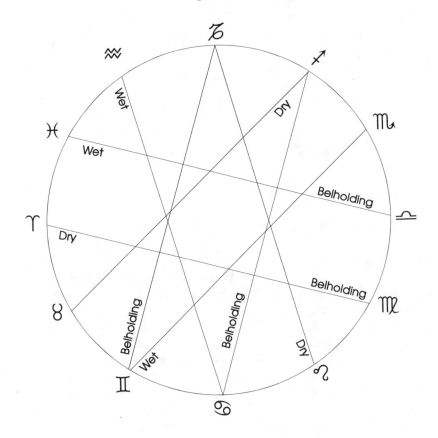

Semi-sextile Affinities

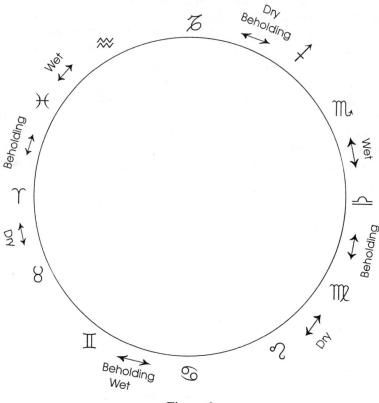

Figure 2

What is the advantage of commonality? Well... Aries has more in common with Virgo—dryness—than with Scorpio. As a result, in the midst of disagreement, the Aries person and Virgo person are more likely to notice their disagreement, and through noticing, dissociate enough to diffuse the situation. Meanwhile Aries and Scorpio are still trying to kill each other!

The idea is rather like the meditation theory used by many Eastern religious traditions. Through observation of thoughts, one tends to dissociate from the egoic issues associated with those thoughts. The observer position is one of equanimity: this resembles the beholding Quincunx or Semi-sextile. Beholding—like meditation—doesn't "solve" anything. But any time there is commonality by quality, the process is easier. But even without commonality, through beholding, the observation process makes the situation easier to bear.

Both the Quincunx and Semi-sextile are believed to be "new" aspects, by which we mean that they were not used by Classical Astrology. This impression is partially wrong. Ptolemy specifically mentioned the distance represented by one sign or five signs. It was interpreted, but it was not considered an aspect. Even William Lilly used a Semi-sextile in a horary reading[5] to indicate hope.

Before we continue, let's review what we've learned.

- Summer (Northern) Signs
  Aries, Taurus, Gemini, Cancer, Leo, Virgo
  The Sun rises to the Northeast
  The day length is greater than or equal to the length of Night
  Commanding
- Winter (Southern) Signs
  Libra, Scorpio, Sagittarius, Capricorn, Aquarius, Pisces
  The Sun rises to the Southeast
  The night length is greater than or equal to the day length
  Obeying

Now the kicker. Ptolemy went on to discuss what Robbins translated as "disjunct signs" and Ashmand translated as "signs inconjunct." In the Ashmand translation (and Robbins agrees in substance):[6]

> All signs, between which there does not exist any familiarity in any of the modes above specified, are inconjunct and separated.
>
> For instance, all signs are inconjunct which are neither commanding nor obeying, and not beholding each other nor of equal power, as well as all signs which contain between them the space of one sign only, or the space of five signs, and which do not at all share in any of the four prescribed configurations, viz. the opposition, the trine, the quartile, and the sextile. All parts which are distant from each other in the space of one sign only are considered inconjunct, because they are averted, as it were, from each other; and because, although the said space between them may extend into two signs, the whole only contains an angle equal to that of one sign: all parts distant from each other in the space of five signs are also considered inconjunct, because they divide the whole circle into unequal parts....

Ptolemy's system therefore recognizes three classes of Quincunxes/Semi-sextiles:

- signs commanding-obeying (contra-antiscia)
- signs beholding, or of equal power (antiscia)
- signs inconjunct (the remainder).

While Ptolemy defined the sign relationship represented by the

Quincunx and the Semi-sextile, he did not define them as aspects, but rather, as the *lack* of aspect. Before considering the ramifications of these three classes, I should mention that the terminology changed somewhat in the period after Ptolemy, but when the concepts were still in use. In the 17th Century, Lilly, Ramesey, Coley, and Partridge all defined antiscia and contra-antiscia in the same fashion as Ptolemy, and listed the commanding and obeying signs without pairing them as contra-antiscia. The difference was that the later authors used "beholding" to mean "not inconjunct"; i.e., two planets in aspect, antiscion or contra-antiscion relationship. Clearly this was the standard usage of "beholding" by the 17th Century.

While historically Ptolemy's usage should prevail, since it is oldest, I prefer a slight variation on the Renaissance usage as shown in Table 2. The reason for my departure is that it is simply too useful to have a single term for the combination of "in aspect or Solstice point or contra-antiscion" relationship. In the Renaissance they defined beholding to mean just that. Thus, it is easier to use "beholding" that way than to invent yet one more word. However, I have rescued Ptolemy's alternate terminology for Solstice Points, namely Signs of Equal Power.

Table 2. Nomenclature for quincunx and semi-sextile types, and aspects.

	Ptolemy	Renaissance	Lehman
Contra-antiscial	Commanding & Obeying	Commanding & Obeying	Commanding & Obeying
Antiscial	Equal Power or Beholding		Equal Power
Ptolemaic aspect, contra-antiscial, or anticial		Beholding	Beholding

Applications in Practice

Now that we have survived this somewhat tortured historical phase, the take-home message is this: the lesson from Ptolemy is that planets in Antiscion or Contra-antiscion degrees (and signs!) share a relationship every bit as powerful as planets in aspect. The *nature* of that relationship is determined by the relationship between the signs involved. There are only three possible natures for Antiscion and Contra-antiscion signs:

- Signs which are Semi-sextile (e.g., Aries-Pisces or Gemini-Cancer)
- The Fixed signs which square each other (e.g., Taurus-Leo or Taurus-Aquarius)
- Signs which are Quincunx (e.g., Aries-Virgo or Pisces-Libra)

This has translated into the following muddle in practice. Because we have good, solid ideas for the meaning of the square aspect, it has been possible to ignore that the fixed squares may also be beholding each other by Antiscion or Contra-antiscion, depending on the degrees involved. Accordingly, fixed squares which have wide orbs may be functional because they are nonetheless beholding, as one planet at 4° Taurus beholds another at 26° Leo.

On the other hand, the definition of the Quincunx and Semi-sextile are much more amorphous. This resulted in the muddle about sixth House versus eighth House Quincunxes as we discussed previously. So what does it really mean? Let's examine some examples of true Inconjuncts versus Quincunx/Semi-sextiles that behold each other.

Nicholas II

The only example in Nicholas II's chart was Neptune semi-sextile Pluto, which did not configure strongly with his Inner Planets, and so we will move on.

Mary Shelley

Mary Shelley had Mercury and Venus in contra-antiscion relationship to each other as well as being in an out-of-sign conjunction. It is especially interesting because both planets are in dignity by sign as well. Venus is in the 5th House of enjoyment and children, while Mercury rules the 5th. Venus is the second sign ruler of the 5th, and rules the 12th, where Mercury is the second sign ruler. Thus, Mercury and Venus are very intertwined in their meanings in Shelley's chart. We can begin to consider this quite simply: being in love (Venus) with writing or writers (Mercury)? Writing (Mercury) about love (Venus)? Notice that Venus is in an obeying sign, while Mercury was in a commanding sign, so this should imply that the writer was the dominant persona, since otherwise the two are about equally dignified. The theory is that an obeying sign will more readily consider other's opinions than a commanding sign would.

Let's sort out these themes. One obvious 5th House theme is children. Shelley had four children: three of them died. The 12th House is the 8th from the 5th: the death of the children. Here we see the same planets ruling the 12th as the 5th. Now, so what? We have already seen that the late degrees of a sign were considered to be malefic, and Shelley's 5th House cusp is 29°! Also, her Occidental Mercury is Void of Course. Specifically, Mercury is applying to a nonbeholding quincunx to Pluto in Aquarius. The Air Signs are Hot and Wet; the Earth signs are Cold and Dry. Mercury and Pluto have nothing in common, so they have difficulty finding common ground. This is as if you are introduced to someone at a party, and find that you cannot find a single topic to discuss. Not that you disagree: you cannot even find anything in common, even by disagreement. Yet you continue to try to relate, because it would appear impolite if you did not. While this "aspect" is applying, it is not beholding, so it is certainly not going to mitigate the void qualities of Mercury. However, it does suggest that there will be destruction of children, potentially. Thus, we have a couple of warning signs about problems with 5th House matters. And naturally, Neptune here does not help! Mary's one surviving son, Percy, was not considered to be especially talented, certainly not an intellectual equal of his parents. However, he was interested in theater.

On the other hand, we have the creation of Frankenstein and his monster: Mercury (the power of mind), Venus (desire), Neptune (spiritual), and Pluto (destruction) become the nexus for this novel. Also, Mary wrote her best prose when she was in mourning for the death of various people in her life!

Prince Charles

Prince Charles has one non-beholding semi-sextile. His Sun and Mars are inconjunct. His Sun is conjunct the 5th House cusp. Mars is in the 5th House, ruling the 5th, and disposed by a very dignified Jupiter, also located in the 5th. Clearly, Charles' line-up as far as children are concerned looks much happier than Shelley's. Mars rules the 10th House as well as the 5th House, and in Charles' case, there is a dynastic consideration here.

The peregrine Sun rules his Ascendant, and disposed by Mars, as well as semi-sextile Mars. The two planets together rule the 10th House: by Sign and Almuten. Mars is also peregrine, but at least disposed by a highly dignified planet, namely Jupiter, so Mars is not *quite* in as bad shape as the Sun. One almost wonders whether Charles will turn out to be more significant through his children than through his own direct contributions.

Muhammad Ali

Muhammad Ali has one out-of-sign quincunx that just *may* be relevant: Mars-Neptune! In his case, the quincunx is non-beholding, since

Mars is in Taurus, a fixed sign. Neptune in the 2nd House does not usually result in clarity about personal finances! However, in Ali's case, Mars was the means of accumulating personal finances to begin with. Mars is his most elevated planet, and Mars rules the 4th and 9th Houses. It is Almuten of the 6th House as well. Saturn, the sign ruler of the 6th, is not in much better shape than Mars. Ali's travelling was definitely as a result of his profession. We strongly surmise that his health problems are Mars-induced. But back to the Quincunx. While we are within an orb of about 3°, here the two quincunx bodies are in signs of the same element, so there is considerable commonality. This gives the Neptune as soft a landing as possible. The Sun is approaching a trine to Neptune, again in Earth. This is as easy a Neptune as we could get from an aspect standpoint. Thus, while we know generally that boxers historically are ripped off by their trainers and managers, Ali's case was *not* worse, despite the placement in the 2nd House.

George Foreman

George Foreman does not have any quincunxes or semi-sextiles between his planets.

Union Carbide

Union Carbide's chart shows a true Inconjunct Quincunx between the Scorpio Sun and Gemini Moon; they do not behold each other. However, both water signs and air signs are wet, so there is some level of relationship between the signs. We have already noticed *vis-a-vis* a chemical company that it is the wet ties that bind, and the Scorpio-Gemini combination natally is certainly one of the more interesting combinations. The Moon in Gemini is disposed by Mercury, which is in Scorpio, combust. To begin, this is a company that will approach problems by stonewalling: we may remember the admonition to begin secret affairs with a combust Significator! The Sun is in mutual reception with Mars, a topic we will cover in Chapter 11. For now, we will simply note that Mars is in the 29th degree, a dangerous place.

Just as Mercury is conjunct the Sun, Jupiter is conjunct the Moon, so we have a double quincunx pattern here. Curiously, despite being in Detriment in Gemini, Jupiter is the most comfortable planet in this configuration by quality: Jupiter is hot and wet, in a hot and wet sign. The Sun is the most out of quality, being in nature hot and dry, but placed in a cold and wet sign. The Moon is naturally cold and wet, in mixed condition, since Gemini is wet, but hot. The Sun only rules the 3rd House, and is placed in the 9th House. If the Sun is uncomfortable by quality, that discomfort is going to play out in foreign countries (the 9th House), or its immediate environment (the 3rd House). In addition to Bhopal, there has been at least one other serious accident stateside. On the other hand, with the Sun so close to the M.C., the company is at least prominent.

The 1st Trade Chart has Sun semi-sextile Jupiter, non-beholding. Jupiter in this chart rules the public or public stockholders (7th House), and the public's money (8th House). The little guy does not always see eye-to-eye with the higher ups (Sun as natural ruler). Jupiter is peregrine, so we would expect that investors will not always do well, or even consistently.

Mercury, the chart ruler, is quincunx Neptune. Mercury, we have seen, is not happy in Pisces. With the Quincunx to Neptune, hopes and fantasies have a great deal to do with the perceived worth of the stock.

On to the gas leak at Bhopal. The Sun for Bhopal was directly opposite Union Carbide's natal Moon-Jupiter, clearly triggering the corporate chart. Natal Mars is square the transiting Nodes, a configuration we shall examine further in the next chapter. There are no quincunxes or semi-sextiles to consider. Not unexpected. Here we have a chart for a disaster mainly characterized by *every* planet being weak by essential dignity, mutual receptions aside. The only planet with *any* intrinsic essential dignity is Jupiter, which is also in Fall. Such a weak chart, but such a terrible result! But what happened? Things fell apart— a condition of weakness! Peregrine planets find it difficult to deliver the goods, no matter how well intentioned! This is especially true in the case of an event, a horary, or an electional, where, unlike natal, there isn't time for development and experimentation.

Each of the quincunx pairs of Union Carbide has a planet disposed by Mars: Mars is at the notoriously dangerous 29°, a position that was triggered by the transiting Nodes in the gas leak chart.

We may observe that Union Carbide's true inconjunct of Sun-Mercury and Moon-Jupiter does not herald good news for Union Carbide stockholders when those points, especially the Moon, are triggered. This does not show a comfortable aspect. In fact, it represents a basic inability of the powers-that-be at Union Carbide to "behold" the consequences of their actions.

We can summarize the practical applications of these non-aspect methods of beholding as follows:

- Two planets related by commanding and obeying or by signs of equal power relationships interact as strongly as if they were related by Ptolemaic aspect.
- If two planets are doubly beholding (by aspect *and* either antiscion or contra-antiscion), the two planets' interaction is doubly important.

- The nature of the interaction between the two planets is of the nature of the Ptolemaic aspect between the two signs. Thus, planets in fixed signs that are also in antiscion degrees will have the nature of planets in square.
- Signs commanding (Summer signs, Aries-Virgo) may be thought of as the initiators to the signs obeying (Winter signs Libra-Pisces).

This whole analysis suggests another area for study. Whenever you have a situation where a particularly significant aspect also involves a Solstice Point or Contra-antiscion, you should expect an extra emphasis on that aspect because it is then *doubly beholding*. And while Solstice Points or Contra-antiscia do not appear between the planets of every chart, or even most charts, when they do appear, they are important. By ignoring them, the Astrologer misses an important dimension of chart analysis.

In the next chapter, we shall take up yet another neglected topic: the nodal cycle.

Endnotes

1   *Op. cit.*, p 113.
2   *Op. cit.*, page 59.
3   *Op. cit.*, page 61.
4   Lilly, *CA*, page 109.
5   Lilly *CA*, p 390.
6   Book I, Chapter 19.

—— Chapter Ten ——
The Nodal Cycle: from Ptolemy to Rudhyar

Agassiz says that when a new theory is brought forth, it must go through three stages. First men say it is not true, then that it is against religion, and then in the third stage, that it has long been known.

K. E. von Baer[1]

How does the typical astrologer use the Nodes? First, there is the idea that the Nodes have something to do with karma and reincarnation. Then there is the horary idea that the exact degree of the Nodes in any sign is a degree of fatality. The North Node is considered good, or the place the Native is going toward in this life, or the evolutionary path. The South Node is bad, or the past life karma of the Native, or the retrogressive path. Others, such as Cosmobiologists and Uranians, use the Nodes simply as connections with other people, without much if any differentiation between the North and South Nodes.

Now just suppose that you don't believe in reincarnation, or these other meanings leave you cold. Then what do you do with the Nodes? It turns out that there are *cycles* associated with the Nodes which can greatly enhance our ability to delineate with them. Awareness of these cycles goes back to at least the ancient Greeks. Later, the psychological dynamics of the nodal cycle were worked out by Rudhyar and his school, possibly without acquaintance with the original Greek system, but surely with some influence of Carl Payne Tobey. Whether independently or by restatement, the ancient and modern systems have certain intriguing similarities, and by understanding both systems, we can extend our knowledge of the Nodes considerably.

As we study the history and significance of the Nodes, it is proper to point out something which is so obvious that it is often forgotten: like Fortuna, you cannot "see" the Nodes when you observe the Heavens. In astronomy, the North and South Nodes of any body (including the Moon) are formed by the intersection of the plane of the orbit of that body with the plane of the ecliptic. This is shown in Figure 1.

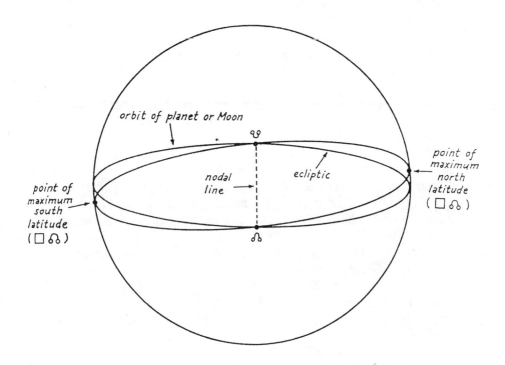

Figure 1

The interpretations given by Greek astrologers Ptolemy or Dorotheus of Sidon would not look strange to a modern astrologer. However, what did become lost in the intervening centuries was that the Greeks recognized the Nodes as belonging to a cycle. While their interpretation of cyclic nature is not the same as our modern one, it still has interest.

The first cycle involving the Nodes is the so-called Metonic cycle, named after the Greek astronomer/astrologer Meton, who was given credit for codifying it. This is the nineteen year "synodic" cycle: it takes approximately nineteen years to have a lunar nodal return. In fact, awareness of this cycle is older than Meton. It is also a cycle recognized by other cultures as well.

The second cycle is the one we will emphasize here: the latitude cycle. Ptolemy said, "Again, if the luminaries, together or in opposition, move toward the maleficent planets upon the angles, or if the maleficent planets move toward the luminaries, particularly when the moon is at the nodes or her bendings, or in the injurious signs..., there comes about deformations of the body such as hunchback, crooked-ness, lameness, or paralysis..."[2]

Lameness? Paralysis? And what's a "bendings" anyway? The word Ptolemy used for "bendings" was καμπίων *(campion)*, or καμπή *(campe). Campe* has several meanings: the winding of a river; flexing or bending of a limb; the turning-post in a race, or a sudden change in a musical passage.[3] Astronomically, the bendings are the points square the Nodes, as shown in Figure 1. Let us defer from discussing the mean-ing of the bendings too much until we also consider the modern treat-ment.

From Raphael I in the beginning of the 19th Century until the mid-20th Century, there was little mention of any latitude cycle. Barbara Watters said, "In horary astrology, any planet falling in the exact de-gree of the Nodes, *regardless of what sign it is in*, is a *fateful* testi-mony." (Her emphasis.)[4] While this included the bendings, it was not restricted to it.

The modern treatment of this cycle comes from the transpersonal school: Dane Rudhyar and Alexander Ruperti. Rudhyar revitalized the concept of planetary cycles, building a philosophical approach to cycles which used the seasonal and lunation cycles as the primary models. In this system, the beginning of the cycle occurs at the New Moon, in which the nature of the unfolding cycle is only intuited at best, the theme is germinated and developed up to the time of the Full Moon. In the second half of the cycle, that which is learned or done in the first half is given to others: the prizes won are bestowed upon the commu-nity. As the waters are poured out, the vessel empties, in preparation to be filled in the cycle which follows. While this generic cycle is more developed than any ancient statement as such, it is consistent with the ancient descriptions of the seasonal cycle of growth and development.

Rudhyar began his description of the latitude cycle by explicitly comparing it to the seasonal cycle.[5] In the Spring (in the Northern Hemi-sphere) the Sun crosses to Northern declination. This corresponds to the North Node of the lunar nodal cycle, or the North nodal cycle for any planet. The culmination at the Summer Solstice—the point of maximum Northern declination—corresponds to the Northern bend-ing point.[6] From this time, the movement of the Sun is Southern, al-though it still occupies Northern declination until the Fall Equinox, when the Sun crosses to Southern declination. This corresponds to the South Node. The Sun continues South, reaching to the point of maxi-mum Southern declination at the Winter Solstice, corresponding to the

Southern bending. Here the movement turns Northward, although the declination is still Southern, until it becomes Northern at the time of the next Spring Equinox, the equivalent of the North Node in the Nodal cycle. For quick illustration, consult Nicholas II. His North Node is at 0° Virgo: his South Node is at 0° Pisces. If you begin at the North Node and count *forward* in zodiacal longitude until you get to the South Node, you have the northern signs of his cycle. So: Virgo, Libra, Scorpio, Sagittarius, Capricorn, Aquarius... all these signs comprise the northern declination area. The southern area starts at the South Node. So; Pisces, Aries—and here we find his Moon. So Nicholas II's Moon was in the Southern region of the cycle. Mary Shelley's North Node was at 18° Gemini; her South Node was 18° Sagittarius. Her Moon was in the later degrees of Sagittarius, so her Moon was also in the Southern hemisphere. Prince Charles' Moon is conjunct the North Node, but at a lower degree of Taurus, so his Moon is Southern as well. Aleister Crowley's Moon was also Southern.

What this means, among other things, is that it is easy to visualize where in the nodal cycle a planet or light falls. Find the North Node. Proceed forward in zodiacal degree to the South Node. If the planet or light falls between the North Node and the South Node, it has Northern position. If it falls between the South Node and the North Node, it has Southern position. If the body falls between the North Node and the square to the North Node (the Northern Bending), then the body is North-North. It is in the Northern hemisphere, and still moving North. If it is between the Northern Bending and the South Node, it is North-South: Northern latitude, but moving South. If it is between the South Node and the Southern bending, it is South-South. Finally, if it is between the Southern bending and the North Node, it is South-North. Please be aware that this is not a statement of true latitude, but *relative* latitude to the nodal axis.

This cycle is the second primary cycle of the Moon: secondary only to the phases of the Moon. The nodal cycle has special significance for both the Sun and the Moon because it is derived from both: the (lunar) nodal axis is defined as the intersection of the plane of the Moon's orbit, with the plane of the Sun's orbit. It still has significance for the other planets, as we shall see. In any cycle, Rudhyar defined the Northern point (in this case, the North Node) as the point of intake, while the Southern point (the South Node) was the point of release. But intake and release of what? He defined the cycle as follows:

> One of the most significant ways of thinking of the nodes is to consider them as two 'gates.' When a planet is at its north node, its essential function and quality in the solar system is focused

upon our Earth-space which is then most able to absorb and
assimilate it. When the planet is at its south node what is released as 'substantial' factors are the results of the relationship
between the characteristic nature of the planet and whatever in
the Earth-space has absorbed its power.... As to the moments
when the planet reaches the points of maximum latitude, these
represent turning points or moments of inner decisions.[7]

Isn't it curious that the only nodal axis that came down to us was
the *lunar* nodes, when all the planets have them, and these nodes are
readily accessible? In fact, all the planetary nodes work, but the special significance of the lunar nodes is that they mark a coordinate system as important for our astrological understanding as the seasonal
cycle of the Sun. It is also heartening to those feminists who have en-
dured the trivialization of the Moon as having, after all, only reflected
light, to reflect on the implication of the Moon (and the other planets
as well) having two primary cycles, while the Sun only has one!

Rudhyar illustrated the concept by using the nodal cycle of Uranus
and its effect on mundane events in the USA. He then returned to the
lunar latitude cycle. In the process, he made one very important statement for how these cycles work: the latitude cycle shows the Moon
within her own orbital plane, and thus, shows *pure* lunar activity, unfil-
tered by her connection to other bodies. Thus, at the bendings, the
Moon is as far from the Earth as possible, which means that she is the
most withdrawn from Earth-bound processes, and simultaneously most
engaged in her own functions.

In general, Rudhyar believed that when the Moon had North latitude, the Native would attempt to conform to the environment, which
could result in ambition, the desire for control, concern about social
status, and the desire for fame or acknowledgement. If the Moon was
located in the South, then one's approach to the environment is more
impersonal, if not taken for granted altogether. In the South, one oper-
ates through a power, either internal, or external; one is the agent for
the power, not its source.

Alexander Ruperti and Marief Cavaignac expanded on Rudhyar's
ideas in a work which has yet to be translated into English. The critical
passage which explains the meaning of the hemispheres may be translated as follows:

One may say, by analogy, that the hemicycle which goes from
the South Node to the North Node, with the Moon in southern
latitude, corresponds symbolically to the seasonal period Au-
tumn-Winter. It is the period in which the results come to pass.
This corresponds to the *liberation* of the seed, and the *discharg-
ing* of undesirable elements, or of the loss of creative initiative

under the compulsive weight of habits and unconscious automatism.

And the hemicycle which goes from the North Node to the South Node, when the Moon has northern latitude, corresponds symbolically to the seasons Spring-Summer. This is the period in which one *receives* the new energies which are *assimilated* after the point of maximum northern latitude.[8]

Ruperti has added one critical element to the discussion, one that is implicit in Rudhyar's system, but not explicitly stated with respect to the latitude cycle. There are actually *four* separate parts to the cycle:

- Reception (North- going North)
- Assimilation (North- going South)
- Liberation (South- going South)
- Discharge (South- going North)

We have two systems of thought. In Ptolemy's wording, *any* planet square the Nodes is in a critical, that is to say, dangerous position. In the Transpersonal system, the points square the Nodes are also critical, but as turning points in the cycle of the Moon. These two views do not contradict. Ptolemy's citation may, in fact, have been part of the inspiration for Rudhyar's later development of the cyclic analysis.

Since we are not so interested in the medically pathological manifestation of the bendings, let us generalize the meanings. Planets at the bendings represent critical issues which can change the flow of life. Since most people are resistant to change, the usual response is to build up a rigidity around these planets, which makes the issues represented by them problematic. In extreme cases, this rigidity can have physical/medical manifestation.

Notice that I said, "*planets* at the bendings." Although we shall be learning this cycle through the position of the Moon in the nodal cycle, planets at any of the critical points (conjunct either Node or at either bending) acquire the character of that placement with respect to the issues represented by that planet. For example, a person with Venus at the bendings is someone who will be challenged by issues of love, or generically, women.

The nodal axis is the plane of existence, reduced to a line. The points of maximum latitude, the bendings, produce a line perpendicular to the nodal axis. This figure forms a cross, a primary figure of physical manifestation, as well as a reflection of thesis-antithesis. If the nodal axis is the plane of existence, then the bendings are the primary challenge to that existence, which is also a challenge to growth and change.

Unfortunately, Rudhyar did not give a very detailed approach to understanding this cycle in practice, other than to note the important caution that the operation of the cycle is somewhat subtle, and therefore, easily masked by other factors in the chart. For example, he stated that President Lyndon Johnson, with his Moon in northern latitude, was more personally ambitious than General Charles de Gaulle, who with the Moon in southern latitudes, tended to see himself as the agent of France. This is perhaps a start. He then contrasted Lenin and Bismarck, southern types, with Khrushchev, Stalin and Hitler, northern types. The problem with this characterization is that it is impossible to view Hitler, Stalin and Khrushchev without the bad-guy blinders. It looks from this as if personal ambition is *bad*. The more benign, or at least less offensive aspect, of personal ambition becomes clearer when I add the following northern leaders: Henry Ford, Napoleon, Elizabeth II of England, Abraham Lincoln, George Washington, Winston Churchill, and George Patton. The concept that Rudhyar was attempting to support with his southern choices of Lenin and Bismarck, was that these were men who acted as the agents of their age/society/nation/party. Curiously, this is a position which is much more akin to what Hitler actually expressed when he talked about *Volk*: the spirit of the people or the nation, or in his case, unfortunately, the race. Now again, it is curious that the prime exponent of that idea, Friedrich Nietzsche, was also a northern type! But perhaps it is not so curious. The counterpoint to *Volk* was the image of the hero, or Superman in Nietzsche's system. The hero is *not* an agent. In fact, the Hero(ine) is one of the best images for the first Quadrant of this latitude cycle: the Quadrant from the North Node to the Northern bending.

Ego is a delicate issue. Charles de Gaulle did not appear ego-less! The more appropriate statement may be that the southern latitude person *acts as agent of his/her time* more than does the northern person. In contrast, the northern latitude person *becomes the embodiment of her/his time* by acts of personal will. Thus, Lincoln *became the hero* of his age not by who he was, nor by manifesting the underlying archetype of his age, but by the courageous application of will and principle to the issue of slavery, on which the country was hopelessly divided, with no consensus whatsoever. Stephen Douglas could be said to have embodied his age much more closely than the more radical Lincoln.[9]

Southern type Mussolini acted as an agent of fascism, and would never have achieved the power that he had without Hitler's success. Richard Nixon rode Senator Joseph McCarthy's anti-Communism bandwagon to prominence and the Vice Presidency. Barry Goldwater in the early Sixties was the agent for the nation's fear of unbridled conflict with Communism; later he came to represent the conscience of Conservatism. As for Louis XIV, he became the extension of that which was already set in motion by his predecessors: France, the prime European continental power, dominant even to the use of French as the principal court and diplomatic language throughout the Western world.

Rudhyar also listed several Indian spiritual masters—Ramakrishna, Vivekananda and Aurobindo—who were South Node types. The danger here is that this implies that southern types are more "spiritual." It may be that southern types are more stereotypically spiritual, but that has to do with appearance, not substance. While the South is also graced by Omar Khayyam, Teresa of Avila, Aleister Crowley, Pope Paul VI, Oral Roberts, and Pope John Paul II; the North gets Maimonides, Joan of Arc, Thomas More, Mohandas Gandhi, and Pope John XXIII. There is a certain subtle difference between the two groups. One of the most notable qualities of both Gandhi's and More's spirituality is how hard they "worked" at it. In Gandhi's case, this was as extreme as going to bed with nubile young women in order to deliberately tempt him away from celibacy; the heroics were in the resistance. Joan of Arc engaged in a level of bravery that was startling for her time. Leading armies does not exactly look like spirituality in the same way as Teresa of Avila's more stereotypical monasticism and prayer.

So how should we understand the cycle of the Nodes in interpretation? First, we should begin with the nodal axis itself. One of the curious things about the Nodes is that they hardly rule anything directly. A perusal of classical texts shows that there are almost no items that either Node rules.[10] Instead, the Nodes seem to act as a focusing lens for the items ruled by the Houses that the Nodes occupy. The position of the North Node was held to result in an increase in the affairs of that house; the position of the South Node presented dangers to the affairs of that house.

This concept meshes well with one of Rudhyar's analogies for the generic functioning of a cycle. He talked about how the cycle of digestion and elimination works in the body, as an example of this type of cycle.

Moon at the North Node

The point of intake is the North Node. This corresponds well with classical delineation, because that which is eaten *increases* the size or energy of the body. The first step of this cycle is intake, and this is the function of the Quadrant that runs from the North Node to the Northern bending. When the Moon (or another planet, if we are looking symbolically, and not just at the cycle) is conjunct the North Node we experience the creation of "new" systems that begin a cycle. But these systems may not in fact be new, and may not in fact accomplish that which the inventor intended. Witness Henry VIII: dubbed "Defender of the Faith" by the Pope, he later defied Catholicism and invented the Church of England when thwarted in his marital plans. His creation is different from all other Protestant sects: a catholic, but not a Catholic church. And curiously, one that in the 20th Century caused the downfall of an anointed King, Edward VIII, because of the Church of England's non-acceptance of the possibility of a Queen who had been divorced. Not what was intended?

Moon North, going North

When the Moon is in the North, going North, we have the Hero(ine)'s Journey. This quadrant values action, systematizing, courage; the "right stuff." There is an emphasis on philosophical purity. The activity is extracting the gold from the dross. Contact with the divine is like that of a priest: a mediator for the redemption of others. The challenge is to bring in the knowledge or feelings of others to create a system. Spiritually we see Gandhi's sexual heroics (by *inaction*, no less!), or the systematizing of Pope John XXIII. We have both Alfred Witte and Reinhold Ebertin creating new systems in astrology. We have the quintessential heros Charles Lindbergh, Napoleon; we have the writers of heroics: Jules Verne, Nietzsche, F. Scott Fitzgerald, Goethe, George Bernard Shaw and even Jacqueline Susann. We have the "men of action" school of politics: Oliver Cromwell, Harry Truman, Lyndon Johnson, Henry Kissinger and George Bush. We even have the anti-hero characters of Bela Lugosi and Vincent Price!

Moon at the Northern Bending

Approaching or at the Northern Bending: the individual becomes the embodiment or personification for a theme which permeates the era. However, prominence does not necessarily equate to popularity, or "success" as we might be tempted to define it. Here we see Lincoln, who worked his way to prominence in a difficult period. And then on the other hand, we have Jimmy Carter (7° applying to the bendings) and Herbert Hoover (7° separating), two practitioners of the politics of scarcity.

And speaking of the politics of scarcity, how about the literature of scarcity? Charles Dickens—the best of times, or the worst of times? Or the experience of scarcity? How about Mozart, whose music has blessed those of us who followed, but who hardly drew an easy "lifestyle."

On the more spiritual side, consider L. Ron Hubbard, the founder of scientology. A respectable science-fiction author, he managed to synthesize a secular religious system, that is structured to keep members once they sign up, by taking advantage of a sophisticated knowledge of psychology and manipulation, both positive and negative. Secular religion? Certainly an embodiment of the age.

Moon North going South

With a Northern Moon going South, we have the architect. This person builds, or pushes a system to the limit, straining the boundaries as far as they will go. The second Quadrant is the phase of *assimilation*, in which the substance brought in by the first Quadrant (digestion) is incorporated into the body. The body is built from its component parts. At the Northern bending we find a perfect embodiment of the second Quadrant: the architect John Ruskin. The next theme of this Quadrant is the carrying of an idea to its logical limit, which is rather like the testing of a physical building. Here the idea is the ultimate; and there may be a trace of martyrdom.

And what do Leonardo da Vinci, Charles Baudelaire, August Strindberg, O. Henry, Gertrude Stein, Lewis Carroll, Percy B. Shelley, Bertrand Russell, John Lennon and Muhammad Ali have in common? Pushing your medium to the limit? And for architects, how about Johannes Kepler, for the first reasonably mathematically accurate heliocentric system, and James C. Watson, of DNA fame? How about George Washington, whose profession was surveyor? Or Winston Churchill, who built the British wartime system? Or Nicholas Culpeper, whose herbals have not gone out of print since he first published them in the 17th Century?

Moon conjunct South Node

When the Moon is conjunct the South Node, the hero is the dictator for the collective. Here we can make an interesting contrast. Karl Marx had his Moon conjunct the North Node. Marx, along with Engels, invented the concept of Communism. V. I. Lenin had his Moon conjunct the South Node. Lenin was the first to "successfully" apply Communism to the government of a country. Now we must put successful in quotations, because it is important to understand that what Lenin created was not Marx's Communism. Marx wrote that Communism is the outgrowth of Capitalism's last gasp. Russia had never achieved a capitalist state which could then reincarnate to Communism. What Lenin created was a new system, the Dictatorship of the Proletariat with a bureaucracy which was not exactly proletarian. Lenin, like Hitler (another South Node type) was supremely confident in his own vision, and was willing to buck even his fellow Communists, who believed that the first successful Communist revolution would take place in Germany because Russia was too backward.

The Moon conjunct the South Node does not generally produce

monsters of the Hitlerian type. It often is difficult, however, and it is generally accompanied by a degree of self-confidence which borders on, or crosses over to, megalomania. The hero (usually, yours truly) has become the agent for the collective. In Richard Wagner's case, the hero was of mythological proportions, played out on the stage where all potentials may be realized. In Oral Robert's case, it means a kind of charisma which makes him believable to millions. In von Bismarck's case, it was the confidence to take the lead in diplomacy and the military, to forge a united Germany.

For the rest of us, who do not occupy the world stage, this configuration can denote someone who is willing to completely throw out the *status quo* in the process of building a new system. Used constructively, it is the configuration shared by Michel and Francoise Gauquelin, who tirelessly gathered thousands of birth records in order to look at astrological symbolism anew, through the lens of statistics. In fact, two of the most successful applications of this conjunction are through art and science. And joining them at the South Node, another astrological light, Carl Payne Tobey, who had the Sun, Mercury and Mars conjunct the South Node. He and his students worked with large data sets: perhaps not in a formal statistical sense, but as a way to acquire new knowledge, unprejudiced by tradition.

Moon South going South

The South Node begins the third Quadrant, the quadrant of *elimination*. How does one live a life of elimination? In this phase of the South Moon, going South, there are several models. The first is the sex god(dess). The projections of others make these people seem bigger than life. Here we see Caruso, Valentino, Zelda Fitzgerald, Marilyn Monroe, Greta Garbo, Marlene Dietrich, James Dean, Elizabeth Taylor, and even Neil Armstrong. These people achieved fame–and legend—not through any personal merit or talent, but because of the public's ability to identify with, empathize, or simply mythologize. All are enigmas. They are compelling simply because they exist, and not because we know them. The Eternal Mystery that is Marilyn is a mystery we must solve within ourselves. Here we, the public, have eliminated the person in favor of the persona. They each become a symbol for a yet bigger riddle.

Then we have the Soul or Conscience of the Era or Nation. Garibaldi the symbol of Italy; FDR, the symbol of America in World War II; John F. Kennedy, the symbol of Camelot. This is but another reflection of the enigma that we allow these people to be.

So far, I have merely touched on how this Quadrant looks from the standpoint of people looking in. How is it to a person who has it? How does one experience elimination as a lifestyle? The metaphor may best be described as throwing the sticks for the I Ching, or laying a spread for Tarot.

The challenge is to put out everything one has, everything one knows. The person is a living sacrifice. Through throwing everything away, one achieves direct contact with the divine. Seldom does this mean the sacrifice of life and limb. Even so, metaphorically Monroe, Dean, and Kennedy *were* sacrificed in the tradition of the Druids. Fertility is maintained through the sacrifice of one member of the community. On a less extreme level, this individual throws out life-energy in order to experience directly the meaning of life. Knowing is the gift of throwing everything away, not the product of years of accumulation. Training may be useful, but only in the sense of Zen or a martial art: the training is a method of distracting the mind while a channel for knowledge is prepared. The Native falls into this channel by giving everything away.

Moon at the Southern Bending

I mentioned that the Gauquelins have the Moon conjunct the South Node, and one of the other greats of statistical astrology, Paul Choisnard, had his Moon conjunct the Southern bending. How is this concept of sacrifice connected with statistics, or perhaps science in general? The process of statistics is to collect a mass of data, and then to throw it away! Throwing it away in this case means throwing it into a series of operations which then allow that data to be characterized in ways that may not have been at all obvious during the collection of the data.

One of the most prominent scientists of all, Isaac Newton, had his Moon at the Southern bending (7° applying). We also know that Newton was not content to only study those disciplines that post-Enlightenment Science has labelled as such. He had a distinct metaphysical side, one that he considered at least as important.

If the Southern hemisphere is considered the more subjective, then the Southern bending represents the pinnacle of subjectivity. Here we experience the deep tones of Franz Schubert, and the rich interiors of Victor Hugo and Tennessee Williams.

Southern Moon going North

Finally, we enter the fourth Quadrant, the southern Moon, going North. The function of this quadrant is the alchemist; the process is *restructuring*. Here, all the preliminary processes are complete, and we finally may achieve the merging of the one and the All. One becomes the perfect vessel of inspiration or invention. And in this moment of reaching, of transcending, one may dare to reach beyond the moment and grasp, or at least intuit, the next cycle.

Here we experience the genius of Galileo, as he forged ahead into the brave new world of experimental science, and the braver new solar system of heliocentricism. And the later genius of Einstein, who warped ahead into the relativistic universe. We have the computational genius of Ada Byron, the invention of Alexander Graham Bell. And then there are the artists, William Blake, Samuel Coleridge, William Wordsworth, Paul Gauguin, Marcel Proust, Richard Strauss. The tone is surreal, primitive, romantic. We have Martin Luther King's dream, Jack Kerouac's vision of life on the road, Doyle's coked-up detective, and Goldwater's conscience of Conservatism.

Let's see how we use this cycle in delineation. As we do so, we will be examining planets that highlight the critical points. As usual, we begin with Nicholas II.

Nicholas II

Nicholas II had Mercury and Saturn at the Bendings, with Saturn at the Northern Bending, and Mercury at the Southern Bending. Remember: the Northern Bending is the crisis of one's own making; the Southern Bending is the scapegoat of the Age. Saturn is always authoritative rule, in Russia's case, the autocracy of the Czar. Nicholas was the embodiment of the crisis that was brewing in Russia: could this system survive and thrive in the 20th Century?

Nicholas did not create the autocratic system in Russia: he was not even its most extreme practitioner. However, with the growth of a Middle Class, with the influx of more progressive ideas from the West, and with the fanatic organization of the Bolsheviks, the crisis that had resulted in the death of his grandfather, that had been brutally repressed by his father, came home to roost with Nicholas.

Mercury was at Nicholas' Southern Bending, the scapegoat position. Mercury ruled Nicholas' Ascendant. Next question? As if we need more, his son, the Czarevitch Alexis had Pluto at the bendings!

As we have already observed, in terms of the lunar cycle, Nicholas was South-South (Southern latitude, going South). So he got to be the druidic sacrifice, and look how much romance is *still* associated with the last Romanovs!

Mary Shelley

Mary Godwin Shelley had Uranus near the Northern bending. We have certainly seen how she was seen as a rebel for her era, and how her lifestyle scandalized her contemporaries.

Like Nicholas, Mary was also a South-South lunar person. She, however, didn't have to die for it, even if she got to experience sacrifice first hand, between her husband and her children. Consider, however, how appropriate this is when we recall that Mary was the living enbodiment of the Romantic Era: and what a perfect literary movement to produce the legends that cling to this placement!

Prince Charles

Prince Charles' Moon latitude phase is the almost the same as that of Edward VIII: his Moon is approaching the conjunction with the North Node, metaphorically the start of a new cycle. With Jupiter in the last degree of Sagittarius, in a tight approaching opposition to Uranus, in the degree of the most recent Saturn-Uranus conjunction, one must at least say that the speculation about whether Charles will serve as king - or serve out a reign as king - is justified. Certainly, in line with the conjunction of the Moon and North Node, Charles' life has seen a whole new era in the relationship of the Royal Family to the world, as the press has turned increasingly obtrusive. Gone is the veil of mystery. Charles, and all his personal thoughts and actions is known to all in ways that earlier royalty could not even contemplate.

Charles' Moon in Taurus again speaks to the strength of women in his life, but this time, it includes the more usual lunar symbolism, Mum. His mother, the Queen, is literally the guiding force in his life. The Moon is disposed by Venus; Venus is in Libra: again we see the strength of women—in this case the wife—in his life. But his 7th House is ruled by Saturn, and Saturn is weak in this chart. This is the contradiction in his chart with regard to his wife: on the one hand, she is strong, on the other hand, she is also weak. With Charles' Scorpio Sun, we have to at least wonder about how capable he is of personal vindictiveness. Charles' Mercury is conjunct the South Node, and as we have seen, the South Node is the point where one "throws it all away." Now how do we interpret this with Mercury? Well one way to throw it all out, is to *talk about all of it!* Thus, we have a counterpoint to the normal reticence of the Scorpio Mercury to say *anything* of importance: the compulsion that somehow confession is good for the soul.

Aleister Crowley

Aleister Crowley had no planets near either the Nodes or the bendings. The antiscion of his Moon was the South Node. His Moon was also in the final phase of the South-North Quadrant: coming to conjunction with the North Node. Metaphorically, this phase is analogous to the Balsamic phase of the Lunation Cycle: the end of the current cycle with the birth of the next.

Of all of the members of the Golden Dawn, Crowley has come down to us as the most significant, as a result of his Tarot deck and his other writings. This deck seldom fails to evoke an emotional response even today, and it may have been much more shocking in his own era. Crowley succeeded in conveying an integration of sexuality into Western occultism that was always there, but very repressed by Christian culture.

Catherine de Medici

Catherine de Medici had the Moon at the North Node, like Prince Charles. In Catherine's case, the lunar issues were a bit different than those confronting Charles. While Charles has spent a long time waiting in the wings because his mother has enjoyed such a long reign, Catherine could only exercise power *because* she was the mother of the King. Catherine had little power as long as her husband was alive: Henry was repulsed by her looks, preferred his mistress, and didn't even father a child with Catherine until ten years into the marriage. Thus, Catherine was put in the position of having to intrigue in order to exercise power at all. The Moon was contra-anticial to her 10th House Saturn, ruling her 10th and 12th.

George Foreman

George Foreman has Mars at the Southern Bending. Unlike Nicholas, Foreman has not needed to be anybody's *real* scapegoat. He did not become a media darling like Ali: he was just a fighter. But even so, he created a sensation by coming back at age forty, a champ older than the usual martial range! His Mars is disposed by Saturn, which is conjunct Foreman's Ascendant: there is no question Foreman is capable of hard work! If we remember that planets at the Bendings represent sore spots in the life, then Foreman himself has provided the answer for how this works out in practice: he has talked about how he had to overcome his own anger, and how anger has been the real stumbling block in his life.

Foreman's Moon is in the North-Node Quadrant, the he-man, the macho man. But significantly, it also represents the start of a new cycle, and Foreman *did* break new ground in regaining his championship: he was one of the vanguard who showed us that top atheletes don't have to be young.

Muhammad Ali

Muhammad Ali has Jupiter at the Southern Bending. Ali's Jupiter is disposed by Mercury. Have we managed to forget Ali's Mercury? All the bad poetry? *Lots* of bad poetry, since we are talking about Jupiter in Gemini! Ali's challenge is exaggeration. Next?

Ali's Moon is in the North-South Quadrant, where the operative expression is: taking things to the limit.

Union Carbide

Union Carbide has Pluto at the South Node. In mundane events, the South Node is often taken as a malefic point: a planet at the South Node was considered to be destroyed.[11] Here we have the great destroyer at the place of destruction. Hmm! The Moon was in the North-South Quadrant when Union Carbide was incorporated. Building is part of the process of business: building a company, or building a molecule.

In the chart for the Gas Leak at Bhopal, Saturn is near the South Node. The North Node itself is at the nasty fixed star Algol. Saturn is structure, or skeletons: here the structure of the physical plant was compromised - or destroyed. At this time, the Moon was in the South-North Quadrant—the ending of the old cycle.

Union Carbide's 1st Trade Chart has no planets at the Bendings.

Thus, we see through these examples how it is possible to interpret the Nodes using both the classical and modern interpretations of the cycles. The modern concept of cycle has been enhanced by emphasizing the crisis nature of the cross-points represented by the bendings, an interpretation that comes straight out of Ptolemy. We have now teased out how to distinguish the Northern and Southern crisis points, something that was left ambiguous in Rudhyar's and Ruperti's works. And we have noted through Ptolemy's usage that these points are not exclusive to the cycle of the Moon *by herself*—they may be interpreted as other planets fall at these points: natally, by transit, progression or direction. The cyclic analysis has expanded the way that planets at the bendings—or at the Nodes themselves—can be interpreted, because now the flavor given to that Quadrant in the latitude cycle proper may be applied to other planets falling at those points.

Fine. But is this classical? If classical is defined as only precise renderings from sources of the 17th Century or earlier, then the answer is: mostly, no. However, if we define classical to include methods of delineation founded on classical concepts, using a logic consistent with classical operations, then the answer is: yes.

I believe that cautious extension of classical methods does nothing but keep the method alive. Lilly and Bonatti were free to evaluate the method as they received it, to note what seemed to work and what didn't, and to extend the method to new situations as applicable. We are doing nothing more radical than that here. If Astrology is to remain meaningful, it must be a living craft. However, I would argue strongly that its foundations *must* be understood and respected if we wish our own techniques to survive well into the next Millennium.

In the next chapter we will take up the challenge of mutual receptions, and see what we can do to understand this puzzling phenomenon.

Endnotes

[1]   Bull, Acad, Imp. des Sciences St. Petersbourg.

[2]   *Op. cit*, page 325.

[3]   Liddell & Scott.

[4]   *Op. cit.*, page 96.

[5]   Rudhyar, 1980.

[6]   Rudhyar did not use the term "bendings, but it will clarify our discussion to use it nonetheless.

[7]   *Ibid.*, page 256.

[8]   *Op. cit.*, page 97. Translated by JLL.

[9]   Douglas' date was given by Luke Broughton in his "Monthly Planetary Reader" for August 1, 1860 as April 23, 1813. Broughton rectified his chart to 11:50 am. This gives Douglas an early Moon in Aquarius, approaching his South Node at 16° Aquarius. That put Douglas' Sun on Lincoln's South Node, and his Moon at Lincoln's Northern bending.

[10]   Lehman, 1992.

[11]   See Ramesey, page 276.

—— Chapter Eleven ——
What is Mutual Reception, anyway?

For some time, there has been a disagreement, principally among Horary Astrologers, about the nature of mutual reception. Specifically, do planets in reception swap places?

The purpose of this chapter is to trace this concept by examining what various Astrologers have said about mutual reception. We may then decide whether this is the best meaning we can derive from mutual reception. We will then examine our chart examples to see how these ideas work out in practice.

We begin by defining mutual reception the "old-fashioned" way: from William Lilly. He said:

> Reception is when two Planets that are significators in any Question or matter, are in each others dignity; as ☉ in ♈, and ♂ in ♌; here is reception of these two Planets by Houses; and certainly this is the strongest and best of all receptions. It may be by triplicity terme or face, or any essential dignity; as ♀ in ♈, and ☉ in ♉; here is reception by triplicity, if the Question or Nativity be by day: so ♀ in the 24th [degree] of ♈, and ♂ in the 16th [degree] of ♊; here is reception by terme, ♂ being in the terms of ♀, and she in his termes.
>
> The use of this is much; for many times when as the effecting of a matter is denied by the Aspects, or when the significators have no Aspect to each other, or when it seemes very doubtfull what is promised by □ or ☍ of the significators, yet if mutuall Reception happen betwixt the principall significators, the thing is brought to passe, and that without any great trouble, and suddenly to the content of both parties.[1]
>
> ...if the *Significator* of the Querent, or thing sought after, or ☽, or Planet to whom she is joyned, whether she is a *Significatrix*, or hath participation in the Question, be joyned to an unfortu-

nate Planet, *viz. Retrograde, Combust, Cadent*, then observe if *Reception* intervene; which if there be, it signifies the perfection of the matter, though with wearinesse and much solicitation: If no reception be, the matter will come to nothing, though there have been much probability of its performance.[2]

The classical understanding of reception was a bit different from that which we have inherited through modern filters. Obviously, the existence of five essential dignities from which reception can occur is different. In addition, we have almost always inserted "mutual" in front of reception. There have been two connotations to "mutual." The first, which would have found acceptance classically, refers to both planets receiving each other. This is the usage that Lilly used for "mutuall" reception" on page 372, where he was distinguishing between the effect of mutual reception and one-way reception in the resolution of lawsuit horaries:

> But if one receive the other, and he that is received, receive not the other *Significator*, they shall agree without Suit of law, but not without intermission of a third party or more; and those that intercede, for the most part shall be his Friends or Acquaintance that did receive the other Planet.... If the lighter Planet be joyned to the more weighty, and receive him not, but the superior Planet receive him, it argues, he that receives would accord whether his Adversary would not.

The other usage implied by "mutual" is that the type of dignity used is the same in both cases: in other words, ruler-ruler, exaltation-exaltation, but not ruler-exaltation. This was *not* a classical restriction, as we can see from Lilly's example charts. Thus, on page 402 he used a reception between Mars and the Moon where Mars was in Cancer (the Moon's sign), while the Moon was in the Term and Face of Mars.

Saunders (1677) listed another way of classifying reception: *fortis* (strong) and *debilis* (weak).[3] Strong reception is when the significators receive each other by Sign, Exaltation or Triplicity; weak is when the reception is by Term or Face. Obviously, this terminology shows that reception by Term or Face was suspect as far as its ability to perform: we see above in Lilly's example that he used weak reception, but when it was by *both* Term and Face. He said:

> Reception is of two sorts, **perfecta & imperfecta**; perfect Reception, otherwise called mutual Reception, is when two Planets aspect one the other, either of them being in the Dignity of the other; as if Mars were in Leo and the Sun in Aries, here Mars receiveth the Sun and the Sun also receiveth Mars.

Imperfect Reception is when a Planet beholds another in his Dignity; as if the Moon were in Gemini and Mercury in Pisces, here the Moon doth receive Mercury with a square.

Also Reception is divided into two other kinds, *fortis* and *debilis*.

Fortis Receptio is, when two Planets do receive each other by the Dignity of House or Exaltation.

Debilis Receptio, is when two Planets receive each other by the dignity of Triplicity, Term, or face.

Dariot/Spark (1653) used the same distinction as Saunders:

> Reception is of two sorts, strong and weak: the strong reception is, when a Planet doth apply to the Lord of a House or Exaltation of *Triplicity* from the place where he is, and that likewise hath some dignity in the place where the Lord is placed, and if both two be in dignities one of another, having also dignities in the place where they are, and their application be by a *Trine* or *Sextile* Aspect, the Reception shall be the better and more perfect. For example, the *Moon* being in *Cancer*, and beholding *Venus* in *Taurus* with a *Sextile* aspect doth receive *Venus* in her Exaltation, and *Venus* the *Moon* in her *Triplicity*; but when this application is, the Planets being in their lesser dignities, as in their terms or faces, then their reception is weak and impotent. It is also to be noted according to the minde of *Ptolemy*, though Planets may be in each others dignities, yet they are not said to be in reception unless they be likewise in aspect with one another.[4]

Ramesey (1653) gave essentially the same definition as Lilly:

> Reception is when two Planets are in each others dignities; for then they are said to receive on the other; and this may be accomplished in many ways as here are dignities of a Planet: as *Saturn* in *Aries* and *Mars* in *Capricorn* by house, *Aries* being the House of *Mars*. & *Capricorn* the House of *Saturn*; so also *Jupiter* in *Capricorn*, and *Mars* in *Cancer* is reception by exaltation, *Capricorn* being the exaltation of *Mars*, and *Cancer* of *Jupiter*: In like manner *Saturn* in *Aries*, and *Sol* in *Gemini*, is reception by triplicitie; the fiery triplicity being the *Suns* by day, and the a'ry *Saturns*, &c. in like manner term and face.[5]

Now we are ready to consider the controversy between modern practice and classical method. It all seems to begin with Ivy Goldstein-Jacobson. She said "... but the mutual reception with Mercury puts Venus in Taurus 10 in another house... "[6]

The late Derek Appleby said "When reading a horary chart we can allow them [i.e., planets in mutual reception] to exchange signs so that each planet moves to the sign where it is most powerful, but they retain their original degrees."[7]

Olivia Barclay said yes, after a fashion: "If you find, when examining a chart, any two planets are in each other's dignities, this is called *mutual reception*. The planets can then be read as if back in their own dignity. When this happens, they exchange degrees—not actually, but as if it were by reflection— with the planet with who they are exchanging places."[8] Thus, we see that the difference between Barclay and Appleby is that Barclay exchanges both sign and degree, while Appleby exchanges only sign. In fact, Barclay's statement may be read as an attempt at refuting Appleby; her point being that if only exchange of sign is allowed, then what happens to dignities like term and face that are dependent on degree?

Not all modern Astrologers agree on this point. Barbara Watters (1973) mentioned mutual reception in three examples, and did not exchange the positions in any of them. Likewise, Jones (1943),[9] Simmonite (1896)[10] and Wilson (1880) mentioned no exchange of sign. Of course, when we deal with the negative, we cannot expect an unambiguous statement like, "There is no exchange of sign."

We have already seen Lilly's definition and usage. Lilly used reception in his horary examples on page 387 and 402 with no clear indication of exchange of place. Other 17th Century sources—Ramesey, Saunders, the Englished version of Dariot by Sparks, Gadbury, Coley and Partridge—defined reception without any indication of exchange of place.

Perhaps the clearest description of what a reception *meant*—as opposed to how to find one, or how to use it— came from al-Biruni (1029):

> Reception. When an inferior planet arrives in one of the dignities proper to a superior one, and makes known to it the relation thus established, there is an exchange of compliments such as 'your servant' or 'neighbour'. If further the superior planet happens to be in a situation proper to the inferior one, mutual reception takes place, and this is fortified, the richer the situation is in dignities, especially when the aspects indicate no enmity nor malevolence. When reception does not take place the result is negative.[11]

While perhaps a little flowery for day-to-day purposes, the image of the neighbor does not evoke exchange.

This being the case, how did this idea evolve? To answer this, we must turn to Ptolemy. Page 189 of the Robbins translation reads:

> Such are the effects produced by the several planets, each by itself and in command of its own nature. Associated, however, now with one and now with another, in the different aspects, by the exchange of sign, and by their phases with reference to the sun, and experiencing a corresponding tempering of their powers, each produces a character, in its effect, which is the result of the mixture of the natures that have participated, and is complicated.

This translation is not accurate. The Ashmand translation is more accurate:

> Each of the planets, when fully exercising its own separate and distinct influence, will properly produce the peculiar effects above ascribed to it; but should it be combined with others, whether by configuration, by familiarity arising from the sign in which it may be posited,* or by, its position towards the Sun, the coming event will then happen agreeably to the admixture and compound temperament which arise from the whole communion actually subsisting among the influencing powers.

The asterisk (*) refers to Ashmand's footnote: "That is to say (technically speaking), by reception, or by being posited in a sign in which another planet has a certain dignity or prerogative."

The only part of the Robbins translation that I prefer to Ashmand is the reference to phases, the word being *phaseis*, which literally means the "phases of the Moon." Ashmand is even more accurate than Robbins in portraying the sentence structure in this paragraph!

The word Robbins translated as "exchange" was *enalloiosis*, alteration. The problem arose because this word is very close to *enallasso*, translated by scholars as "exchange domicile."[12] Further examination of this root shows the use of the word "exchange" as "swap" was not truly descriptive: the sense is more that of being altered as an adjective modifies a noun. Other words and definitions that come from this root are "interchange," "alternate," "to have alternations of fortune," "variation," "in inverted order, upside down," "turned aside, diverted," and "cross one another, of veins and arteries," and yes, "give in exchange" and "receive in exchange." Notice that within the context of these definitions, "exchange" is used in the sense of "to exchange gifts," not in the sense of "to change places." The sense of this passage is that dispositions and receptions modify the workings of the planet in question, possibly by giving the planet something it does not already have.

We therefore posit that the origin of this concept of "exchange" as synonymous with "swap" was from a misunderstanding of the English definition of "exchange." Funk & Wagnalls *Standard College Dictionary* defines "exchange" as "swap" only as the fifth definition; the first was "to give and receive reciprocally: to *exchange* gifts." Given the multiple meanings associated with the word "exchange," it is scarcely surprising that interpretation was in the eye of the beholder. Persons reading only the English translation of the word *enalloiosis* had no way to know what Ptolemy actually said. If this is true, only sources after Liddell and Scott—or their sources—would contain this idea. Wilson, although not an enthusiast for reception, nonetheless knew Greek well enough to translate Ptolemy—sort of. Yet he did not mention this idea. Ashmand's translation was the standard source for much of the 19th Century, and his translation preceded Liddell and Scott.

I think we would all agree that planets in mutual reception are "altered:" in fact the whole classical teaching on the disposal of one planet by another produces an alteration in the interpretation of that planet. Saturn disposed by Mars is different from Saturn disposed by the Moon!

Joan Quigley, who knew Goldstein-Jacobson during her period of San Francisco residency, confirms that she was a great fan of Ptolemy.[13] It seems likely, therefore, that Goldstein-Jacobson's idea of swapping places probably came from Robbins' translation, which was in print during this period. However, since Goldstein-Jacobson died without explicitly stating this (and why would we expect her to address it, since the question wasn't asked until after she died!) my surmise must remain conjecture, however plausible.

Appleby's twist may also be seen as a different interpretation of Ptolemy, since in the Robbins translation the expression is "exchange of sign," which does not necessarily include degree as well. However, Appleby did not list Ptolemy as a primary source. He did list Goldstein-Jacobson, so we might wonder if his version is a second generation concept.[14] Barclay's usage was largely in response to Appleby;[15] however, while it addressed the issue that some essential dignities are dependent on the actual degree (as opposed to sign), it did not clarify the overall meaning of reception.

We may also reflect that none of these variants seem to address a condition which is occasionally encountered: multiple receptions. For example, suppose you are examining a chart with the Moon in Capricorn, Saturn in Cancer, and Mars in Taurus. The Moon is in mutual reception with both Saturn (by sign) and Mars (by exaltation). What do you do about this?

Everyone agrees that a reception may grant a perfection when there is no beholding, collection, rendering, or translation. Swapping places is irrelevant to this fact, unless the Astrologer then attempts to garnish a perfection from an approaching aspect with a Significator to the swapped planet. However, since Lilly freely grants perfection by reception, the aspect from or to the third planet is scarcely necessary. It is possible that timing could be obtained from this secondary aspect. But is this swapping technique primarily a case of gilding the lily?

Let us continue our search for meaning by seeing how other classical authors define mutual reception. First, John Gadbury:

> Reception is performed by House, Exaltation, Triplicity and Term: and it is a sign of a propitious Nativity, where all the Planets are mutually received of each other. This may be, first by House; as Saturn in Taurus, and Venus in Capricorn: and of all Receptions this is the best. Secondly, it may be by exaltation; as Venus in Capricorn, and Mars in Pisces: and this is a good Reception also. Thirdly, it may be by Triplicity; as suppose the Nativity to be by day, and Venus in Aries, and Sun in Taurus: and this is good, though not so excellent as the other. Fourthly, Reception may be by Term, thus; Mars in 16° of Gemini, and Venus in 24° of Aries: here Mars and Venus are in Reception by Term. This is the meanest of Receptions; yet is better then none at all: *Half a loaf is better than no bread.* In Nativities, respect the Planets that are in Reception, and the Houses they are Lords of; and if you finde the Lord of the Ascendant in Reception with the Lord of the Fourth, say, The Native and his Father shall agree well: the stronger the Reception is, the more durable shall their agreement be.[16]

So what does "strength" of reception mean? There are two answers. On the one hand, as Gadbury mentions, reception can be by any dignity. A reception by sign (domicile) is stronger than by term. Secondly, there is the issue of how strong the planets in reception are *apart* from their reception.

One other thought. In Gadbury's day, two planets would be considered to be in mutual reception if they shared *any* dignity between them. Thus, Mars in Libra was considered to be in mutual reception with Saturn in Scorpio. Saturn is in Mars' sign, while Mars, in addition to being in Detriment, is in Saturn's exaltation.

Morinus was the first to use the term mutual reception *only* if the reception was of the same type, e.g., both in each other's exaltation. He denied the usage of "mutual reception" if the reception was of a different type for each planet. Thus, Morinus was the source of this portion of our modern idea. Now we would be tempted to call sign-exaltation "mixed."

Mutual reception is easy to grasp as a concept, but more difficult to understand in practice. Lilly, Gadbury and the rest state that a mutual reception is a good thing. But how good?

The clue to the meaning of al-Biruni's definition quoted earlier came from understanding the context of al-Biruni's culture: the Medieval period. Dismissing the cultural norms of sexism *et al*, pretend you are the Medieval lord of the manor. (After all, Astrology is written for nobles. They can pay!) So you have this land and this castle which you must defend it from other lords who covet it. How do you do this? You rely on your allies: your vassals, your immediate relatives, and your wife's relatives. The question is, how good are your allies? They may or may not show up when they say they will. They may not be numerous enough to dispel the enemy. Or, one of your allies may be strong enough so that once he helps you dispatch your enemy, he then dispatches you and takes over![17]

A planet in mutual reception is your ally. How good an ally is dependent on how well dignified the other planet is *apart* from the mutual reception. Let's examine some charts to see what we *can* do with reception.

Nicholas II

Nicholas II had the Sun and Moon in mutual reception by Exaltation, with neither planet having any dignity otherwise. Symbolically (and especially in so-called traditional society), the Sun and the Moon represent the Male and Female, and thus, locally the husband and wife. Nicholas and Alexandra were very close: all their personal journals and writings show this. She was his closest confidant and advisor. However, Nicholas' Moon was in Aries, with no dignity other than the mutual reception. The Moon was also applying to a conjunction with Neptune. Alexandra was under the influence of Neptune, no doubt personified by Rasputin. The Moon was also applying to a tight square with Uranus. What kind of aid could she give him? Erratic and idealistic. Not much help.

What could he bring to her? With the Sun in Taurus, he could provide her with material wealth, with luxury and ease. But what, ultimately, was the substance behind it?

Mary Shelley

Mary Godwin Shelley had a mutual reception between Mercury and Mars by Term, with Mercury having significant dignity otherwise, and Mars, none. Did this give Mary a sharper tongue than otherwise? Perhaps. But the square between the Moon and Mercury would certainly produce a stronger effect! Since the reception is by Term, it would merely put her in the position to exercise Mercury-Mars. So this means that she gets things in her life to complain about? Who doesn't?!

Prince Charles

Prince Charles has two receptions involving the same planets: Mars and Jupiter. Mars in Jupiter's sign and triplicity and Jupiter is in Mars' term. This is not a very strong linkage, but it may make the conjunction of the two bodies a little stronger than it would be otherwise. Mars is peregrine in Charles' chart: with Mars' dispositor Jupiter strong by sign and triplicity, Mars is not as malefic as it might otherwise be, certainly a good thing, since Mars rules Charles' Midheaven.

Aleister Crowley

Aleister Crowley had Moon - Mars in mutual reception by Triplicity, with Mars dignified by Exaltation, and the Moon otherwise peregrine, and in Mars' Term and Face too. The Moon and Mars are in a partile sextile in any case. The Moon is placed in the 9th House of religions, Almuten of his 11th House of friends, and sign ruler of the 12th House of witchcraft and sorcery. In this case, the Moon has a powerful ally in Mars, aid that the Moon would get anyway through the sextile. So, Crowley's strength of will can aid his spiritual quests, fortify his friends, and aid his 12th House explorations. But can the Moon help Mars? Not very well!

Catherine de Medici

Catherine de Medici's Mercury was peregrine, but was in reception with two planets: Mars and Jupiter. The Mercury-Mars reception was double: by Term and Face. The Mercury-Jupiter was a double cross of Rulership-Triplicity and Triplicity-Rulership. Mars otherwise had dignity by Triplicity, while Jupiter had dignity by Term. In addition, Catherine's Mercury was cadent—in the 12th House of conspiracies, to be exact.

Was Catherine beautiful? No! (And Venus was in Detriment in any case, so she wasn't going to score points through being a blushing violet, either.) Was she brilliant? No! (Mercury was in Detriment and Fall in Pisces, no less.) Was she a hereditary ruler? No! (But she was of the right class, with her exalted Sun.) Did she have the uncanny ability to land on her feet? You bet! With dignified Saturn in the 10th, she was certainly capable of long term planning, as the situation warranted. And what did the situation warrant? Conspiracy, murder, and mayhem, not a bad list for Mars in Triplicity and Fall!

Now I don't want to imply that everyone with Mars in Cancer and Saturn in Capricorn is going to engage in the kind of amoral *Realpolitik* which Catherine allowed to result in the deaths of thousands of innocent people. However, her angular cardinal cross, with the tight Sun-Saturn square was not one which would brook opposition lightly.

Catherine was a survivor if nothing else! And who is to say that her opponents, had they succeeded, would have been any less ruthless?

Notice the involvement of Jupiter and Mars with Mercury through reception. Here is Mercury in Detriment and Fall. Mercury in Pisces *wants* to grasp the whole picture. (While Virgo is accused of not seeing the forest for the trees, Pisces isn't always clear that the forest is composed of trees!) The totality, or the bigger picture, has more immediate reality than the constituent parts. Thus, if the goal is power, then the details are not important. With the mutual reception with Mars, what needs to be done will be done. Mars with mixed dignity and debility will alternate between forthright and sneaky. Add to that the reception with Jupiter, ruling the 9th House, the use of religion to further the will to power is just inevitable. Jupiter in Term is merely Jupiter following form. Form in religion is merely the outer appearance of piety: rather like going to church on Sunday, then knifing one's fellows the rest of the time!

Muhammad Ali

Muhammad Ali has two planetary pairs highlighted by reception: Venus-Saturn by sign, and Moon-Saturn by sign and Exaltation/Triplicity. Venus has no essential dignity, and Saturn only has Face. In addition, Venus and Saturn are square. Does the reception make the square easier to deal with? According to Lilly, yes, but neither does it resolve the conflict completely. Venus rules Ali's 3rd House from the 7th, while Saturn rules his 7th from the 10th. Did his poetic (Venus) rhetoric (3rd) enhance his reputation (10th) through his confrontation with his opponents (7th)? Probably! We can achieve almost the same synthesis with the other mutual reception, with Moon conjunct Mercury (the quips), with Moon Almuten of the 10th House in reception with Saturn, ruling the 7th of open enemies. But is this literature?? No - there's not enough dignity here to allow for proper crafting!

George Foreman

George Foreman shares the Mercury-Saturn reception with Ali, except that his is stronger, being by sign, and exaltation as well in one case. However, there is now no 7th House involvement, so Foreman can skip directing his rhetoric at his opponents! Mercury rules his Ascendant, and Saturn is right there, so now the Mercury-Saturn reception becomes a more personal statement of who Foreman is. Foreman has chosen to become a mouthpiece (Mercury) to combat the effects of growing up poor (Saturn) through his preaching and his youth center.

Union Carbide

Union Carbide has a very strong reception between the Sun and Mars, by every combination of Sign and Triplicity. Mars is co-Almuten of the chart, and with greater dignity than co-Almuten Saturn, a better ruler in any case. Remember the relationship we have already discussed between Mars and chemistry? The Sun, however, lacks dignity otherwise. The Sun is Almuten of the 3rd. Does this position in Scorpio suggest absolute truth and candor in explaining company policy and objectives, especially when the Company is embroiled in a controversy?

So what is the meaning of reception in this chart? On an almost trite level, Mars/chemistry supports the whole company institution/Sun. The tendency of the company when faced with adversity will be to stonewall (Sun-Mercury in Scorpio). If this doesn't work, then the next plan is to combat or counter-attack (Mars). But with the Moon-Jupiter conjunction in wet Gemini, doesn't this suggest a company subject to leaks? Someone is just going to have to gossip about what's really going on!

At the time of Bhopal, Mars and Saturn were in reception by Sign, and also Triplicity in the case of Saturn. It's such a joy in mundane when the two malefics come together in any way, when they are both peregrine, and hence, maximally dangerous and capable of the greatest mischief!

We interpreted reception as the bringing together of potential allies, with the abilities of the allies shown by the intrinsic dignities of the planets apart from the reception. Can two heads be better than one? Sometimes *any* help seems better than no help. However, it is also true that all help is not of the same quality.

Endnotes

[1]   Lilly, *CA*, page 112.
[2]   *Ibid.*, page 185.
[3]   *Op. cit.*, ,page 5.
[4]   *Op. cit.*, page 49.
[5]   *Op. cit.*, , page 111.
[6]   Goldstein-Jacobson, Ivy. 1960. *Simplified Horary Astrology*. Severy Publishing: Alhambra, CA, page 152.
[7]   Appleby, Derek. 1985. *Horary Astrology*. Aquarian: Wellingborough, page 35.
[8]   Barclay, Olivia. 1990. *Horary Astrology Rediscovered*. Whitford Press: Westchester, PA, page 102.
[9]   Jones, Marc Edmund. 1966. *Problem Solving by Horary Astrology*. Sabian Publishing: Stanwood, WS.
[10] Simmonite, W. J. 1896. *Horary Astrology*. AFA: Tempe, AZ.
[11] *Op. cit*, page 312 (Point 507).
[12] See Liddell and Scott.
[13] Personal communication.

[14] When I published some of this material in *Astrological Quarterly Vol 64* (3): 53-58 (1994), the editor commented following my piece that Goldstein-Jacobson had been *the* primary reference in horary in England prior to the rediscovery of Lilly in the 1980's. This included both use by Appleby and Barclay.

[15] Personal communication.

[16] *Op. cit.*, page 43.

[17] Rob Hand has informed me that he has found a reference in Bonati (unpublished) to the effect that a mutual reception between planets in their own Detriment would be *worse* than no mutual reception at all. Clearly, here is a case where *bad* help is worse than *no* help.

—— Chapter Twelve ——
The Ancient Medical Model and its Meaning in Wellness & Psychology

... beneath what the mind chooses to admit to itself lie convictions that shape our lives.

Robertson Davies[1]

It is impossible for us to approach the topic of psychology in the total absence of our 20th Century biases that developed in the wake of Freud and later psychologists and psychiatrists. In the first place, we believe for the most part, that only a pale form of proto-psychology existed in the eras prior to the later Masters. In the second, our language for discussing psychology is colored by later meanings, meanings that only make sense in the context of our capitalistic, industrial, or post-industrial world view.

Would it be correct to assert that, prior to our own age, knowledge of human nature was embryonic at best? Of course not! Were this true, how could our literature, from Sophocles to Shakespeare, and on to Melville, or Whitman make any sense? Are we attracted to these works *solely* based on the quality of language, or are we also engaged by what these authors have to say of the human condition? I would contend that Jane Austin had far more practical psychological knowledge and understanding than most people do today, with or without psychological training.

We are thus left to the conclusion that what is "new" about psychology is not the content when it comes to the study of motivations, but the attempt to put such study on a scientific footing. The *advantage* of the scientific approach is in the process of creating thought experiments. The *disadvantage* is in the general rationalistic tendency to create a fictional world peopled by events that only contain one variable at a time!

The question that I propose to discuss in this chapter is what, if anything, classical methods can add to a discussion of psychological astrology. I believe this is an open question for several reasons.

First, from the standpoint of classical astrology: if classical astrology is inherently more predictive than its modern counterpart, then it does not necessarily follow that classical methods would do as well at character delineation. We have Patrick Curry to thank for tracing this point so thoroughly.[2] Briefly, Curry has shown that Alan Leo, in an unsuccessful attempt to forestall additional prosecution (and to stay out of jail) under England's fortune-telling laws, deliberately changed his astrological writings and presentation. After this legalistic metamorphosis, Leo claimed that the purpose of astrology is character delineation and *not* to predict the future. We can see therein the genesis of psychological astrology as we know it today. But if Leo had to change his techniques in order to accomplish his "goal" of character delineation, the question remains as to whether predictive astrology is very good at *describing* as well as *predicting*.

Second, from the standpoint of psychology, classical astrology represents an entirely different kettle of fish. Most modern counseling is based on the conviction that, however deep-seated and unconscious the neurotically-based behavior of the patient, through understanding of the circumstances which led to the current impasse, the patient is *free* to *choose* a different mode of behavior. Thus, in any moment, the patient may *choose* to be *free*. How can this be reconciled with a style of astrology that says, yeah, but the Native is *still* going to be sick for much of this year?

That which we in the secular West regard as an existential philosophical or psychological dilemma about freedom has been the subject of much religious study in the East. First, consider that there are multiple models for spiritual or religious practice. However, one of the major themes consists of the idea that in all of us there *is* the divine spark, and our quest is to discover it in ourselves and other people. In this model, there is no concept of perfectibility, because there is nothing to be perfected.

In Zen Buddhism, there is the concept of sudden enlightenment. The student is given a *koan*, or riddle, one which is designed to have no rational answer. The student grapples with it, and finally, reaches an intuitive understanding in a flash! This flash, or satori, is a moment, or an eternity, of enlightenment.

This immediate, indwelling sense of the divine, is achievable through many religious paths, Eastern and Western. Even in this time when we can talk about such a thing as the technology of enlightenment, it is my observation that very few people walk around in an enlightened state at any point in time, *even if that state is completely possible*. Why? Basically, because in our human state, it is easier to walk around being mesmerized by all the pretty *maya*. Now... is this any different from exercising free will? If I say that the astrological chart is nothing but a road map of *the path of least resistance*, how many people at any point in time feel inclined to go to the trouble of going against the traffic? Free will says that in this moment you *can* do anything you want. But inertia says that the odds are: you won't.

Thus, we see that the modern psychological emphasis on free will may be no different from a classical perspective, except in degree.

If you subscribe to the other great theme in religion: then your God (most notably male) is so much *more* powerful, wise, etc., than you are, that you, as a mere creature, cannot even *begin* to imagine the depth and immensity of the godhead, much less share in it. You do *not* share in any commonality with the Divine, you are completely at the disposal of your Creator. In this scenario, there is no freedom anyway, so then maybe astrology is simply a system of reading your Deity's inertial guidance system.

We shall return to the issue of free will in the final chapter. However, for now, I think we can safely assert that the difference in viewpoint between the counseling classical astrologer and the counseling therapist may be one of degree. A portion of this difference is inevitable to the different perspective of each professional type. Thus, the classical astrologer may downplay free will more than necessary, because the nature of a classical astrological reading *demands* prediction. Similarly, the therapist may overestimate the degree of free will possible, because the therapeutic process *demands* that the client *choose* to respond to the therapy.

Now that we have established that just *maybe* it might be possible to reconcile the classical and psychological perspectives on free will, we will spend the rest of the chapter addressing whether classical astrology has anything worth saying to the psychologist in the first place!

We have already presented our opening salvo in the psychological department in Chapter 3, with the introduction of the qualities and the temperaments. This system, firmly rooted in ancient and medieval medicine, was the basis for not only classical medicine, but also classical psychology as well. And it is here that we can approach one of the truly remarkable personages who made the Renaissance what it became: Marsilio Ficino (1433–1499).

Ficino is now being hailed as the Father of Psychology. That is perhaps one of the few overstatements it is possible to make about this man. Ficino lived at a time of major change in Europe: changes which saw the flowering first of the Renaissance, and then later of the Reformation. Ficino's own contribution to the mix was to translate works of Plato and Plotinus from Greek into Latin. It was in this period of time, the 15th Century, that theologians were beginning to realize the importance of works heretofore available only in languages other than Latin. Prior to the Renaissance, hardly any Western Christian scholar knew any languages except the vernacular and Latin. The Greek originals of Aristotle or Ptolemy were virtually completely unknown. The Latin translations were the only standard texts. They were also beginning to explore a back-to-basics concept with respect to the *Bible*, since the New Testament was originally written in Greek and Aramaic. Thus, we see Erasmus (1466?–1536), Humanist extraordinaire, and lifelong Catholic, bringing his not inconsiderable talents to the translation of the New Testament from Greek. It was left for the next generation— Martin Luther's (1483–1546)— to add Hebrew for the Old Testament, so that by the 16th Century, the scholarly Catholics were classically bilingual (not counting, of course, the various vulgar tongues like German or English!) while the scholarly Protestants were classically trilingual.[3]

So... by translating the Neo-Platonists like Plotinus into Latin, Ficino was making this work available to the *literati* a couple generations early. Besides the scholars, there were the elements of the nobility, like Ficino's patron Cosimo de' Medici, who were unlikely to go to the trouble of learning Greek in any case, but were delighted to have the fruits of Ficino's labors nonetheless. Thus, we have the Renaissance equivalent of our own Project Hindsight.

Ficino was installed as the head of the Platonic Academy of Florence, which three generations of de Medicis bankrolled. The importance of this upsurge in interest in Platonism and Neo-Platonism stands in contrast to the dryer emphasis on Aristotle that had characterized much of the Western scholastic system. Ficino and his school re-introduced Plato's perspective which was a breath of fresh air, in no small part because it represented a viewpoint deliciously pagan, far more attractive to the cosmopolitan Italians than scholastic piety.

Critical as this period was to the development of many Western philosophical systems, it was *not* of particular import astrologically. Ficino's astrology was absolutely in tune with the astrological river as it passed through his time. Thus, we see the following in a letter to his student, Amerigo Corsini:

> Astrologers consider [that] there is mutual attraction between those at whose birth the sun and moon were in complementary positions; for instance, if at my birth the Sun was in Aries and the Moon in Sagittarius, and at your birth the Sun was in Sagittarius and the Moon in Aries. Such attraction also occurs in

those born under the same sign or a similar one, and with the same planet or a similar one in the ascendant; or again if the benign planets make a similar aspect to the Ascendant or if Venus was placed in the same house and degree at birth.[4]

Now aside from the translator's uncertainty about what astrological terminology to capitalize, we could encounter this statement in any work from 200 B.C.E. to today and we would not even be able to tell when it had been written, or by whom! This ignorance on the part of scholars and translators has, I believe, resulted in the odd idea that Ficino is somehow the originator, or at least popularizer, of a form of psychology which was invented by the Renaissance. Thus, we see Thomas Moore tracing Ficino's psychology to Neo-Platonism.[5] Yet the psychology that he then goes on to explicate in Part Two is standard astrology, pretty much the same astrology that would have been used by any Medieval practitioner of the Arte. There is no question that Ficino's deep study of the Neo-Platonists pervaded the whole of his knowledge. But when Ficino finds that "scholars are subject to phlegm and black bile"[6] he is scarcely breaking new ground! Thus, we may conclude by extension that, if Ficino's "psychology" is illuminating in a 20th Century context, then so is the *entire* corpus of Medieval medical astrology, because that is what Ficino did: he applied the system of medicine as developed through the centuries to the problem of creating the balance of qualities that Hippocrates discussed as the basis for health in the 5th Century B.C.E.!

It is interesting that Ficino has been credited with inventing a psychological astrology, given that he lived in a period with stunning similarities to that of Alan Leo, the *modern* inventor of psychological astrology.

Leo's problem was legal. He was rightly afraid of being prosecuted for fortune-telling. Ficino's problem was theological. He was working in an era when the Catholic Church was shoring up the concept of Free Will and penning in Astrology at the same time, since prediction was anathema to Free Will.

Both situtions challenged the ability of the Astrologer to successfully predict the future. In Ficino's case, such an ability would fly in the face of the need of the Christian to *choose* God and Jesus Christ. In Leo's case, such an ability would fly in the face of scientific thinking, and hearken back to ignorant superstition. In both cases, the solution was to pull back. Ficino backed away from the Free Will dilemma by emphasizing Astrology from a *medical* standpoint. Leo backed away by emphasizing character delineation.[7]

Well, if we accept the premise that the psychology as practiced by

Ficino is just regular, old, classical astrology, then why don't we *just do it?* I thought you'd never ask!

Camille Paglia

Let's begin our classical romp with brassy, trashy, sassy Camille Paglia, the bane of certain prominent Feminists. Paglia has driven certain elements of the Feminist movement nuts by calling key points in their agenda into question, most notably a form of politically correct belief that men are responsible for certain despicable practices, such as nonmonogamy. Paglia has a much more pro-sex approach than most Feminists find comfortable. While bi-sexual, she has no problem with the idea of having fun with the phallus. In her book *Sexual Personae,* she developed the theme that sexual role-playing is often practiced, that it can be fun, that it need not be exploitive, and that women often have as good a time as men. What a concept! For those of you who have not read her works, I should also mention that Paglia has a solid working knowledge of astrology, and occasionally uses it overtly.

Let's begin by examining her qualities, shown in Table 1.

Table 1. Camille Paglia's Qualities.

	Triplicity	Seasonal	Traditional
☉	hot & dry	hot & wet	hot & wet
☽	cold & dry	hot & dry	hot & dry
☿	cold & wet	cold & wet	hot
♀	cold & wet	cold & wet	hot & wet
♂	cold & wet	cold & wet	hot & dry
♃	cold & wet	cold & dry	wet
♄	hot & dry	hot & dry	cold & wet
Asc	hot & wet	cold & dry	hot & wet
M.C	cold & wet	hot & dry	cold & wet
⊗	cold & dry	hot & wet	cold & dry

Paglia is predominantly cold and wet by Triplicity, the melancholic temperament, despite being a Sun sign Aries. This is the first anomaly. However, by season she is *absolutely balanced* (tell that to her critics!) This means that she has all temperaments at her disposal. The amount of work that has gone into the literature and criticism she has reviewed is prodigious, and this is probably best done by a cold type. A hot type is just too likely to get distracted by something else. However, she can enjoy bursts of energy and controversy when she wants them! Her basic contribution is a new synthesis, which is one way of saying that she has found new ways to *connect* the dots between different eras and authors: in other words, a wet approach. Yet her writing style has the wryness that we associate with dry skepticism. However, if you don't want to admit that Paglia might be balanced, you can use the Traditional system, in which she comes out strongly sanguine. However, then you have to deal with the idea that sanguine is the most popular temperament!

Back to the chart. Her basic life theme through her Sun is impulsive, and with the Sun trine Pluto, we know that she will stand up for what she believes. This is not indicative of someone backing down easily. However, with the Sun opposite Neptune, she is also idealistic; possibly misguided from time to time.

Her Ascendant is ruled by Venus, with Saturn as co-Almuten. Venus is highly dignified, being in Exaltation and Term. Located in the 5th house of Sex! (Next question!) Saturn, meanwhile, has the accidental dignity of being angular, in the 10th House, but in Detriment in Leo. It is at least saved from peregrinity by being in Term and Face. In any case, with Saturn in Detriment, Paglia is distrustful of authority, tending to place the self as the highest authority. It wouldn't be a bad placement for an anarchist.

These two chart rulers, Venus and Saturn, are in a non-beholding quincunx. Saturn rules her 4th House, which is generally Dad. Does this imply some struggle with Dad (but likely not as overt as a square or opposition) which has tempered her sense of self? Probably.

Now is any of what I just said foreign from the standpoint of a modern, "psychologically" based reading? Where a classical reading would part company with a modern one is *not* over whether the Native's motivations and character can be, or is, delineated, but over the inclusion of other information. For example, a classical reading is probably going to take health issues into account more extensively. In Paglia's case, with the Sun in the 6th House opposite Neptune in the 12th, she is going to be more sensitive to drugs than the average person, and her short-term illnesses will be directly related to issues of esteem or work. Now clearly, Bonatti and Lilly did not use Neptune, so they would not comment on her sensitivity to "physic," as they would say!

The other major differences in reading style are:

- The classical reading was typically done by going around the houses and reading the affairs of each house, a very systematic approach.
- While solar returns and progressions were known, two systems

were used in addition, and to a greater degree: primaries, and profections. Unfortunately, finding sources who agree on how to calculate primaries is problematic. This is an area where I believe we need some time to sort out the techniques, because we may subsequently discover that the most satisfying methods mathematically produce the least satisfying results in delineations. Therefore, in this work we shall treat only profections, and these will be discussed in Chapter 14.

Let us continue by studying Paglia's diurnal-nocturnal mix. This is shown in Table 2. The only planet that Paglia has in Hayz is the Moon, which has substantial dignity anyway by Triplicity. Actually, both Paglia's Sun and Moon are fairly strong by dignity, which gives her a definite advantage to begin with. Having the Sun and the Moon both dignified means that the person comes into life in a strong position, although of course life can change all this! It generally denotes support from both parents, which is no guarantee of later success, but a definite help!

The Aries-Virgo quincunx is an interesting one, both between people and in one individual. This is also a good one for illustrating the effect of planetary dignity and how it affects the signs. Paglia's combination with the Sun in Aries gives her a daring quality, an impulsiveness that is tempered by Virgo's database, rather like Captain James T. Kirk being tempered by Mr. Spock's facts. Consider the reverse, in which neither Sun nor Moon has dignity. Now the natural phlegmatic Earth conservatism (or shyness/hesitancy) of Virgo is interrupted by flashes of emotional impetuousness. Now Captain Spock is trying to run everything in an even manner, and brash Commander Kirk keeps interrupting. Shipboard morale is disrupted! Both Aries and Virgo are commanding (Northern Hemisphere Summer) signs, so neither one tends to give way to the other. It's just that the dignified combination works better with respect to others. The Virgo with Aries Moon is often dismaying to colleagues, because this nice reliable person periodically has fits of impulsiveness. On the other hand, the Aries who occasionally temporizes is not going to offend anyone by the process of temporizing!

Paglia's "offensiveness" quotient comes not from the Sun-Moon combination, but from Moon and Venus at the bendings. (The tendency to speak her mind, as well as her tactlessness, *is* an Aries trait. But Paglia has aroused a level of resentment far greater than one would expect for the mere exercise of her First Amendment rights.) A planet at the bendings is rather like an angular planet: it forces itself into prominence, regardless of its essential dignity. The Moon in Virgo and Venus in Pisces *do* have dignity. In Paglia's case, this means that her

Table 2. Camille Paglia. Chart is Nocturnal. "Preference" denotes the planet's natural sect.

	Preference	Placement	Sign	Comment
☉	Day	(Nocturnal)	Diurnal	
☽	Night	Nocturnal	Nocturnal	*Hayz*
☿	Mixed	Diurnal	Nocturnal	Oriental = diurnal
♀	Night	Diurnal	Nocturnal	Oriental = diurnal.
♂	Night	Diurnal	Nocturnal	
♃	Day	Diurnal	Nocturnal	
♄	Day	Nocturnal	Diurnal	

issues are primarily with women. Interesting, for someone who has been declared a pariah by many feminists! Since both have dignity, this does not mean that Paglia has difficulty with women's strength, she has difficulty with women's weakness! Since this is a bit counter-intuitive to much of our modern understanding of the sign Pisces (and Virgo!), let's study this in more detail.

The modern conception of Pisces is inextricably linked to the modern belief in the "rulership" of Pisces by Neptune. As we have already discussed in Chapter 5, the classical sign ruler of Pisces is Jupiter. The assignment of Neptune with Pisces is unfortunate because Rafael I used the word "rulership" to denote this process of attempting to equate the qualities of sign and planets. Had he chosen a neutral term like "similitude," we could have saved a lot of grief in astrology. The grief in this case is because the Neptune similitude has resulted in the assignment of Neptunian traits to Pisces that don't belong there. Not all Pisces are victimized, or sympathetic to victimization, nor are they necessarily space cadets. Pisces are generally very enthusiastic, positive, curious people, who can show a real zest for life when they are not put upon. The downside of Pisces is that they can easily turn into a watery puddle when under stress.

Just as a person with Sun-Pluto or Mars-Pluto can be *very* sensitive to the dynamics of power plays, a Piscean can be *very* sensitive to the process of exclusion, a trait that has been astrologically transformed in the modern context into sensitivity to victimization. What is the difference? Consider the Mercury-Jupiter difference, especially Mercury as manifested in Virgo. Virgo classifies everything into boxes. If substance 1 is in Box B, it is not in Box A: it has been excluded. Pisces is intrinsically against the process of exclusion, and is hypersensitive emotionally to the psychological dynamics of exclusionism. Pisces also is intrinsically oblivious to a lot of the criteria that many people use to classify people as "good," such as looks. Thus the Pisces reputation for picking "losers" or "victims:" Pisces is simply not observing the societal prejudices for how to judge a book by its cover. Thus we have Piscean Albert Einstein in his quest for the *unified* field theory that will unite all of physics. Of all the signs, Pisces is the mystic, the one sign that *knows* that everything ultimately goes together.

Paglia's dignified Venus is in Pisces. For Paglia, women cannot merely *be* playthings, although with her Piscean placements, she is quite capable of advocating that women (and men) should have the right to *play* at being anything. What was she taking about in *Sexual Personae* but the intrinsic human right to play at being anything we want in our sex lives? Paglia has unmasked the masks as such, but then she says, why can't we mix and match as we want! Talk about threatening the feminist movement that has always had ambivalent attitudes about recreational sex!

Virgos and Pisces play. Differently, of course! Virgo tends to go in for more verbal play, Pisces more visual. Neptune the God, on the other hand, like most of the Greek deities, took himself *very* seriously. Hubris was close to a mortal offense! Consider how this works with her Mercury in Pisces. Mercury in Pisces is the *least* dignified placement of Mercury possible, because here it is in both Detriment and Fall. Now... does this make the person stupid? No! First the bad news. Lilly says this about Mercury in Pisces in horary:

> If the Lord of the Question or the Moon be in a Signe opposite to his own house, as Mercury in Sagittarius or Pisces, etc., the Querent hath no good hopes of his demands, he despaires, nor doth he delight in it, nor doth he care whether it be performed or not.[8]

Lilly was clearly referring to horary in this aphorism, but there is a kernel of relevance to natal. We have already stated that having a planet in Detriment puts the Native a step behind others at the start of the race. Basically, the planet acts in a way opposite to its strongest or easiest path. In the case of Mercury, Virgo has a reputation for sweating the details, while Mercury in Pisces has a reputation for not even noticing that there are details! This, however, is not really true.

The first key to understanding this is to consider the rulers of the possible sign oppositions. There really *is* an antagonism between the Sun and Moon to Saturn. There really *is* a tension between Venus and Mars, although it might be closer to refer to it as being competitive than combative. There is the *least* difficulty between Mercury and Jupiter. Why? Well, among other things, as we have gone through the various delineation systems, Mercury keeps avoiding classification. Mercury is mixed in quality and mixed in sect. Who can draw a bead on it? Jupiter may be ponderously philosophical by comparison, but is Mercury going to stay away from a discussion of *anything?*

Bearing this in mind, is Mercury in Pisces going to approach writing or speaking in a different fashion from Mercury in Virgo? Of course! Mercury in Pisces, being wet, is more likely to dwell on the connections between things, than Mercury in Virgo, which, being dry, will emphasize the differences. Mercury in Pisces needs to be edited by cutting down on the verbiage, Mercury in Virgo by being told to expand. Mercury in Pisces does have a tendency to gloss over some of the details in the course of an argument. It is more important to proofread the accuracy of numeric tables from Mercury in Pisces, but not because the concept is unsound, but because sloppiness can creep in. Meanwhile, Mercury in Virgo is being maddeningly literal!

If we examine Paglia's work *Sexual Personae*, there is a stunning amount of detail, and yet a broad brush presentation of attitudes and literature over a staggering time frame and a multitude of languages. Paglia's writing is nothing if not memorable: who else would have the *chutzpah* to call Emily Dickenson the "Marquise de Sade?"

So, does this mode of delineation tell us anything about the psychology of the person?

King Ludwig II

Even if you happen to disagree with Paglia, you are not likely to call her insane—wild, maybe; outrageous, certainly! But not a few bricks short of a load...

On the other hand, let's consider someone who arguably was: Mad Ludwig of Bavaria, 19th Century friend of Richard Wagner, and builder of Neuschwanstein castle, certain inspiration for the Disney logo and my favorite subject for jigsaw puzzles! Madness ran in his family. His younger brother Otto was too mad to ascend the throne after Ludwig's death. Several of his closer cousins and other relatives also manifested the tendency, known in that period as being of a "sensitive" nature. While one is extremely tempted to ascribe this madness to the degree of inbreeding experienced by Europe's royal houses, one cannot dismiss that the stress of being raised as a crown prince, with all its attendant lack of privacy, protocol, and ego issues can contribute to the problem.

Look at Ludwig's chart, with its Virgo Sun square Moon in Gemini, and Cancer rising; the chart virtually *screams* sensitive! High strung! His father, Maximillian II, ascended the throne in 1848 when Ludwig's grandfather, Ludwig I, was forced to abdicate after he flaunted his especially tacky mistress Maria Montez too strongly in conservative Catholic circles. Ludwig II ascended the throne when his father died unexpectedly March 10, 1864 at 11:45 am after an illness of seven days. Curiously, Ludwig I was still alive at this time, allowing interesting contemplation of what might have been...

Ludwig had difficulty relating to women, other than his female relatives, his mother (whom he adored), and certain female friends, who he seemed to view platonically. His friendships with men, on the other hand, were romantically homophilic, if not homosexual. His (male) friendships tended to follow a pattern of obsessive closeness, followed by some slight, then distance, which may then be followed by reconciliation, or perhaps not. Given frequent references in his private journal to "kissing," one has to wonder how much further things went.

His friendship with Wagner nearly cost him his throne earlier, because Wagner's political radicalism was not appreciated in his kingdom. Ludwig was a hopeless romantic, and completely taken by the German mythology that Wagner incorporated into "Lohengrin," "Tristan and Isolde" and the "Ring" cycle. He was also obsessed by Louis XIV and Louis XVI of France. As time went on, Ludwig was increasingly more and more at home in his world of semi-pagan myth, and less and less at home in the real world, in which Prince von Bismarck was consolidating Germany into one country under his boss, the Prussian Kaiser, Wilhelm I. Ludwig was, however, aware enough of his position to conduct affairs of state, negotiate for the rights of Bavaria, correspond with his royal counterparts, instruct his councilors, and commission reports.

Finally, in part through trumped up charges (but with a kernel of truth) concerning his diminished sanity, Ludwig was forced to abdicate in 1886. He apparently committed suicide two days later, after killing the psychiatrist who had provided the insanity diagnosis, a diagnosis given without bothering to examine him. Just before he died, he was reported to have said, "I can bear that they take the Government from me, but not that they declare me insane." Since his brother Otto had been committed, Ludwig had a mortal fear of becoming insane.[9]

How do we interpret his chart? We can begin by examining his qualities, given in Table 3. Ludwig is cold by Triplicity, with equal mixtures of wet and dry. In his seasonal qualities, he is slightly hot, and evenly mixed between wet and dry. He does not stand out as being extreme on either scale. By the Traditional system, Ludwig was cold and wet. Other than in his romances, Ludwig does not appear to have been impulsive. He was a great planner. With the Moon in the 12th

House, sign ruler (although not Almuten) of the Ascendant, he had a strong private emotional life. Given the 12th House Gemini placement, we are not surprised to discover that he wrote about his emotional problems and challenges in a secret journal!

Ludwig's Sun and Moon are square, which would normally indicate some stress between his parents. This did not appear serious, at least in accounts from contemporaries. We note, however, that the two signs involved are both Mercury-ruled, and that can go a good way toward alleviating the less edifying effects of the square.[10]

Table 3. Ludwig II's Qualities

Ludwig's diurnal and nocturnal placements are shown in Table 4.

	Triplicity	Seasonal	Traditional
☉	cold & dry	hot & dry	hot & dry
☽	hot & wet	hot & wet	cold & wet
☿	cold & dry	hot & dry	dry
♀	cold & dry	hot & dry	wet
♂	hot & wet	cold & wet	hot & dry
♃	cold & dry	hot & wet	wet
♄	hot & wet	cold & wet	cold & wet
Asc	cold & wet	hot & dry	cold & wet
M.C	cold & wet	cold & wet	cold & wet
⊗	cold & dry	cold & dry	cold & dry

Table 4. Ludwig II. Chart is Nocturnal. "Preference" denotes the planet's natural sect.

We know that Ludwig had problems with women; clearly, Venus

	Preference	Placement	Sign	Comment
☉	Day	(Nocturnal)	Nocturnal	
☽	Night	Nocturnal	Diurnal	
☿	Mixed	Nocturnal	Nocturnal	Occidental is defined as nocturnal
♀	Night	Nocturnal	Nocturnal	Occidental = nocturnal. *Hayz*
♂	Night	Nocturnal	Diurnal	*Hayz* in the later style
♃	Day	Nocturnal	Nocturnal	Out of sect.
♄	Day	Nocturnal	Diurnal	

in *Hayz* is not able to deliver the goods very well. With Mars possibly in *Hayz* (i.e., new style), and Mars co-Almuten of his 11th House of friends, the male companions may be obvious, but not of a consistently good quality. So the *Hayz* of Mars doesn't help much either. Further, the ruler of his 7th House, Saturn, is dignified, so it should have given him fewer problems. There was often an age differential with his romantic "friends," because Ludwig was quite taken by youthful beauty.

The Sun is as out of sect as it can be (being below the horizon and in a nocturnal sign), and the Sun is Ludwig himself. The Sun has dignity only by Face, which we have already seen isn't much. This is a man worried about whether he measures up, a man obsessed with heroics! Furthermore, Ludwig was wild about Louis XIV, the *Sun* King of France!

The modern astrologer would probably expect to see a prominent Neptune, given Ludwig's rich fantasy life. In fact, Neptune is the most elevated planet. Mars is conjunct Neptune—romanticized friendships with men, especially martial types, which most of them were? Neptune is also in a nonbeholding quincunx with Mercury, the Dispositor of Ludwig's Sun. The nonbeholding quincunx in question is the most extreme sort, because no qualities are in common between Aquarius (hot and wet) and Virgo (cold and dry). The Mars-Neptune conjunction is at the Bendings. Clearly, men were the challenge of Ludwig's life!

So far, we have said little about physical health. Health in a chart is given by the 1st House, short-term illness is shown from the 6th House, while long-term or chronic disease is given from the 12th House.

Ludwig's health is ruled by the Moon by Sign, and Jupiter by Almuten. Both are peregrine.[11] Therefore, Ludwig's health is subject to ups and downs, which is the natal interpretation of a peregrine planet's wandering path through life. With Jupiter placed in the 11th House, we see that his friendships can affect his health. Given the amount of passion he put into them, this is scarcely surprising. More importantly, the Moon is in the 12th House of chronic disease in the sign Gemini. Here is Ludwig's "high-strung," "sensitive" nature, because what sign could top Gemini for high-strung and nervous? This also implies immediately that concern about mental problems are a chronic condition. Mercury ruled his 12th House. Mercury was at least strong in Virgo. Ludwig could be *very* perceptive about the world around him, and was certainly nobody's fool politically, even if personally he was quite capable of making a mess.

His personal "mess quotient" is shown by the conjunction of Mercury with Venus, in Mercury's sign, Venus's Fall. One could begin a treatment of Venus in Fall by suggesting that this person will tend to "fall" for inappropriate people. Does this deny relationship? Not necessarily. Does this deny happiness? Not necessarily.

Jupiter, besides being Almuten of his Ascendant, ruled the 6th House. Thus, peregrine Jupiter also ruled short-term or acute illnesses, often brought on by emotional turmoil (Moon in mutual reception with Jupiter; neither dignified). Ludwig was almost constantly sick as a child, colds and nasal problems, nothing serious. But notice that Taurus rules the throat, and that is where these illnesses lodged. Ludwig was never particularly athletic, not surprising given his cold temperament. However, he was over six feet tall, and did ride well, until he was thrown from a horse and reacted by never riding again.

Let us turn next to his education. In examining his chart, what could we have recommended to his father the king as a way to train him? The Sun rules the 3rd House of childhood education, and the Sun is disposed by Mercury, which is strong in Virgo. Reading, writing, 'rithmetic? Ludwig did pretty well at the three "R's." The problem was that Maximillian chose to educate Ludwig with a chief tutor whose idea of education was rigidly conservative, who believed that the first step in the educative process was to break the will of the pupil. Now this is clearly a saturnian style of education, and we see that Saturn and Mars bracketed Ludwig's 9th House cusp, with Neptune close as well. Later on, Ludwig also got instruction in military matters, so there is the Mars effect.

But here is the problem. La Rosee, the author of this "educational" regimen became Ludwig's instructor when Ludwig was *eight years old*. Ludwig's Saturn was dignified in Aquarius, so discipline certainly was an appropriate thing for him to learn. However, ruling the 9th House and being conjunct the cusp, the chart indicates that Ludwig should not have been subjected to this until he was older, at least past his Saturn opposition. Here was a case where 9th House education eclipsed 3rd House education, and basically ruined the process thereby. Ludwig's response to La Rosee's discipline was to turn inward, a tendency that he already had in spades with his 12th House Moon. Being forced ever more into himself, with the Virgoan tendency toward introversion, Ludwig was channeled down a path which, by overindulgence, simply precipitated his later mental problems more than his chart dictated. (Turning back on himself? How is that for an expression of a strong Saturn *retrograde*?)

Ludwig's childhood experience of education, then, was conducted in almost the opposite fashion from the form of enlightened psychology advocated by Ficino, or earlier astrological practitioners. Their position was to know the chart, and use the chart to develop a regimen which strengthened body and mind *at the right time* as well as in the appropriate ways. *This* is the creative way to approach the psychology of a chart classically: to understand the person's natural strengths and weaknesses, and then to fortify the strengths, and temper the weaknesses, giving the individual the *choice* to maximize her/his potential.

Have we in fact established anything about Ludwig's mental state? I think that part of our difficulty here is in assessing exactly what our aims might be in a psychologically-based reading. We have established certain character traits that plagued Ludwig's life. But does the chart say that he was mad?

I would argue that the chart says that Ludwig was emotionally sensitive, tending toward a rich interior life, with an active imagination. The chart shows some difficulty in relating to women, and an unrealistic, or idealistic, view of foreign policy (Mars-Neptune conjunction in the 9th House). His finances are likely to be unstable with a 12th House, cadent, peregrine Moon. The chart has a strong Saturn, ruling the 5th, 7th, 8th and 9th Houses. Saturn, among other things, is building, land, real estate, etc., and Ludwig was certainly obsessed in this department!

Madness as a concept is now clinically defined. As a psychiatric condition, it shifts according to whatever the current models of sanity and insanity may be. Since astrology is an independent system of viewing the individual apart from the psychological model, I am not convinced that the two have a direct correspondence. Accordingly, I would be reluctant to take any chart and judge the sanity of the person in question, even if I feel completely comfortable discussing the kinds of life questions which will likely command the greatest attention from the individual.

In the next chapter, we will continue our delineation examples as we examine more deeply how to interpret the houses.

Source for Data

Camille Paglia: from her, quoted by Lois Rodden to Marion March (personal communication).

Ludwig II: Birth data of the Bavarian monarch from the "official announcement" cited in "AAM" for Feb. 1956 and Feb.1970. Cited in Blackwell Database, Astrolabe: Brewster, MA.

Endnotes

[1]   *Op. cit.*, Page 47.

[2]   See especially Chapter 5.

[3]   For a more complete account of this interesting period, see Heiko A. Oberman. 1994. *The Impact of the Reformation*. Eerdman Publishing Co.: Grand Rapids, MI, Section III. This also contains a full accounting of the related issue of the impact of learning Hebrew on the nature of intellectual Anti-Semitism, but that is another story completely!

[4]   Letters, Volume 1, Number 129, page 169.

[5]   For example, pages 96-97 in Thomas Moore. 1982. *The Planets Within*. Lindisfarne Press: Great Barington, MA.

[6]   *The Book of Life*, page 5.

[7]   For a fuller discussion of the theological dimensions of Ficino's time, and how it affected his astrological practice, see Cesare Vasoli, "Marsilio Ficino e l'Astrologia," pages 159-186 in Istituto di Studi Umanistici Francesco Petrarca. 1992. *L'Astrologia e la sua Influenza nella Filosofia, nella Letteratura e nell'arte dall'et^ Classica al Rinascimento*. Nuovi Orizzonti: Milano.

[8]   Lilly, *CA*, page 301.

[9]   Biographical material presented here comes from Desmond Chapman-Huston. 1993. *Ludwig II The Mad King of Bavaria*. Barnes & Noble, New York.

[10] Consider the interesting circumstance that the two Mercury-ruled signs, Gemini and Virgo; and the two Jupiter-ruled signs, Sagittarius and Pisces; are square each other. The mutual squares within planetary rulerships are certainly a different case than squares between signs that do not share planetary rulerships. These two in-planet squares share friction and camaraderie at the same time, like two siblings confronting their similarities and differences simultaneously.

[11] A reminder that the scoring of dignities on the charts from PrintWheels that are presented here is not the system I would use. In the PrintWheel charts, *any* mutual reception releases a planet from peregrinity. Furthermore, the point values for *all* mutual receptions count in the score. In Ludwig's case, the Moon and Jupiter have dignity *only* by reception: with each other, and the Moon with Mercury, which *is* dignified. I would interpret this as Jupiter only getting useless assistance (talk, in the form of a Gemini Moon, rather than action) while the Moon gets some assistance from Mercury, which also disposits the Moon. This would mean that Ludwig could talk himself out (Mercury) of some emotional problems and challenges (Moon).

—— CHAPTER 13 ——
BEYOND ASPECTS: HOW TO READ A HOUSE

"We may never define it," Bickel said. "But that doesn't mean we can't reproduce it."

Frank Herbert[1]

Houses are one of the most poorly understood concepts in modern astrology. It is no wonder that a typical reading places so much emphasis on aspects! The typical astrologer begins with the Ascendant, maybe proceeds to the Ascendant ruler, then quickly passes on to something other than houses, unless they are subsumed under the twelve letter zodiac. This is generally because, while all introductory books give extensive lists of the affairs of each house, there is little understanding how to approach these affairs.

Fortunately, this is not the case with classical. We can begin by listing the possible ways to delineate houses.

- The **house cusp** itself. The house cusp gives a sign associated with the house. Planets may aspect that degree. The sign on the cusp has seasonal and Triplicity qualities, as we have seen.
- The **sign ruler** of the house cusp. This planet can be used in several ways. For example, the cusp of Camille Paglia's 3rd House is 14° Sagitarrius. The sign ruler is Jupiter.
- We can interpret the house **location** of that ruler. Paglia's Jupiter is in the 2nd House; she makes money from writing
- We can interpret the **dignity** of the sign ruler. Jupiter has no dignity in its placement in Scorpio, but it is in mutual reception with Mars, Mars being further dignified by being in Pisces.
- We can interpret the dignity of the **dispositor** of the sign ruler. This is generally only done if the ruling planet has little or no dignity on its own. In Paglia's case, the dispositor of Jupiter is Mars. Mars is already in mutual reception with Jupiter, and

Mars has dignity. She will make *good* money from her writing.

- We can interpret the **Almuten** planet or the dispositor of the Almuten planet in the same fashion that we have done for the sign ruler.

- We can interpret **planets in the house** as showing information about the affairs of the house. Paglia has Uranus in the 9th House, which shows that she will be a disruptive influence on higher education, or her own process of education will be interrupted.

- We can interpret **aspects to either planets in a house or to a ruler (or Almuten) of a house** as showing other affairs impinging on the operation of the house. Paglia's Mars is also trine her Jupiter in the 2nd House. Mars is located in the 5th House. Paglia will benefit financially from writing about 5th House affairs, *i.e.*, sex.

Notice that this system of delineation has already eliminated one of the "problems" invented by modern astrology: the empty house. Now on the one hand, with asteroids and comets, there really is no such thing as an empty house. But restricting ourselves to planets, an "empty" house is simply a house without planets. It is not "vacant" or "absent," because there are so many other ways to interpret the house. An empty house can hardly be considered problematic when all that it does is reduce the number of ways to interpret the house to four from five!

The typical natal delineation, as late as William Lilly's time, consisted of a series of judgments on the affairs of each house. For example, the reading would begin with a statement on the overall health of the Native, shown by the 1st House. (Health is the 1st, disease is the 6th.) Financial affairs would be read from the 2nd House, brothers and sisters from the 3rd, etc. This style of reading certainly demonstrates that there was no omission of a house if there were no planets there!

Robert Zoller's assessment of the Medieval position on house rulers in natal astrology is that a planet's placement in a house is more important than a planet ruling a house. In other words, if there is a planet in a house, he will consider that planet *preferentially* as the ruler of affairs in that house over the ruler of the cusp of the house. If there is no planet in the house, then he goes to the ruler of the house as the next step. My assessment from working with Renaissance horary is that the ruler of a house (Almuten or sign, whichever is more dignified) is the more important. Are these positions actually in conflict? Do we have a case of either/or or both/and? How do we rate the importance of house placement versus house rulership?

We can go back and examine some of the people we have been studying throughout this volume. However, before we do, I would like to add one more example: Mickey Mantle.

Mickey Mantle

Hall-of-Famer Mickey Mantle had a tough job when he came to the New York Yankees: replace Joe DiMaggio. Mantle blossomed in his second year after DiMaggio's retirement. He turned into a superb power hitter, hitting .298 lifetime, and in April 1953, hitting one home run 565 feet. During most of his playing years, he partied as hard as he played, and became an alcoholic. In 1995 he was diagnosed with liver cancer, received a liver transplant, and died barely two months later of cancer which had metastasized.

For now, we wish to examine three charts: Mantle's birth, his liver transplant, and his death. We shall also examine another death chart in the next chapter. I don't want to give the impression that this in any way represents the most significant element of Mantle's life. However, if we are going to do classical astrology, we do come to grips with the fact that historically, death was predicted routinely. In this particular case, I publicly predicted Mantle's death based on the transplant operation chart. Whether this is a form of prediction that any astrologer will choose to use in working with clients is a different question entirely. I certainly would have pulled my punches considerably had Mantle been my client. But I would not have elected that surgery time either!

Mantle's birth data is class C^2 in Lois Rodden's scale. However, the death chart suggests that we are probably off by only a matter of a couple of degrees on the houses.

Mantle's peregrine Sun was in Detriment in Libra, conjunct peregrine Mercury. His peregrine Venus was also in Detriment. All three of these debilitated planets are in the 11th House. Friends? It was with his buddies that he got into the hard-drinking pattern which ultimately cost him some years. Venus in Fall ruled his 6th House. A benefic in Fall is still a benefic, but his 6th House ruler is disposed by Mars. From a medical perspective, Mars rules accidents. Venus could only mitigate the size of the injuries. It was mainly little injuries which plagued him through his playing years in the 60's.

By far, Mantle's strongest planet is Mars, certainly appropriate for a great athlete! His Mars is in a Gauquelin sector, in and ruling the 12th House. Mars is in a partile trine to Pluto, which certainly gave him the discipline to develop himself physically: the word powerful was often applied, and his muscle development was commented on in that pre-steroid era. In addition, Mars is in an approaching partile square with the Moon.

Mantle credited his success to his father, who worked hard to make him into a successful baseball player. The Almuten of his 4th House is

Mars, so here we have the sporting interest right off the proverbial bat. The sign ruler, Jupiter, is in kingly Leo, technically dignified only by Face, but Jupiter is the nighttime Triplicity ruler of Leo, so Jupiter is stronger than his points would indicate. Dad is also shown by the Fortuna-North Node conjunction in the 4th House: he was certainly a *good* influence! But he had an erratic side, shown by Uranus in the 4th House. The harmony of purpose between the two of them is shown by the sign ruler of the Ascendant and 4th House being the same planet, namely Jupiter, which, being the greater benefic, denotes a benevolent influence.

Unfortunately, all the modern emphasis on Uranus ruling Aquarius has blinded us to the fact that Aquarius *is* a fixed sign, and the Aquarius Moon can be very stubborn. With Libra Sun and Aquarius Moon, Mantle was not quick to jump to conclusions, but once he made up his mind, there was no going back. The Moon-Mars square certainly gave him determination, and quite a level of competitiveness. His Sun and Moon are in an approaching trine, which suggests a good relationship between his parents, a helpful thing for getting an early start in life.

Saturn in dignity ruling and located in the 2nd House shows financial stability, but only if he worked for it. With the square to Uranus, one would expect some ups and downs.

Let us now examine the transplant operation chart. The operation itself is shown by the 1st House. (The event itself is by definition the Ascendant). We observe the South Node in the 1st House, which already gives us a clue that things are not getting off to a good start. We can, in effect treat this as a horary chart of Mantle's prognosis. Health is given by the 1st House. Mars is sign ruler and Co-Almuten: Mars is in the 6th House and peregrine. The Sun, the other Co-Almuten of the 1st House is in the 2nd House, also peregrine. Mars is in the 6th, ruling the 8th House: not a good sign. Cancer is a prolonged illness, (a 12th House matter) and the sign ruler of the 12th House is in the 8th House. Also not a good sign! Venus is the Almuten of the 12th, in the second and dignified, but fairly close to the lovely fixed star pair, Scheat and Terebellum. Oh dear! Does this look like an operation that would get the whole cancer? Not with Saturn peregrine in the 12th, it doesn't!

In medical astrology, the 10th House represented the "physic," which we may translate as the course of treatment, and the success of the method of treatment. Peregrine Saturn in the 12th House rules the treatment. Is this going to be effective? No way! Furthermore, Neptune and Uranus are in the 10th House, indicating misdiagnosis (Neptune) and erratic changes (Uranus). Should you believe a doctor who says "We think we got the whole cancer" with this kind of supporting evidence?

The strength of Venus, one ruler of the 12th, and Mercury, ruler of the 6th House, bodes well for the immediate outcome of the operation. This was not looking like death on the operating table! The problem was that the chart showed that the root problem was not being excised, so that, while the operation itself would prove successful, the overall prognosis was poor.

Finally, we arrive at the death chart itself. The Ascendant-Descendant angles are approximately reversed; not an unusual occurrence at death. In Hellenistic astrology, the Ascendant represents the Portals of Life, while the Descendant is the Portals of Death. Here we have Jupiter conjunct the Portals of Death. Cosmobiologists have been some of the best in the modern context at reminding us that Jupiter does represent release in death charts, and that Jupiter will generally be active. Malefics alone mean suffering, not death!

Transiting Mars came to the Descendant of the operation chart, so Mars effectively transited the entire 6th House of the operation chart. There is a partile square of Mercury and Jupiter, with Mercury ruling the Ascendant, and Jupiter the Descendant. The ruler of the 8th House, peregrine Saturn, is just being joined by the peregrine Moon, which is in a partile separating trine from Mantle's natal Pluto and Mars. And of course, elsewhere in Baylor University hospital, surely someone was being born as Mantle was dying.

In all this delineation, which was more important: house ruler or house placement? That is a truly hard call, because both were so important! Mantle was a martial hero: so which is more important, his Mars in the 12th House, or being sign ruler of the 5th and 12th, or Almuten of the 4th? Clearly, most planets will rule more than one house, so the rulerships give a wider breadth for the activities of the planet.

I propose next to give one of our usual suspects in the style of House delineation that was practiced by William Lilly, or some of his astrological ancestors. Before I begin, let me mention what I am *not* going to cover. In classical times, great emphasis was placed on the calculation of the *Hyleg*, which, as Lilly said, "that Planet, or place of Heaven, which being directed by his or its Digression, we judge of Life or the state thereof."[3] Once the Hyleg was calculated,[4] it was then easy to determine the *Alcochoden*, or Giver of Years; the Alcochoden was the Almuten of the Hyleg in most cases. The Alcochoden was used to determine the length of life. Each planet was considered to have three periods associated with it: a short, medium, and long period as shown in Table One. In my own case, the Alcochoden is Mercury: the three lengths of life associated with Mercury are 20 (least or short; I've already outlived this), 48, and 76. Which period to use is basically determined by examining the dignity of the Alchocoden: since my

Mercury is highly dignified in Virgo, I would expect to live 76 years.

The use of the Hyleg was with the system known as primary directions: this was a system for directing planets or cusps (mainly the angles) to natal positions: again, the method of calculation varied.

Now beyond the observed fact that people do not die exclusively at 21 different ages (the ones predicted in the tables), the length of life seldom comes up as an issue in any of the natal readings that I do! Accordingly, I am not sure of the emphasis to be placed on these concepts anyway, other than the obvious possibility of treating transits, directions, or progressions to the Hyleg as representing points of danger or crisis.

Table One. Length of Life from the condition of the Alchocoden. Source: Gadbury.[5]

Planet	Old Years	Mean Years	Least Years
Saturn	57	43	30
Jupiter	79	45	12
Mars	66	40	15
Sol	120	69	19
Venus	82	45	8
Mercury	76	48	20
Moon	108	66	25

In a natal reading of the classical type, the calculation of Hyleg and Alchocoden was considered part of the analysis of the nature of the 1st House. We shall take up the 1st House in our example after this point, in order to emphasize affairs of the house.[6]

Mary Godwin Shelley

First House: Affairs of the 1st House include the length of life, the temperament or complexion, the awareness and understanding of the Native, the Native's stature, and the general fortune of the Native.

Mary's Ascendant was ruled by the Moon, in the 6th House, conjunct the 7th House cusp. Saturn was in her 1st House. The Ascendant ruler in the 7th (since the Moon is conjunct the cusp) according to Gadbury, "inclines to strife, quarrels and contentions."[7]

The Significator of Manners (we might say behavior), according to Lilly, is that planet (not a light) which is located in the 1st

254 How to Read a House

House, preferably in the sign ascending. If there is more than one planet ascending, then the strongest one shall be the principal, but the others will contribute. In Mary's case it's easy, because only Saturn is in the 1st House. Saturn is in its Detriment, hence unfortunate: "Men of abject spirits, il-favored, having a low conceit of themselves, repiners, negligent, timerous, lovers of solitarinesse, sorrowfull, envious, pertinacious, inispicious, backbiting, slanderous, superstitious, deceitfull, malignant, rough-hewen fellows."[8]

A bit extreme? I would be more tempted to say that, given the 1st House Saturn detrimented, she was likely to have life filled with many sorrows, of a serious nature, but occasionally leavened by the Moon in Sagittarius.[9] She might have a tendency towards depression, given that Saturn placement, as well as the Moon in partile contra-antiscion to the Ascendant. With Saturn ruling her 7th House, her partner would not be of the same age, probably older, with some difficulties of his own. And that is what she got!

Second House: the affairs of the 2nd House are those of wealth.

Mary's 2nd House was ruled by the Moon, already an indicator of changeable fortune. It was common to include the Part of Fortune in this discussion, since Fortuna was the alternate indicator of wealth. Fortuna is primarily disposed by Jupiter, which in Mary's case has dignity by Triplicity. She got some lucky breaks financially. We moderns observe the opposition of Fortuna with Uranus: surely lucky breaks from something unusual or unexpected. Was *Frankenstein* supposed to be a best seller? Yet even with this work, she was not exactly settled for life: with the Moon applying to the square with Mercury, she had to contribute articles to otherwise uninteresting annuals, merely because they paid reasonably well.

Third House: the 3rd House shows siblings, neighbors, and short journeys.

Mary was the only child of her parents, but when her father remarried, she accumulated step-siblings, and later, half-siblings. Notice that Leo is on the cusp, a barren sign,[10] and the Sun is the ruler, the Sun being mostly barren. However, to play a little horary game here, note that the Sun is with three other planets in the same (4th) House: the Sun has companions in the 4th House. So Mary grows up with companions in her own household. All are in feminine signs, but one is Mars: one boy, the rest girls. One other interpretation: the ruler of the 3rd in the 4th: her closest "sibling," or in this case, "surrogate sibling," was her father, the person of the 4th.

Fourth House: the 4th House shows parents, the patrimony of the father, whether the parents agree, whether the Native will waste his/her inheritance, and of fortune to be made from land and real estate.

Like her 3rd House, Mary's 4th House was ruled by the Sun. The Sun, Dad, *was* the major focus of her life growing up. The Sun was in the 4th House. Not only did Mary work at home during her adult years as a writer, but so had her father. The Sun *as* Mary's father had dignity only by Face, and Mary's father did not live an easy life: he was constantly being hounded by creditors.

Whether the Native will enjoy a good patrimony[11] is determined by examining the aspects of the Sect Light to the two benefics: in Mary's case, the Moon is Sect Light, and the Moon is past the sextile to Venus, and applying to an out-of-sign square to Venus, a square within the Moon's Detriment, and the Moon is past the trine to Jupiter. This is extremely interesting. Reading in a horary fashion, this would mean that the patrimony is past (a past aspect to the Moon means events in the past), and what the future portends is problems. That was exactly what occurred. Godwin was in much better financial shape before Mary was born, and he left her mainly bills when he died.

Lilly stated that Saturn could be used as an alternate nocturnal Significator of the patrimony to the Moon.[12] If we apply this idea, then Venus is approaching a square to Saturn (no good!) and Saturn and Jupiter will come together by square just before Jupiter turns direct—also no good!

Fifth House: the 5th House rules children: will the Native have children, what genders, how healthy, and so forth.

Mary had Venus and Neptune in the 5th House. With respect to the condition of her children, we have to consider Neptune a malefic. About the traditional malefics, Gadbury says: "Saturn and Mars in the Fifth or Eleventh, or in Opposition from these Houses, do quickly kill the Native's Issue; and if the Sun having Dignity in the Fifth shall be joyned unto Saturn or Mars, it leaves not one Child alive.... The Sun, *Saturn*, and *Mercury*, in Conjunction in the *Medium Coeli*,... in Quartile or Opposition to the Moon, is an assured argument of the death of the Native's Children"[13]

Mary had a malefic in the 5th House, and detrimented Saturn and the Moon coming to opposition of each other, so despite the ruler of the 5th, Mercury, being strong by dignity, her children did not fare so well. Of the seven aphorisms that Gadbury gave for the death of one's children, only two involved the ruler of the 5th House. One of them is a bit indirect: that if the ruler of the 5th is in the 8th, the children will pre-decease the Native.

So it worked in this case. But I have to point out that Mary lived in a time when infant and child mortality was much higher than it is now. These rules for children *must* be tempered in the age of antibiotics. Thus, it would be more appropriate now to consider these factors as indicators of children having serious or significant disease *as* children, diseases to which we may now have perfectly good cures.

Sixth House: the 6th House rules the Native's illnesses.

Mary's 6th House was ruled by Mars, but the Moon is in the 6th, if only barely. Lilly lists the ruler of the 6th before planets in the 6th in his list of significators of infirmities, but whether this list was ranked is impossible to know.[14] Mars as Significator rules the left ear, gall bladder, kidneys, veins and the genitals.[15] There are also a series of diseases especially associated with Mars: various fevers, plague, fistulas, and wounds and scars to the face. I do not know whether Mary had any of these: her biographer didn't say. She *was* subject to depression, and that would be the Moon in the 6th House. Also the Moon: "Despite two years in the city, she was still so sensitive to Nature that she invariably knew when the tide ebbed and flowed by the fluctuations in her own vitality."[16]

Seventh House: the principal affair of the 7th House is marriage, or as we define it now, a live-in or committed relationship. The 7th shows whether the Native shall marry, how many spouses, the nature of the spouse, whether the two shall agree, and of the nature of the Native's public enemies.

We have already observed Saturn, ruler of Mary's 7th House in the 1st in Cancer: an older man with money problems (Saturn also rules the 8th, the spouse's money, and Saturn is in Detriment). Being in poor condition, he dies first. This also shows that Mary's open enemies are older men (another Saturn idea!) and certainly the leading candidate was Percy Shelley's grandfather, who had cut the couple off financially in life, and continued to make life miserable for Mary and Percy Junior after Percy Bysshe's death.

Eighth House: the 8th House rules the death of the Native, and the spouse's "portion" (i.e., the resources brought to the marriage).

Mary's 8th House sign ruler was in the 1st, but the Almuten of her 8th, Mars, was in the 4th. Gadbury says this of the ruler of the 8th in the 4th: "The Native's Parents will be strangers; they will also be sickly, and of short life; but for the Native, it denotes that he shall die in his own proper Countrey or House."[17] Even though Mary spent a substantial amount of her life abroad, she did die in England in her own house. As for her parents: we already know the fate of her mother Mary Wollstonecraft: bingo! As for Godwin, he lived 78 years, but not comfortably.

Ninth House: the 9th House rules journeys and religion, although Rob Hand has remarked that the religion given by the 9th House is the dominant religion of the culture, while repressed religions or heresies are given by the 3rd House.

> Among the arguments that Lilly gave for whether the Native shall travel is to observe Mercury and the Moon, what we would classify as the two wanderlust planets. If the Moon and Mercury are in mutual reception, it is an argument for travel. In Mary's case, Mercury receives the Moon by Triplicity, but not vice versa. However, the next consideration is whether the ruler of the 9th is either in reception with, or conjunct Mercury or the Moon. In this case, Saturn, ruler of the 9th is in Cancer. The Moon is in Saturn's Face: weak, but present. Another argument for travel is the ruler of the 9th in the 1st. OK! We have our indicators.[18]

> The ruler of the 9th is Saturn, and Saturn is unfortunately placed in Cancer, even if this is handy from a travelling perspective. But it is Saturn and that means that travel and life abroad will not be entirely pleasant, which it wasn't.

> As for religion, according to Lilly, the first bulwark is to examine planets or the Nodes in the 9th or the 3rd; Mary doesn't have any there. The next step is to try Jupiter, which had dignity by Triplicity. This would denote the state Lilly referred to as "good minded."[19]

Tenth House: the 10th house gives honor and dignity, or what Lilly called preferment. We would probably designate the latter concept as "promotion."

> Again, Saturn rules the roost. Part of Mary's reputation lies on her editing of her husband's posthumous works. And Pluto is here, oh joy! Pluto did not do wonders for Mary's dignity in her life, as she was reviled from some of the best hypocritical circles in England! To posterity, however, Fortuna triumphed, and made her place secure in the annals of literature.

Eleventh House: the 11th House rules friends.

> Mary had Jupiter ruling the 11th, and in the 11th, although out-of-sign with the cusp. Jupiter had moderate dignity by Triplicity. Despite her social outcast status, she did have friends throughout life. Her Jupiter was in Aries, whose antiscion was conjunct Uranus and sextile Saturn. Many of her male friends were hot-headed: a group of them fought for Italian independence, a most romantic cause in those days. Jupiter was retrograde, and they were not always reliable or predictable. But she seldom lacked for friendship or company.

Twelfth House: the 12th House rules confinement and secret enemies.

> The Almuten of Mary's 12th House was the Moon, while the sign ruler was Venus. Moon applied to a square to Mercury: there were times when her writing made her a virtual recluse. Venus was ruling the 12th, in the 5th House. After Percy's death, for the sake of what little money she could get out of Percy's family for her son, she was forced to live as a recluse, because Percy's family wanted her (and the memory of Percy) to be as obscure as possible. However, with Venus dignified, this quiet life was not at all distasteful to her, so the circumstances were not as onerous in reality as Percy's relations had hoped.

Discussion

I believe it would be impossible in these examples to attempt any kind of realistic ranking of primacy between placement and rulership. Clearly both apply. Consider Saturn in Mary's chart. Saturn was in her 1st House, and ruled one entire quadrant: from the 7th to the 10th Houses. In a very real sense, this *did* represent a theme. All of the time Mary lived abroad was with Percy: almost as soon as he died, she went back to England. Percy, shown by the 7th House ruler, sits in her 1st House: a major theme of her life, although he didn't even live through most of it! Thus, we can truly say that the meanings of the house rulers interweave with the meaning of the houses of the planetary placement.

However, I think there is a fairly straightforward explanation for the horary preference for ruler over placement, which may also have a direct bearing on other interrogatory charts, *i.e.*, events and electionals. The key is given in Lilly's description of the 4th House:

> "The Signe of the fourth [house] denoteth the Town, the Lord thereof, the Governour..."[20]

This little trick, very useful in horary, allows us to distinguish between a *person* given by a house, and *things* of the nature of the same house. For example, it may be advantageous to be able to distinguish between one's allies in a lawsuit (allies are the 2nd House), and potential monetary outcome of said lawsuit (also 2nd House). The allies can then be given by the ruler of the 2nd, while the monetary considerations are shown by either the sign on the cusp of the 2nd, aspects to the 2nd House cusp, or by planets in the 2nd House. Thus, we can dissect multiple themes applicable to the question that stem from the same house.

This is not a process which is especially necessary or desirable in natal. Themes ebb and flow throughout the life, and, given time, many different facets and combinations can take their place on center stage. Thus, natal provides us with the opportunity to observe *many* of the different possible combinations, not merely the *one* that applies to the question.

In the next chapter, we will continue our study of houses as we learn how to move them, through the predictive technique known as profection.

Endnotes

[1] Frank Herbert. 1966, 1978. *Destination: Void.* Ace: New York, page 58.

[2] The simplified version of the Rodden's classification scheme, given in *Astro Data II (The American Book of Charts)* is that A = Accurate data (birth certificate, from the person or close family member); B = Biography or autobiography; C = Caution (no source of origin); and DD = Dirty Data, date(s) or time(s) conflicting.

[3] Lilly, *CA*, page 527.

[4] Part of the reason I am giving such short shrift to this concept is that the method for calculating the Hyleg varied. However, the basic scheme was to begin with the Sect Light, and determine whether it was in what was considered to be a hylegical place, generally the 1st, 10th, 11th, 7th or 9th House. If the Sect Light is not within one of these houses, or within 5° of one of these houses, then the same check would be performed on the alternate Light. If the alternate Light also failed the test, then the Ascendant or Part of Fortune could be used: here the multitude of variants comes into play.

[5] *Op. cit.*, page 92.

[6] There are two computer programs which allow you to explore some of the dimensions of these concepts: CCRS, which calculates the Hyleg and Alchocoden using the somewhat simplified method of Henry Coley; and Chart Wheels 3, which uses the more complex Medieval system.

[7] *Op. cit.*, page 106.

[8] Lilly, *CA*, page 539.

[9] Occasional, because the Moon is not constant.

[10] The barren signs are Aries, Gemini, Leo, Virgo, and Capricorn. See Lilly, *CA*, pp 565- 566.

[11] Patrimony in this sense really refers to an inheritance of property or land, which in Lilly's day was generally inherited patrilineally.

[12] The idea that Lilly gives in *CA*, page 572, seems a little questionable, since Saturn is given as a diurnal planet, not a nocturnal one.

[13] *Op. cit.*, page 118.

[14] Lilly, *CA*, page 576.

[15] The full list of the parts of the body and their rulerships is given in Lilly, *CA*,

pages 579- 580, as well as in a host of other sources, including *The Book of Rulerships*.

16   Sunstein, page 308.
17   *Op. cit.*, page 149.
18   These ideas about travel are found in *CA*, pages 606-611.
19   Lilly, *CA*, page 612.
20   Lilly, *CA*, page 53.

—— CHAPTER 14 ——
PROFECTIONS: THE EASY WAY TO SPIN THE CHART

To offer a mass of undigested facts, of names not identified and places not located, is of no use to the reader and is simple laziness on the part of the author, or pedantry to show how much he has read. To discard the unnecessary requires courage and also extra work, as exemplified by Pascal's effort to explain an idea to a friend in a letter which rambled on for pages and ended, 'I am sorry to have wearied you with so long a letter but I did not have time to write you a short one.' The historian is continually being beguiled down fascinating byways and sidetracks. But the art of writing—the test of the artist is to resist the beguilement and to cleave to the subject.

Barbara Tuchman[1]

Well, it's Chapter 14 and so far, I have successfully resisted the temptation to do more than barely mention Primary Directions in the last chapter![2] I present instead the other main system for moving the chart that astrologers have neglected since the 17th Century: profections.

In addition to working with a system of advancing the chart, which has much older roots than secondary progressions or solar arc directions, we are now ready to overtly consider one of the fundamental differences between Hellenistic method and the later Arabian-Medieval-Renaissance system: whole sign versus degree-based systems.

When Ptolemy and other Hellenistic writers discussed aspects, or antiscia, they referred to them by sign: thus, Aries is sextile Gemini. The concept of orb came later. Similarly, the oldest systems of house divisions were whole sign. ("Systems" is plural because not all early house systems began with the Ascendant: for example, the Circle of Athla, as we have seen, begins with the Part of Fortune.) This system of whole sign aspecting is also used in Vedic Astrology.[3] We have already seen in Chapter 2 that the Babylonians did not originally work with degree units of measurement, but instead used asterisms of about 10° each, which they may well have acquired from the Egyptians. Thus, although the zodiac *itself* is not the original locator system, the smaller units of measurement were passed over for what the Greeks perceived as the truly obvious units of sign, which differed by Rulership, Exaltation, Triplicity and Quality. The only system which utilizes subdivisions of signs (apart from the actual *calculation* of Ascendant or Lot) is the Essential Dignities, which subdivide the signs into either five sections (Terms) or three (Faces). This, by the way, suggests that the Essential Dignities, or at least the Terms, are only as old as the subdivision of the circle into 360°. And we may also understand that the unit used in the Faces goes back to the original asterisms used by the Egyptians and Babylonians.

Although we don't call it such, this whole sign system has survived even to the 20th Century, especially as a general system for transits. Thus, we have astrologers such as Doris Hebel pointing out that an opposition of Saturn to a natal placement begins when Saturn enters the opposing *sign*, and does not fully complete until Saturn leaves the opposing sign.[4]

To cut to the heart of the question, are we necessarily better off in our delineation when we work with aspects with orbs, or with whole signs? I think that the answer is relative, meaning that it depends on what we are trying to get out of the system. As Betty Lundsted noted in her discussion of orb size, the answer may just sort itself out depending on the nature of the technique involved.[5] Thus, midpoints by their very nature *require* small orbs, because otherwise the method would be drowned with so much noise that any real hit would simply be undetectable. However, there is little doubt that an Outer Planet entering a sign represents a sea change!

Thus, I encourage the reader to go back over the Circle of Athla in Chapter 8 from the standpoint of whole signs, *i.e.*, the beginning of the sign that contains Fortuna. I present material in the Medieval/Renaissance fashion, which is with actual degree symbolism, because that is the system I personally use, but I recommend that you try both systems to see which one you prefer.

Profections are a system for moving the chart to examine how emphasis in the chart will shift from year to year, month to month, day to day, or by some other interval. The specific method is this: the 1st House gives the first year of life, the 2nd House, the second, and so forth. The problem is that we often think of our lives in age, not year of life, and the 1st year of life equals age zero. These age correspondences are shown in Table One.

The beauty of this system is that it is easy to do by hand. All you need to know is the person's age, and you can easily find the starting point to the profection by casting out 12's. Thus, if I am 41 (as I am right now, in the closing days while writing this), I can either cast out 36, and calculate 41-36=5, which I then add to the 1st House represented by age 36 to get the 6th House, or I can go into the table. In either case, the period from my 41st birthday until my 42nd birthday is a 6th House year. My 6th House cusp then becomes an alternate Ascendant to show issues specific to the year. I may read that chart in full using all houses from this derived Ascendant starting point. Please note that I do *not* recompute a chart for this new Ascendant, but read the radix cusps exactly the same way I might use derived houses in horary. Thus, my income for a 6th House year (a 2nd House issue) is the 7th House, and my partner (a 7th House issue) is the 12th House. This is *exactly* the way derived houses work in horary. I can graph this situation as shown in Table Two.

Table One. Correspondence between House rulership and age in profection calculation.

House	Age	Age	Age	Age	Age	Age	Age
1	0	12	24	36	48	60	72
2	1	13	25	37	49	61	73
3	2	14	26	38	50	62	74
4	3	15	27	39	51	63	75
5	4	16	28	40	52	64	76
6	5	17	29	41	53	65	77
7	6	18	30	42	54	66	78
8	7	19	31	43	55	67	79
9	8	20	32	44	56	68	80
10	9	21	33	45	57	69	81
11	10	22	34	46	58	70	82
12	11	23	35	47	59	71	83

Table Two. Profected Houses for Lee's 42nd year (age 41). The top
        line gives the house that you want to examine: the bottom
        line gives which house this represents in the radix chart.

1	2	3	4	5	6	7	8	9	10	11	12
6	7	8	9	10	11	12	1	2	3	4	5

The whole idea embedded in this system is that none of us have
ideal charts from all perspectives, and we will have issues which, at
one time in our lives, might be trivial, which in another period can be
absolutely earth-shaking.

Profections can be delineated using the following model:

> • The first consideration is to remember which year it is rela-
> tive to the radix, because this will tell something about themes.
> In my own case, because this is a 6th House year, I should
> expect health problems. My 6th House contains no planets, and
> is ruled by Saturn, which is exalted in Libra. Thus, lacking
> debilitating aspects to my natal Saturn, the dignity means that
> the health effects will not be totally debilitating or worrisome:
> the worst of the effects I encountered were a bone bruise, a
> broken toe, and some temporary gray hair: annoying, but hardly
> debilitating.

> • The second way to interpret the chart is as I indicated above:
> by reading the whole chart and its house meanings in the de-
> rived position. Thus, acute illnesses or accidents are shown by
> the 6th House from the 6th House profected Ascendant: this
> works out to the 11th House. Thus, my (radix) 11th House is
> ruled by the Moon, which is moderately dignified by Triplicity
> in Virgo (nighttime birth), but Uranus is found there. Again, no
> major problems, but susceptibility to accidents. Bingo!

> • The third consideration is to know what the transits are doing
> to the natal planets, because this shows how this *particular*
> twelve-year cycle differs from any previous or future ones. In
> my case, transiting Neptune is opposing natal Uranus, so I
> should expect more than the usual amount of carelessness as-
> sociated with the accidents, and probably lower energy level
> overall, especially as transiting Neptune is also squaring my
> natal Neptune.

Let's illustrate these ideas by example. Before we resume our study
of the usual suspects, I would like to add another example: one of our
dearly missed astrologers, Nancy Hastings.

Nancy Hastings

Rob Hand used to joke that he used Nancy's chart to test his dial programs, because her tight cardinal grand cross had a way of blowing up all but the hardiest software. When she was alive, we all kidded about what a difficult chart she had, and there is no question that aspects of her life *were* difficult. However, Nancy was too good a friend for me to consider all of her life as merely a prelude to her death, so let us celebrate the life first. Table Three is a set of dates which we can use for illustrative purposes.

Table Three. Significant dates in Nancy Hastings' life.

1974 -	Became professional astrologer.	Age:29	Profected house: 6th
1980 -	Separated from husband.	Age: 35	Profected house: 12th
1984 -	Published *Secondary Progressions*.	Age: 39	Profected house: 4th
1989 -	Published *The Practice of Prediction.*	Age: 44	Profected house: 9th
1990 -	Diagnosed with colon cancer.	Age: 45	Profected house: 10th
1991-	Died.	Age: 46	Profected house: 11th

Before we begin spinning the chart, let me present a full table for profectional houses, to ease the pain of following the process. This is given as Table Four.

If we begin with 1974, the year she became a professional astrologer, already the fact that this was a 6th House year suggests hard working, virtual servitude as one possible scenario. Nancy's 6th House is ruled by debilitated Jupiter, but it contains exalted Venus. In this year, she had her first Saturn Return, with Saturn in her profected 4th House (the radix 9th), and ruling her profected 8th (Almuten), 11th and 12th Houses. Therefore, this particular 6th House year is going to be characterized by more work and nose-to-the-grindstone characteristics than other such 6th House profectional year.

Nancy was separated from her husband in a 12th House profectional year, which already suggests that the circumstances were difficult. Her 12th House was ruled by Mercury, with Jupiter in the 12th. Her husband is given by that Jupiter, ruler of her profected 7th House (the radix 6th House). The essential signature for the year 1980 was the Jupiter-Saturn conjunction, which occurred sequentially from 9 through 4 Libra in its three passes. This conjunction involved the very planet representing her husband, as well as conjoining her Neptune and squaring Saturn. This conjunction also squared Mars. What does Mars rule? In her profected chart, Mars is Almuten of the 5th and in the profected

5th (the radix 4th). So the issue was her children! Squares, of course, show conflict and strife, so here we see conflict and strife between the marriage partners due to the activation by the Jupiter-Saturn. Nancy and her husband had substantial disagreements about child support.

Table Four. Profected Houses for any year. The first column in each row gives the profectional year. Refer to the top line to pick the house you want to examine. The column in your profectional row is then the correct radix House. For example, if you want the 8th House in a 7th House profectional year, go down to the row that begins with a 7, find the 8 in the top row, and follow it down to the 8th row. The answer is the 2nd House.

1	2	3	4	5	6	7	8	9	10	11	12
2	3	4	5	6	7	8	9	10	11	12	1
3	4	5	6	7	8	9	10	11	12	1	2
4	5	6	7	8	9	10	11	12	1	2	3
5	6	7	8	9	10	11	12	1	2	2	4
6	7	8	9	10	11	12	1	2	3	4	5
7	8	9	10	11	12	1	2	3	4	5	6
8	9	10	11	12	1	2	3	4	5	6	7
9	10	11	12	1	2	3	4	5	6	7	8
10	11	12	1	2	3	4	5	6	7	8	9
11	12	1	2	3	4	5	6	7	8	9	10
12	1	2	3	4	5	6	7	8	9	10	11

Nancy's first book was published in 1984, a 4th House year for her profectionally. Now of course, this means she was writing it in a 3rd House year! Nancy had Mercury, natural ruler of writers and writing, in her natal 3rd House but conjunct the I.C., so by itself this heralded the importance of writing during this time. As far as her 3rd House year, the 3rd from the 3rd, or the radix 5th House, rules writing for the year. Her 5th House is ruled by Saturn, in her radix 9th House of publishing. During 1983, transiting Saturn was trining her own natal Saturn on and off, thereby giving her a bit more discipline and hard work than she experienced normally.

In 1984, the profected 4th House year, we may first remember that the 4th House, being the second from the 3rd House, gives the (first!) fruits of the writing process. Nancy's radix 4th House ruler, Saturn, is in the 9th House, so she didn't always get the opportunity to stay at home as much as perhaps she would have liked. (She did see clients at home, a manifestation of the 7th House ruler, Mars, being in the natal 4th.) Mars, one of her 4th House planets, being dignified by exaltation shows that she received recognition. This was the year that Jupiter triggered her grand cross.[6] In this case, Jupiter was doing the triggering from its Fall in Capricorn, so the result is more likely disappointment over heightened expectations, rather than untrammeled success.

1989 marked the publication of her second book in a 9th House profectional year. Nancy's 9th House is sign-ruled by Venus, which is exalted in her chart, while the Almuten is the Moon, which has dignity only by reception with a planet in Fall, thus peregrine to my way of thinking. The publication would be the 9th (publishing) from the 9th (profected 1st House), which translated to the 5th. Her 5th House was ruled by Saturn, which was in her radix 9th House. In 1989, Neptune was still afflicting Mars, while Uranus was getting ready to start mixing it up with her cardinal cross. It was in 1989 that Nancy first observed the symptoms of what was later diagnosed as cancer: not only do the afflictions of both Uranus and Neptune qualify as serious stress, but Pluto was trining her Venus. The significance? In this profectional year, her health (6th) was given by the radix 2nd House, already debilitated by the late degree on the cusp, but further, the house is ruled by Venus, which is being impacted by Pluto.

Nancy spent most of 1990 fighting the cancer, and at times, even succeeding. She managed to be well enough to speak at both the American Federation of Astrologers Conference in Orlando, and the Seven Hills Astrological Conference in Lynchburg, VA. A 10th House year is supposed to be a "preferment" or at least an "honors" year, and Nancy got plenty of recognition as she fought her battle. Remember, in this year, her health, given by the profected 6th House, is the 3rd House, ruled by exalted Mars.

The battle turned against her in 1991, an 11th House year. Now her health was given by the radix 4th, the 6th from the 11th House, or profected 1st. The 4th House is ruled by Saturn, one of the two stunningly debilitated planets in her chart. Her profectional 7th was likewise ruled by Saturn. The second seriously debilitated planet, Jupiter, ruled her profectional 8th House. In this year, Pluto was aspecting her Nodes, and Neptune was sextiling Venus. While the symbolism isn't going to be the same for every twelve-year cycle, remember that the 7th House cusp is the "Portals of Death" just as the 1st House cusp is the "Portals of Life."

Prince Charles

Some events in Prince Charles' life are shown in Table Five. We are going to be especially interested here in the repetition of houses in different cycles.

Table Five. Events in Prince Charles' life.

1958, July 26: Became Prince of Wales.	Age: 9	House: 10th
1981, July 29 at 10:18 a.m. GMT, London: Married Diana Spencer.	Age: 32	House: 9th
1982, June 21, London: Son born, Prince William.	Age: 33	House: 10th
1984, Sept. 15, London: Second son born, Prince Harry.	Age: 35	House: 12th
1987, March 10: Almost dies in an avalanche which kills a close friend.	Age: 38	House: 2nd

Now obviously, becoming Prince of Wales is a clear 10th House sort of thing. The monarchy is always associated with the 10th House, so this is a clear hit. Let's remember that, in Charles' case, the Sect Light, the Moon, is in the 10th House, and when that is not referring to his mother, the highly dignified Moon speaks well for him. His 10th House rulers are the Sun and Mars, the quintesscentially male planets. We are talking *Prince* of Wales here, not *Princess*, a prerogative still reserved in British law for the eldest male heir. At this time, transiting Mars had passed into his radix 10th House, and was in a partile conjunction to Charles' North Node, and trine his Saturn.

In Charles' profected chart, his 10th House is the radix 7th, ruled by Saturn. Transiting Saturn in July 1958 was approaching to within a degree of his natal Mars, a degree in which Saturn then retrograded. In horary, this would be a refranation, but here, of course, the sense is more in keeping with the symbolism of the office: the Prince of Wales is waiting to become King. He has not yet arrived.

His marriage to Diana Spencer was a 9th House matter profectionally. Ninth? Charles' 9th House ruler, Jupiter, is posited in his radix 5th, the house of children. It's the dynasty, isn't it! His marriage partner is given by his 3rd House, the 7th from the profected 9th. Mercury rules the 3rd House: transiting Venus was sextile Charles' Mercury, but more importantly, partile conjunct his Saturn (and Di's Pluto), which probably says a great deal about the outcome of the marriage. Transiting Mars was just past the trine to Charles' Mercury, and approaching Diana's Sun. The Jupiter-Saturn conjunction that year was falling in Charles' profected 7th, so of course everybody had grand hopes for the marriage!

Prince William was conveniently born eleven months later, in another 10th House profectional year for Charles. Now, one would suspect that 5th House years might be associated with children, but remember here that the significance of Prince William's birth was dynastic, which is *always* a 10th House matter, royally speaking. However, in 1958 the symbolism evoked by the transiting planets concerned the radix 10th House and the profected 10th House. This time, transiting Saturn conjoined Charles' natal Venus-Neptune conjunction in the profected 7th House. Didn't Di's stock go up when William was born! Thus, while the event had dynastic considerations, it was of greater import for Diana than for Charles.

Prince Harry was born in a 12th House profectional year. Charles' 12th House is ruled by the Moon, which as we have seen, is hands down the most dignified planet in his chart. With William's birth, Charles' Venus-Neptune conjunction was activated by transit; here, that conjunction is in Charles' profected 5th House of children.[7] Furthermore, transiting Venus, sign ruler of the profected 5th House, has just passed the conjunction to Charles' Venus-Neptune. And transiting Pluto was in partile opposition to the Moon, his profected Ascensional ruler.

Finally, we consider a personal event, or from his standpoint, almost event. Charles was nearly killed in an avalanche that did kill a close friend. This happened in a 2nd House profectional year for him. Why? Well consider that Charles' 8th House ruler, Saturn, is posited in his radix 2nd! Transiting Saturn was conjunct Charles' Mars. Transiting South Node was conjunct Charles' I.C. and Neptune. Charles' 8th House profected ruler, Jupiter, as well as his radix 8th House ruler, Saturn, were unaffected, but then the avalanche didn't toll for him. However, in profected houses, his friends are the radix 12th. A friend's death is the 8th from the radix 12th, the radix 7th. And Saturn rules his 7th, with transiting Saturn doing his Mars.

Muhammad Ali

Table Six shows Muhammad Ali's title fights. From his first heavyweight boxing title in 1964, he successfully defended the title until 1967, when it was stripped from him because of his refusal to serve in the military. (The lawsuit this would evoke now boggles the mind!) When he returned to the ring in a title bout in 1971, he was defeated, but then once he won the title back in 1974, he retained it until 1978, when he was defeated by Larry Holmes. Thus, he maintained the title for three years, got it back seven years later, and then retained it again for three more years. We have a seventeen year period, which means that there was a repetition of profectional years from the beginning part of his championship career until the end.

Table Six.. Events in the life of Muhammad Ali.

1964, Feb. 25: Won world heavyweight title by defeating Sonny Liston.	House: 11th
1965, May 25: Retained his title by defeating Sonny Liston in a re-match.	House: 12th
1965, Nov. 11: Retained his title by defeating Floyd Patterson.	
1966, March 29: Retained his title by defeating George Chuvalo.	House: 1st
1966, May 21: Retained title by defeating Henry Cooper.	
1966, Aug. 6: Retained title by defeating Brian London.	
1966, Sept. 10: Retained title by defeating Karl Mildenberger.	
1966, Nov. 14: Retained title by defeating Cleveland Williams.	
1967, Feb. 6: Retained title by defeating Ernie Terrell.	House: 2nd
1967, March 22: Retained boxing title by defeating Zora Folley.	
1967, April 30: Stripped of World Boxing Association heavyweight title for refusing military service.	
1971, March 8: Defeated by Joe Frazier in 15 rounds.	House: 6th
1974, Oct. 30: Wins back heavyweight title by defeating Joe Foreman.	House: 9th
1975, March 24: Retains title by defeating Chuck Wepner.	House: 10th
1975, May 16: Retained title by defeating Ron Lyle.	
1975, June 30: Retained title by defeating Joe Bugner.	
1975, Oct. 1: Retained title; beat Joe Frazier.	
1976, Feb. 20 in San Juan, PR: Retained title by defeating Jean-Pierre Coopman.	House: 11th
1976, April 30: Retained title by defeating Jimmy Young.	
1976, May 25: Retained title by defeating Richard Dunn.	
1976, Sept. 28: Retained title by defeating Ken Norton.	
1977, May 16: Retained title by defeating Alfredo Evangelista.	House: 12th
1977, Sept. 29: Retained title by defeating Ernie Shavers.	
1978, Feb. 15: Defeated by Leon Spinks, Ali loses title.	House: 1st
1978, Sept. 15: Wins world heavyweight title by defeating Leon Spinks.	
1980, Oct 2: Defeated by Larry Holmes in attempt to take Holmes' title.	House: 3rd
1981, Dec. 11: Defeated by Trevor.	House: 4th

Ali first won the world title in 1964, when he was 22 years old. This corresponds to an 11th House year. I find it fascinating that Ali's radix 11th House is ruled by Mercury, given his subsequent reputation for what we now refer to as "sound bites." In an 11th House year, Ali's opponents are given by the 5th House (a 7th House relationship), ruled by Jupiter. Mercury in Ali's chart is conjunct the Moon, Ali's Sect Light, while Jupiter is in Detriment, albeit the lesser Detriment, in comparing the relative qualities of Jupiter in Gemini versus Virgo. In 1964, Saturn in Aquarius was transiting Ali's 7th House: it remained in his 7th House until just before his successful rematch against Sonny Liston. In 1965, a 12th House profectional year, Ali's Fortuna was in his profectional 1st House; conjunct Pluto. It suggested financial success by demolition. In 1966, Ali celebrated his 24th birthday and his profectional return. Now Saturn rules his opponents, and transiting Saturn spent the year hovering around Ali's South Node, while Uranus was transiting in the neighborhood of his North Node, and Neptune was opposing his natal Saturn. Thus, Saturn was not in the best of shape. In 1967, Ali began the year successful, but then lost his title to governmental intervention. This was a 2nd House profectional year. In the first part of the year, represented by the first part of the 2nd House,[8] we see the North Node, but the second part of the House has Neptune. Talk about blindsiding? He was convicted on June 20, 1967, his defense being that he claimed exemption as a *Black Muslim minister.* Neptunian enough? At this time, Jupiter had just finished conjoining his 12th House (incarceration) Pluto, and Neptune was opposing his Saturn. Both Uranus and Pluto were transiting his 2nd House. He was ultimately vindicated by the Supreme Court on June 28, 1971, just three months after being defeated in his first world title comeback attempt by Joe Frazier. The Lord giveth, the Lord taketh away? 1971 was a 6th House profectional year. On March 8th, for his defeat, transiting Mars was square his Fortuna-Pluto conjunction. Transiting Saturn, ruling Ali in his profectional chart, was at 0° Aries, and hence just having gone into Fall. This position is also in exact antiscion to Ali's Neptune, so we can presume his expectations were way out of whack. Transiting Neptune was trine Ali's natal Saturn, so we have reciprocal Saturn-Neptune hits. Meanwhile his Moon, representing his opponents in this year, was completely unscathed. Judges in lawsuits are the 10th House: his 10th profectional House cusp was, appropriately, Libra, the scales of Justice. Transiting Mars in Libra was trine Ali's natal Venus. Transiting Jupiter had just passed his Fortuna-Pluto.

Ali got back into the black in 1974, when he won the heavyweight title from Joe Foreman. In 1974, Ali was 32, a 9th House profectional year, Among the 9th House qualities was that the title bout took place in Zaire. Ali is given by Mars, ruler of his radix 9th. Transiting Mars was coming to trine his natal Mars, while transiting Venus was conjoining Mars, in Mars' sign. Mars is in a Gauquelin plus zone in Ali's natal chart, and dignified by *hayz.*

Ali then began his second successful round of title defenses, running until 1978. Again, it was a three year period. This time, it ran through the profectional 10th, 11th and 12th Houses, whereas the first run was 11th, 12th, and 1st. The 11th House again is ruled by Mercury, with Jupiter being the opposition. Transiting Neptune was roughly opposite Jupiter this entire year, thereby weakening his opponents. In 1977, his 12th House profectional year, the Moon ruled Ali, and Saturn, his opponents. In 1977, Saturn was transiting Ali's profectional 1st House, thereby putting his enemies in his court.[9] Furthermore, Saturn in Leo is in Detriment, so his opponents were not strong in any case.

When we get back to the 1st House profectional year, 1978, now we have Ali as the Sun, and his opponents as Saturn. For his defeat by Leon Spinks, both the transiting Sun *and* Saturn were in Detriment, and even within 1° of exact opposition, so Ali's edge was reduced. With this opposition square Ali's Uranus, a change was in the cards. Furthermore, transiting Mars was coming to oppose Ali's natal Sun. Later in the year, he got a rematch, but this time, the Sun and Saturn were both in Virgo, with transiting Sun coming to the trine of Ali's natal Sun, and transiting Jupiter was coming up to Ali's Fortuna. This being in the portion of the year represented by Virgo,[10] the competition at this point was Mercury-Jupiter: we have already seen financial benefit to Ali (Fortuna) coming from his opponent (Jupiter). Transiting Uranus was squaring Ali's natal Moon-Mercury conjunction, another indication of an upset to the status quo.

Two years later, at the age of 38, Ali lost the title for the final time to Larry Holmes. Age 38 is a 3rd House profectional year. Ali is Venus, his opponent is Mars. Transiting Venus was in Leo, square Uranus, indication of another change of state. Mars was far more dignified, at 23° Scorpio, opposite Ali's Saturn, and conjunct transiting Uranus. And so it goes...

Catherine de Medici

And now for something completely different. Some events in Catherine's life are shown in Table Seven. Of course, now we tend to view marriage at fourteen as being early, but then it was commonplace. However, given that this is the time of the Saturn opposition to natal Saturn, it is definitely indicative of a match made in Saturn rather than in heaven. Husband Henri *hated* her. The long interval before the birth of the future Charles IX was because Henri refused to sleep with her. However, annulment would have required returning the de Medici dowry...

Marriage in a 3rd House profectional year puts the marriage partner as the 9th House, ruled by Jupiter in Catherine's chart. Natally, Jupiter is conjunct the 7th House cusp, so it is certainly appropriate symbolism between the natal and profected chart. Transiting Jupiter was going through her profectional 7th House, again appropriate. This transit of Jupiter was to her natal 5th House, and of course, the whole purpose of the marriage was to provide a royal heir.

Table Seven. Events in the life of Catherine de Medici.

1533, Oct. 27: Married Henri, Duke of Orleans.	Age: 14	House: 3rd
1544, Jan. 19: The future Francis II born.	Age: 24	House: 1st
1547, March 31: Husband becomes Henri II, king of France.	Age: 28	House: 5th
1550, June 27: Her son, the future King Charles IX of France, born.	Age: 31	House: 8th
1559, June 30: Husband mortally wounded in a joust.	Age: 40	House: 5th
1559, July 10: Husband died. Succeeded by Francis II.		
1560, Dec. 5: Francis II died, leaving Catherine as Regent.	Age: 41	House: 6th
1563: Charles IX (at 13) declared of age; Regency "ends."	Age: 44	House: 9th
1572, Aug. 24: St. Bartholomew's massacre began	Age: 53	House: 6th
1574, May 31: Charles IX of France died. Succeded by Henri III.	Age: 55	House: 8th
1589, Jan 5: Catherine dies.	Age: 69	House: 10th
1589, Aug. 2: Henri III assassinated. Valois dynasty ends.		House: 11th

However, *her* ruler was Mercury, which was in Detriment and disposed by Jupiter. Even though Jupiter (her spouse) was retrograde, he was in his own Terms, so he was still stronger than she was. In this sort of dynastic marriage, Catherine was but a pawn, certainly not in control of her own destiny. Transiting Mercury was retrograde, opposite her natal Venus, a first indicator that reality wasn't going to match "The Plan." Neptune had just completed the conjunction to Mercury (entering the natal 11th House of expectations and hope), so there is no doubt reality was a let-down. Furthermore, transiting Saturn was square Venus, as well as roughly opposing natal Saturn. Now things are starting to look distinctly unhappy.

Prince Henri successfully avoided sleeping with Catherine for ten years. When he finally got down to his "duty," she conceived and bore the future Frances II in a 1st House profectional year, at age 24. Her child would be both the radix and profected 5th House, ruled by the Moon. The child was born with a Mars-Jupiter conjunction in Scorpio, squaring her Fortuna and Neptune. Prince Francis' Saturn was conjunct Catherine's South Node, and his Uranus was at her Northern Bending. Neptune was conjunct her Sun. Pluto was trine her Jupiter. Transiting Mercury was conjunct her Saturn. Now all of this does not exactly sound like blissful bonding between mother and child. The reason? Francis was sickly. The child's health is the 6th from the 5th House, or the 10th House. Now we see Saturn and Pluto popping up, and now we can understand the context and the meaning of these transits for Catherine.

The profectional 1st House year represented an opportunity for Catherine to come into her own. In those days, producing a son and heir would be considered just that for a woman. But a sickly heir was a danger, and a smudge on her character.

Catherine got "promoted" to Queen of France at the age of 28, a 5th House profectional year. Catherine is given by the Moon, ruler of the radix 5th House. Catherine's elevation is the 10th from the 5th (the radix 2nd House), ruled by Venus, or the Moon again, being posited there. Catherine's natal Saturn is dignified in Capricorn, and conjunct the 11th House cusp. Transiting Venus had just gone direct at 18° Pisces. Transiting Jupiter beheld natal Venus by contra- antiscion. Transiting Saturn, ruler of the profected 7th House, was trine natal Venus. Transiting Uranus had just passed natal Venus. Transiting Pluto was just coming to her Fortuna. Not bad! Catherine still had not consolidated her position enough to have held onto the throne had Henri died at this point. That level of consolidation came only later. Beyond the issue of profections, it is interesting that Catherine married with the Saturn opposition, and became queen with the Saturn return.

That consolidation began three years later with the birth of her second royal son, the future Charles IX. It did *not* happen with the birth of the future Francis II because he was sickly: this was held against Catherine. Charles' birth was an 8th House year for her. The 8th House is ruled by Mars, of mixed dignity in her radix 4th House. A child of this year would be the 5th from the 8th, or her radix 12th. Saturn rules: Fortuna is here, but so are Neptune and Mercury. Transiting Venus at 2° Gemini was conjunct her natal North Node. Transiting Mars at 11° was conjunct natal Uranus. Transiting Jupiter at 17° Gemini was trine natal Jupiter at 16° Libra: and don't underestimate Jupiter when it comes to fertility! Transiting Saturn, ruler of the profected 5th House, at 8° Aquarius was partile trine her natal Moon, ruler of her natal 5th House.

Catherine became Queen of France in a 5th House profectional year: in the next 5th House year 12 years later, she became a widow. Catherine is again given by the Moon, ruler of the radix 5th House. What is the difference between this cycle and the last? In the last cycle, the emphasis by transit was on Catherine's profected 10th: preference or elevation. This time, Henri II is given by the 11th: the 7th from the 5th, and Henri II's death is shown by the 6th, the 8th from the 11th. The 11th House—Henri II— is ruled by Saturn, or Mars as Almuten. Henri's death is given by the Sun. Transiting retrograde Mars at 5° Sagittarius was moving from conjunct the South Node, to opposite the Moon,

Catherine's ruler. Transiting Saturn was partile conjunct Catherine's North Node in her profected 10th House at the time of Henri's Mortal Combat. Transiting Uranus was partile opposite her natal Uranus. Transiting Neptune was square Catherine's Neptune. Transiting Pluto beheld Catherine's Sun by contra-antiscion. Thus, we see the transits are affecting Henri, not Catherine directly. After the history between them, it is difficult to imagine Catherine *really* being that broken up by Henri's death.

The succession of Francis II was not exactly wonderful for Catherine, because the parties who became his Regents were not sympathetic to her interests. Francis died a year later, a 6th House profectional year. Her son is the 5th from the 6th (the 10th House); his death is the 8th from the radix 10th, or the radix 5th. Transiting Venus was coming to her 10th House Pluto, transiting Mars was sextiling Pluto, Jupiter was stationary direct, squaring her Mars and opposing her own Jupiter; transiting Saturn was conjoining her Moon, ruler of the radix 5th, and the profected house of her son's death. Transiting Uranus at 22°, Scorpio (her natal 8th House cusp, and the profected end-of-the-matter) squared her Fortuna; Neptune at 29° was still square her natal Neptune. Pluto at 7° Pisces sextiled her natal Pluto, and squared her Moon. Saturn and Pluto attacking the ruler of her children's house, accidentally the house of the death of children in the profected chart? The symbolism is clear.

Her eldest son Francis II's death meant that Catherine actually became more powerful as Regent for the underage second son Charles IX. The Regency of Charles IX ended three years later, a 9th House year. As a 9th House year, Catherine was ruled by her Jupiter, dignified by Triplicity, but in Mars' Detriment. Her son got Catherine's radix 1st House, easily the strongest in her chart, ruled by Mars. Still, this house is Catherine's radix 1st: things for Catherine did not really change that much: she simply ruled from behind the scenes, given her influence over Charles, rather than in her own right. Transiting Mars at 12°, Aries opposed her natal Jupiter, dignified only by Term; transiting Jupiter at 16°, Cancer had just passed her natal Mars; Mars was the sign ruler of Charles in the profected chart. In addition, transiting Saturn squared Catherine's Sun and opposed her 10th House Saturn, so naturally her official standing diminished at this time.

We now continue to the St. Batholomew's Day Massacre. While this has gone down in history as one of the more heinous religious events of the period, it was in the midst of a series of religious/political wars. The issue was not as simple as Catholic *vs.* Protestant because various noble houses had aligned with the Huguenot Protestants, and it was *those* houses that Catherine wished to destroy, far more than the

Huguenots themselves. In any case, the event triggered the Fourth Religious War in France, with skirmishes continuing until the end of the Century.

The massacre occurred during a 6th House profectional year for Catherine. Her open enemies are therefore the 12th House, and this was no secret conspiracy, at least at far as the Court was concerned. They were accordingly ruled by Saturn, with Neptune and Mercury aboard as co-conspirators. I think it is probably appropriate to consider the persecuted Huguenot pawns to be Neptune. Transiting Venus, ruler of her profected 2nd House, was square her Saturn, with the transiting South Node conjunct Saturn. The enemy is destroyed! Transiting Saturn was opposite her Uranus and transiting Uranus was conjunct her Pluto. (One bold and unexpected stroke?) Further, transiting Pluto was partile conjunct her Mercury. Her natal Sun, representing her in this year, and located in the 8th House, is untouched at the time except for the mild opposition from Venus. Guess who won!

Catherine died 5 January 1589, still in her 10th House profectional year. The 8th from the 10th is the 5th, ruled by the Moon, and her radix 8th is ruled by Mars. Transiting Venus at 20° was opposite Saturn. Transiting Saturn had just finished conjoining her Moon. Transiting Uranus had just completed the sextile to her Saturn, and was approaching the conjunction to her Mercury, ruler of the profected 6th House. Transiting Pluto was squaring her Mars, and conjunct her radix Ascendant.

In the same year, her son Henri III died, and with him, the Valois dynasty. On his deathbed, he named Henri of Navarre as his successor. Henri of Navarre, who became Henri IV, was married to Catherine's daughter; after his succession he divorced her and married yet another de Medici. It took Henri IV a while to consolidate his own reign, following a foray into Protestantism. But after he did, he became the founding father of the Bourbons, the final dynasty prior to the French Revolution.

Can we see any of this from Catherine's chart, given that she died before her son was assassinated? Let's see. As an 11th House profectional year, her son would be given by the 5th from the 11th; this is the radix 3rd. His death would be the 8th from the radix 3rd, or her radix 10th. Her 10th contains Saturn and Pluto, perhaps already suggestive of the ultimate effect she would have on a dynasty! Her 3rd is ruled by Mercury. We have already seen that Catherine's Mercury was the least dignified of all of her planets, so 11th House years were not likely to be great ones for any of her sons! Transiting Mars at 18° Scorpio was opposite her Part of Spirit. (Yes! Spirit!) Transiting Jupiter was coming to opposition with her natal Mercury. Transiting Saturn had finished with her Moon, and was now applying to trine Jupiter. Uranus was applying to her Mercury. Pluto had finished with her Ascendant. The symbolism here is not as good as for her death. Either her profections truly died with her, or the death of the dynasty was of little import for her. From the female side, the Bourbon dynasty continued to be genetically linked to Catherine; even when Henri IV divorced Catherine's daughter, he married her cousin. Perhaps this is the ultimate revenge from the sinister side of the gene pool.

Mickey Mantle

Like our previous example with Muhammad Ali, Mickey Mantle, as a sportsman, had a professional life truncated into a relatively few years: in his case, from his debut with the New York Yankees in 1951, until just before the beginning of the 1969 season.

Key events, mainly during that time, are shown in Table Nine. We begin with his rookie year, when Mantle was put into the stressful position of being new kid on the block during the very popular Joe DiMaggio's final year. Mantle was already tapped to be Joe's successor, and the fans were skeptical at best—until Mantle distinguished himself.

While neither Mantle nor DiMaggio's birth data is of the best quality from our standpoint—both are "C" in their Rodden Ratings—one interesting observation is that they both have early Sagittarius Ascendants: Joe's is about 1°, Mickey's about 7°.

Mickey's rookie year was an 8th House profectional year. The Almuten of his 8th House is Jupiter, technically with dignity only by Face, but being nighttime Triplicity ruler. Jupiter is diurnally placed in a diurnal chart in a diurnal sign: it is in *hayz*. During the course of 1951, Pluto had been transiting this Jupiter. This transit was not universally good for Mantle, because he ended up spending part of the season back down in the Minor Leagues when he acquired a hitting slump.

In an 8th House profectional year, Mantle's accident susceptibility is given by the 6th from the 8th House, which is the radix 1st, also ruled by Jupiter. On the day of his knee injury during the World Series, the transiting South Node was conjunct his natal Neptune. The cause of injury? He tripped over a partially buried drainage pipe! Transiting Mercury and Saturn has just finished conjoining his natal South Node, so he definitely had a double South Node whammy. For good measure, Saturn (knees) ruled his profected 3rd House of locomotion.The good thing for him earlier in the season was that transiting Jupiter was going over his Fortuna and North Node, and trining his radix Ascendant. He *did* manage to acquit himself very well in this year, despite the injury.

Table Nine. Events in the life of Mickey Mantle.

1951. Mantle's rookie year. Injured knee during the World Series.	Age: 19	House: 8th
1951, Dec. 23: married Merlyn Louise Johnson.	Age: 20	House: 9th
1952, May 6: Father died.		
1953, Apr. 18: hit home run 565 feet.	Age: 21	House: 10th
1953, Oct 4: grand slam in the World Series.		
1953, Nov. 2: knee operation that costs him 24 games in '54.	Age: 22	House: 11th
1956: Triple Crown of Batting, Most Valuable Player for AL.	Age: 24	House: 1st
(Award given November, which is next profectional year.)		
1957: second consecutive MVP	Age: 25	House: 2nd
1961: in contention for Babe Ruth's one-season home run record; until injuries took him out of the lineup in September; played hurt in the World Series.	Age: 29	House: 6th
1962, May 18: muscle tear; out 30 games. Wins Gold Glove.	Age: 30	House: 7th
1963, June 5: breaks third metatarsal in left foot; out 5 weeks.	Age: 31	House: 8th
1964, Oct 10: breaks Babe Ruth's record for most homers in the World Series.	Age: 32	House: 9th
1967, May 14: hits his 500th home run.	Age: 35	House: 12th
1969, Mar. 1: announces his retirement.	Age: 37	House: 2nd
1974: inducted into the Hall of Fame.	Age: 42	House: 7th
1995, June 8: receives a liver transplant.	Age: 63	House: 4th
1995, Aug 13: dies of cancer which had metastasized.		

After the season was over, he married, and several months later, his father died. This was a 9th House year. Mantle's 9th House is ruled by the Sun, and Jupiter and Neptune are in the 9th House. At the time of his wedding, the transiting Moon was conjunct his Sun-Mercury. In Mantle's natal chart, Mercury rules his wife. Transiting Mercury was trine Mantle's Jupiter and Uranus. In this profectional year, Saturn and the Moon rule his marriage partner. Transiting Neptune was trine his Moon, and square his Pluto, while transiting Mars was square his Saturn and opposite his Uranus.

His father died about 6 months into this 9th profectional year. His father was given by the 4th from the 9th House, or the 12th House: his father's death by the 8th from the (radix) 12, or the 7th House. (It's interesting that Mantle's wife and his father's death are both the radix 7th House in a 9th House profectional year.) In his natal chart, the death of the father is the 8th from the 4th, or the 11th. In both radix and profection, his father is given by Mars: Mars rules the profected 4th, and is Almuten of the radix 4th. Mars is an appropriate Significator, because Mutt Mantle had drilled his son in baseball since before Mickey was six. Mutt's death as shown in the profected chart, Mantle's radix 11th, can be given by the Almuten Saturn (dignified in Capricorn), or by Mercury or Venus, the later sign ruler of the 11th and posited there. Since we are talking about death, I would prefer to use Venus, since she is in Detriment. Transiting Mars was conjunct Mantle's Venus the day his father died. Transiting Pluto at 19° Leo was still hovering around Mantle's Jupiter, one of his own Significators. Clearly, the death of one's father can be a shattering experience.

The following year, Mickey's profectional 10th House year, was marked by pyrotechnics. He was capable of hitting absolutely towering home runs, and on April 18, 1953 he hit a monster estimated at 565 feet. Mercury, ruler of his profected 1st House and profected 10th House had just entered Aries to conjoin his Part of Fortune and North Node! Profection or not, I think a feat like that is unequivocally Mars, and transiting Mars was opposite his natal Mars, sextile his Pluto. Throughout this season, the Saturn-Neptune conjunction of the year was hovering around, opposite Mickey's Sun-Mercury and square his Pluto, while transiting Uranus was squaring his natal Uranus and conjoining his Pluto. Mickey's tightest aspect configuration was his Mars trine Pluto, with his Moon square Mars and quincunx Pluto. A little activation of this configuration was evidently a good thing!

By the World Series Saturn had come up to conjoin Mickey's Mercury, ruler of both the profected year house (10th) and the profected 10th from the radix 10th House, the 7th. Saturn had spent most of the baseball season transiting his 11th House, the radix house of dreams and wishes.

After the end of the '53 season, and after his birthday, Mickey had a knee operation which kept him out of the first month of the '54 season. In the 11th profectional year, the 6th from the 11th is the 4th House, (sign) ruled by Jupiter, with Mars Almuten, and Uranus in the house. The transiting nodal axis was square Mickey's Mercury, while transiting Uranus was a few minutes from exactly trine his natal Mars, and transiting Neptune was at its own contra-antiscion. Transiting Uranus was contra-antiscial to his Ascendant.

In 1956, Mickey had his best year yet, and arguably the best of his career, winning his first Most Valuable Player Award, but also achieving the batting Triple Crown, a feat much rarer. This was a 1st House profectional year. Throughout the Season, Pluto was occupying the 26th degree (until July) and then the 27th degree (until mid-August) of

Leo, sextiling Mickey's Sun, and then Mercury. Transiting Neptune retrograded back as far as his Mercury, turning stationary Direct *exactly* on his Mercury on July 9th. Mercury rules Mickey's 7th House, his opponents or the opposing team, so all that station did was make him invisible to his opponents! Functionally speaking, what does that mean? It means that they didn't know how to pitch him, or how to play against him. Not a bad camouflage! Who says Neptune transits can't be "good!"

1957 was the second consecutive MVP year, a second House profectional year. Now Mickey's opponents were given by Pluto, Jupiter, or the Moon, depending on whether we assign the planet in the profectional 7th, the Almuten, or the sign ruler of the profected 7th. Transiting Neptune was occupying the low degrees of Scorpio: Mickey was no longer confounding the other team the same way he had the previous year. Transiting Pluto never quite got back to sextiling his Mercury, but made its first pass into Virgo. Transiting Uranus was trining his Fortuna, North Node, and Ascendant. Mickey himself was given by Capricorn, profected 1st House ruler, and transiting Saturn was retrograding back over his Saturn antiscial degree, going direct conjunct his natal Ascendant. Thus, we see two consecutive years of significant stationary direct points partile in his chart, even with Saturn crossing his Ascendant, the profected 12th House.

1961 began as a very good year for Mickey, as he and Roger Maris both began a quest for Babe Ruth's single season home run record. Mantle was actually ahead of Maris when injuries forced him out of the race in September: Maris went on to claim the new record. 1961 was a 6th House profectional year, which already warns of events of a 6th House nature: *i.e.*, injuries. Mantle's 6th House ruler, Venus, is in Detriment, diurnally placed, and sextiling Neptune. None of this gives support to Venus. During 1961, transiting Neptune had passed over Mickey's natal Venus, and was retrograding back towards her, turning stationary Direct just one degree away (8°)—*so* close. In horary, this would be a refranation, although in the reverse direction from the way it is normally considered. (Normally, a refranation occurs when the transiting planet goes retrograde prior to forming the aspect, not here where it turns direct before conjoining.) However, as Neptune was teasing his Venus, transiting Pluto was doing the deed by sextile from early Virgo.

So the question: why was it a good year up to the later half of the season, when injuries mounted up? If we look at Mickey's 6th House, the house itself occupies 23°. The portion with Taurus ascending is 15/23 = roughly 2/3. That's 8 months. So, counting from October, this means that through June, Taurus was the profected Ascendant sign, with Gemini beginning roughly in July. The season opened with transiting Uranus opposing his Moon, turning Stationary Direct less than a degree away from the opposition on April 29th. Now the breaking of any established record could be considered a Uranian matter. Mars had charged up and conjoined his Pluto this month, and transiting Jupiter and Neptune were hovering around square each other, square and opposite Mickey's Venus. In a 6th House profection year, Venus rules both Mickey's profected 1st *and* his profected 6th, so health and injury are more closely connected than usual. Once again, Mickey was being invisible to the pitchers. Then in July we add Mercury and Jupiter to the mix, as the profected 1st/7th House rulers begin to change. And so what is going on with Mercury? How about a square from transiting Saturn! Mantle had his Saturn return in the off-season, but now Saturn was retrograding back to square his Mercury and Sun. Bye bye, health! Just coincidentally, Saturn retrograded back and turned Stationary Direct a degree from opposite Mickey's natal Pluto, one of the three critical planets in his 22° power configuration of Moon-Mars-Pluto.

The next year, injuries continue in his 7th House profectional year, yet his fielding is good enough for him to win a Gold Glove. Transiting Pluto is living on Mickey's Neptune for the season, squaring his Ascendant. Neptune is staying off his chart: pitchers can see him, but I suppose this *did* help his fielding!

If Pluto doing his Neptune isn't enough in '62, things get even more grim in 1963, when he breaks a bone in his foot. And he doesn't get a Gold Glove! Now it's an 8th House profectional year. Mickey's health is now at the disposal of Pluto, Moon and Jupiter. Saturn was transiting his Moon, squaring his Mars, and quincunx his Pluto. Any questions?

The next year, fireworks of a better kind were in store, when in a 9th House profectional year, he broke Babe Ruth's record for the most lifetime home runs in the World Series. This was a cycle up from his second year in the Majors, when he finally established himself as not just another flashy rookie. In 1952, Mantle batted over .300 for the first time, batting .311. In 1964, Mantle batted over .300 for the last time, batting .303; also leading the League in On-base percentage. Being a 9th House year, Mantle is given by the Sun, Jupiter and Neptune, ruler of and planets in the 9th House. On the day he broke Ruth's record, the transiting Sun was partile opposite Mickey's Uranus.

From then on, his career declined. He never again led the League in any percentage. Even so, we highlight one more playing accomplishment, one which is a function of longevity: his 500th home run. In a 12th House profectional year, with Mars ruling his profectional 1st, Mickey did the deed with transiting Neptune partile conjunct his Mars!

The use of Neptune transits in Mickey's case illustrates a humorous side to Neptune transits. One of the side-effects of a Neptune transit is that on some level, you cannot be seen. Now, most of the time, from the standpoint of accomplishment and success, this is not such a good thing. However, Mickey's situation shows the positive side. The game of baseball involves the constant dual between pitcher and batter. The ability of one to confound the other can spell out success. There is a long history of particular hitters who could nail particular pitchers, and pitchers who could nail particular hitters. In Mantle's case, one such pitcher who had his number was Dick "Monster" Radatz, a relief pitcher. In 1962–1966, Mantle managed only one hit (a home run) in 63 at bats, striking out 47 times. Radatz was born 2 April 1937,[11] with Venus dignified in Taurus, conjunct Uranus, opposite Mickey's Venus, Mars in Sagittarius, just the 12th House side of Mickey's Ascendant, Jupiter square Mickey's Sun-Mercury, and opposite Mickey's Pluto, and Pluto partile square Mickey's Sun.

At any rate, while Neptune transits could add to Mickey's success, we have to remember two things. First, he already *was* recognized. Had he been a Minor League player, transiting Neptune might simply have made him *more* obscure. Second, baseball is one of those rare things: a job in which performance is meticulously measured year after year, player after player, with countless statistics that are mostly unaffected by judgment calls. Thus, if Mickey had more home runs in any year than anyone else, there was no way to hide it. How many of the rest of us have our lives so objectively measured? Thus, Mickey could benefit from Neptune in a way that few of us can: by taking advantage of confounding others. Of course he also spent these years confused and in an alcoholic haze, as we now know.

When Mickey retired in 1969, it was a 2nd House profectional year, ruled by Saturn. Transiting Saturn-Venus was square his Pluto, quincunx his Mars, and sextile his Moon for the announcement. In 1974, he was inducted into the Hall of Fame with transiting Neptune conjunct his Ascendant!

Finally, we consider his last months. We have already examined the chart for his transplant operation in the last chapter. Mantle was in a 4th House profectional year: his health was ruled by Mars (Almuten ruler), Jupiter (sign ruler) or Uranus. During this health crisis, Uranus and Neptune were variously squaring his Sun-Mercury in his profected 8th House. Transiting Jupiter was prominent, going over his natal Ascendant and squaring his Neptune. Jupiter transits are not real welcome when the diagnosis is cancer. In the profected chart, the 8th House is the 8th from the 4th, or the radix 11th House. Transiting Uranus was partile square his Mercury, one of his 8th House profectional rulers. At the time of his death, there was a Moon-Saturn conjunction in 22-23° Pisces, that aspected his power degree, the degree of his Moon, Mars and Pluto. This conjunction was right on Mickey's 4th House cusp, his physical body in a 4th House profectional year. His radix 8th House Almuten was Jupiter; transiting Venus, ruler of the profected 8th House, was conjunct his natal Jupiter in his profected 6th. Transiting Jupiter was conjunct the Ascendant.

Comments

The obvious question to ask at this point is why, since profections are so easy to do, did they drop out of Astrology? I think we shall find the answer in John Partridge.

Why Partridge? As I discussed in *Essential Dignities*, John Partridge was Rafael I's link to classical method.[12] Partridge discusses profections in his *Vade Mecum*.[13] His explanation of the method of calculating profections is correct, given that it follows the Medieval official practice of profecting each house cusp by 30° per year. But notice that this is not what we have done here. The 30° rule essentially assumes equal houses, and in fact goes back to the Greek system of whole sign houses. Thus, in a whole sign system (or even equal houses off the Ascendant or M.C.), moving the Ascendant 30° *is* equivalent to moving exactly one house in sequence. In Mantle's case, the 2nd Year profectional Ascendant would be 7° Capricorn, the 3rd 7° Aquarius, the 4th 7° Pisces, and so forth. Now this starts getting complicated, because the profectional house cusps are *not* falling on the natal cusps. Now we have to draw a new chart. This system ceases to be so nicely simple unless we either use equal houses or dispense with the 30 ° rule.

Furthermore, it is important to consider what Partridge actually proposed doing with profections. He proposed using this 30° per year system to direct the angles to critical placements in the chart, like Saturn. This then becomes a stand-in system for that bane of calculational systems, primary directions.[14] Used in this fashion, profections are essentially a pain in the butt to work with on a manual basis, *i.e.*, without a computer.

Now, I hasten to emphasize that Partridge's definition was correct for the time, and true to usage as it was understood in the 17th Century. Lilly's description was more complete, since he also gave the systems of monthly and diurnal profections, adding that diurnal profection is "more scrupulous than necessary,[15]" *i.e.*, more trouble than its worth.

This is perhaps one of the most glaring cases in practice where we run up against the philosophical difficulty posed by unequal houses. Does a profection really mean one sign for a year, or one house for a year, because when the technique was developed, *these two statements were equivalent.* As long as the use of profections was as a directional system, awkward as that may be in practice, the incompatibility of whole signs and unequal houses did not have to be addressed. However, if we are to use profections descriptively as I have used them in this chapter, the difference is glaring.

Essentially, I have demonstrated the technique of profection within the context of a modern reading, not a classical one. The style I have used, of highlighting particular houses, and then examining transits to the house rulers or planets in the house, is a contemporary style. I have bowed to classical method in using classical rules for determining house rulers (ancient rulers and Almutens). The *idea* of a house for a year derives from profection, even if it has been developed in independent ways by modern astrologers like Bruno and Louise Huber.

Working with profections in the truly classical manner, as a system for directing hylegical placements is a system I have found to be of mixed value at best. Frankly, I get better hits more consistently with Solar Arc directions. For experimentation, however, I do recommend working with the 360° or the 90° dial, because that is the easiest way to visualize either type of direction.

Of course, we could solve this dilemma completely by adopting the Greek system of whole sign houses. It may be that, as more people work with profections, this will be the preferred solution. But maybe not!

In the next and final chapter, we shall return to this important question of putting classical method into context, as we attempt to integrate the Old with the New as we face the next Millenium.

Source for Chart Data
Nancy Hastings: from herself. Time of her death was reported by her daughter.

Source for Ancient Positions for Catherine de Medici
Trédaniel, Guy, Ed. 1985? *Les Grandes Éphémérides. Tome Premier 1500-1699.* Gabriel.

Endnotes
[1]   Barbara Tuchman. 1981. *Practicing History.* Knopf: New York. Page 18.
[2]   The reason I have not chosen to cover primaries, one of the principal classical systems for directing the chart, is in large part because of the controversy about how to calculate them. Until we have a chance to work with the Directions once the calculational controversy has died down, it is better to defer judgement on the technique.
[3]   Braha, page 233.
[4]   For example, her talk "Transits from Saturn on Out" at the United Astrology Congress, April 13-18, 1995 in Monterey, California. Note that Doris is a trained

cosmobiologist, and thus generally one who favors tight orbs. Even so, she has worked with whole sign aspects successfully with her clientele.

5   *Op. cit.*, pages 7-8.

6   Note that, unlike the other manifestations of profectional interaction with transiting planets, Jupiter transits *will* tend to repeat from cycle to cycle, because the sidereal cycle of Jupiter is approximate 12 years, so Jupiter is in synch with the profectional cycle by definition.

7   The modern tendency to step around the chart in units of two houses is not a classical Western technique, but a Vedic one. The Western classical tendency for examining a second child in this case would be one of two: either to take the second sign ruler of the 5th House (or radix 4th in this case), Mars ruling Scorpio, or to take the second Triplicity ruler for the cusp. In that case, we would use Saturn, the daytime Triplicity ruler of the air signs, since Libra is on the cusp.

8   Like many predictive techniques, profections had a system for predicting when, during the time interval in question the appropriate events would occur. In the case of profections, the general idea is to calculate the relative position of the planet within the house. Thus, the North Node in Ali's chart is 4° into a 26° house: thus, the "exact" profectional hit would be 4/26 = about 56 days into the year (Jan 17 + 56 days = Mar 14). Both of his successful defenses for the year occurred during this segment. If we were to use whole sign house profection, then this hit would occur just over halfway through the year, 194 days after his birthday (16°/30°). Ali was stripped of his title April 30. The North Node hit was complete in the later form of profection, but not in the earlier Hellenistic whole sign profection. But see discussion leading up to note 12, later in this chapter.

9   In all contest horaries and electionals, your opponent's Significator in your house means that the opponent is at your disposal. The ball is in your court, so to speak.

10   Using the portion of the House as a time indicator, the beginning of Virgo would come at 12°/23°, 12° being the number of degrees remaining in Leo from the 1st House cusp of 18° Leo, or late June.

11   Birth dates of professional sports players are available through a number of sources; the standard source in the United States is the *Sporting News*, but many countries have compendia of biographies and lifetime statistics on their major sports: these listing usually include the birth date and location.

12   *Op. cit*, pp 98-100.

13   *Op. cit.*, pp 218-224.

14   Now does this system work? I used this system to calculate Mickey's profectionally directed M.C. at the time of his death, and it came out to 16° Capricorn 45', close enough to his Saturn to be within rectification range! When he broke his metatarsal in 1964, the profected Ascendant in this system came up to 26° Cancer, square his Sun and in his 8th. But directions are supposed to be by conjunction. Checking his profections for his marriage, the only significant hit was profected Moon directed to 17° Libra, opposite his Uranus and square his Saturn, not *exactly* the symbolism we would have in mind for a marriage. So shall we consider this method to produce rather "mixed" results?

15   Lilly, *CA*, page 716.

---- CHAPTER 15 ----
CHANGES

What was that popping sound?
A paradigm shifting without a clutch.

Scott Adams[1]

In your clothing, your food, your habits, your feelings, fi-
nally even your language you have repudiated your ances-
tors. You are always praising antiquity, but you renew your
life from day to day.

Tertullian (160?–230?)[2]

If Classical Astrology succeeds in becoming a major style of modern technique, it will be because of a paradigm shift in Astrology. In
this chapter I would like to consider this topic directly, and also what
this paradigm shift means to astrologers.

The term paradigm was popularized in Thomas Kuhn's 1962 work,
The Structure of Scientific Revolutions. This work, which has received
much attention both by scientists and philosophers of science, attempted
to define what constituted "normal" science. By studying "normal" as
well as "extraordinary science, Kuhn was able to reach a number of
conclusions about how scientists conduct scientific enquiry.

Kuhn studied the historical record and concluded that science is
practiced within a framework. This framework may be called a paradigm. A paradigm is a set of beliefs about how the world works. The
idea is simple: scientists (like everyone else) view the world through a
certain set of assumptions. These assumptions may be labelled paradigms. The assumptions one holds affect the kinds of questions one
can ask, the experiments one can think to perform, and the conclusions
one reaches.

For example, if I believe that God created the world in seven days, then I am not going to be especially concerned with how He did it. However, if I believe that the world evolved by contraction from a cloud of gases during solar system evolution, I may well be concerned with what kinds of attractive forces were operating to permit this contraction.

As long as I admit that I am making an assumption, little trouble will come of it. However, when I begin to believe that my assumptions are self evident, and that everyone else is deluded, then we have the basis for an inquisition or at least repression. I begin to believe that I am dealing with the facts, and that everyone else is chasing chimeras.

This danger is twofold. First is the danger that my assumptions look so "real." The other is simply that I have these assumptions for so long that I take them as given, rather than as provisional. Kuhn applied this reasoning to science (heretofore scientists had limited this methodology to "superstitious" religionists or metaphysicians). He found that when he examined the history of science, scientists operated within belief systems. These systems served a constructive purpose in suggesting certain questions to investigate, such as the question of contractive forces given above. However, the underlying paradigms at some point would prove to be imperfect. Evidence which could not be explained within the context of the paradigm would accumulate. Initially, this evidence would be treated as "anomalous," and attempts would be made to explain it away, or the evidence would simply be ignored. Eventually, enough contrary evidence would accumulate, and then a new paradigm would be put forward. Initially, experiments would be designed to test the predictive ability of the new paradigm (predictiveness is considered a necessary element of a paradigm, because without it there is nothing to investigate, and hence, no science), and if the new paradigm "worked," then the process of paradigm shift would occur. This shift process is more or less painful, because the scientists who "grew up" under the older paradigm usually find it difficult to switch. Scientists do not willingly forsake an old paradigm until they absolutely have to: inertia works with scientists, as well as everyone else. In the interim, most will do anything to ignore or discredit any evidence that suggests that their assumptions are out of whack. This is why Kuhn referred to paradigm shifts as revolutions: they represent a major discontinuity in "thought."

It should be obvious that scientists are not alone in resisting change to their cherished assumptions. It is dangerous when people fail to recognize that they are operating out of belief systems, just as the groups they oppose are operating out of belief systems. Unfortunately, there is no way to prove a belief system wrong, so instead of proof, one resorts to ridicule, falsification, or simply repression. The ability to embrace a new belief system appears to decline as one gets older and more entrenched in one's current system.

During the resistance phase, almost any tactic is used to prevent the dreaded paradigm shift. If a scientist makes an assertion, it does not follow that the scientist is acting in a "scientific" fashion. The tactics of ridicule and exception-finding - so common in the diatribes against astrology - are in fact the common ploys of desperate scientists. Stephen Jay Gould documented such tactics in the battles over evolution and recapitulation in nineteenth century biology:

> Natural history does not refute its theories by cataloguing empirical exceptions to them (while working within a paradigm that engendered the theory in the first place). With millions of potential examples in a discipline second to none for its superabundance of empirical information, how can a catalogue of counter cases ever refute a theory - especially when the theory itself allows a "reasonable" number of exceptions? Proponents can always furnish their lists as well. And since each list must include a ridiculously small percentage of all possible cases, how can a theory of natural history be rejected by simple enumeration? ... The biogenetic law [recapitulation] was not disproved by a direct scrutiny of its supposed operation; it fell because research in related fields refuted its necessary mechanism. If these arguments offend some scientists' beliefs about the way science should operate, they reflect, nonetheless, the way it does operate.[3]

The relevance of Kuhn's theory to astrologers lies in the fact that we appear to be living during one of the most profound paradigm shifts encountered in the past two thousand years. (I will refrain from speculating about what this has to do with the Age of Aquarius, but then, I'm certain the reader is awash with speculations!) Kuhn noted that there are hierarchies of paradigms: that is, a major paradigm, known as a metaparadigm, is the basis to which "lesser" paradigms are anchored. If the metaparadigm is successfully challenged, then the whole group falls like a house of cards.

The shift I refer to is of a metaparadigm which has been so entrenched for so long that it is virtually unconscious: the assumption that there is such a thing as an objective observer, in other words, the entire underpinning of the reductive approach.

The consequences of the reductionist metaparadigm to Astrology are quite interesting. Astrology is not inherently reductionist, although portions may be explored using reductionist methods. That very recognition goes a long way towards explaining the rabid hostility shown by the skeptics, who have so persistently engaged in publicity stunts such as circulating petitions to scientists stating that astrology is a form of superstition. Of course the scientists who sign are merely showing how low their own standards of rigor are by condemning something they have never studied. But the point is that the acceptance of astrology pushes the reductionist paradigm past the breaking point.

Astrology is not alone on the other side of this alleged boundary. We are "over there" with Eastern philosophy, Jungian psychology, quantum physics, fringe ecology, and numerous mystics through the ages. Not such a bad place to be.

As our society is confronted with a challenge to our collective belief system, so Astrology is being challenged with a possible paradigm shift of its own. For the last eighty years, the character delineation model of Alan Leo has reigned supreme. Astrology of the 20th Century has confronted the age by hitching its wagon to what was, at the beginning of the century, the rising star of the new science of psychology. Now, psychology is firmly entrenched in academia, and astrology is not. Whether Astrology provides the better model of personality may be debatable; in any case, the attempt to move astrology away from fortune-telling laws by aligning it with science has simply not worked.

And what have we lost in the process but a large portion of our art and craft? Mundane, horary, and electional astrology could never fit under the psychological umbrella anyway. These fields were allowed to atrophy to the point of embarrassment at the time of World War II (remember the predictions of "no war"). Further, they were relegated as "specialties," which was merely an excuse for not being proficient in them. Granted, today we have more access to timed birth charts than any of our predecessors, so horary is perhaps not as essential in daily practice. However, nothing beats either horary, or event astrology (such as sports forecasting) for honing technique!

As the 20th Century has progressed and we have put together our global society, the methods of different countries and regions are rubbing shoulders with each other more effectively than ever before. We live in the age of the visual, a tendency enhanced by television and film. Thus, dial techniques of Uranian astrology and cosmobiology have become common, precisely *because* they make it easier to visualize the hard aspects and midpoints. The computer age has allowed us to work with techniques like Astro*Carto*Graphy® that, while developed manually, would be too much hassle to work with without computers. It is no accident that the classical essential dignities and Almutens have come back into common usage in the aftermath of the appearance of these tables in popular astrology programs.

And just as the computer age has brought us speed and accuracy not to mention, the technique of the week, we have also seen the mushrooming of interest in going back to the future through Classical, aided and abetted by the massive translation of material previously unavailable to English-speakers.

In the course of this book, I have taken examples of techniques from as early as the Babylonians, through the 17th Century, with occasional forays into modern parallel developments. Is there anything that we can say about the rationale for using a technique from the Hellenistic period, or its later modification by the Arabs or the Renaissance astrologers?

In general, the Greeks favored a much simpler system of houses, primarily whole sign, compared to some rather hairy house systems developed later. In general, the Greeks favored aspects by sign, while later astrologers developed the concepts of orbs and degrees.

Who is right? As we have seen, both systems are in modern usage simultaneously, but with a different flavor to them. Aspects by sign are used to understand basic compatibilities, and then aspects by degree or orb are used to emphasize when the effect will be particularly strong.

Yet another wrinkle in this system is understanding the nature of how our forebears dealt with the concept of malefic planets. Having Saturn strong in your chart did not make you intrinsically evil. But Mars and Saturn were treated differently. For example, Saturn was given a sect of day because Saturn is *weaker* by day, being cold, while the day is warm. Mars was given to the night because it was better to cool off hot-headed Mars. In other words, the sect assignment was meant to tone down the more malefic qualities. Mars in a hot and dry sign like Leo was *too* excessively Mars, while a Mars in Pisces, being less effectively Mars, was considered less dangerous. Mars in sect is *less* martial, but also less problematic; Mars out of sect is *more* martial, and hence, more dangerous. A strong Mars, in other words, was a malicious or dangerous Mars. A weak Mars might be less martial, but more effective.

Part of the difficulty that we encounter now as we study these ideas is the full appreciation of the linguistic difficulties of studying so long a time frame in the multiple relevant languages. Greek is a very difficult language to us modern Romance language types, because ancient Greek was a very dense language. Each word had multiple meanings, and the meanings changed, often dramatically, over time. Furthermore, the Greeks engaged in a fundamentally different approach to naming new concepts than we do. When we have to describe a new thing, we invent a new name, often by relying on a mix of Latin and Greek roots. The Greeks did something else: they took a word which was already in use, and added a new meaning. Thus, the same word in Greek could apply to a completely mundane object, or to an advanced philosophical topic. Take the word *moira*, usually translated as fate.

Moira, like many Greek words, shifted considerably in meaning over time as philosophical schools came and went. If we begin in the pre-Homeric period, we have the following, according to Greene:

> For there stands behind the gods a shadowy reality, a fixed order rather than a power, a divine conscience, at times gathering moral grandeur, at times dreadful and oppressive to man, the reality known as *Moira*. If *Dike*, in the pre-Homeric world, stands for a rhythm in the time-flow of things, *Moira* suggests their orderly division in space, - men's lands and just portions, the roles and prerogatives of men and gods.... The exact color of the word *moira* depends, of course, on its context in each case; sometimes neutral, sometimes suggesting what must be and therefore should be, it often tends, particularly when it refers to the one lot that all must accept, the *moira thanaton*, to acquire, like *daimon*, an unfavorable meaning, and is given uncomplimentary epithets. Thus, in a polytheistic world *Moira* keeps order and assigns limits; she is just, or at least, not capricious...[4]

Please notice that *moira*, or Fate, applied to the Gods as well. At the Homeric stage, no possible conflict was conceived between the idea of Fate and the free will of Zeus or the other gods and goddesses: at this point in time, once established, the deities were just as subject to fate as mere mortals.

Homer lived before the time when Astrology had permeated Greek thought. As we move through the centuries to Plato, we find a completely different sense of the position of Man [*sic*] in the world. Gone is the overwhelming sense of Fate: Plato is concerned with the Soul (*nous*). Plato invokes the Demiurge, a creator God, a step in the direction of a kind of proto-monotheism. The Creator is not bound by Fate: "God indeed does what he can to impart his goodness to the world, by the continuous ordering of given materials..."[5] Plato, following Socrates, refers, whether seriously or in jest, to "divine dispensation" or "divine chance" (*theia physis, theia moira,* or *theia tyche*) which sometimes allays the likely results of human frailty or stupidity. Greene reminds us that even modern Greeks give credit for good luck to *"Agathe Tyche,* whose name they ejaculate when an issue hangs in the balance, and to whom, sometimes in association with *Agathos Daimon,* they in time give a cult."[6]

By Plato's time, the time of Hellenistic Astrology, the outlines which will remain familiar in Christian teaching are in place, and now good luck and Fortuna, not to mention grace and virtue, can modify and temper the impersonal consequences of Fate. Later, the Stoics adopted the more pessimistic position that Free Will is an illusion. Every action binds us into a chain of causality, until the very idea of Free Will is illusory. Now, all we can control is our attitude toward the inevitable:

> This ultimate connection of every last detail in the universe, past, present and future, here and in remotest space, with every other detail, - for example of the aspects of the stars with human actions, - is a bond of 'sympathy' between all the parts of the universe, and serves, together with the providence of Zeus, as the basis of the Stoic belief in the possibility of foretelling future events by divination. Chance (*tyche*) is excluded from serious consideration, as merely a cause inaccessible to man's reckoning.[7]

Later, of course, especially during the Roman Empire, Stoicism was softened to allow a degree of Free Will and a limit to Fate, although the ethical and moral position of indifference to the vagaries of fortune was maintained.[8]

So we see that the conception of the importance of Fate varied considerably during different Greek philosophical periods. But why do we care about all this, other than simply as interesting asides? The reason is that *moira* is the word the Greeks ascribed to degrees (as in, degrees, minutes, and seconds!) *Agathos Daimon* (literally, good spirit or demon) is the 11th House . We begin to appreciate that the very act of *measuring* the Heavens through the 360° circle had sacred considerations, according to whatever level belief one had in Fate and Free Will. We observe from the earliest meanings in the pre-Homeric period that "degree" had spatial connotations, but also *degrees* of Fate. Good luck, or Good Fortune were found in the chart in particular places or abodes, but were only accessible if your philosophical system allowed for escape from the wheel of causality.

As astrological writings moved out of Greek, and into Latin, Arabic, and finally modern languages, these sacred connections built into the Greek language were lost. To what extent did we maintain this knowledge? Or alternatively, to what extent is this "occult" meaning significant to our astrology and our culture? This is, to a great extent, a question of the relevance of the Hellenistic world-views to our own.

The concept of "progress" is a monotheistic, and possibly a Christian, artifact. Until then, time was cyclic. The next Golden Age might even be inhabited by identical people to the last Golden Age. The birth of Jesus created a gulf between time before His birth and time after. The serpent no longer swallows her tail, but instead creeps upward toward the Light.

Can we succeed in bridging the gulf between a sacred Hellenistic Astrology and a Metaphysical Astrology, midwifed by the Theosophical Society and several New Ages? And how important is either kind to the understanding of daily existence on the physical plane?

Consider, for example, a chart in which the Sun is at 0° Libra and the Moon is at 28° Aries. Is this an Opposition, or a Quincunx? If whole signs are used, it's an Opposition, but if orbs are used, it's a Quincunx. Ptolemy would describe this as an Opposition, and so we would then be free to discuss the polarity of the Qualities of Aries (Warm and Wet by Season, Fire by Triplicity) and Libra (Cold and Dry by Season, Air by Triplicity). In this case, we would emphasize the polarity of Fire and Air, the issues raised of relationship of self to others. Most moderns would see this as Quincunx, and now the issues of adjustment would come up: the difficulty of integrating. In this case, the seasonal qualities would more accurately describe the difficulties represented by the adjustment.

And yet both descriptions are true. The whole sign approach may turn out to be the key to understanding the metaphysical dimension of existence, because it emphasizes the qualities *per se*, without recourse to the *measurements* (degrees, *moira*) imposed by fate.

In this book I have essentially taken three courses: first, I defined some of the astrological conditions posed by classical astrologers, by providing a time line for various astronomical observations and philosophical developments, with their ensuing impact on techniques. Then, I presented a survey of some of the critical classical techniques and concepts, such as essential dignity, accidental dignity, sect, mutual reception and the Part of Fortune. Finally, I used classical method and technique as a jumping off point for a modern synthesis of such concepts as the quincunx, nodal cycle, and profections. In this third part, I illustrated the possibility for integrating classical concepts in ways that were never done in the classical period.

This sequence mirrors my own wanderings through classical method. I only took this path because I found that classical techniques provided answers I was not getting - or was not satisfied with - from modern methods. I only stayed on the classical path because I found that it provided me with deeper insights into the meaning of a chart. And I only combined classical concepts with modern styles of delineation when I found that *both* could be enhanced by the combination.

By studying the history of ideas, it becomes obvious that theories, speculations, and methods are inextricably enmeshed in a network of other theories, speculations and methods. An idea taken out of context often looks silly or superstitious. This is why we cannot simply bring back past methods without studying them, and ultimately adapting them:

we have not found that the entire cultural milieu of these techniques is totally worth emulating. Plato did not provide us with the only, nor even necessarily the best solution to leading a good life. Greek society had slaves. Women were chattel. Plato was a sexist pig by our modern standards!

Even so, we should not make the mistake of taking the present as the measure of the past, and so evaluate past ideas and methods outside their proper context. Thus, I do not dwell on Plato's sexism, even if it keeps me from romantically inserting myself into a daydream of the Academy of Athens!

We also have to recognize that there may be good reasons a technique has lost favor, and it is important to bear this in mind before unconditionally accepting a past practice. In this volume, I mentioned hurling-of-rays as an example of techniques best left to the pages of the Project Hindsight volumes, rather than incorporated into practice. Certain ideas about sect and spear-bearing may ultimately fall into this category, although not, I suspect, the entire doctrine!

As we learn about old techniques, or new ones, for that matter, we should attempt to answer certain questions:

1. Does the technique work consistently in contemporary charts?
2. If this is an old technique, why did it lose prominence?
    a. Was the technique eclipsed by other, better techniques?
    b. Are the questions addressed by the technique obsolete?
    c. Was the technique simply too difficult to calculate? (This is now easily fixed.)

Anthropologists tell us that we create our own culture. Through the process of that creation, we are changed. May Sarton expressed this concept beautifully when she describes how to write a novel:

> If you are not changed by your novel, if it does not teach you something you did not fully understand until you came to grips with it through setting your characters to work it out as if they really live and you lived through them all, then there is small chance that it will magnetize readers to the troubling questions it has asked.[9]

I would extend her observations to astrology by stating: if a device or technique does not change your way of looking at the world, if it does not extend your grasp on the human condition, if it does not provide you with new informtion, then that technique doesn't change you. And if that technique doesn't change you, it isn't worth your time.

Endnotes

[1]   *Dilbert* Aug. 25, 1995.
[2]   Cited in Boorstin (189), page 56.
[3]   *Op. cit.*, pages 167-168.
[4]   Greene, pp 13-14.
[5]   *Ibid.*, page 298.
[6]   *Ibid.,* pp 298-299.
[7]   *Ibid.*, page 340.
[8]   Cramer, pp 146-149.
[9]   May Sarton. 1980. *Writings on Writings*. Orono, Maine.

References

Note: several of the sources used as references in this work, although technically out-of-print, are available in xerographic edition from John Ballantrae. His address is P.O. Box 152 Station A, Brampton, Ontario L6V 2L1, Canada; (905) 450-7998. There are also some books available from Just Us & Associates, 1420 N.W. Gilman Blvd. #2154, Issaquah, WA 98027; (206) 391-8371. These books are noted as such, below.

Aaboe, Asger. 1980. "Observations and Theory in Babylonian Astronomy." *Centaurus* 24: 14-35.

Agrippa, Heinrich Cornelius. 1531, 1533. *De Occulta Philosophia Libri Tres*. Antwerp: J. Grapheus and Paris: Christianus Wechelus (both first book only). Cologne: Johannes Soter (full three books, 1533).

Agrippa, Henry Cornelius. 1651. *Three Books of Occult Philosophy*. Translated by J.F. London: R.W. for Gregory Moule.

al-Biruni, Abu'l-Rayhan Muhammed ibn Ahmad. 1029. *The Book of Instruction in the Elements of Astrology,* translated by R. Ramsay Wright, Luzac & Co.: London, 1934. Available from Ballantrae.

Alexandrinus, Paulus. circa 378 C.E. *Introductory Matters*. Translated by Robert Schmidt. Project Hindsight: Golden Hind Press: Berkeley Springs, WV, 1993.

Antiochus of Athens. 1993. *The Thesaurus*. Translated by Robert Schmidt. Project Hindsight: Golden Hind Press: Berkeley Springs, WV.

Aristotle, from W.D. Ross, ed. 1928. *The Oxford Translation of Aristotle*. Oxford: Oxford University Press.

Ashmand, J. M. 1822. *Ptolemy's Tetrabiblios or Quadripartite*. Private Reprint by Astrolabe: Orleans, MA. Also available from Wizards Press: San Diego.

Aveni, Anthony F. 1984. A View from the Tropics, pp 253-288 in E. C. Krupp, Ed. *Archaeoastronomy and the Roots of Science*. AAAS Selected Symposium/Westlake Press: Boulder.

Barnes, Robin Bruce. 1988. *Prophecy and Gnosis: Apocalypticism in the Wake of the Lutheran Reformtion*. Stanford University Press: Stanford, CA.

Barton, Tamsyn. 1994. *Ancient Astrology*. Routledge: London.

Bills, Rex. 1991. *The Rulership Book*. American Federation of Astrologers (AFA): Tempe, AZ.

Benjamin Jr., Francis S. and G.J. Toomer. 1971. *Campanus of Novara and Medieval Planetary Theory*. University of Wisconsin Press: Madison.

Bishop, John. 1689. *The Marrow of Astrology*. Fisher: London.

Blagrave, Joseph. 1671. *Astrological Practice of Physick*. Obad. Blagrave: London. Available from Just Us.

Boer, Charles, Translator. 1980. *Marsili Ficino: The Book of Life*. Spring Publications: Irving, TX.

Bonatti, Guido. *Tractatus Sextus*. Translated by Robert Zoller in successive issues of Astrology Quarterly 62(3): 33-38, 63(1): 15-25, 63(2): 35-45, 63(3): 16-22 (1992-1993).

Bonatus, Guido. 1676. *The Astrologer's Guide*. Translated by Henry Coley. Facsimile printing of the 1886 edition in 1986 by Regulus Publishing Co., Ltd.: London. Also available from Just Us.

Boorstin, Daniel J. 1985. *The Discoverers*. Vintage - Random House: New York.

Boorstin, Daniel J. 1989. *The Creators*. Random House: New York.

Bouché-Leclercq, A. 1899. *L'Astrologie grecque*. Culture et Civilisation: Brussels.

Braha, James T. 1986. *Ancient Hindu Astrology for the Modern Western Astrologer*. Hermetician Press: Miami.

Brock, Arthur John. 1916, 1979. *Galen: On the Natural Faculties*. Loeb Classical Library: Harvard University Press: Cambridge, MA.

Burnett, Charles, Ed. 1987. *Adelard of Bath. An English Scientist and Arabist of the Early Twelfth Century*. Warburg Institute: London.

Cardan, Jerome. 1663? *The Book of my Life (De Vita Propria Liber)*. Translated by Jean Stoner, 1929. Available from Ballantrae.

Cherniss, Harold and William Helmbold, Translators. 1957, 1984. *Plutarch's Moralia XII: On the Principle of Cold*. Loeb Classical Library: Harvard University Press: Cambridge, MA.

Choisnard, Paul. 1983. *Saint Thomas d'Aquin et 'Influence des Astres*. fditions Traditionelles: Paris.

Coopland, G. W. 1952. *Nicole Oresme and the Astrologers*. Liverpool University Press: Liverpool.

Coley, Henry. 1669. *Clavis Astrologiae, or a Key to the whole Art of Astrology: In Two Parts*. Joseph Coniers: London.

Coley, Henry. 1676. *Clavis Astrologiae, or a Key to the whole Art of Astrology. New Filed and Polished in Three Parts*. Thomas Sawbridge: London. Available from Ballantrae and Just Us.

Cramer, Frederick H. 1954. *Astrology in Roman Law and Politics*. The American Philosophical Society: Philadelphia.

Culpeper, Nicolas. 1655. *Astrological Judgment of Diseases from the Decumbiture of the Sick*. American Federation of Astrologers: Tempe, AZ.

Cumont, Franz. 1911, 1956. *The Oriental Religions in Roman Paganism*. Dover: New York.

Cumont, Franz. 1912, 1960. *Astrology and Religion among the Greeks and Romans*. Dover: New York.

Curry, Patrick. 1992. *A Confusion of Prophets*. Collins & Brown: London.

Daniel, Clifton, ed. 1987. *Chronicle of the 20th Century*. Chronicle Publications, Inc.: Mount Kisco, NY.

Dariot, Claude. 1583. *A Brief and Most Easy Introduction to the Astrological Judgement of the Stars: Whereby Every Man May With Small Labor Give Answers to any Question Demanded*. Translated by Fabian Wither. Reprinted 1992 Just Us & Associates: Issaquah, WA.

Dariot, Claude. 1653. *A Brief Introduction conducing to the Judgment of the Stars, wherein the whole Art of Judiciall Astrologie is briefly and plainly delivered*. Translated by Fabian Withers and enlarged by Nathaniel Spark. London.

Dariot, Claude. 1558/1990. *Introduction au Jugement des Astres suivie d'un Traité des élections propres pour le commencement des choses*. Adapted to modern French by Chantal Etienne. Pardès: Puiseaux.

Davidson, Norman. 1985. *Astronomy and the Imagination*. Routledge & Kegan Paul, London.

Davies, Robertson. 1985. *What's bred in the Bone*. Penguin: New York.

Eade, J. C. 1984. *The Forgotten Sky: A Guide to Astrology in English Literature*. Clarendon Press: Oxford.

Ebertin, Reinhold. 1982, 1989. *Astrological Healing: The History and Practice of Astromedicine*. Samuel Weiser, Inc.: York Beach, ME.

Edlin, Richard. 1668. *Observations Astrologicae, or an Astrological Discourse of the Effects of a Notable Conjunction of Saturn and Mars*. Billingsly & Blagrave: London.

Ficino, Marsilio. 1975, 1978, 1981. *The Letters of Marsilio Ficino*. Three volumes. Preface by Paul Oskar Kristeller. Gingko Press: New York.

Forster, E.S., Translator. 1955, 1978. *Aristotle III: On Coming-to-Be and Passing Away*. Loeb Classical Library: Harvard University Press: Cambridge, MA.

Gadbury, John. 1658. *Genethlialogia, or The Doctrine of Nativities Together with The Doctrine of Horarie Questions*. Printed by J[ohn] C[oniers] for William Larner. In production: Regulus Publishing Co., Ltd.: London. Horary portion available from Just Us.

Garin, Eugenio. 1976, 1983. *Astrology in the Renaissance*. Routledge & Kegan Paul: London.

Gardner, F. Leigh. 1929. *A Catalogue Raisonné of Works on the Occult Sciences. Vol. II, Astrological Books*. Privately printed in London. Known to all its users as *Bibliotheca Astrologica*, available from Ballantrae.

Godwin, Joscelyn. 1994. *The Theosophical Enlightenment*. State University of New York Press: Albany.

Goold, G.P., Translator. 1977. *Manilius: Astronomica*. Loeb Classical Library: Harvard University Press: Cambridge, MA.

Gouchon, Henri-J. 1975. *Diccionario Astrologico. Iniciaci—n al levantamiento e interpretaci—n del Horoscopo*. Luis C‡rcamo: Madrid.

Gould, Stephen Jay. 1977. *Ontogeny and Phylogeny*. Harvard University Press: Cambridge, Mass.

Greene, William Chase. 1944. *Moira: Fate, Good, & Evil in Greek Thought*. Haper Torchbooks: New York.

Hand, Robert S. 1995. *Night & Day: Planetary Sect in Astrology*. ARHAT Monograph #1: Golden Hind Press: Berkeley Springs, WV.

Hellemans, Alexander and Bryan Bunch. 1988. *The Timetables of Science: A Chronology of the Most Important People and Events in the History of Science*. Simon & Schuster: New York.

Hephaistio of Thebes. Circa 415 C.E. *Apostelesmatics. Book I*. Translated by Robert Schmidt. Project Hindsight: Golden Hind Press: Berkeley Springs, WV, 1994.

Heydon, Sir Christopher. 1603. *A Defence of Judiaciall Astrologie, in answer to a Treatise lately published by M. John Chamber, &c.* Cambridge.

Hinze, Oscar Marcel. 1983. *Tantra Vidyā*. Aurum Verlag: Freiberg.

Howe, Ellic. 1984. *Astrology & the Third Reich*. Aquarian: Wellingborough.

Johndro, L. Edward. 1934. *A New Conception of Sign Rulership*. Reprinted by American Federation of Astrologers: Washington, D.C.

Jones, W.H.S., Translator. 1939, 1984. *Hippocrates I*. Loeb Classical Library: Harvard University Press: Cambridge, MA.

Jones, W.H.S., Translator. 1923, 1981. *Hippocrates II*. Loeb Classical Library: Harvard University Press: Cambridge, MA.

Jones, W.H.S., Translator. 1931, 1992. *Hippocrates IV*. Loeb Classical Library: Harvard University Press: Cambridge, MA.

Julevno. 1912. *Nouveau Traité d'Astrologie Pratique avec Tableux, Figures et Tables astronomiques Permettant d'ériger un Horoscope scientifique d'établir très facilement les dates des événements de la Vie*. Bibliothèque Chaornac: Paris.

Kirby, Richard and John Bishop. 1687. *The Marrow of Astrology*. London: Joseph Streater for John Southby. Available from Just Us.

Kitson, Annabella, Editor. 1989. *History and Astrology: Clio and Urania Confer*. Unwin Paperbacks: London.

Knappish, Wilhelm. 1967, 1986. *Histoire de l'Astrologie*. Translated by Henri Latou. Vernal: Philippe Lebaud.

Kuhn, Thomas. 1962. *The Structure of Scientific Revolutions*. University of Chicago Press: Chicago.

Lagarde, André and Laurent Michard. 1985. *XVIIIe Siècle. Les grands Auteurs français du Programme Anthologie et histoire littéraire*. Bordas: Paris.

Lehman, J. Lee. 1989. *Essential Dignities*. Whitford Press: West Chester, PA.

Lehman, J. Lee. 1992. *The Book of Rulerships*. Whitford Press: West Chester, PA.

Liddell, Henry George and Robert Scott. 1951. *A Greek-English Lexicon*. Revised by Henry Stuart Jones and Roderick McKenzie. Oxford University Press: Oxford.

Lilly, William. 1647. *Christian Astrology*. Reprinted in 1985 by Regulus: London. Also available: Just Us & Associates.

Lilly, William. 1652. *An easy and familiar method whereby to judge the effects of the Eclipses, Either of the Sun or the Moon*. Company of Stationers: London.

Lindberg, David C. 1992. *The Beginnings of Western Science*. University of Chicago Press: Chicago.

Little, Lucy. 1974. *Astrosynthesis. The Rational System of Horoscope Interpretation according to Morin de Villefranche*. Zoltan Mason Emerald Books: New York

Lundsted, Betty. 1984. *Planetary Cycles. Astrological Indicators of Crises & Change*. Samuel Weiser: York Beach, ME.

Massie, Robert K. 1967. *Nicholas and Alexandra: An Intimate Account of the Last of the Romanovs and the Fall of Imperial Russia*. Athenium Books: New York.

Maternus, Firmicus. 334. *Ancient Astrology Theory And Practice: Matheseos Libri VIII*. Translated By Jean Rhys Bram. Noyes Press: Park Ridge NJ. 1975. Available Ballantrae.

Moore, Thomas. 1990. *The Planets Within: The Astrological Psychology of Marsilio Ficino*. Lindesfarne Press: Great Barrington, MA.

Morin, Jean Baptiste (also known as Morinus). 1661. *Astrologia Gallica Principiis et Rationibus propriis stabilita atque in XXVI Libros distributa, Nonsolum Astrologiae Judiciariae Studiosis, sed etiam Philosophis, Medicis, et Theologis monibus per necessaria...* Hagae- Comitis.

Neugebauer, Otto. 1969. *The Exact Sciences in Antiquity*. Dover: New York.

Neugebauer, Otto. 1983. *Astronomy and History. Selected Essays*. Springer-Verlag: New York.

Neugebuaer, Otto and Van Hoesen. 1959. *Greek Horoscopes*. The American Philosophical Society: Philadelphia.

O'Neil, W. M. 1986. *Early Astronomy from Babylonia to Copernicus*. Sydney University Press: Sydney, Australia.

Oppenheim, A. Leo. 1969. "Divination and Celestial Observation in the Late Assyrian Empire." *Centaurus* 14(1): 97-135.

Paglia, Camille. 1991. *Sexual Personae*. Vintage/Random House: New York.

Partridge, John. 1679. *Mikropanastron, or an Astrological Vade Mecum, briefly Teaching the whole Art of Astrology - viz., Questions, Nativities, with all its parts, and the whole Doctrine of Elections never so comprised nor compiled before, &c.* William Bromwich: London. Available from Just Us & Associates.

Pelikan, Jaroslav. 1978. *The Growth of Medieval Theology (600-1300).* University of Chicago Press: Chicago.

Pelikan, Jaroslav. 1984. *Reformation of Church and Dogma (1300-1700).* University of Chicago Press: Chicago.

Potter, Paul, Translator. 1988. *Hippocrates V.* Loeb Classical Library: Harvard University Press: Cambridge, MA.

Potter, Paul, Translator. 1988. *Hippocrates VI.* Loeb Classical Library: Harvard University Press: Cambridge, MA

Potterton, David, ed. 1983. *Culpeper's Color Herbal.* Sterling Publishing Co.: New York.

Préaud, Maxime. 1984. *Les Astrologues à la fin du Moyen Age.* J.-C. Lattès: Paris.

Ptolemy, Claudius. 2nd Century A.D. *Tetrabiblos.* Translated by F. E. Robbins. Harvard University Press: Cambridge. 1971.

Raphael I Et Al. 1827. *The Astrologer Of The Nineteenth Century.* W.C.Wright: Edinburgh.

Ramesey, William. 1653. *Astrologia Restaurata; or Astrology Restored: being an Introduction to the General and Chief part of the Language of the Stars.* Printed for Robert White: London. Available from Just Us.

Rudhyar, Dane. 1971. *The Lunation Cycle.* Shambhala: Berkeley, CA.

Rudhyar, Dane. 1980. *Person-Centered Astrology.* ASI: New York.

Ruperti, Alexander & Marief Cavaignac. 1984. *Les multiples visages de la Lune.* ƒditions universitaires: Paris.

Salmon, William. 1679. *The Soul of Astrology. Horae Mathematicae seu Urania: the Soul of Astrology, containing that Art in all its parts, in Four Books, &c.* London. Available from Ballantrae.

Sambursky, S. 1956. *The Physical World of the Greeks.* Princeton University Press: Princeton.

Sambursky, S. 1959. *Physics of the Stoics.* Princeton University Press: Princeton.

Sambursky, S. 1962. *The Physical World of Late Antiquity.* Princeton University Press: Princeton.

Saunders, Richard. 1677. *The Astrological Judgment and Practice of Physick, deduced from the Position of the Heavens at the Decumbiture of the Sick Person, &c.* Thomas Sawbridge: London.

Schmidt, Robert, Translator. 1995. *The Astrological Record of the Early Sages in Greek.* Project Hindsight: Berkeley Springs, WV.

Schoener, Johannes. 1539, 1994. *Opusculum Astrologicum.* Translated by Robert Hand. Golden Hind Press: Berkeley Springs, WV.

Schwickert, Friedrich "Sinbad" and Adolf Weiss. 1972. *Cornerstones of Astrology.* Sangreal Foundation, Inc.: Dallas.

Sepharial. 1962. *The Manual of Astrology.* W. Foulsham & Co.: London.

Sibly, Ebinezer. 1817. *A New and Complete Illustration of the Celestial Science of Astrology; or the Art of fortelling future Events and Contingencies by the Aspects, Positions and Influences of the Heavenly Bodies.* The Propietor, at #17, Ave-Maria Lane, St. Pauls: London. (12th, or Posthumous Edition).

Sidonius, Dorotheus. 1976. *Carmen Astrologicum,* translated by David Pingree. B. G. Teubner Verlagsgesellschaft: Leipzig. Also available: Ascella: Nottsh.

Siraisi, Nancy G. 1990. *Medieval & Early Renaissance Medicine*. University of Chicago Press: Chicago.

Star, Ély. 1888. *Les mystères de l'Horoscope*. E. Dentu: Paris.

Stein, Werner. 1975. *The Timetables of History*. English language edition updated by Bernard Grun. Simon and Schuster: New York.

Sunstein, Emily W. 1989. *Mary Shelley: Romance and Reality*. Little, Brown & Co: Boston.

Tester, Jim. 1987. *A History of Western Astrology*. Boydell: Bury St. Edmunds.

Carl Payne Tobey. 1973. *Astrology of Inner Space*. Omen Press: Tucson.

Tompkins, Sue. 1989. *Aspects in Astrology*. Element Books: Longmead.

Thompson, R. Campbell. 1900. *The Reports of the Magicians and Astrologers of Ninevah and Babylon in the British Museum*. Volume II. Luzac & Co.: London. Available from Ballantrae.

Thorndike, Lynn. 1923-1958. *A History of Magic and Experimental Science*. 8 volumes. Columbia University Press: New York.

Tito, Placido. 1657, 1883. *Primum Mobile*. Translated by John Booker and originally published 1820. The Institute for the Study of Cycles in World Affairs: Bromley, Kent.

Trager, James, ed. 1979. *The People's Chronology*. New York: Holt, Rinehart & Winston.

Tuchman, Barbara. 1966. *The Proud Tower*. Bantam Books: New York.

Valens, Vettius. 2nd Century C.E. *The Anthology, Book I*. Translated by Robert Schmidt. Project Hindsight: Golden Hind Press: Berkeley Springs, WV, 1993.

Valens, Vettius. 2nd Century C.E. *The Anthology, Book II*. Translated by Robert Schmidt. Project Hindsight: Golden Hind Press: Berkeley Springs, WV, 1994.

Valens, Vettius. 2nd Century C.E. *The Anthology, Book II (concl.) & Book III*. Translated by Robert Schmidt. Project Hindsight: Golden Hind Press: Berkeley Springs, WV, 1994.

Vickers, Brian, Editor. 1984. *Occult and Scientific Mentalities in the Renaissance*. Cambridge University Press: Cambridge.

Vidal-Naquet, Pierre, ed. 1987. *The Harper Atlas of World History*. Harper & Row: New York.

Water, W. G. 1898. *Jerome Cardan: A Biographical Study*. Lawrence & Bullen, Ltd.: London. Available from Ballantrae.

Watters, Barbara. 1973. *Horary Astrology and the Judgment of Events*. Valhalla: Washington, DC.

Weiss, Adolpho. 1946, 1987. *Astrologia Racional*. Editorial Kier S.A.: Buenos Aires.

Wharton, Sir George. 1683. *The Works of that Late Most Excellent Philosopher and Astronomer, Sir George Wharton, Bar. collected into one Entire Volume*. Collected by John Gadbury. H.H. for John Leigh: London. Available from Just Us.

Whitrow, G. J. 1989. *Time in History*. Oxford University Press: New York.

Wilson, Collin. 1984. *Religion and the Rebel*. Salem House: Salem, NH.

Wilson, James. 1820, 1880. *A Complete Dictionary of Astrology*. Reprinted by Samuel Weiser: New York, 1974.

Withington, E.T., Translator. 1928, 1984. *Hippocrates III*. Loeb Classical Library: Harvard University Press: Cambridge, MA.

Zoller, Robert. 1980. *The Lost Key to Prediction: The Arabic Parts in Astrology*. Inner Traditions: New York.

Zoller, Robert. 1992. *Fate, Free Will and Astrology*. Ixion Press: Cliffside Park, NJ.

Key & References

** Items in the Englished Dariot that were added by Withers; i.e. items not in the original Dariot text

Lilly example charts:
(ex) page reference refers to example
* Lilly mentioned condition (including indirectly)
! Lilly did not mention condition
+ Lilly misidentified condition

AA = Antiochus of Athens. 2nd Century C.E. *The Thesaurus.*

AB = al-Biruni, Abu'l-Rayhan Muhammed ibn Ahmad. 1029. *The Book of Instruction in the Elements of Astrology.*

B = Bonatus, Guido. 1676. *The Astrologer's Guide.* Note: numbers are aphorism numbers.

C & CN = Coley, Henry 1669. *Clavis Astrologiae, Or A Key To The Whole Art Of Astrologie.* CN is used for the Section on Nativities.

CA = Cardan, Jerome. 1676. *The Choicest Aphorisms from the Seven Segments of Cardan, edited by William Lilly.* Note: numbers are aphorism numbers.

D = Dariot, Claudius. 1653. *Dariotus Redivivus, or a Briefe Introduction conducing to the Judgment of the Stars, wherein the whole Art of Juiciall Astrologie is briefly and plainly Delivered.*

DF = Dariot, Claude. 1558/1990. *Introduction au Jugement des Astres suivie d'un Traité des élections propres pour le commencement des choses.*

DS = Dorotheus of Sidon. 1976. *Carmen Astrologicum.*

F = Maternus, Firmicus. 334. *Ancient Astrology Theory And Practice. Matheseos Libri VIII.*

G & G2 = Gadbury, John. 1658. *Geneth lialogia, or The Doctrine of Nativities Together with The Doctrine of Horarie Questions.*

GBTS4 = Bonatti, Guido. "Tractus Sextus." Part 4. Translated by Robert Zoller in Astrology Quarterly *63*(3): 16-22.

JS = Johannes Schoener. *Opusculum Astrologicum.*

HT = Hephaistio of Thebes. Circa 415 C.E. *Apostelesmatics, Book I.*

L = Lilly, William. 1647. *Christian Astrology.*

MM = Manilius.1st Century C.E.? *Astronomica.*

P = Partridge, John. 1679. *Mikropa nastron, or an Astrological Vade Mecum, &c.*

PA = Paulus Alexandrinus. circa 378 C.E. *Introductory Matters.*

Pt = Ptolemy, Claudius. 2nd Century C.E. *Tetrabiblos.* Translated by F. E. Robbins.

R = Ramesey, William. 1653. *Astrologia Restaurata; or Astrology Restored: being an Introduction to the General and Chief part of the Language of the Stars.*

RS & S2= Saunders, Richard. 1677. *The Astrological Judgment and Practice of Physick, deduced from the Position of the Heavens at the Decumbiture of the Sick Person, &c.*

V1 = Vettius Valens. 2nd Century C.E. *The Anthology, Book I.*

V2 = Vettius Valens. 2nd Century C.E. *The Anthology, Book II.*

V3 = Vettius Valens. 2nd Century C.E. *The Anthology. Book II (concl.) & Book III.*

Classical Sources Index

1st House...L50, L129-167, C54-55, C76-79, D68, D75-76, D90-92(ex), DF65, DF72, DF95-96, P41, P61-62, G41-46, G242-249, R107
in elections...R132-134
Lord of Ascendant...G105-107, B50, B61, B77, B128

2nd House...L51-52, L167-187, C55, C80-83, CN106-110, D68-69, D76-77, D93-95(ex), DF66, DF72-73, DF97-98, P42, P62-63, G47-48, G107-110, G249-252, R109, B78, V2:17-18
accidents...L171
in elections...R134-139

Lord of, placement...L175, G108-109, B119

3rd House...L52, L187-201, C55, C82-84, CN111-113, D69, D95-100(ex), DF66, DF99-100, P42, P63-64, G48-49, G110-114, G253-258, R109, B8, V2:16-17
in elections...R140-141
Lord of, placement...G113-114

4th House (also see "End of matter")...L52, L202-222, C55, C85-87, CN114-116, D69, D100-103(ex), DF66-67, DF101-102, P43, P64-65, G50-51, G114-117, G258-263, R109, B8, V2:15-16
in elections...R142-151

Lord of, placement...G116-117
5th House...L53, L222-242, L602-606, C55, C88-
        90, CN128-130, D69-70, D103-105(ex), DF67,
        DF103-104, P43, P65-66, G51-52, G117-121,
        G263-268, R109, B8, V2:15
    in elections...R152-159
    Lord of 5th afflicted in 7th...B109
    Lord of, placement...G119-120
6th House...L53, L130, L131, L243-297, C55, C90-
        92, CN116-120, D70, DF67, DF105-106, P44,
        P66-67, G53-54, G121-129, G269-273, R109,
        B5, V2:14
    in elections...R160-174
    in marriage...DS274
    Lord of, placement...G128-129
7th House...L54, L130, L131, L297-404, C55, C93-
        100, CN120-127, D70-71, D105-108(ex),
        DF68, DF107-108, P44, P67-70, G54-56,
        G129-140, G273-283, R108, B6, V2:13-14,
        V3:1-6
    in elections...R175-188
    Lord of 7th in illness...B68
    Lord of, placement...G139-140
    Lords of houses in 7th...B109, B119, B120
    unfortunate planet in...L302
8th House...L54, L404-422, C55-56, C101-102,
        CN148-152, D71, D108-113(ex), DF68,
        DF109, P45, P70, G56-59, G140-150, G283-
        285, R108, B5, V2:12-13
    in elections...R189-190
    Lord of...L302, B114, B115
    Lord of, placement...G148-149
9th House...L55, L130, L422-444, L606-614, C56,
        C103-104, CN131-135, D71, D113-116(ex),
        DF68, DF111-112, P45, P70-71, G58-59, G150-
        158, G285-288, R108, B5, V2:11-12
    in elections...R190-196
    Lord of, placement...L130, L175, G156-158
10th House...L55, L130, L444-457, L615-634, C56,
        C105-107, CN135-141, D71-72, D117-120(ex),
        DF68-69, DF113-114, P46, P71, G59-61, G158-
        165, G288-290, R108, B8, V2:11
    in elections...R196-198
    infortunes or S. Node present...L298, C74
    Lord of, placement...L175, G164-165
11th House...L56, L130, L457-459, L634-639, C56,
        C107-108, CN142-145, D72, D120-123(ex),
        DF69, DF115-116, P46, P71, G61-62, G165-
        171, G291-292, R108, B8, V2:10-11
    in elections...R199-200
    Lord of, placement...L175, G170-171
12th House...L56, L460-482, L639-643, C56, C108-
        109, CN145-147, D72, D124-126(ex), DF69,
        DF117-118, P47, P72, G62-63, G171-178,
        G292-294, R108, B5, V2:10
    in elections...R201-202

Lord of, placement...G176-179
5 degree rule (i.e., planet within 5° of a house cusp
        is in the next house)...L391

—A—

Abortion...L229, L233, L604
Abcess, impostumations in the stomach/
        cancer...L95
Abduction...L463-464
Abscissor of life...G142-143
Abscissor of light...L184, DF54, JS46
Absent person, dead or alive?...L151, L156, L404-
        407, L417-418, C78, C112, D90-92(ex),
        DF95-96, P63, P314, G245-246
    brother L189, L196-199, D90-92(ex)
    condition...L430-431
    location...L153
    time of return...L407, L417-418
Accidental Debilities...D59-60, DF57-58, P29, P57
Accidental Dignities...L115, C35, D56-58, DF59-
        60, G88, P28-29, R66-67, AB315-317, HT32-
        33
Accidents, and timing...L130-132, L138, L140,
        L146, B2
    2nd House accidents...L171
    dead or alive...L197
    for good or ill...L148
    in the past, example...L138-139
    in the future, example...L140-142
    sudden happenings...L155
    timing...L198
Accidents & casualities...L134
Achernar...Pt57, R94
Acquire desired object?...C116
Adversaries...L383-385, P45, P277, P284
Advice, quality of...L194, C120, G257-258
Aestival (see "Estival")
Affairs, romantic...DF67
Affliction(s), ...P282, P325, P338, B5, B6, Pt267,
        Pt285, Pt431
    all manner of...L56
    to Moon...L301
Age, i.e. which is best...L134, L138
Al Hecka (see "Fixed Stars, Al Hecka")
Al Jabhah (see "Fixed Stars, Al Jabhah")
Alamac...R95
Albirto...R102
Albubater...L647
Albumazer...R124
Alchodon...L530, CN89-90, P80-81, P168, P81,
        P176, P251, P295, P307, G91-92, B141
    Table...CN89, G92
Aldebaran (see "Fixed Stars, Aldebaran")
Alderamin (see "Fixed Stars, Alderamin")

Alfridaries (also fridaria)...L733, P223, AB239, AB319
Algareb (see "Fixed Stars, Algareb")
Algenib (see "Fixed Stars, Algenib")
Algol (see "Fixed Stars, Algol")
Alioth (see "Fixed Stars, Alioth")
Alkes (see "Fixed Stars, Alkes")
Almugea (Faces as used by Ptolemy)... D53-54, DF57, JS41
Almuten (i.e., planet with greatest amount of dignity in a given zodiacal degree)...L49, L352, L511-512, L749, L758, L818, CN90-91, D77-80, DF75-77, P22, P30, P84, P298, G92-93, R111, B124, AB308, JS62
　Almuten different from House ruler...L152!, L162!, L165!, L177!, L196!, L200!, L219*, L240*, L286*, L415!, L421!(co), L442!(co), L452!(co), L455!, L473!
Alnilam (see "Fixed Stars, Alnilam")
Alphard (see "Fixed Stars, Alphard")
Alphecca (see "Fixed Stars, Alpheca")
Alpheratz (see "Fixed Stars, Alpherarz")
Alrucaba (see "Fixed Stars, Alrucaba")
Altair (see "Fixed Stars, Altair")
Althazer...R111
Ambassadors...L53, L235-238
　reason for meeting...L235
Ammunition...L53, L56
Amphibious signs...MM99-101
Anabibazon (North Node)...L49
Anaphora...L52
Anareta...L527, L529, L531, L694, L764, L829, CN150-151, P251, P309, AB324, Pt281-287
Angelus, John...CN80
Angetenar (see "Fixed Stars, Angetenar")
Angle of the Earth...L53
Angles...L48
　erect...AB150
Anguish...L299
Angular...L48, L130, P46, P68, P72, P149, P151, P152, P154, P155, P158, P211, P247, P296, P310, P320, P332, P343, P344, P345. MM145-149
Angularity, of significator...L301, Pt239
Animals
　if escape pound...L328
　if fled by self...L322
　if large or small...L324
　if in pound...L324, L325, L326
　if stolen...L321-323, L326, L334, L335
　large...L56, C137
　location...L326
　not stolen...L325
　small...C92, C126, CN118-119, G128, G272-273
　strayed...L319
　where...L327
Antares (see "Fixed Stars, Anatres")

Antiscia...L90-92, C20-21, P35-37, P202, P317, R76-77, AB227-228, G64-65, F58-68, AA19-20, JS53-54
　example...L164, L181, L186-187
　of the Moon...L299
Apheta...L527, L650, L700, CN87-88, P251, G90-91, R100, V3:27-57
Aphorisms...L298-302, C72-75, P264-348
　children...G120-121
　elections...C151-155, P264-274
　fixed stars...L648-650
　for physicians...L282
　friendship...CN143-144, G169-170
　health & sickness...L282-286, L577-581, D108-112, G121
　manners or conditions...G94-97
　marriage...L303, CN122, G136-137, V3:1-9
　nativities...CN75-77
　profession...CN138-139
　recovery...L356-L358
　revolutions...G212-215
Apogee...L31, D58, AB88-89, AB93-94, AB104
Appearance...(see "Physical characteristics")
Application...L107-108, C39, D45-47, DF49-50, G42-43, R110, B31, AB313, Pt113-117, Pt169, Pt209
　by square or opposition...L205
　donor...AB313
　follower...AB313
Aquarius...L98, C15-16, P9, P36, P46, P65, P76, P87, P97, P98, P282, P302, P335, G87, R90-91, B5, F296-298, MM243, V1:15-16, PA4, HT21-23, JS19
　diseases...L246
Arabicall...L307
Arcturus (see "Fixed Stars, Arcturus")
Argol, CN155, CN160, P106, P107, P178, P202, P203, P204, P210, P212
Aries...L93, C9, P4, P19, P35, P36, P41, P52, P65, P66, P73, P87, P97, P100, P279, P282, P287, P310, P311, P333, P343, G83, R86, B5, F282-283, MM233, V1:7-9, PA1-2, HT3-5, JS14
　diseases...L245
Arrest & Imprisonment...DS287-289
Artist, recognition...L298
Ascendant...L51, L129, L130, L131, L132, L620, P28, P38-P40, P44, P277, P279, P281-285, P287, P288, P290-294, P296-298, P300-302, P304, P307-309, P311-319, P324, P329, P331, P332, P337, P338, P340, P342-345, P347, AB149, B112, B125, B128, B133, B135, Pt229-235
　Crooked (CP-GE) or straight (CN-SG)...DS262-263
　degrees...L301
　near Significator...B67
　late degree...L298

Lord sq or opposite Ascendant...C73
  sign...B110
Ascendant lord...L48
Ascension, long and short...L92, V1:30-32
  square as trine...L181, L220
Ascensional Difference...C42
Aselli ((see "Fixed Stars, Ascelli")
Asking the Question...B1, B2
Aspects...L25-27, L105-107, C6-7, D42-43, D45-
  47, DF45-47, R92-93, F53-56, F184-203, Pt73-
  75, JS36-38
  application & separation...AB303-304, G42-43,
    AA27, PA37-39
  between pairs of planets
  Jupiter & Mars...V1:48, F185, F189, F195, F199,
    V2:27-28
  Jupiter & Mercury...V1:48-49, F185, F190, F195,
    F200, V2:23-24
  Jupiter & Moon...V1:48, F185, F189, F195, F200
  Jupiter & Saturn...F184, F187, F195, F197,
    V2:25-26
  Jupiter & Sun...V1:48, F185, F189, F195, F199,
    V2:18-19
  Jupiter & Venus...V1:48, F185, F189-190, F195,
    F199-200
  Mars & Mercury...V1:50, F186, F191, F196,
    F200-201, V2:24-25
  Mars & Moon...F186, F191, F196, F201, V2:20-
    21
  Mars & Saturn...V1:46-47, F184, F189, F190,
    F193-194, F196, F197-198, V2:26-27
  Mars & Sun...F186, F190, F196, F200, V2:20
  Mars & Venus...V1:49, F186, F196, F200
  Mercury & Moon...V1:50, F187, F192-193,
    F197, F203, V2:22
  Mercury & Saturn...V1:47, F184, F188, F194,
    F199, V2:22-23
  Mercury & Sun...V1:50, F201-202
  Mercury & Venus...V1:49, F192, F202
  Moon & Saturn...V1:47, F184, F194, F199
  Moon & Sun...V1:50-51, F191-192, F196, F202
  Moon & Venus...V1:49, F187, F196-197, F203,
    V2:21-22
  Saturn & Sun...V1:47-48, F184, F188, F194,
    F198, V2:19-20
  Saturn & Venus...V1:47, F184, F188, F194, F198,
    V2:25
  Sun & Venus...V1:49, F201, V2:19
  to bring to perfection...L124-128
  calculation of...L47
  coition...L106
  complex...F210-219
  congresse...L106
  conjunct eclipse...L301(30)
  conjunction not an aspect...G32
  diametrical radiation...L106
  opposition...L106
  out-of-sign aspect...L152, L196
  partile...L106, G42
  platick...L107, G42
  quadrangular...L106
  quadrate...L106, D42
  retrograde...L107
  squares of long ascension...L181, L219(ex),
    L289(ex)
  synod...L106
  to House cusp...L455(ex)
  unaspected planets...L140
Assistants...L51
Astrologer's Errors...B7
At home, is a party?...C78-79, C112
Athla, Circle of...MM171-175, V2:7-14
Attending planets...Pt241-243, AA23-24, AA39,
  HT35
Authorities...L55
Autumnall...L48, DF21
Azimene or deficient...L118, L121, L250, P244,
  G40-41, B5
Azimuth...AB134

— B —

Bargains...L297
Barren...L53, V3:10
Barren signs...L89, L96, L604, C4, D5, P3, P6, P9,
  P117, P118, P119, P124, P135, P138, P257
Baten Kaitos...R94
Beginnings...DS290-291
Beholding...L109, P35, P51, P63, P65, P70, P85,
  P86, P91, P99, P100, P111, P120, P126, P131,
  P138, P140, P141, P142, P154, P167, P181,
  P206, P213, P225, P237, P238, P240, P267,
  P288, P290, P292, P296, P303, P307, P319,
  P343, P344, P345, Pt77, PA27-31
Being away from home...V2:54-62
Bellatrix (see "Fixed Stars, Bellatrix")
Benan Elkered (see "Fixed Stars, Benan Elkered")
Bendings (i.e., points square the Nodes)...Pt325
Benefaction...AB310
Benefice...L432, L433, L734, C104, C134, G287-
  288
Benefics...P46, P89, P113, P131, P175, P192,
  P193, P202, P205, P206, P211, P213, P214,
  P224, P226, P226, P262, AB232-233
Besieging...L114, C41, P22, P29, P311, P322, G45,
  R111, B5, AB309, DS166, JS 41-42
Best part of life...G243
Bestial signs...L89, P4, P6, P244, P276
Betelgeuze (see "Fixed Stars, Betelgeuze")
Bethem...P274, P322
Betrayal...L473
Bicorporeal signs...L89, P3, P8, P69, P295, P301,
  P304
Biquintile...L32, C6, D42**

Birth
  bonding...L234
  condition after...L233
  day or night...L232
  defects...L269, G102-104, Pt261-265
  difficulties before...L226, DS162-163
  premature...323
  time of...L231, L232, L242
Blindness, incl. fixed stars...L581, CN117, P280, B129, Pt323, AA7
Body
  afflicted parts...L244
  constitution of...L51
  injuries...Pt317-333
  parts...L50, L269, C34, G125, RS14-16, F56
  table...L119, RS37-38, AB217-218
  planetary significators...L246-47, L269, RS14-15
Bondage & chains...DS287-289
Borrowing money...L173, DS278
  in elections...R134-135
Bos (see "Fixed Stars, Bos")
Bringing water to the house...L214
Brotherly love...L188
Brother(s)...L52, L187, L566, DF99-100, P42, P48, P63-64, B78, V3:11, JS87-88
  absent...L189, L196-199, C83, G254-255
  agreement or love...L188, L201, C82-83, C119, CN112-133, P63, G112, G253-254, DS179
  brothers and sisters...L564-568, G111, Pt251-255, DS178-182, V3:11
  discord or harmony...L195, L201
  electing to make friends of...R140-141
  fortune of...L566
  health of...L189-190
  significator of...L190-191
  status of...L197-199
  whether or not...L195, L201, CN111-112
Building
  a building...DS267
  a ship...DS281-286
Bum-bailies...L633
Business (see "Partnership" and "Lawsuits")
  if profitable...L446
  if shall gain...L370
  resources of...L457-8
  which is best...L371
Buying, mainly real estate
  animals...R172-174, DS270
  agreement of buyer & seller...L205
  buying & selling...L376-77, DF101-102
  if deal will be concluded...L205
  in elections...C155-156, P241-242, R136-138, R146-147, R172-174, DS270
  commodities...L376-377
  price...DS322
  real estate...L204, L219-222, DF101-102
  relocate...L371
  ships...DS281-286

— C —

Cadent...L48, L52, L54, L56, L130, DF61, P42, P51, P62, P296, P322, P323, P332, P340, AB149, B5, DS172, Pt239
  fortunes...L299
  Significators...L300, L301
Cancer...L95, C10-11, P5, P32, P35, P36, P43, P57, P65, P74, P83, P87, P100, P119, P135, P138, P141, P145, P167, P212, P219, P220, P230, P239, P241, P256, P259, P261, P269, P282, P287, P293, P296, P298, P302, P316, P334, P338, P344, G84, R87-88, B8, F286-287, MM235-237, V1:11-12, PA3, HT9-11, JS15-16
  diseases...L245
Canopus (see "Fixed Stars, Canopus")
Capella (see "Fixed Stars, Capella")
Capricorn...L98, C14, P8-9, P35, P36, P46, P65, P66, P76, P87, P100, P119, P135, P141, P145, P158, P167, P169, P220, P231, P239, P253, P260, P279, P294, P296, P299, P335, G86, R90, B5, F294-296, MM241-243, V1:14-15, PA4, HT20-21, JS18-19
  diseases...L246
Captive or slave...L463
Captivity...(also see "Imprisonment") L463-464, L642, G174-176
Caput Medusa...(see "Algol")
Cardin, Jerome...L647
Cardinal Signs...L300, DF21, P3, P8, P278, P285, P288, R81, Pt65-69, DS263
  in elections...R126
Career...L444
  if profitable...L445
Catabibazon (South Node)...L49
Cataphora (cadent)...L56
Cattle...L53
  strayed...L320-21, L325
  Moon as...L20
Cauda Draconis...L173
Caution...L132
Cazimi (i.e., located within 16' of conjunction with Sun; an accidental dignity)...L113, L300, L752, L761, C41, P21, P29, P251, R111, AB296, P278, G44, JS38
  lawsuit...L374
Change...G243
Chart, how to erect...L33-42, L519-523, C47-53, CN15-75, D80-84, DF79-83, G35-38, D112
Child, legitimacy...L318
  relationship to parent...L234
  sex of unborn...L228, L230-231, L240-241, C89, D104-105(ex)
  when will birth be?...L231-232, L240-242
    by day or night...L232-233
  whether shall live...L228-229
Child-bearing...L222-229, L231-233, L240-242

Children...L53, L602-606, C88, CN128-130, P43, P65-66, G120-121, G264-267, F251-252, Pt409-413, DS207-211, V3:10
  boy or girl...L53, L227, L228, L230, L232, L241(table), DF103-104, G118-119, G266, DS210211
  disobedient...L53
  gender...G266
  health of...L53
  how long until having...L223
  if man will have by wife or any...L225
  if querent should have...L222, L238-L240
  if shall live or die...L225-226, L228, L233
  Jupiter as natural significator...L230
  length of life...G118
  lies about...L234
  not reared...Pt265-271
  number of...DS207-
  part of...L231-232
  paternity...L318
  twins?...G266
  when...L223-224, G264-265, G266-267
  whether a man shall by wife...L225-226
  will ever have?...L222-225, L238-240, C123, CN128, D103-104, P264, G117-118
Choleric signs...L48, C4, P4, P6, P8, P12, P13, P14, P39, P66, P335
Chronocrator...L733, F57-58, Pt451
Crooked (CP-GE) or straight (CN-SG)...DS262-263
Circles of position...C42
City (and country) Rulerships...L52, C157-160
Clergy...L55
Clergy question...L432, L437, L439
Clothes, color of...L51
Cold...L48, L298
Color...L50, L52-54, L86, C37
Collection...L126-127, D87-88, P50, P51, B4
Colors, of planets and signs...L86, C37, AB219
Coma Berenices...L581, R99
Combustion...L113, L123, L129, L130, L131, L132, L300, C41, C73, D53, D59, P21, P29, P51, P66, P69-70, P310, P322, P323, P325, P338, P340, P342, P345, G44, B5, AB64, AB296, R111, DS165, DS189, DS264, DS321, JS38-39
  health...L129
  Lord of Ascendant...L123
  Moon...L301(35), AB64-65, V1:37
  secret matters...DS264
  significator...L300(23)
    when combust planet is dignified...AA31
    worse if applying...DS221
Comet...L530, MM71-75
Commanding signs (AR,TU,GE,CN,LE,VI: See "Signs, Commanding & Obeying)
Commodities, buying & selling...L376-377
Common signs (see "Mutable signs")... L130, L131
Commotion...L132
Conception & infertility...L229, L238(ex), Pt323, Pt325

Conception, time of...L231, C12-14(table), D104-105(ex), AB329-330, V1:60-63, V3:60-66
  electing...R152-153
  if possible...L223, L226
  how long since...L231
  whether...L229
Condition of situation...L299
Confidence...L56
Congresse (i.e., conjunction)... L106
Conjunction...L26, L27, L106, L130, R92, B31, AB150-15-152, AB260, AB304-305
  opening the doors (opposing natures conjunct)...AB315
Considerations before judgment...L121-123
Constellations...MM269-
Contention (opposite of Hayz)...AB308
Contests, electing to win...R185-186
Contra-Antiscia...L92, P35, G64-65, R76-77, AB227-228, AA19-20
Contradiction...L299
Contrariety (retro aspects)...D51, DF53-54
Controversies...L297
Co-significator...L49
Cor leonis...(see "Fixed Stars: Regulus")
Corporature
  descriptions of...L84-86, L135-136, Pt307-317
  Jupiter...L63
  Mars...L66
Co[n]significator...L49, L51, P41, P42, P43, P44, P45, P46, P47
Counsel given: whether good or bad...L194
Countries, foreign...L55
Country (and city) Rulerships...L93-99, C157-160, P73-76, MM269-289
Country, where best to live...L137
Courts (see "Lawsuits")...L371-376
  who shall win...L373
Cowardice...DS195
Crisis in disease...L290-296
Critical days...L294-296
Critical years...V3:58-60, V3:70-71
Curable disease...L53
Cure...L53
Cusp, fortitudes...JS61-62
Cusp, planet near...L151

— D —

Daily motion of planets...L42
Damage...L51
  to querent...L302
Danger...L130, L157
  from that feared...L414
  by water...L132
Dariot...L258
Day...L53
  planetary...PA41
Dead Degrees...B58, AB304, Pt273

Deafness...L582, CN117-118, P11, P127, G127

Death...L54, L130-131, L156, L228, L274, L408-411, L527, L644-650, L763-764, C101-102, C132, P40, P45, P52, P66, P81, P82, P116, P120, P279, P280, P285-289, P296, P310, P321, P323, P344, P346, G140-148, G283-284, B16, B92, RS39-64, RS72-80, JS86-87
  arguments of...L255-258
  dead or alive...L151, L322, L404
  due to illness...L253-258, L286(ex), L289(ex)
  in marriage...L310
  in war...L368
  kidnapped...L322
  manner of death...L412, L419-420, G143-145, G284, Pt427-437, F193
  obtain spouse's portion...G284
  of parents...F244-245, DS176-177
  of querent...L408-411, L419
  of spouse...L411, L415-418(ex)
  of woman...L302
  pronouncement of...L132
  time of...L249
  violent...CN148-151, G145-148, F256-260, V3:11-26
  which spouse will die first...L411-412, L415-416, C102, C132, G285

Debilities of the planets...L105, L115, C35, G88, B4, JS55-60

Debilities of Fortuna...L145, C37, G89

Debt & the payment thereof...DS278

Decans...AA11-12, MM245-251. See also "Essential Dignities, Face."

Deceit by parties...L194

Decile...C6

Declination...L49, C42, P202, AB59-60sion")

Decrease...L174
  in Light...C42, D57, JS33
  in number...JS34

Decumbiture (a chart taken for the moment a sick person takes to bed)...L268-286, P66, P312, DS291-292, DS317-318

Defendant...L54

Deferred judgment...L300

Degree(s)...L28, Pt109-111, MM255-263
  ascensional...MM263-269
  azimene or deficient...L118, L121, L250, D40, DF38, P244, G40-41, B5, JS53
  deep...L116, L118, D39, JS53
  increasing or diminishing fortune...G40-41, AB271
  late...DS168
  light & dark...C6, D39, DF37, G40-41
  masculine & feminine...C5-6(table), D39, DF37, G40-41, AB269-270, F150-151, V1:36
  pitted...L116, L118, L121, P35, P299, G4, B5
  smoky...L116-117, C6, D39, DF37, G40-41, AB270, B5
  void...D39-40, DF37, G40-41

Delays...L299, L300, B6

Delight, house of...L53

Delphinus...L538

Demolishing a building...DS267

Deneb (see "Fixed Stars, Deneb")

Deneb Alchedi (see "Fixed Stars, Deneb Alchedi")

Deneb Algedi (see "Fixed Stars, Deneb Algedi")

Denebola...L666, R99

Derived Houses...L126-128, C70, D75, DF71-73, P51-52

Descriptions
  of people...L100, CN97-104
  table of sensitive degrees...L116

Destroyer of the question...L185, B92

Determining time of question...L166

Detriments...L130, L301, L452(ex), P27, P28, P98, P100, P102, P132, P148, P152, P167, P170, P189, P214, P244, P286, P338, P345, B4, AB237

Devoutness...(see "Religious")

Dexter (backwards in signs)...L108- 109, C7, D45-47, P24, P298, P309, P318, P323, P339, P341, AB225, AA22

Diametrical radiation...L106

Dignities, in perfection...G235, B5

Dignities of the planets...(see "Accidental and Essential Dignities")

Dignities of Fortuna...L145, C37, G89
  accidental...L103, L115 (table)
  essential...L101
  mixed...L387, L402

Direct (forward)...R110

Direct ascension...(see "Right Ascen

Direction, compass...L607-608, P65
  aspects for distance...L392(ex)
  finding...L202-204
  from sign of Significator... L390(ex), L392(ex), L470(ex)
  quarter of heaven...L139, L154, L204, L364-65, L392(ex), C37

Directions...L651-741, CN152-183
  converse...CN155
  duration of effects...L654-656
  latitude...CN156-158
  measure of time...L708-715, CN175-185, G206-209, G208(table)
  of the Ascendant...L656-668, CN171-172, P175-183, G183-190
  of the Midheaven...L668-679, CN172, P183-188, G190-193
  of the Sun...L679-691, CN172, P189-194, G193-198
  of the Moon...L691-703, CN172-173, P194-198, G199-205
  of Fortuna...L703-708, CN173, P199-202

Discord...L299

Disease (see also "Illness")...L54,
  L576, L577-581, C32-33, CN116-118, P4-15,
  P17, P18, P32, P40, P44, P52, P66, P112, P115,
  P125, P126-132, P172, P176, P177, P183,
  P189, P190, P192, P194, P196-198, P229,
  P295, P315, P321, AB223, Pt317-333, DS316-321
  application of the Moon to planets...S2:8-10
  by house...L245, G123-124, RS66-67, S2:24-45
  by planet...C32-34, P44, P66-67, P315, P321,
    G122, B68, RS19-22, S67-68, S2:10-18, JS28
  by signs...L245-246, RS16-18, RS127-192
  chronic...L248
  condition...DS319-321
  curable, incurable...L53, S2:19-24, S2:58-59,
    S2:79-80, DS316-317
  hot and dry...L248
  ill omen...L253
  in body or mind...L264-266, S2:80-85
  infirmities, physical...F243-244, F254-255
  leading to death...L252, RS39-64, RS72-80
  length of...L247, L248-249, L253
  on left or right...L263, L264
  quality of...L261
  recovery...L250, RS64-66, D108-113(ex), DS290
  recurring...L248
  related to setting malefics... Pt321
  short...L248
  treatment of...DS314-316
  visiting the sick...S2:68-76
Disjunct signs (see "Inconjunct")
Disobedient children...L53
Dispersion of substance...L52
Disposition, one-way...L219(ex)
Dispositor...P12, P81, P88, P89, P90, P91, P92, P95,
    P99, P100, P105, P106, P112, P115, P122,
    P150, P201, P208, P211, P229, P239, P243,
    P277, P300, P304, P308, P316, P334
  of significator...L300
Disputes (see "Lawsuits")
Distance...L154
Diurnal...L43, L178, P4, P5, P6, P7, P8, P9, P10,
    P11, P14, P80, P121, P122, P290
Divine matters, electing to study...R141
Dodecatemoria
  planetary...MM141-143, PA44-46
  zodiacal...MM137-141
Dowry...(see "Portion, Wife's")
Dragon's head (see "Nodes, Moon's")
Dragon's tail (see "Nodes, Moon's")
Dreams...L55, L434-435, L436(ex), CN133-135
  interpretation...L55, L434-437
  true?...G155-156
Dry...L48, L298
Duels...L54
  second...L51
Dwads...Pt109

— E —

Early degrees ascending...L122
Eclipses...L266, L409, L794, P41, P42, P44, P204,
    P207, P237, P298, P301, P308, P320, P340,
    AB154-160, Pt161-195, DS172, DS264,
    MM289-291, HT37-52
  before birth: relationship to
Ecliptic...L530, P1, P10, P14, P18, P22, P35, P90,
    P152, P221
Education, will it profit querent?...G286-287
Electional Astrology...C147-156, DF125-134,
    P235-271, R121-202, JS65-80
  1st House...R132-134
  2nd House...R134-139
  3rd House...R140-141
  4th House...R142-151
  5th House...R152-159
  6th House...R160-174
  7th House...R175-188
  8th House...R189-190
  9th House...R190-196
  10th House...R196-198
  11th House...R199-200
  12th House...R201-202
  alchemical...JS79-80
  baths & haircuts...P260-261, R133, JS70
  beginning any work...R124-125, R127-128,
    JS75-76
  beginning...JS73
  bloodletting & cutting...P257-259, R170-171,
    JS67-68
  borrowing or lending money...R134-136
  building a building...P248-254, R142-145,
    DS267, JS76
  building a ship...R194-195, DS281-286
  buying, selling & hiring...C155-156, P241-242,
    R136-138, R146-147, R172-174, JS77-78
    animals...R172-174, R202, DS270, JS73-74
    arms...R184
    price...DS322
    ships...DS281-286
  cardinal signs...R126, MM213-219
  chemical work...R139
  conception of children...R152-153
  cutting & felling wood...P240
  cutting an unguent...JS70-71
  demolishing a building...R145-146, DS267
  endurance...R125
  entering upon office...P262
  exorcism...R151
  fishing...P241, R187-188
  fixed signs...R126
  fowling...P241, R187-188
  gaming...R185-186
  gifts, giving or receiving...R155
  going to war...R179-181

hair cutting...JS70
hiring servants...JS73-74
horse- or foot-racing...P243-248
hunting...P240, R187-188
installation in office...R196-197
journeys...P262-264, DS278-281, R140, R190-193
learning sciences, music...R195-196, R198
making peace...R182-183
marriage...P261, R175-178, DS271-274, JS72-73
medicine administration...P259-260, R162-168, S2:52-55, S2:60-66
mutable signs...R126
obtaining favor...R197-198
partnership or agreement...R178-179
planets in, general significance...JS66-67
removal...P242, R138
renting...R149
quick dispatch...R125
seeking fugatives...R184-185
sending messengers...R159
ship launching...P254-256
sowing & planting...P239, R148-151, JS71-72
surgery...R169
taking a drug...JS68-69, JS71
to know clandestine practices of others...R185-186
traveling...JS78-79
venereal sports...R178
weaning an infant...JS72
will, making...R189
writing letters...R158
Elements (or more properly, Trigons)
sect...AA10-11, HT30
Elevated...P135, P297, P299, P309, P315, JS47-49
Emissaries (see "Messengers")
Emplacement...L126, D93, DF91-93
Emplacement horary examples...L135-142, L152-156, L162-166, L177-187, L196-199, L199-201, L238-242, L286-290, L390-403, L415-420, L436-437, L439-444, L452-457, L467-471
with Moon translating...L126-27
Empty and Full Degrees...F147-150
End of the matter...L52, L142, L209, L420(?), DF67, DS289
if get job...L446
lawsuits...L375, DS293
Enenecontameris (90° degree)...F267-268
Enemies...Pt413-421
of planets...C37, G88, JS50
open...L297, L383-385, C95-96, CN126-127, P72, P279, P294, P322, P323, P325, P328, P347, G135, G278, B54
secret...L56, L460-461, C136, CN145-146, D122-123, DF117-118, G172-173, G293

shall enemies prevail?...G136, G174
Engonasin (See "Fixed Stars, Engonasin")
Enif Alpheracz (see "Fixed Stars, Enif Alpheracz")
Ephemeris, use of...L27-32
Epistles...L52
Equinoctial...P3, P158, P284, AB56-57
Escaped animals...L328
Essential Debilities...P28-29, P309, AB257-258, AA9-10
Essential Dignities...L101-105, L130, L298, C29-32, CN91, D29, DF25-36, P23-28, G34, R65-67
by Exaltation...L102, D31-32, DF27-29, P20, P21, P23, P25, P26, P28, P84, P89, P102, P114, P118, P149, P246, P286, P315, P339, R69, B6, F32-34, AB256-258, AB306-307, Pt89-91, DS162, AA7-8, V2:29, HT30-31
Exalted degrees...V3:43
Happiness from...V2:29-30
by Face...L103, B6, CN80-85, D35, DF31, R73-75, AB262-263, Pt111-113, AA11-14, PA11-12, MM245-251, JS52
by House...L101, D29-31, DF25-27, R68, Pt79-83
by Term...L102, L389, D34-35, DF30, P21, P26, P27, P28, P57, P319, R71-73, B5, B6, AB265-266, F36-38, Pt91-107, AA15-16, V1:18-24, PA6-10, V3:49-54
by Triplicity...L87, L102, L298, D33, DF29, P21, P27, P28, P299, P302, P316, R70, B5, B6, AB259, Pt83-87, DS161-162, DS196, V2:1-6
example of adding points...L178-181, CN91-96, AB306-307
fortunes in...L300
none...L299
Table...L104, L115, C30, C35, D37-38, D61-63, P26, G35, JS30
thrones of the planets (greatest dignity)...D54
Estate...L572
argument of an...L52
means to obtain...G109-110
of father, what will happen...L210-211, L572, CN114-115, G115, B86
Estival...L48, C4, DF21, P2
Event, good or bad?...L148, L155, C114
Events, timing of...JS88-93
Events, tracing of...L140
Eyes, hurt to...L132, G126
Exaltation (dignity), (See "Essential Dignity, Exaltation")
ex. more favorable than rulership by sign...F34
Example horaries
Accidents...L130
Attain the preferment desired?...L456-457
Battle outcome horary...L399-400
Bewitched?...L464, L468-469
Bewitched...L464
Change of residence...L212

Charles out of Ireland?...L455-456
Dog missing, where?...L392-394
Essex goes West...L473
Brother is absent...L189
Fish stolen...L397-399
Fugative servant, where? return?...L390-392
  Horse lost or stolen? Recoverable?...L467-468,
  D123-124(ex)
If attain the philosopher's stone?...L442-444
If have the portion promised?...L421-422
  If he should obtain parsonage?...L437-438
If husband at sea alive? where?...L417-418
If pregnant, sex, and time to birth, L240-242
If the Querent ever have children?...L238-240
If the Querent should be rich, etc...?L177-187
Is the party at home?...L152-155
If Presbytery shall stand?...L439-442
Is the rumor true (King-Cambridge)?...L199-201
Is the sudden event good or bad?...L152-155
Is the absent one dead or alive?...L152-156
Money lost? Thief? Recoverable?...L395-396
Prisoner escaped? Direction? Catch?...L470-471
Prisoner: will he be released?...L471-472
Rupert or Essex in war?...L452-454
Shall the Querent live long, etc...?...L135-142
Ship at sea, sunk or living?...L162-164, L165-166
Should I purchase Mr. B's houses?...L219-222
Should the lady marry man desired?...L389-390
Sick doctor, what disease, curable?...L286-288
Sudden happening...L148
Terrible dreams...L436-437
What manner of death for Canterbury?...L419-420
Whether dead or alive...L404
Whether man or wife shall die first?...L415-416
Whether the Sick would live...L289-290
Where an absent brother was?...L196-199
Will Essex take Reading?...L401-403
Would the lady marry man desired?...L385-388
Exorcism...DS314
Exposed infants...F234-237

— F —

Face (see "Essential Dignities, Face")
Face, shape, etc...L50, L548-549, L577, G105
Facies ("see Fixed Stars, Facies")
Fall (debility)...AA7-9
  application of Moon to planet
  in...L299
    Moon in...L301
    Significator in...L301
Fall (season) signs (LI,SC,SA)...PA3-4
Falls...L585
False...L192
False evidence...L132
False writings...L132
Fat or Thin...L549-550, P7, P8, P11, P333, P335,
  P337

Father...L569-570, B98, MM157
  inheritance from...L210-211, L572, CN114-115,
  G115, B86
  if loved by...L211, CN115-116, G114-115
  wealth of...L53
Favor, to ask for a...DS271
Felony cases
  sentences...F260-261
Feminine...L48, L52, L53, L54, D55, DF21, P4,
  P5, P6, P7, P8, P9, P15, P17, P35, P39, P43,
  P44, P45, P46, P47, P53, P125, AB211,
  AB234, F150-151, Pt41, Pt69-71, DS167
  malefics in feminine signs...DS165
  old age...L48
Feminine degrees...(see "Degrees, Masculine &
  Feminine")
Feral signs...L89, DF58, P3, P146, P171, R81-82,
  AB310-311
Fertility of ground...L206-207
Fertility, shall a woman conceive...L223
Fight, planet of...L453
Finances in life...L167-176, L178-184(ex)
Finding, directions to...L202-204
Finding a person at home...L147
Firdaria (see also "Alfridaria")... P223, AB239,
  AB319
Firmicus...D43, D75, DF46, DF71, P83
Five degree rule (i.e., planet within 5_ of a house
  cusp is in the next house)...L391
Fixed Signs...L130, L131, L300, DF21, R81, Pt65-
  69
  in elections...R126
Fixed Stars...L130, L131, L537-538, L620, L623,
  L648-649, L665-668, L677-679, L689-691,
  L701-703, CN262, P309, B9, B10, G96, G188,
  R93-106, AB59, AB68-81, Pt47-59, F183-
  184, F271-281, F300-301, HT28-29, JS7-8
  Al Hecka...L690, R96
  Al Jabhah...L667, R99
  Achernar...Pt57, R94
  Alamac...R95
  Albirto...R102
  Alchenib...R95
  Aldebaran...L257-258, L536-537, L564, L616,
  L620, L644, L649, L677, L690, L694, L725,
  L748, L751, L759, L761-764, L774, L829,
  P119, P152, P169, P285, P316, G96, G193,
  G198, AB80, Pt47
  Alderamin...L648, R94
  Algareb...R100
  Algenib...R94
  Algol...L115, l145, L257, L536, L564, L620,
  L644, L648, L649, L679, G40-41, G96, G188,
  G193, P29, P57, P169, P285, P316, R95, B132
  Alioth...R99
  Alkes...L667, R99
  Alnilam...L537, L581, L649, L666, P182, P188
  Alphard...L649, L667, L701, R98, AB81, Pt57

Alphecca...L703, R101
Alpheratz...L648, L649, R94
Alrucaba...R96
Altair...L537, L649, L702, R102, AB79
Angetenar...R94
Antares...L257, L537, L581, L616, L620, L623, L644, L649, L677, L689, L694, L703, L725, L769, L808, L812, L819, P188, G96, G198, R102, Pt51
Arcturus...L621, L649, L666, L678, P183, P188, G193, R100, Pt55
Aselli...L668, L690, P230, G188, G198, R98
Baten Kaitos...R94
Bellatrix...L677, L702, R96
Betelgeuze...L621, L644, L677, Pt57
Benan Elkered...R99
Bos...L537
Canopus...L678, AB81, Pt57
Capella...L547, L677, P188, R96, AB79
Caput Medusa...(see "Algol")
Coma Berenices...L581, R99
Cor leonis...(see "Regulus")
Delphinus...L538
Deneb...L538, P231
Deneb Alchedi...R104
Deneb Algedi...R105
Denebola...L666, R99
Engonasin...R101
Enif Alpheracz...R104
Facies...L581, R103
Fomalhaut...L621, Pt57
Hircus...R96
Hyades...L620, L623, R96, MM309-311
Iota Puppis...L647, L666, G188
Lans Australis...(see "South Scale")
Markab...L649, R105
Menkar...R95
Milky Way...L130-131, L581, P230-231
Mirach...R94
Nashira & Deneb Algedi...L678
Orbs...L179
Palilicium...L257
Perpetual apparition & occultation...AB131-132
Pleiades...L257-258, L536, L581, L618, L620, L649, L667, L679, P181, P187, P230, P280, G96, G188, R95, AB80, MM311-313
Pollux...L537, L616, L623, L644, L649, L690, L703(?), P188, G96, G198, R97, Pt49
Praesaepe...L581, L667, L691, G198, R98, Pt49
Princeps...L665, R100
Procyon...L537(?), L621, L649, L666, L689, R97, AB80, Pt57, MM317
Ras Alangue...R102
Ras Algeti...R102
Rastaban...L702, R102
Regulus...L115, L135-136, L145, L537, L616, L619, L707, L756, L795, P182, P188, G96, G188, G193, R98, B145, Pt49

Rigel...L678, L689, L701, G198, R96, Pt57
Sadalsuud...L649
Scheat...R105
Schedar...R95
Seginus...L702, R100
Sirius...L537, L621, L649, L678, P182, P188, G188, G193, G198, R97, AB80, Pt57, MM319
Size...AB115
South Scale...L257, L616, L624, L644, L690, L707, L750, L761, L772, L779, L798, L799, R101
Spica...L115, LL145, L537, L616, L618, L620, L667, L678, L690, L701, L707, L725, L759, L771, L778, L808-809, L822, L824, P29, P57, P91, P152, P182, P188, P231, G96, G188, G193, G198, R100, Pt51, MM323-325
Stream or Wave of Aquarius...L581, R105
Subra...L667, R98
Trica...R99
Unukalhai...L702, R101
Var...Pt57
Vega...L537, L649, L748, L750, L765, L771, R102
Vindiamatrix...R100
Yed Prior...L702, R101
Fomalhaut (see "Fixed Stars, Fomalhaut")
Fortitudes and debilities, table of...L115, G88, JS55-60
Fortuna (see "Part of Fortune")
Fortune...L551-561, DF98
  argument of...L52, CN107-110, G107-108, DS189-190
  good or bad...L140, CN104-110, G107, AB309, DS183, DS184-189, DS190-193
  increase of...DS292
Fortunes...L298, L299, L300
  assistance of...L300, B12
  as significators...L298, L299, B4, B37, B38
  by House...B106, B118
  cadent...L299
  equal in strength to Infortunes...L182, B83
  ill placed...L299, L300, B42
  retrograde...L299
Found...L319-320, L323
Fourth, sign of...L53
Friends (also see "Partnership")... L51, L56, L457, L459, L634-639, CN142-144, P42, P46, P51, P71, P72, P347, G166-170, Pt413-421
  aphorisms...CN143-144, G169-170
  endurance...L370
  fortunate in...C136, 291
  is the "friend" real?...D123(ex)
Friends, of planets...C37(table), G88, AB260-261, JS50
Fruitful signs...L89, L201, L222, L565-566, C4, D5, P3, P65, R81
Frustration...L112, C40, D51-53, DF54, G44, R111, JS47
  in marriage charts...L305

of significators...L301(38), L305
Fugitives...L297, L323, L328, L390, L394
    fugatives...L323, L328, L390
    gone which way? return?...C129, G279-280
    if shall be caught...L328, L329
    if shall return...L328, L329
Full and Empty Degrees...F147-150

— G —

Gadbury, John...P70, P149, P202, P203, P252, P274,
    P275
Gain the item?...L51, L173, C116
Gambling...C124, L132, G268
    electing to win...R186-187
Gemini...L52, L94, C10, P5, P21, P36, P42, P57,
    P65, P73, P87, P282, P293, P316, P333, G84,
    R87, B5, F285-286, MM235, V1:10-11, PA2,
    HT7-9, JS15
    diseases...L245
Genitures
    kingly...G163-164
Glaucoma...Pt323
Good or evil things attending life...G242-243
Goods, obtaining...L173
Gout...L585
Government position attainable?... L444-447, L456-
    457
    continue in present office?...L447-448
    return after expulsion?...L448-450
Grounds, quality of...L52-53

— H —

Hair color...L547
Haly...L647, P62, P237, P240, P248, P249, P253,
    P263
Happiness...L132, P286, P290, P303
Harpocratiacs (see "Hermaphrodites")
Having children (see "Children")
Hayz (i.e., feminine planet in feminine sign below
    horizon or masculine planet in masculine sign
    above the horizon, a kind of minor
    dignity)...L113, L416, D55, DF58, P22, G45,
    R111, B40, AB308, JS39-41
Health...L129-130, L243-253, L268-295, P322,
    JS84-85
    aphorisms...L282-286, G121
    combust...L129
    of brother...L189-190
Heart, honest...L194
Height...L546-547
Help or hinder...B9
Herbs
    of Jupiter...L64, R52
    of Mars...L67, R54
    of Mercury...R62
    of Moon...R63

of Saturn...L59, R50
of Sun...R57
of Venus...R58
Hermaphrodites...Pt263, Pt325
Hermes Trismegistus...L268, P274, P290
Hesperus (inferior planet visibble in evening)...L72
Hidden
    to find...L217
    treasure...L215-217
Hindrance (of matter)...L301, DF62, B9, B101
Hinderance in marriage (see "Marriage")
Hircus (see "Fixed Stars, Hircus")
Homosexuality...F248-249, Pt369-373, DS206-207
Honor...L55, L615-624, CN139-141, DF113-114,
    G158-160, JS85-86
    in revolutions...P211-215
Hope, shall one attain it...L56, L299, L300, L457-
    458, C107-108, C135, D120-122(ex), DF115-
    116, P46, P63, P295, P338, P340, G292, B9,
    DS289-290
Horary
    aphorisms...L298-302
    question, judgment of...L298
Horary useless if natal chart available...G243
Horizon...L47
House rulership by intercepted sign...L165
Houses (of the chart - also see #s)...L33, L47, 50-
    56, L129, L130, L131, C57-63, D64-67, DF63-
    69, G36, R106-109, AB275-278, F42-52,
    F219-226
    5_ rule on cusps...B58, AB304, CA1-22, Pt273
    description of...L347, L348, JS3132
    emplacement as perfection...D93
    evil ones (i.e., 3,6,8,12)...DS169
    of joy...L176
    planets in...G43-63
    relative strength...DS164
    turned...L419
    unfortunate...L54
    when comprised of more than one sign...AB279
Houses (i.e., real estate)...L204, L219-222, C65-
    66, DF101-102
    purchase...G258-259
    quality...G259-260
How money is obtained...L168
Human constellations...Pt315-317
Human signs (AQ,GE,LI,VI)...L89, G39, R81,
    AB212-213, MM95
Humors...C5, CN98-99, DF20, G32, G39, G93-94,
    G97-98, AB240
    active & passive...AB211, Pt39
    adding together (i.e., complexion)...L532-534,
    CN98-99
    compound qualities...L70-72
    constant for a given planet?... AB235
    humoral inbalance...RS81-93
Hunting...L371-372. R187-188
Hyades (see "Fixed Stars, Hyades")

Hyleg (also called prorogator)...L527, L529, L652, L656-665, CN87-88, P81, P83, P112, P168, P175, P204, P215, P219, P221, P287, P290, P295, P307, Pt269, Pt271-281, JS82-84
Hypochondria...L797
Hypocrates...L291

—*I*—

If a rumor is true...L193
If the querent has siblings...L195
If the same planet rules Querent and Quesited...GBTS4-19
If a short trip should be taken...L195
If a man shall marry...L307
If a marriage will happen...L317
If querent will gain the money sought...L174
Ill-disposed...L184
Ill omen...F204-206
Illness (see also "Disease")...L53, L243-253, L286-288(ex)
    aphorisms...L282, S2:1-7
    cause of...L259, S2:8
    chrysmal...L291
    combust...L129
    critical days...L291
    crises...L290-293, RS22-32
    death from...L252-258, L286(ex), L289(ex)
    decretory...L291
    decumbiture (see "Decumbiture")
    end of...L282, L268
    humoral imbalance...RS81-93
    if querent is ill...L259
    indicative days...L292
    judgment...L243, RS32-36
    long or short...L288
    lovesick...L260-261
    medicine administration...P259-260, S2:52-55, S2:60-66
    Moon afflictions...L272-282
    Moon's aspects...L290
    nature...L258, L289(ex)
    of passion...L272
    quality and cause...L53
    showing itself...L292
    significator of...L244-246
    signs of life...L253
    time of recovery...L267-68
    timing of illness...L292
Imagination ("fancy")...L51
Impediting the question...L184-186, L440, P130, P237, P240, P246, P253, P258, P263, P265, P266, P282, P293, P295, P298, P300, P301, P302, P338, P340, P341, P347, B5, B116
Imprisonment...L56, L642, L461-463, CN146-147, G174-176, DS287-289
Imum Coeli...L53

Incest...F247-248
Inconjunct (not beholding each other, i.e., not in aspect nor antiscion nor contraantiscion relationship by sign; also translated "disjunct" by Robbins)...L109, AB225, Pt77-79, Pt253-255, PA2526, HT31-32
Increase...L174
    in Light...C42, D57, JS33
    in motion...L355
    in number...L355, JS34
Inferior planets...R111, AB62-63, AB297-298
Infertility, conception...L229, L238(ex), Pt323, Pt325
Infidelity...L313-316
Infortunes...L131, L132, DF61-62, P10, P12, P18, P62, P141, P175, P202, P206, P208, P213, P277, P282, P285, P290, P291, P292, P295, P296, P300, P302, P303, P304, P306, P307, P311, P322-324, P331, P332, P338, P339, P342, P343, P344, B11, B36, B66, B83, B84, AB232-233
    angular as danger...L162, L200, P106, B16, B45, B105
    as significator...L182, L298, L299, L300, L442(ex), C74, P113, B27, B32, B33, B34, B41, B48, B49, B127
    aspecting significator...L301, L470(ex), P51, P107, B86
    cadent...L301, B113
    dignified...P115, DS164, B32
    ill aspects to Moon...L301
    ill placed...L300, P148
    in masculine and feminine signs...DS165
    peregrine...L301, B40
    retrograde...L301
    when joined...L300
Ingresses...Pt453-457
Inheritance...L52, L210, C87, C116, C121, P43, G262, B139, DS177
    from father...L210-211
Injuries...V2:74-86
    related to oriental malefics...Pt321
Injurious degrees...MM255
Insanity...L264, L583-584
Intellect, quality of...L543, CN101-102, G99-100
Intentions...L194
Intercepted sign house rulership...L165, C121
Interficient (killing) planet (see "Anareta")...L527, L529
Inverted signs (TA,GE,CN)...MM99
Iota Puppis (see "Fixed Stars, Iota Puppis")
Is my son at home or with master?...L153
Is a report true or false...L192
Is a thing happening suddenly for good or bad?...L155
Is the absent person dead or alive?...L156
Is the brother dead or alive?...L197

Is the report true?...L200
Is the husband at sea alive?...L417
Is the querent bewitched...L468
Isoceles configuration...Pt269

— J —

Job, employment...C105-107
  if profitable...L445
  will I get...L444-45
Journey, long...L55, L423-424, L428-429, C103-
    104, C133, D113-116(ex), DF111-112, P45,
    P143-148, B57
  cause...L428, G153
  length...L429
  time until return...L424-428, DF111-112
  where...L431-432
Journey, short...L52, L195, C83-84, C119, P42, P63-
    64, G112, G256
  if good to go...L195, L300
  in elections...R140
Journeys...L606-611, CN131-132, P175, P178,
    P180, P181, P191, P192, P200, P201, P214,
    P219, P236, P238, P262-266, P293, P298,
    P311, P327, P346, G151, Pt423-427, DS278-
    281
  best location...L196
  departure...DS279-280
  if safe...L367, B72
  in elections...P262-264, DS278-281, R140, R190-
    193
  Moon impedited...L301
  which way...L195, CN132, G151
  inland...L52
Joys...L51-56, L176, DF59, C20, B5, B8, AB309,
    DS162
  of planets (see also "Thrones")... R75, HT30
Judgment of a question...L123, C68
Judgment...B143
  aphorisms...L298-302
  beginning...L123
  considerations before...L121-123
  deferred...L300
  quick...L146
  strictures against...L121-123, L298
Jupiter...L52, L61-65, L84, L130, L132, L540, C24,
    D19-20, DF24, P11-12, P97, P99, P207-214,
    P224, P294, P295, P296, P298-302, P308,
    P315, P322, P325-331, P336, P339, P341,
    P343, P344, P345, P347, G67-68, R52-53, B5,
    F78-82, AB240-257, V1:3, Pt183, DS222,
    DS226-227, DS232, JS21-22
  animals of...L64
  angular...DS226-227
  as dispositor of significator...L300
  condition of...L298
  conjunctions with planets...DS221-222

corporature of...L63, L84
dignities of...L62-63
dignified...L298, L302
diseases...L63, L246, L262
heats & humidifies...Pt37
house of...L302
in the houses (by ruler)...G75-76, DS232
medicines...L270
occidental...L63
oriental...L63
plants and trees of...L64
sextile of...L298
significator of children...L230
stones of...L64
trine of...L298
triplicity of...L62

— K —

Kepler...L32, P23, P24
Kings...L452(ex), L455(ex)
Knowledge, kind and success...L429
  attain Philosopher's Stone?...L442-444

— L —

Lands...L52
  cheap or expensive...L208-209
  if good to buy...L208-209
  of buying and selling...L204
  of quality of...L205-209
  quality of the ground...L206-207
  trees and timber on land...L52, L206-209
  running water on...L214-215
  what land yields...L206-208
Lans Australis (see "Fixed Stars, South Scale")
Late degrees ascending...L122, L298
Latitude
  Moon's...AB101, DS171, DS172
  planetary...L49, AB60, AB102-104
Launching a ship...DS282-286
Lawsuits (see "Business" & "Partnership")...L54,
    L297, L369, L372-376, L403, C95-96, C128,
    P42, P44, P185, P191, P200, P300, G277,
    DS292-295
  cazimi...L374
  defendent...L54, DS293
  end of matter...L375, DS293
  friends or assistants...L51, L375, DS294
  go to court?...L372-376
  judge...L374-376, DS293
  who'll do best...L369, L372, L375, DS294
Learning...L55
  strength of...L374
  will substance be obtained...L173
  victory...L375
Lease...L132

Lending money or goods...G251-252, DS278
  in elections...R134-135
  litigation concerning...DS294-295
Length of life...L129, L136, L146, L311, L525-527
  C76-77, C111, CN85-91, G89-90, G242, F56-
  57, Pt271-307, MM209-213, V3:67-70
Leo...L95, C11-12, P6, P20, P22, P24, P25, P36,
  P43, P57, P65, P74, P83, P87, P100, P287,
  P302, P308, P317, P334, G84, R88, B8, F287,
  MM237, V1:12-13, PA3, HT11-12, JS16
  diseases...L246
Leprosy...Pt327
Letters: contents?...D96-98(ex)
Liberty...L140
Libra...L96, C12-13, P7, P32, P36, P44, P65, P75,
  P87, P282, P294, P310, P331, P334, G85, R89,
  B5, F289-290, MM239, V1:14, PA3, HT14-
  16, JS17
  diseases...L246
Lies...L192-194
  time to cast chart for...L193
Life
  divisions of...Pt437-459
  length of...(see "Length of Life")
  live longest...L311-312
  long life...L51, L129-130
Liking...L51
Lilly, William...G246-249, G257-258, G282
Lilly example charts:
  * Lilly mentioned condition
    (including indirectly)
  ! Lilly did not mention condition
  + Lilly misidentified condition
  Almuten different from House ruler...L152!,
    L162!, L165!, L177!, L196!, L200!, L219*,
    L240*, L286*, L415!, L421!(co), L442!(co),
    L452!(co), L455!, L473!
  out-of-sign aspect...L152, L196
  peregrine planets used as Significator...L135*,
    L152!, L165!, L196*, L419!, L436!, L437!
  planetary hours
    no match...L135, L238, L238,
      L286, L385, L390, L397, L417,
      L437, L439, L442, L470, L471
      (12 examples)
    hour ruler matches triplicity
      of sign on the Ascendant...
      L240, L289, L473
    hour ruler matches ruler of the
      Almuten of the Ascendant...
      L196, L392, L436
  timing by degree...L419
  timing by ephemeris...L152, L196, L385, L415,
    L417
Lisp...(see "Mute")
Location
  best place to live...L132-133, L137

directions...L133
  relocation...L370, L371
Location, of absent brother...L198
  of mislaid item...C122, C129, G262-263
Location of goods...L350-354
Longitude, planetary...L49, P22, P169, P230, P255
  mean & corrected...AB95-96
  of thief...L364-365
Long life...L51, L129-130
Lord of Action...Pt381-393
Lord of Geniture...L531
Lord of the Ascendant...L48-49, L130, L131, L132,
  L298, B128, P345-347
  cadent...L300(25)
  not in sign of own sex...P347
  out of dignity...L300(25)
  peregrine...L300(25)
  unfortunate...L298, B50, B77, P347
  with nodes...L300-301, B61
Lord of 8th...L130, L131, B114
  impedited...L302, B115
  in the 8th...L302
Lord of 4th...L130
Lord of the hour...L298, C145-147, CN77-80
Lord of 6th...L130, L131
Lord of 12th...L130
Loss...L51, L331-334
Lost things, servants, beasts...L202-204, L319-366,
  L390-392, P68-69
  (see "Stolen", "Recovery", "Mislaid", "Theft",
    "Treasure")
  alive?...L322, L325
  articles...L202, L319, L323, L334
  condition...DS299-301
  direction...L204
  distance from owner...L330, L350
  fugitive, shall he be taken?...L328-330
  general rules...L323, L325
  hid or mislaid...L202-204
  how item was lost...L321
  if found...L319, L355, L356, L359
  if lost or stolen...L335-336
  in owner's hands...L349
  location of lost item...L320, L323, L326, L350-
    353, L392-394
    type of ground...L327
  locked up (protective custody)...L325, L327-328
  luminaries under earth...L257
  mislaid (treasure)...L217
  quality of location...L347
  recovery?...L323, L325, L355, P69, DS297
    Lights under the Earth
      rule...DS297
    sudden...L357-358
    use of 2nd House...L467(ex)
    when will recover...L356
  retrograde...L357

stolen?...L321-323, L326, C97, G280-281
strayed?...L323-324, L326
theft (see "Theft")
to find...L217
treasure...L215-218
where lost...L347, L353
wife fleeing husband...L330
with thief...L349
Love...DF67
brotherly...L188
neighborly...L188
questions of...L54
who loves best...L305
Lucifer...L72
Lunar mansions...AB81-87, JS62-64
Luminaries, aphorisms...L617

— M —

Madness...L132, L264
Malefic(s)...(see "Infortunes")
Mansions...(see "Houses")
Many marriages...L307
Markab (see "Fixed Stars, Markab")
Marks, moles...L148-150, L155-156, L221, C69, C114, P53, G240-241
Marriage...L54, L297, L302-319, L587-602, C93-95, C126, CN120-127, D105-108(ex), DF107-108, P44, P67-68, P133-134, P180, P185, P190, P191, P193, P197, P236, P237, P256, P257, P261, P268-270, P286, P289, P299, P302, P328, P329, AB214, G136-137, G273-276, Pt393-409, DS197-206, DS271-274, V3:1-9
agreement after marriage...L308-309-L311, C95, CN124, P141-142, G134-135, G275, DS273-274
benefits one of the partners...DS272, DS274
broken off...L305
chaste...L312
contention...L308
death of partners, timing...L311
description of partner...CN123-124, P138-141, G275
divorce or ending of marriage?...L310-311
ease of courtship?...P136-137
hatred after marriage...DS274
have the desired party...C128
help of friends...L304
hindrance...L305
honesty of partner...L314
if marriage is legitimate...L309
if perfected...L317
in questions of...L302
location (geographic) of partner...L308
loss of fiance...L311
lover, does the other have one?...L313, L314-316, DS272

man as querent...L302
Moon impedited...L301
Moon sign & viability of marriage...DS272-273
more than one marriage...G274, F247, F249-250
murder of spouse...F250
number of spouses...L307, CN121-122, P138, G131, DS204-205
perfection...L303-305, L317-318
preventing the marriage...L305-307, C93
quality of...L308, G132-134, F248, F250-251
separation...L308
should she marry the man...L389-390
significators...L302
of the man...L302, L303, L304
of the woman...L302, L303, L304
threat to...L302
use of 6th House in interpretation...DS274
virginity of prospective spouse...L312-313
wealth of spouse...G149-150
when...L302, L307, CN124-125, P137, G274
where does spouse come from?...G138-139
whether dowry comes through...L421-422
whether legitimate marriage...L308
whether spouse or lover returns...L318-319, DS275-276
whether the other is in love...L305
whether the other loves another...L305
whether the two shall marry...L301, L303, L307, L385-388, C93, D107-108(ex), G130-131, G273-276, P135-136
whether s/he be rich...L308, L412-413, C94, C127
who dies first...L311-312, G139-140
who is master...L308
who is more noble...L308
who loves more...L305
widows...L311
woman as querent or native...L302, P142-143, CN125
Mars...L54, L65-68, L84, L299-300, L540, C24-25, D20-21, DF24, P12-13, P41, P42, P45, P46, P49, P53, P57, P62-65, P68-71, P81, P86, P87, P90, P93, P97-99, P275-284, P287-291, P294-299, P303, P307, P310, P311, P313, P316, P317, P318, P320, P325-331, P336, P337, P339, P343, P344, P345, G68, R54-55, B5, F82-88, AB240-257, Pt183-185, Pt311, V1:3-4, DS222-223, DS227-228, DS32, JS22-23
angular...L300, B91, DS227-228
as impeditor...L440
as dispositor of significator...L300
as fighting planet...L453
as significator...L182
aspects to Algol...B132
condition of...L298
conjunctions with planets...DS221-222

corporature of...L66, L84
daily motion of...L45
death...L647
dignities of...L66
diseases...L67, L246, L262-263
disobedient children...L53
dry & hot...Pt37
exalted...L299
fever...L262-63
fixed stars...L131-32
good...L164
health...L130, L262-63, L277-82
herbs of...L67
in house of joy...L54
in human sign...G248
in second...L52, B107
in seventh...L54
in tenth...L298, B107
in the Houses (by Ruler)...G77-78, DS232
medicines...L270, L272
nature of...L66
occidental...L66
of ill influence...L298
orientall...L66
performing...L299
professions of...L67
significator of men...L600
stolen goods...L354
terms and faces...L66
triplicity...L299
Masculine...L48, L51, L52, L53, D55, DF21, P4,
    P5, P6, P7, P8, P9, P10, P11, P12, P14, P35,
    P39, P42-46, P53, P65, P69, P124, P125,
    P246, P316, Pt41, AB211, AB234, Pt69-71,
    DS167
malefics...DS165
Masculine degrees...C5-6, D39, G40-41, AB269-
    270, F150-151
Matter not ripe for judgment...L298
Matter of question elapsed...L298
Matters brought to perfection...L176
Matters impeding...G239
Matutine & Vespertine planets...F38-39, Pt40-41,
    AB62
Maxima elongatione...L31
Mean and true anomaly...AB94-95
Mean rate of planet...AB94
Means to obtain object...C116
Measure of time...L131
Meddle, do not...L298
Medicine...L269
  to give...L295
Mediocrity, deliberate...L300
Melancholic signs...L48, L264, C4
Memory...L51
Men, significator of...B131
  Mars...L600

Sun...L302, L600
Men, Women, Masculine & Feminine Signs...P4,
    P5, P6, P7, P8, P9, P15, P17, P35, P39, P43,
    P44, P45, P46, P47, P53, P125, B131
Menkar (see "Fixed Stars, Menkar")
Mental deficiencies...F252-254
Mental illness...L134
Mercury...L51, L54, L72-73, L76, L85, L132, L541,
    L543-546, C27, D25-26, DF24, P15-17, P41,
    P44, P49, P85, P86, P89, P90, P91, P95-100,
    P275-278, P280-285, P287, P288, P291, P292,
    P297, P299, P300, P303, P304, P310, P316,
    P326-331, P336, P337, G71, R61-62, B8, B14,
    B126, B137, F99-113, AB240-257, Pt187-189,
    Pt311, V1:5-6, DS224, DS 230-231, DS233-
    234, JS24-25
angular...DS230-231
as dispositor of significator...L300
aspects...B14,B137
conjunctions with other planets...DS221-224
corporature of...L78, L85
daily motion of...L46, L47
diseases...L247, L263
in the Houses (by ruler)...G81, DS233-234
medicines...L270, L272
motion...AB98-99
Meridian...L47, L48
Meridional descending...L29
Meridional latitude...L49, D56, DF20
Merriment, house of...L53
Messages...DS286-287
Messenger...L52, L81, L235-236, C90, C124, G267
  for money...L236-238
  for Republics...L53
  safe journey or impeded...L236-238
  when shall return...L237
Midheaven...L619-620, P28, P38, P40, P83, P183,
    P187, P204, P211, P215, P219, P244, P248,
    249, P279
Milky Way (see "Fixed Stars, Milky Way")
Mines, quality of...L216-217, L575
Minutes...L28
Mirach (see "Fixed Stars, Mirach")
Miscarriage...L233, Pt323
Misery of Native...L551
Misfortune...L130, L131, CN104-110
  as significator...L182
Mislaid items...C65, C87
  (see "Lost", "Stolen", "Recovery", "Theft", "Re-
    lationships")
  articles...L202-204, L332, L333-334
  as 4th house...L202-204
  directions to find...L202-204
Missing persons...L147, L151, L153, L196-199
  condition of...L430
  if at home...L153-155, L202
  if a stranger...L154

location of person...L198
significator of...L404
timing news...L198
Moiety, degrees by planet...L107, DF50, P20, P24
Moles...L148-150, L155, L221
and scars...L221
facial...L51
Money...L51, L421(ex), D93-95(ex), P42, P46, P51, B75
lent...L51
borrowed...L173
Money lent: will it be returned?...C118, G262-263
Months...L130
Moon...L52, L80-81, L86, L129, L130, L131, L132, L619, C27-28, C73, D26-27, DF24, P17-18, P276-278, P280-282, P284-294, P296, P298, P300-304, P308-311, P313-320, P325-330, P337, P338, P340, P344, P345, P347, G72, R63-64, B5, B113-135, F117-136, F152-154, AB240-257, DS224, DS234-235, JS25-26
Althazer...R111
application of...L299, B22, B23
aspecting malefics...DS264
combustion...L301, B123
corporature of...L81, L86
corruption of...DS264-267
debility of...L298, B77
diseases...L247
signified by sign &
aspect...L273-282
medicines...L270, L273
diurnal motion of...L46, L47
fortunes & infortunes...D60-61
impedited...L301, B5, B50, B63, B75
in elections...R126, R127, R128-131
in her fall...L301
in the Angles...DS224-225
in the houses (rulership)...G82
in Via Combusta...L415, L439, L468, DS265, DS278, DS296
judgable chart...L401
judged when void...L401
motion of...AB96-98
phases...DF60, G94, AB65-68, AB152-153, DS322, V2:71-74, PA34-37
planet separating from...L299
state of...L299
strength of...L299
strength of relative to her ruler...DS265-266
tracing events with...L140
void of course (see)
with nodes...L300-L301
Morinus...C57
Morning stars...(see "Oriental")
Mother...L570-572, P46, Pt251
Moveable goods...L51

Moveable sign...L88, P3, P8, P42, P52, P103, P146, P148, P162, P181, P187, P206, P240, P264, P301, P340, P343, P345
Moving, whether a good idea...L212-214, L370-371, C86, C121
Mundane Astrology...R213-333
annual revolutions...R221-307
aspects of the planets...R290-305
comets...R318-327
eclipses...R308-318

grand conjunctions...R327-332
New Year's Day...R332-333
predictions...R214-220, Pt161-219
Murderer(s)...P13
of spouses...F250
Murders...L132
Mutable signs...L52, L88, L130, L131, L300, DF21, P8, P17, P69, P149, P171, P214, P295, P296, P301, P337, R81, Pt65-69, DS263
in elections...R126
Mute signs...L89, C4
Mutual reception...L112, L185, B39, B56, B82, Pt189
"mixed"...L387, L402, L452(ex)
perfection by...L172, L185-186, B95

— N —

Names...L340-342
Nashira & Deneb Algedi (see "Fixed Stars, Nashira & Deneb Algedi")
Nations, friendship between...L235
Nativities, methods of prediction...Pt235-241
Nature...L131, L298
of the illness (see "Illness")
of planets...L88
Needing help...L116-118
Neighbors...L370, C119, P42, G253-254
agreement or love...L188
quality of...L212-213
New Moon...L301, P343-344
New Moon of the Year...Pt195-201
News, quality of...L192, L199, L200, D95-100(ex)
Ninetieth degree...F267-268
Nodes...L25, L44, L49, L83, L228-229, L353, L432, L535, L687, L700, L706, P18, P29, P41, P42, P46, P57, P63-65, P68, P69, P71, P85-87, P90, P279, P281-283, P288, P289, P300, P337, P341, P343
Moon's...L25, L44, L49, L173, L300-301, DF24, R76, AB233-234
tenth house...L298
planetary...AB91-92, AB105, AB110-111
Nondescript...Pt261
North angle...L53
North Node...L49, L300-301, DF24, P18, P300, R76, B5

Northern signs (i.e., those in which the Sun has Northern declination; AR-VI)...L48, C3, R81, AB88

— O —

Obdescension...C42
Obeying signs (LI,SC,SA,CP,AQ,PI: see Signs, commanding & obeying")
Object hidden or mislaid...L202
Oblique Ascension...C42
  signs of...C4, D2, DF20, R81
  use of...R181
Obstruction...L301
Obstructor...L185
Obtaining...L173
Occidental...L30, L48, L70, L114, L300, C42, D28, DF21, P10-11, P22, P28, P29, P38, P39, P69, P86, P98, P99, P116, P137, P141, P158, P296, P301, P315, P316, P320, P343, G45, G94, G101, R111, B8, AB296-297, AB302, Pt241, Pt391, AA31, JS34-35
  qualities affected by...JS27
Occupations...F145-147, F264-265, Pt381-393
Office, appointed...L456
Office, elected...L447
Officers, in authority...L55
Omen
  illness...L253, L258
  good...L220
Open Enemies...(see "Enemies, Open")
Opposition...L26, L27, L106, L130, L131, DF46, R93, DS218-220
  by Sign...L300, MM115-117
  in perfection...G239, L302, L303, L305, L317
Orbs, degrees by planet...L107, C21-22, DF49, P10, P20, P23, P24, P85, P138, P195, P253, P296
Oriental...L30, L48, L70, L114, L300, C42, D28, DF21, P10-11, P22, P29, P38, P39, P69, P86, P97, P99, P116, P137, P145, P153, P158, P211, P246, P297, P300-302, P315, P316, P320, P345, G44-45, G94, G101, R111, B8, AB296-297, AB302, Pt45, Pt241, Pt313, Pt391, AA31, JS34-35
  qualities affected by...JS27
Oriental Lords of Sun, Moon, Ascendant...B90
Origanus, L647, P41, P203, P214, P236, P249

— P —

Palilicium (see "Fixed Stars, Palilicium")
Paranatellonta...MM303-359
Parents...L234, L569, L573-574, Pt241-251, V2:65-70
  agreement...L573

hostility to...F245-246
pre-deceasing...V2:62-64
Part of Basis...AA33
Part of Brothers...DS179, AA36
Part of Children...L231-232, DS209-210, V3:10, AA34-35
Part of Courage...PA47
Part of Debt...V2:46
Part of Father...DS174, AA35
Part of Fortune...L143-146, L301, L703-707, C46, C75, CN104-110, P43, P44, P57, P63, P69, P112, P122, P208, P209, P319, G248, B9, B85, B123, AB279-281, F135-137, Pt373-381, DS167, DS190-191, AA33, V2:28-29, V2:30-32, AA36, PA46
  as ruler of 2nd House questions... CN107
  calculations for...L143
  if ill dignified...L301(39)
  if well dignified...L301(39)
  in aspect...L703-07
  night...L143-44, DF85
  table of strengths...L144, C36
Part of Marriage...DS199-206, V3:5-9, AA35-36
Part of Mothers...DS174-176
Part of Necessity...AA34, PA47
Part of Nemesis...PA47
Part of Sodomy...DS206-207
Part of Spirit...F137, AA33-35, PA46-47
Part of Theft...V2:46-47
Part of Treachery...V2:47-50
Part of War...R181
Part of Victory...R181, AA33
Partile (less than 1°) aspects...L106, C22, P24, P25, P29, P277, D52, R92, G42, AB260
Partnerships...L369-371, L377-379, C130, G276-277, DS276-278
  (see "Business", "Lawsuits", "Friends")
  Ascendant & Moon sign in judgment...DS276-277
  delineation...L377
  how long...L369, L370
  if beneficial...L369, L370
  if yes or no...L369
  which gains most...L369-370
Parts, Arabic...AB282-295, DF85-86, G178-182
Parts of the body by sign & planet...L119-120, L579-580, P30-32
Parts of the house...L203
Past Events...L138-140, C73
Paternity...L318
Pawn: recovering goods...L173
Peregrine...L112, L298, L299, L301, C41, P16, P21, P28, P42, P46, P51, P62, P63, P66, P68, P69, P71, P98, P100, P102, P103, P107, P115, P122, P126, P132, P137, P139, P148, P149, P154, P158, P164, P166, P168, P207, P210, P211, P251, P265, P267, P298, P337, P339, P340, G44, G281, R111, B6, JS42

as thief...L331
by sign, example...L454
definition...L112, L299
disallowed reception...L439(ex)
sickness/death...L130
significator...L298(3), L299(19), L301(36), B55
used as Significator...L135*, L152!, L165!, L196*,
    L419!, L436!, L437!, L452*
Perfect combustion...L132
Perfection...L124, L298-302, C67, D87-88, DF91-
    94, P50-51, P305, P325, G239, B3, B4, B96
2nd House matters...L184
against perfection...L184-185
by aspect...L125, DF91
by placement...L126, D93, DF91-93
by semi-sextile...L389-90
    example horaries...L152-156, L196-199, L219-
        222, L385-390, L417-418, L421-422, L437-
        438, L456-457, L471-472
    mutual reception...L185, DF91, B95
    stifled by:
        abscission...AB312
        evasion...AB311
        intervention (prohibition)...
        G43, AB311
        prevention...AB312
        prohibition...L110, C40, P20,
        G43, B4
        refranation...L111, C40, P20,
        AB312
        return...AB311
    things brought to...L124-25, L176
    void of course...L153(ex)
Perigeon, i.e., perigee... L31
Persons impeding...G239
Phlegmatic signs...C4, P39, P337
Phlegmatique...L48
Physical characteristics...L84-86, L123, L135-136,
    L150, L156
    description example...L389
    marks, scars...L148, L150, L155-156
    near cusp...L151
Piety...(see "Religious")
Pirates...L151, L422, L648, L649
Pisces...L99, C16, P9-10, P16, P17, P36, P47, P57,
    P65, P76, P280-282, P292, P299, P308, P310,
    P316, P335, P338, G87, R91, B5, F298-300,
    MM243-245, V1:16-17, PA4, HT23-25, JS19
    diseases...L246
Pitted degrees...L116, L118, L121, P35, P299, G4,
    B5
Plaktic (other than same degree) aspects,
    interpretation...L106-107, R92, C22, P25, P118,
    P126, P151, P156, P167, G42
Planet @ 29° having qualities of next
    sign...B30
Planetary dignities (see "Dignities")

Planetary Hours...L474-486, C138-147, DF41-43,
    AB237-238, G238, G294, PA42-44
    good things under that hour...C145-147
    if valid...L298(1)
    in warfare...R181
    Lilly examples RE Asc/PH match
        no match...L135, L238, L238,
        L286, L385, L390, L397, L417,
        L437, L439, L442, L470, L471
        (12 examples)
    hour ruler matches triplicity
        of sign on the Ascendant...
        L240, L289, L473
    hour ruler matches ruler of the
        Almuten of the Ascendant...
        L196, L392, L436
Planetary returns...L738-741
Planets...L25, R77-78, HT25-28
    active power (heating & moistening)...Pt35, Pt39
    cadent from own house...L227, B51, B94
    daily motion of...L42-44, AB105-110
    diurnal & nocturnal (see "Sect")
    diurnal motion of...L178
    evil as significator...L299
    friends & enemies...C37, G88, AB260-262
    heliacal (first) rising...Pt313
    hourly motion of...L44-47
    ill disposed (i.e., "suspect")... L184, B16, B43,
        AB310
    in declension...B24
    in each other's houses...DS225-235
    in houses of joy...L176
    in quadrants...Pt313-315
    inferior as Evening/Morning Stars...B52
    impediting perfection...L184-185
    latitude of...L49, DS161
    longitude of...L49, DS161
    lost item ruler...L203
    masculine & feminine...Pt41
    mean years...V3:71-73
    nature of...L88, D28(table), AB231-232
    passive (cooling & drying)...Pt39
    peregrine (see "Peregrine")
    physical type...L84-86
    postponing evil in a bad nativity...DS183-184
    power of...L48
    properties...D15-17, AB240-257
    retrograde (see "Retrograde")
    same planet rules Querent and Quesited...GBTS4-
        19
    size...AB116-119
    slow in motion...L299, B28
    station...L299
    thrones (greatest dignity)...D54
    true position...AB96
    under the Sun's beams (see "Under the Beams")
    weighing...L178-181

Plant rulerships...G66
Pleiades (see "Fixed Stars, Pleiades")
Plumbing...L214-215
Poles of position...C42
Pollux (see "Fixed Stars, Pollux")
Portion, wife's...DF109
Poverty...L554, P42, G249-250, B133
Praesaepe (see "Fixed Stars, Praesaepe")
Precogator of life (see "Hyleg")
Predomination (see "Apheta")
Preferment(s)...L444-447, L456-4557, CN136-137,
    D117-120(ex), DF113-114, P46, P52, P71,
    P309, G158-160, B110
Pregnant, is she?...L53, L226-230, L232-233, C89,
    C123, D104-105(ex), DF103-104, G265
    no she's not...L228
    yes she is...L226, L227, L228
    will she deliver...DS276
    with twins or multiples?...L230
Presbytery, shall it stand?...L439-442
Present condition...L299
Priest, good parsonage?...L432-434, L437-438,
    B110
Priests, oppression by...L132
Princeps (see "Fixed Stars, Princeps")
Prison(s)...L461, L470, L471, L642, L763, P72,
    P322, P325, P344, B24
Prisoner, released? when?...L461-463, L471-472,
    C108-109, C137, G293-294
    escaped, shall he be captured?...L470-471
Procyon (see "Fixed Stars, Procyon")
Profection...L718-734, CN247-256, P175, P218-
    224, P229, P314, P315, P319, G242-246,
    MM207-209
Profession...L55, L450-451, C105-107, C135,
    CN137139, G158-163, G288-290
    obtain the office sought?...C134, G158-159,
    G288-289
    remain in position?...G159-160, G289-290
    which profession is best?...G160-162, G290
Profit...L51
    in career...L445, L458, G162-163
    from education...L429
Profit or loss?...C117
    by livestock...L53
    from knowledge...L429
Prohibition...L110, C40, D47-48, DF51, P20, G43,
    R110-111, B4
    of significators...L301(38)
Promittor...CN155, P38, P82, P103, P112, P175,
    P183, P189, P194, P199, P215, P218, P221,
    P223, P288
Promotion...(see "Preferment")
Prorogator...(See "Hyleg")
Prosperity...P62, P299, P302, B46
Ptolemy, P25, P81, P100, P104, P243, P246, P263,
    P274, P305, P315

—Q—

Quadrangular...L106
Quadrate...L106
Quadruplicity...L533, DF21, MM11
Quadrants...L47, L48, L87, L132-133, P39, P116,
    P292, P303, AB230-231
Quality (cardinal, fixed, mutable)...L131, L300
Quarrel(s)...L54, L132, P42, P44, P62, P68
Quarter of heaven...L204
Quartile (see "Square")
Querent...L50, L123, L131, C64-66, C73
    death of (see "Death of Querent")
    If the same planet rules Querent and
    Quesited...GBTS4-19
    inferior to quesited...L170
    significators of...G235-236
    strength of...L374
Quesited('s)...L123, P48, P49, P52, P67, P70, P72,
    P331
    If the same planet rules Querent and
    Quesited...GBTS4-19
Quesitor...L54
Questions (see also "Examples")
    by priest...L432-434
    confused...L298
    formulation of...L219, L298
    of love...L54
    really asked...P345-347
    trivial...L298
Quick judgments...L146
Quincunx...L31, L32, L109, L830, C6, Pt77-79,
    MM113-115
Quintile...L32, L790-791, L797, C6, D42**

—R—

Radical & fit to be judged...L121-123, L298-302,
    C68, C72, C73-75, D84-85, DF87, P33-38, P48,
    P50, P52, P67, P341, G237-238, B7, B65
Ras Alangue (see "Fixed Stars, Ras Alangue")
Ras Algeti (see "Fixed Stars, Ras Algeti")
Rastaban (see "Fixed Stars, Rastaban")
Real estate, buying or selling...L52-53, C85-86,
    C120, G258-260, DS268
    buying or selling...L204, L219-222, D100-101,
    DS269
    cheap or expensive...L208-209
    if good to buy...L208-209
    if lands detained will be returned?...D102-103(ex)
    if water...L214-215
    quality...L205-208
    quality for commercial use...L213
    quality of ground...L206-207
    price...L208
    should I buy the House?...L219-222
    timing example...L221

Reception...L112, C40, D49, DF52-53, P20, P28, P50, P51, P62, P63, P64, P65, P67, P68, P70, P71, P97, P276, P284, P285, P288, P299, P332, P339, P345, G43-44, R111, RS5, B4, B5, AB312, JS43-45
   mixed dignities...L387, L402(ex)
   one way...L372
   strong & weak...RS5, D49
   without...L298
Recognition, artist...L298
Reconciliation...L318
Recovery...L354-359
   (see "Lost", "Stolen", "Mislaid", "Theft")
   aphorisms...L357, L358
   if will be recovered...L328, L329, L332, L355, L356, L359
   sudden...L357-358
   use of 2nd House...L467(ex)
   when...L356
Rectification...L500-508, CN8-11, CN185-226, G29-31
Refranation (i.e., a method of perfection in horary)...L111, C40, P20, R111, JS47
Regiomontanus...L490, L519-523, L574, P202
Regulus (see "Fixed Stars, Regulus")
Relationship...L302-319, L412-413, L421-422, L587-602
   how long...L369
   if beneficial...L369
   separated forever...L330
   wife fleeing...L330
   return of partner...L318, L319
Relatives...L52, L187, L564
Religion...L55, L422, L611-613
Religious or not?...L611-613, CN133, G154-155
Relocation...L52, L370-371
   for business...L371
   should one...L212, L371
Remove...L212-214, L370, L371, G260, C121, DS296
   in elections...P242, R138
Rendering (i.e., a method of perfection in horary; see also "Benefaction" & "Requital")...L387, D50, DF52
Rent owed, will obtain it?...D93-95(ex)
Rental: if good to...L208, DS267-268
   in elections...R149
Reports & rumors...(see "News")
Request a gift...DS271
Requital...AB310
Residence change...L212-214
Retrograde...L42, L107, L114, L130, L299(13), C39, P19, P20, P22, P29, P302, P322, P323, P324, P325, P329, P345, AB191-192, G279, R110, B5, B6, B25, DS165
   confusion...AB60
   contradiction...L299, L301

delay...L419, L462
denoting ill...L299
discord...L299
   follower (inf. retro planet catches sup. retro planet)...AB313
fortunes...L299
happening suddenly...L107, L198, L211, L406
returning...L406, L468
stationary...L299(13)
sudden recovery...L211, L357
surprise...L211
Retrograde significator, example...L220, L439-442, L467
Return of a person...L406-408, L417
Return of virtue...JS47
Revolutions...L734-741, CN228-247, P203-204, G209-241
   aphorisms...G212-215
   health & sickness...P204-207
   honor & dishonor...P211-215
   houses in...G215-232
   planets in...L738-741, G232-237
   wealth...G208-210
Rich(es)...L167-170, L177, L457, L552, DF97, P40, P42, P62, P63, P68, JS85
   revolutions...P208-210
   timing of...L171-172, L563, DF97
   will thing desired be obtained...L173-176
   without marriage...L181
   why won't become rich...L172-173
Rigel (see "Fixed Stars, Rigel")
Right Ascension...C42
   signs of...C4, D2, DF20, R81
   use of...R181
Rivers, changing course of...L214-215
Ruler of the chart...F138-144
Ruler of the Year...V1:35-36
Rulership by sign, description...L101
Rules for physicians...L282-286
Rumors, quality of...L52, L193, L199-201, C84, C120, P343-344, G256-257
   (also see "News")
   example chart...L199-201, D97-100
   time to cast chart for...L193
   true or false...L192-194
Runaways...L54, L322, DS307-314

— S —

Sadalsuud (see "Fixed Stars, Sadalsuud")
Safety of a ship...L157-161
Sagittarius...L97, C14, P8, P16, P24, P36, P45, P57, P65, P75, P81, P83, P87, P92, P100, P281, P282, P293, P297, P302, P335, P338, G86, R90, B8, F292-294, MM241, V1:14, PA3-4, HT18-20, JS18
   diseases...L246

Sanguine signs...L48, L532-534, C4, P5, P6, P7, P8, P9, P39, P85, P87, P88

Saturn...L51, L52, L57-61, L84, L130, L132, L298, L299, L539, C23, D17-19, DF23, P10-11, P41, P45, P46, P49, P57, P62, P63, P64, P65, P66, P68, P69, P70, P71, P86, P87, P90, P97, P99, P273, P275, P276, P278-289, P293-299, P301-303, P307, P310, P315-318, P320, P325-330, P335, P337, P339, P343-345, P347, G66-67, R49-51, B5, F75-78, AB240-257, V1:2-3, Pt179-181, DS221-222, DS225-226, DS231, JS20-21

  angular...L299, L300, DS225-226

  as Ascendant ruler...G243

  as dispositor of significator...L182, L300

  cold & dry...Pt35, AB235, AB240

  condition of...L298

  conjunctions with other planets...DS221-222

  corporature...L58, L84

  disobedient children...L53

  diseases...L246, L261-262

  exalted...L299

  herbs of...L59

  in tenth...L298

  in the Houses (by ruler)...G74-75, DS231-232

  medicines...L269, L272

  of ill influence...L298

  performing...L299

  professions of...L59

  sicknesses of...L59

  triplicity...L299

Scars & moles...L148-150, L155-156, L221

Scheat (see "Fixed Stars, Sceat")

Schedar (see "Fixed Stars, Schedar")

Schoner...L647

Scorpio...L97, C13-14, P7, G86, P7, P32, P36, P45, P65, P75, P83, P87, P91, P279, P282, P291, P292, P331, P334, B5, R89, F290-292, MM239-241, V1:14, PA3, HT16-18, JS17-18

  diseases...L246

Seasons...Pt59-65

Second sign of the House...L436(ex)

Secret enemies (see "Enemies, secret")

Secret Things or Desires...B93

Sect (i.e., diurnal or nocturnal)... Pt43, Pt377, AA5, D55, AB234, V3:45, PA15-16, DS192, DS196

Seginus (see "Fixed Stars, Seginus")

Self undoing...L56

Selling

  commodities...L376, L377

  if buyer and seller be in agreement...L205

  if deal will be concluded...L205

  real estate...L204, L219-222

  in elections...C155-156, P241-242, R136-138, R146-147

Semi-quintile...D42**

Semi-sextile...L31, L289(ex), L390, L785-786, C7, D42**, Pt77-79, MM113

Semi-square...C6, D42**

Separation...L108, L110, C39, D45-47, DF49-50, G43, R110, B4, Pt113-117

  of the Moon...L299

Septentrional (Northern) latitude...L49, D56, DF20

Servant(s)...L53, L56, L243, L296, L586, CN118-120, DF105-106, P44, P67, G128, B111

  electing hiring...R172

  fled...L319

  free from master?...L296-297

  honesty or fortunate in...C92, C126, G272

  if shall get free...L296

Sesquiquadrate...C6, D42**

Sequiquintile...L511-512, L830, D42**

Sex of child...L53, Pt255-257

Sex of person given by translation...G245

Sextile...L26, L105-106, L132, DF45, P23, P50, P57, P64, P67, P68, P70, P91, P97, P273, P285, P286, P303, P328, P344, R92, DS221

Sexual desire...F261-264

Ship...L157-161

  damage of...L157, L158

  location of...L163

  parts of...L158

  sinking of...L165-166

Ship safe or destroyed?...L157-166, C79, C113, P62, P313, G246-249, B61

Short journeys (see "Journeys")

Sickness...L243, L576-586, B122

  (see "Diseases" and "Illness")

  aphorisms...L282-286

  cause...L244-245, L259-261, L287-290, G271

  chronic or acute?...G270

  crisis/critical days...L266-267, L290-296

  decumbiture...L269-272

  duration...L247-253, L267-268, L288

  diseases signified by house...L245

  diseases sign... by sign&aspect...L273-282

  fatal or not...L253-258, L289-290

  mental or physical...L264-266, G269-270

  misdiagnosis...C91

  part of body...L243-244, L263-264, L269, L286-287, C125, G269

  quality of disease...L261

  recovery...C90-91, C125, G271-272

  whether or not sick...L259

Significator...L123, D85-86, DF89-90

  above the Earth as good omen... L163

  below the Earth as bad omen... L165, DS297

  by sign...L538

  emplacement as perfection...D93

  evilly aspected from bad or good places...G242

  in the 8th House...G255

  in the 12th House...G255

  in agreeable sign...L301

Sign(s) ...L25, L28, L50, L93-99, L131, D5-14, R79-86, F39-42, F156-181

9ths of signs...AB266-267
12ths of signs...AB267-268
ascending & descending...AB229
barren (GE,LE,VI)...L89, L222, L565-566, C4, G39, R81, AB214
bestial or quadrupian (AR,TA,LE,SG,CP)...L89, G39, G40-41, R81, AB212-213
commanding & obeying...L90, D3, DF20, R81, Pt75-77, PA21-22, HT31
common (GE,VI,SG,PI)...L88
crawling (CN,SC,PI)...MM103
deformed (TA,CN,SC.SA)...MM103
diurnal & nocturnal...AB211-212, DF20-21, DS263-264, MM99-101
erect...AB212
feminine (CN,CP,TA,PI,SC,VI)...L88, AA3-4, MM95, PA4
feral (LE & last of SG)...L89
fixed (AQ,LE,SC,TA)...L89
fruitful (CN,SC,PI)...L89, G39, R81
human (AQ,GE,LI,VI)...L89, G39, R81, AB212-213, MM95
          long   or   right   ascension (CN,LE,VI,LI,SC,SG)...L92
masculine (AR,AQ,GE,LE,LI,SG)...L88, AA3-4, MM95, PA4
maimed...AB212
manly...L89
moveable or cardinal (AR,CN,CP, LI)...L88
mute (CN,SC)...L89, C4, G39, R81, AB213
Northern (AR,CN,GE,LE,TA,VI)...L88
not beholding...L109
          oblique   or   short   ascension (CP,AQ, PI,AR,TA,GE)...L92, L122, C4, D2, DF20, R81
of equal power (also called seeing)...Pt77, HT31
of long ascension...L181, L220, R81
prolific...L89
right ascension...C4, D2, DF20
seeing & hearing...AA21, V1:32-33, PA18-19, HT31
southern (AQ,CP,LI,PI,SG,SC)...L88
strong & weak...R82
transition from one to next...HT5, HT6, HT9, HT11, HT12, HT14, HT16, HT18, HT20, HT21, HT23, HT25
with voice...AB213
Sign ascending...L131
Significator(s)...L123, L130, L131
above Horizon...B47
aspecting infortunes...L301, B16
angular...L301(34)
behind cusp of Angle 15_...B59
beware if...L300
cadent...L301(34 &L36), B51, B94
cardinal...L300(28)
combust...L113, L300(23)
common...L300(28)
conjunct...L301(37), B20

conjunct eclipse...L301(30)
dispositor...L300(26)
fixed...L300(28)
fortunes as...L298(7 &L8), L299(17), B46
friendly & unfriendly...AB226
frustration of...L301(38)
how to find...L154
    infortunes as...L298(8), L299(16 &L18), L182(ex), B46
in eighth House...B57
in essential dignity...B44
in fall...L301(32), L299(12)
in late degrees...B30
in reception...B39, B56, B82, B95
light & dark degrees...AB270
more than one Significator...B102
moveable...L300(28)
of brother...L190-191
of children...L230
of illness...L244-246
of long ascension...L181
of profession...B124
of things lost...L320
opposition Sun...L300(23), D59
peregrine...L301(36), B55
planet impediting...L301(33 &L38)
prohibition of...L301(38)
quadruplicity...B60
quality of its sign...L300, B58, B80
retrograde...L299(13), L301(36), R223
rising from 12th House...B71
safe and prosperous...B17
slow of course...B28
square the Sun...D59
stationary...B26, B74, L439-440(ex)
succedent...L301(34)
thief significator...L331
Signs
    see and hear each other...F268-269
Sinister (forward in signs)...L108-L109, C7, D45-47, AB225, P24, AA22
Sirius (see "Fixed Stars, Sirius")
Sisters...L52, L187, L564
    agreement or love...L188, L201, C82-83, C119, CN112-113, G112, B139, V3:11
    discord or harmony...L195, L201
    sisters and brothers...L564-568, G111, Pt251-255
    whether has...L195, L201, CN111-112
Skin conditions...AA7
Slander...L302
Slave...L53, L463-464, DS167-170
    buying...DS269-269
    freeing...DS270-271
Salvery...V2:70-71
Slow of motion...L299, G248, B5
Small cattle...G272-273
Smoky...L116-117, C6, G40-41, AB270, B5
Socrates...P139

Solsticial points...AB57
Soul, tormented...L265
South latitude...L29
South Node...L49, L130, L300-301, C75, DF24,
    P18, P300, P337, P341, R76, B5, B139
  conjunctions to as unfortunate... DF61
  house of...L302, B111, B117
  in tenth...L298
South Scale (see "Fixed Stars, South Scale)
Southern signs...C3, R81, AB88
Speak to party, if at home...L147, C112, G244-245
Spear-bearing planets (see "Attending Planets")
Speech, defects of...G127
Spica (see "Fixed Stars, Spica")
Spouse's death...L411
Spouse's wealth...L412
Spring Signs (AR,TA,GE)...PA1-3
Square...L26, L105-106, L130, L157, DF45, P16,
    P23, P29, P49, P51, P57, P62, P63, P66-72,
    P87, P98, P275, P278, P280, P282, P284, P285,
    P287, P289, P295, P297, P311, P316, P327,
    P328, P330, P331, P340, P344, R92-93,
    DS214-218
  between Significators example...L220
  in perfection...G239
  of long ascension...L181, L220
States of mind...Pt333-363
  anger...P333
  anguish...L54
  fear...L54, P92, P93, P94, P214, P322, P323, P335
  haughtiness...L265
  jealosy...P92, P94, P139, P179, P180, P185, P191
  lust...P133, P191, P299, P326
  self conceit...L265, P288
  sorrow...L56, P45, P47, P299, P325
  vanity...L265
Stationary...L114, L299(13), L439-440(ex), P10,
    P22, P323, B25, R110, PA31-34
Station, time of retrograde & direct...L58, L62, L65,
    L73, L76
Stature...L50, L100, L135-136, L546, CN102-104,
    P333-338, G101
Status, decline in...DS193-196
Stolen (see "Lost", "Mislaid", "Recovery", "Theft")
  in jest...L321, L332-333, L467
  intention to steal...L335
  not stolen...L335
  what is stolen...L354
  whether or not...L321-323, L326, L334, L335,
    L336,
Straight (CN-SG) or Crooked (CP-GE)...DS262-263
Strayed animals...L323-328, L392-394
Stream or Wave of Aquarius...L581, R105
Study of divine matters, electing... R141
Subra (see "Fixed Stars, Subra")
Succedant...L48, L52, L53, P40, P43, P45, P46,
    P106, P302, P321, P340, AB149-150
Success...L55

despair of...L298
Sudden distempers...L131
Sudden Resolution...L300, P14, P62, P321
Suicide...P173, HT25
Summer Signs (CA,LE,VI)...PA3
Sun...L52, L53, L69-73, L130, L132, D22-23, DF24,
    P13-14, P43, P46, P62, P67, P69, P71, P80-83,
    P86, P87, P95, P97, P276, P277, P278, P280,
    P283, P285-296, P300, P302, P303, P310,
    P315, P316, P317, P319, P321, P324-330,
    P336, P337, P340, P342, P343, P345, P347,
    C25-26, P13-14, P315-316, P336, G69, R56-
    59, B5, B13, F88-94, V1:1-2, DS223, DS225,
    JS23
  aspects of...Pt45
  cazimi...L300
  conjunct Moon...L301, B123
  conjunct other planets...DS221-223
  corporature...L70, L85
  diseases...L247
  diurnal motion of...L45, L47
  in the houses (rulership)...G78-79
  latitude of...L49
  mean argument...AB90
  mean movement...AB89-90
  medicine...L272
  position of...L42
  significator of men...L303
  under the beams of (see "Under the Sun's Beams")
Superior planets...R111, AB62-63, AB296-301
  combust or fortified...B54
Surgery, election of...R169
Swift of Course...L130, C42, D57, P29, P72, G248,
    G274, B9

— T —

Tables
  alchodon...CN89, G92
  almugea (an accidental dignity)... D53-54
  antiscia & contra-antiscia...C20, P36-37, G65
  ascensional differences, oblique ascensions, dec-
    linations, etc...L494-499, CN262, G2:1-184
  aspects, including dexter & sinister...C8, D46
  circles of position...G2:185
  city longitudes...L832, CN263
  colors by planet...C37
  compass directions by house...C37, D131
  conception...CN12-14
  days of the year...P216-217
  degrees (pitted, smoky, etc.)... D41
    elections according to the aspects of the
    Moon...R129
  fixed stars...CN262, P230-231, G26-28, R93-106
  fortitudes & debilities...L115, L178-180, C30,
    C35-36, D37-38, D61-63, G35, G88-89, R65-
    67
  friends & enemies...C37

houses...L27, L32, CN259-260, G2-25
logarithms...C21-27
masculine & feminine degrees...C5-6
middle motions...C22, D57, G2:186-228
Moon's mansions...R130-131
of the meaure of time (for directions)...L711-715, G208
orbs...L107, C22
planetary hours...L473-482, C139-143
planetary natures...D28
planetary significations...P108-110
  profectional directions...CN248, CN251-253, P222, G243
revolutions...G211, G238-241
right ascension...L492-493, C161-162, CN261
sensitive descriptive degrees...L116, G40-41, P33-34
sign rulership of body...L119-120, C34, P127-130, G125-126
Sun's revolutions...CN230-233
thrones of the planets...D54
Talents...B134
Taurus...L53, L94, C9-10, P4, P36, P42, P57, P65, P73, P87, P98, P294, P333, P338, G83, R86-87, B8, HT6-7 F283-284, MM233-235, V1:9-10, PA2, JS15
  diseases...L245
Teaching Writing or a Science...DS271
Tenants...L53, L206
Term (dignity), description...L102, L389, P21, P26, P27, P28, P57, P319, B5, B6, F36-38, Pt91-107
Theft/thieves...L54, L297, L330-366, L395-399, L467-468, C96-100, D126-134, P16, P35, P44, P64, P68, P69, P71, P145, P146, P157, P190, P191, P196, P197, P199, P201, P210, P346, B142, DS296-307
(see "Lost", "Stolen", "Mislaid", "Recovery")
age of thief...L336-338, L362, C99, D126-127
aphorisms...L361-366
as peregrine planet...L331
best experienced rules...L351
clothes of thief...L339, D126
description of thief...L339-340, L343-344, L360-L361, L362-363, L394-399, D126, P13, P16, P35, P44, P64, P68, P69, P71, DS302-307
discovery of...L358, L360, L365
if caught...L366
distance of...L345, L350
fish...L397-399
flight of thief...L364-366
form and stature...L362, L363
gender of thief...L338-339, L362, C99, D129-130, G281
goods with owner or thief...L349-350
his house...L348
if his first theft...L361
in town or not...L344

if returns things...L346, L366
if suspected...L360
judgement of theft...L332-334
location of goods...L350-354, L349, L363
location of thief...L345-347, L363, L364, D130-131
  house of thief...L347-349
name of thief...L340-342
number of thieves...L339, D129-130, G282
quality of goods stolen...L354-355
recovery...L355-359, L366, L395-399, L467-468, C98, C129, D132-133, G280-281, DS297
  time of...L356, C100, G282-283, DS296
sex of thief...L338, L362
sign of Moon = type of item... DS300-302
significators...L331
took with him...L350
what is stolen...L354
  whether stolen...L334-336, C97, C129, D127(Lilly plag.)**, G281
whether thief carried goods away...L350
whether thief is in town...L344-345
whether thief is of the house...L342, L364
whether thief is a stranger...L342, L343, L360, L364, C99, G282, DS302
whether thief is suspected...L360
who is...L343-344, L360, L364
will thief be caught...L358-359, L365-366
Thin or fat..L549-550
Things happening...L148
Thrones of the planets (greatest dignity)...D54, R75
Time of birth...L231, L232, L242
Time of question...L130, L131, L166-167, L219, C71-72
Timing...L125, L153-154, L171, L176, L198, L242
  accident, time when...L139-141(ex)
  by degree...L419(ex)
  by house...L171, L176, L267(table)
  by sign...L152(ex), L267(table), L307
  ephemeris...L152(ex), L196(ex), L221(ex), L385(ex), L415(ex), L417(ex)
  health crises...L266
  lost or stolen article return...L356
  marriage...L307
  missing person's return...L198
  of recovery...L267
  real estate...L221
  significator changing sign...L268
  symbolic...L221(ex)
  table...L267
  when riches will come...L183-184
Time to perfection...P52, P318, G240
Torture...L648
Transits...CN257-258, P175, P208, P210, P211, P225-229, P287, P310, G246-248
Translation...L111, L125-126, C40, D48-49, DF52, P20, P50, P64, P71, P136, G43, G245, G287, R111, B4, JS45

as perfection...L126, D87, DF91
by friends...L304
by square or opposition...L205
double...L183
examples of...L183, L220, L421, L454
in marriage charts...L303, L304
Travel...(see "Journeys")
Treasure, hidden or buried...L52, L215-218, C122, G260-262, B122
Trepidation...AB101
Trica...R99
Tridecile...L32, C6
Trigon...P3, P9, P323, P324
Trine...L26-27, L106, L27, L132, DF45, P20, P23-25, P29, P50, P57, P64, P67-70, P91, P273, P281, P284-286, P303, P328, P329, P344, R92-93, DS212-214
Triplicity (dignity)...L87, L102, L298, P21, P27, P28, P299, P302, P316, AB230, B5, B6, Pt83-87, DS161-162, DS196
Trotting...L52
Trouble...L299
Trudging...L52
True...L192
True or false
  fears...L192-193
  for good or evil...L192-194
  news...L192-193
  rumors...L192-193
  reports...L192-193
Tumults...L132
Turned chart...L419
  mixed houses...L419-20
Turning (solsticial) points...AB57
Twins...L229, L230, F237-238, Pt257-261

— U —

Unaspected planet...L140
Under the Sun's Beams...L113, L300(26), C41, P300, P302, P324, P344, R111, R222, B43, DS165, DS189, DS222, DS264, Pt285
  fear...L389-90(ex)
  Mercury...L389(ex)
  Secret affairs...V3:4
  Secret matters...L393, DS264
  when USB planet is dignified...AA31
Underweight...L549
Unmarried...L312
Unsure of judgment...L298
Unfortunate...L298
Unukalhai (see "Fixed Stars, Unukalhai")

— V —

Vacua cursus...(see "Void of Course")
Var (see "Fixed Stars, Var")

Vega (see "Fixed Stars, Vega")
Venus...L53, L54, L72, L73, L85, L130, l132, L541, L595-596, C26, D23-24, P15, P43, P47, P57, P62, P63, P65, P67, P69, P81, P86, P87, P276, P279, P281-283, P286, P288-291, P294, P296, P297, P303, P309, P316, P318, P322, P326-331, P336, P339, P341, P343, P344, P345, G70, R59-61, B8, F94-99, F206-210, AB240-257, Pt185-187, Pt311, V1:4-5, DS223-224, DS229-230, DS233, JS23-24
  angular...DS229-230
  as dispositor of significator...L300
  condition of...L298
  conjunct other planets...DS221-224
  corporature...L74, L85
  dignified...L302
  diseases...L247, L263
  diurnal motion of...L47
  house of...L302
  humidifies & heats...Pt37
  in essential dignity...L298
  in the Houses (by ruler)...G79-80, DS233
  marriage indications...L302, L303, CN122, G136-137
  medicines...L270
  sextile of...L298
  significator of women...L303
  trine of...L298
Vernal...L48, C4, DF21-22
Vespertine & Matutine planets...F38-39, Pt40-41
Via combusta (i.e., 15° Libra to 15° Scorpio; an accidental debility)...L122, D59, DF61, AB317
  Moon in...L415(ex), L439(ex), L440, L468(ex), P49, P287, B5, DS265, DS278, DS296
  Ascendant in...L395-396(ex)
Vindiamatrix (see "Fixed Stars, Vindiamatrix")
Virginity...L312
Virgo...L96, C12, P6, G85, P6, P32, P36, P44, P53, P57, P65, P74, P87, P91, P270, P281, P282, P302, P308, P310, P316, P334, R88, B8, F288-289, MM237-239, V1:13-14, PA3, HT12-14, JS16-17
  diseases...L246
Visions...L55
Void of course...L112, L122, L299(9), L385(ex)+, L461-472(ex), C41, P21, P338, G45, G257, R111, B5, B19, F123, AB310, AA28, DS171, JS42
  perfection after sign change...L152-L53(ex)
  performeth somewhat...L122
  planets...L112
  signs work in...L122, L299(9)
Voyage at sea...L422-423
  how prosperous...G285-286
  long or short...G286

— W —

Wages, receipt of...L170, L171, G252
Wan...L51
Wantoness...L132
War & Warfare...L54, L297, L366-368, L379-383,
      L399, L401-403, L452-456, C128, C131, P44,
      P344, G277-278
   ammunition and soldiery in...L56
   effect on status of commander...L452-454
   if return safely...L367
   if benefit from...L368
   in elections...R179-184
   Moon impedited...L301
   Mars as fighting planet...L453
   opposing party...L54
   outcome of battle...L192, L367, L399-400, L453-
      456
   quality of army commanders...L380-383
   shall the armies fight...L383
   whether a place be taken...L379-380, L401-403
Water...L132
   election to bring...R148
   if access to...L214-215
Wealth...L51, L118, L167, L551-561, C80-81,
      C115, P42, P43, P68, P311, P317, G249-250,
      B139, JS85
   maintenance of wealth...L552-564
   means to obtain...L168, L182, L555-561, G250
   mutual reception...L172
   of father...L53
   profit/loss from event...L171
   reasons for not having...L172
   of spouse...L412, L421
   table for measuring wealth...L178-180
   timing...L183, G250
   when during life...L563
   where the Querent may be prosperous...G244
   whether legal...L561
   without marriage...L181
Weather prediction...Pt201-219, HT3-25, HT53-63,
      JS9-13
Weighting planets...L178-181
Weeks...L130
Wells, election to dig...R148
What will happen...L368
What part of life is best...L134
Where to live...L132
Whether Ascendant or Signifying House be
      Stronger...B69
Whether Lord of New/Full Moon be Angular...B70
When the money will be obtained...L175
When a baby will be born...L231
Whether a woman is single...L312
Whether a woman is honest in marriage...L313-316

Whether a person is dead or alive...L151-152
Whether a person will return...L406-408
Who benefits most?...G276-277
Who is loved most...L305
Who will die first...L311
Who will cause trouble...L310
Who will have power in marriage...L309
Who a person will marry...L308, L385-390
Why wealth won't be attained...L172
Widow(s)...P15, P302
Wills...DS321-322
Winds...L160, L423, V1:39-40, PA39-40
Winter, of the nature of...L48
Winter, signs of...DF21-22
Witches & Witchcraft...L56, L250, L263, L464-466,
      L468-469, C138
Woman
   prejudice by...L132
   significator of...L302
   with child...L53
Woody...L53
World days...AB113-114
Write to a person...DS271

— Y —

Years...L13, DS235-245, AB224, AB239
   best of life...L134, L138, L146
   transfer of years...DS245-261
Yed Prior (see "Fixed Stars, Yed Prior")
Yes or No...L124-128
Youthful...L48

— Z —

Zodiac...L86

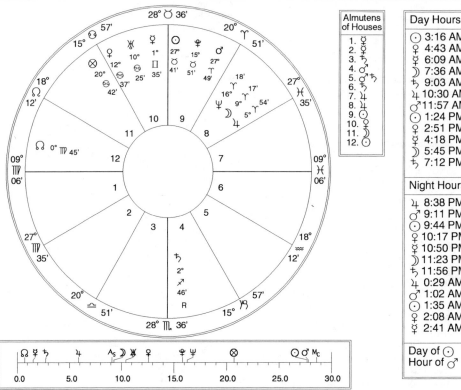

Nicholas II	12:00:00 LMT	May 18, 1868
St Petersburg, Russia	59°N 55'00"	30°E 15'00"
Regiomontanus	3:45:28 S.T.	J.D. = 2403470.9160
Natal Chart	R.A.M.S. = 3:45:28	Obl. = 23°27'23"
Tropical	No Ayanamsha	Geocentric Ecliptic

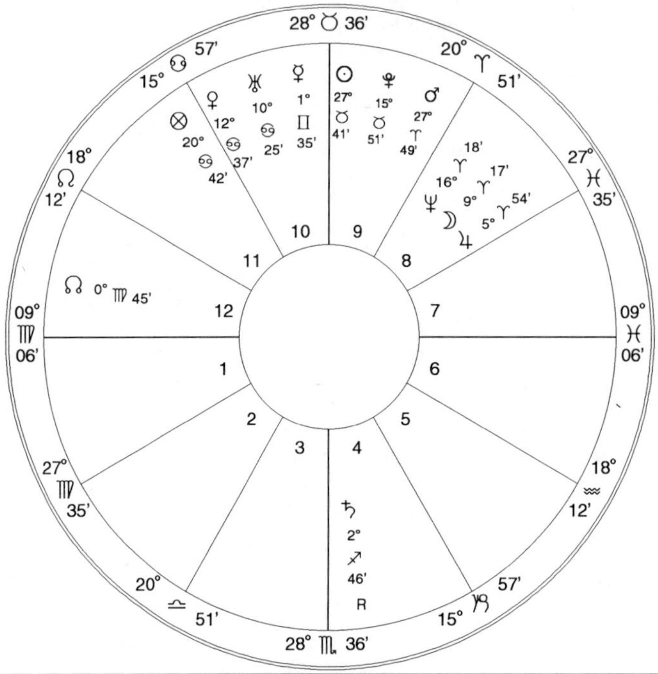

Almutens of Houses
1. ☿
2. ☿
3. ♄
4. ♂
5. ☿ ♂ ♄
6. ♄
7. ♃
8. ♃
9. ☉
10. ♀
11. ☽
12. ☉

Day Hours

☉ 3:16 AM
♀ 4:43 AM
☿ 6:09 AM
☽ 7:36 AM
♄ 9:03 AM
♃ 10:30 AM
♂ 11:57 AM
☉ 1:24 PM
♀ 2:51 PM
☿ 4:18 PM
☽ 5:45 PM
♄ 7:12 PM

Night Hours

♃ 8:38 PM
♂ 9:11 PM
☉ 9:44 PM
♀ 10:17 PM
☿ 10:50 PM
☽ 11:23 PM
♄ 11:56 PM
♃ 0:29 AM
♂ 1:02 AM
☉ 1:35 AM
♀ 2:08 AM
☿ 2:41 AM

Day of ☉
Hour of ♂

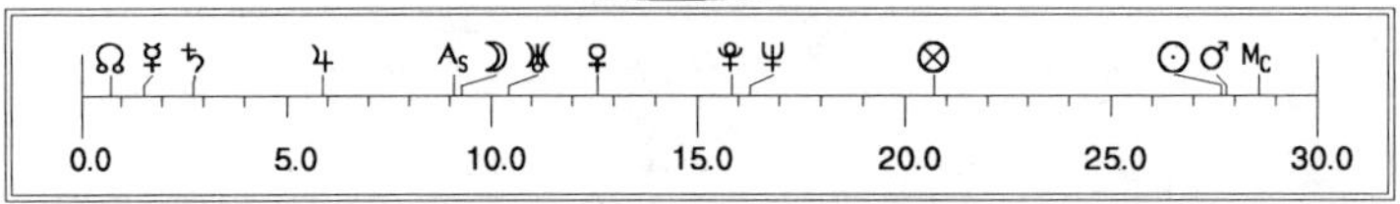

Table of Essential Dignities

Points	Ruler	Exalt.	Trip.	Terms	Face	Detr.	Fall	Score	Solar	Quality of Degree
☉	♀	☽ m	♀	♂	♄	♂	--	+ 4	Occ.	Masc., Light
☽	♂	☉ m	☉	♀	♂	♀	♄	+ 4	Ori.	Masc., Dark
☿	☿ +	☊ m	♄	☿ +	♃	♃	--	+11	Occ. Beams	Fem., Light, Deep
♀	☽	♃	♂	♃	☿	♄	♂	- 5p	Occ.	Masc., Dark, Lame
♂	♂ +	☉	☉	♄	♀	♀	♄	+ 5	Ori.	Masc., Light
♃	♂	☉	☉	♃ +	♂	♀	♄	+ 2	Ori.	Masc., Light, Deep
♄	♃	☋	☉	♃	☿	☿	--	- 5p	Occ.	Fem., Light
♅	☽	♃	♂	♃	☿	♄	♂	--	Occ.	Fem., Light, Lame
♆	♂	☉	☉	☿	☉	♀	♄	--	Ori.	Fem., Light
♇	♀	☽	♀	♃	☽	♂	--	--	Ori. Beams	Fem., Void
☊	☿	☿ m	♀	☿	☉	♃	♀	--	Ori.	Fem., Dark
☋	♃	♀	♂	♀	♄	☿	☿	--	Ori.	Masc., Dark
As	☿	☿	♀	♀	☉	♃	♀	--	--	Masc., Void
Mc	♀	☽	♀	♂	♄	♂	--	--	--	Masc., Dark
⊗	☽	♃	♂	♀	☽	♄	♂		Occ.	Masc., Light

Pl.	Antiscia
☉	2° ♌ 19'
☽	20° ♍ 43'
☿	28° ♋ 25'
♀	17° ♊ 23'
♂	2° ♍ 11'
♃	24° ♍ 06'
♄	27° ♑ 14'
♅	19° ♊ 35'
♆	13° ♍ 42'
♇	14° ♌ 09'
☊	29° ♈ 15'
As	20° ♈ 54'
Mc	1° ♌ 24'
⊗	9° ♊ 18'

J. Lee Lehman, Ph.D. - P.O. Box 501107 - Malabar FL 32950 - (407) 728-2277 Fax -2244

OLDTIME1

(C) 1992 Astrolabe, Inc.

Mary Godwin Shelley	23:20:00 LMT	Aug. 30, 1797
LONDON, ENGLAND	51°N 30'00"	0°W 10'00"
Regiomontanus	21:58:27 S.T.	J.D. = 2377643.4729
Natal Chart	R.A.M.S. = 10:38:28	Obl. = 23°27'56"
Tropical	No Ayanamsha	Geocentric Ecliptic

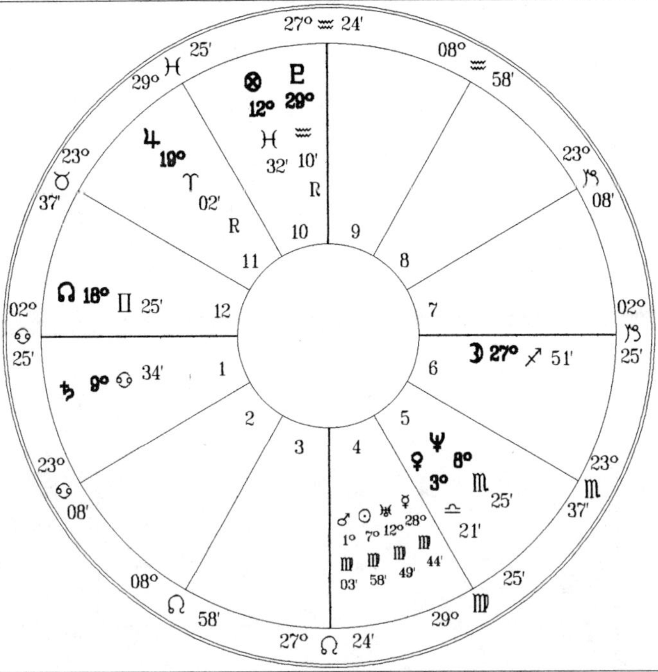

Almutens of Houses
1. ☽
2. ☽
3. ☉
4. ☉
5. ☿
6. ♂
7. ♄
8. ♂
9. ☿ ♄
10. ♄
11. ♃
12. ☽

Day Hours
☿ 5:10 AM
☽ 6:18 AM
♄ 7:26 AM
♃ 8:35 AM
♂ 9:43 AM
☉ 10:51 AM
♀ 12:00 AM
☿ 1:08 PM
☽ 2:16 PM
♄ 3:25 PM
♃ 4:33 PM
♂ 5:41 PM
Night Hours
☉ 6:50 PM
♀ 7:42 PM
☿ 8:33 PM
☽ 9:25 PM
♄ 10:17 PM
♃ 11:09 PM
♂ 0:00 AM
☉ 0:52 AM
♀ 1:44 AM
☿ 2:36 AM
☽ 3:28 AM
♄ 4:19 AM
Day of ☿
Hour of ♃

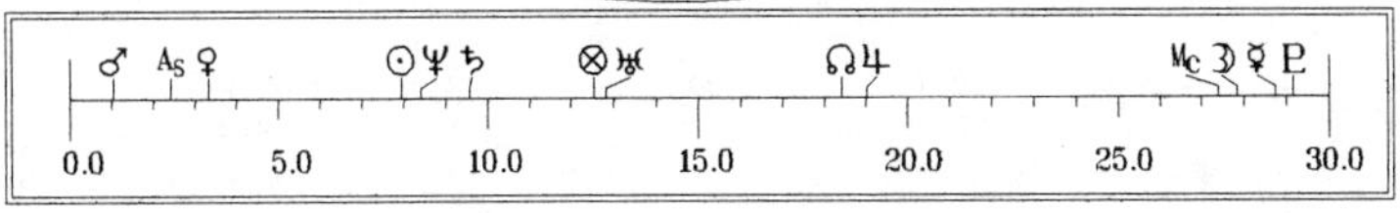

Pl.	Antiscia
☉	22°♈02'
☽	2°♑09'
☿	1°♈16'
♀	26°♓39'
♂	28°♈57'
♃	10°♍58'
♄	20°♊26'
♅	17°♈11'
♆	21°♒35'
♇	0°♏50'
☊	11°♋35'
As	27°♊34'
Mc	2°♏35'
⊗	17°♎28'

Table of Essential Dignities

Points	Ruler	Exalt.	Trip.	Terms	Face	Detr.	Fall	Score	Solar	Quality of Degree
☉	☿	☿	☽	♀	☉ +	♃	♀	+ 1	Ori.	Fem., Light, Deep
☽	♃	☋	♃	♂	♄	☿	--	− 5p	Ori.	Masc., Light
☿	☿ +	☿ +	☽	♂ m	☿ +	♃	♀	+12	Occ.	Masc., Dark
♀	♀ +	♄	☿	♄	☽	♂	☉	+ 5	Occ.	Masc., Light
♂	☿	☿	☽	☿ m	☉	♃	♀	+ 2	Ori. Comb.	Fem., Dark
♃	♂	☉	♃ +	☿	☉	♀	♄	+ 3	Occ.	Fem., Light
♄	☽	♃	♂	♃	♀	♄ −	♂	−10p	Ori.	Masc., Light, Lame
♅	☿	☿	☽	♀	♀	♃	♀	--	Occ. Comb.	Fem., Light, Deep
♆	♂	--	♂	♃	♂	♀	☽	--	Occ.	Fem., Void, Deep
♇	♄	--	☿	♂	☽	☉	--	--	Ori.	Fem., Light
☊	☿	☊ +	☿	♀	♂	♃	--	--	Ori.	Fem., Light
☋	♃	☋ +	♃	☿	☽	☿	--	--	Ori.	Fem., Light, Lame
As	☽	♃	♂	♂	♀	♄	♂	--	--	Fem., Light, Fort.
Mc	♄	--	☿	♂	☽	☉	--	--	--	Fem., Light
⊗	♃	♀	♂	♃	♃	☿	☿		Occ.	Fem., Dark, Fort.

J. Lee Lehman, Ph.D. – P.O. Box 501107 – Malabar FL 32950 – (407) 728–2277 Fax –2244

OLDTIME1

(C) 1992 Astrolabe. Inc.

Prince Charles	21:14:00 UT	Nov. 14, 1948
London, England	51°N 30'00"	0°W 08'00"
Placidus	0:48:57 S.T.	J.D. = 2432870.3850
Natal Chart	R.A.M.S. = 15:35:30	Obl. = 23°26'45"
Tropical	No Ayanamsha	Geocentric Ecliptic

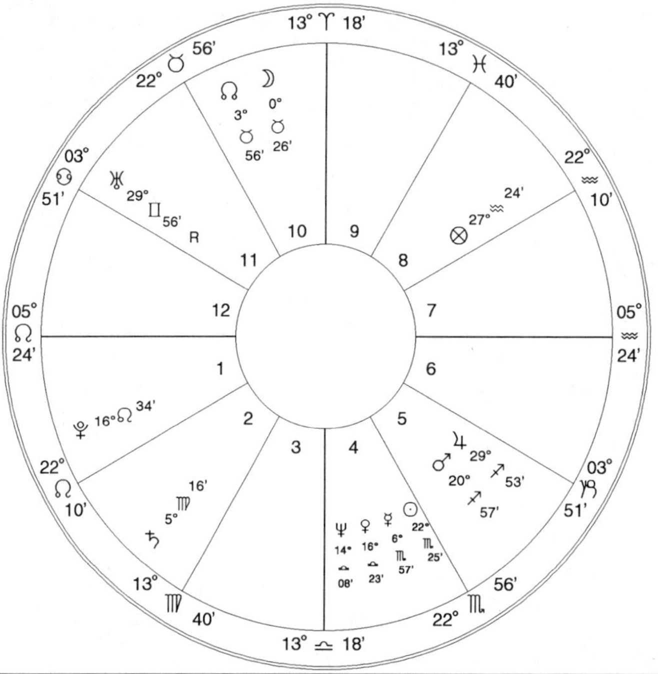

Almutens of Houses
1. ☉
2. ☉♃
3. ☿
4. ♀♄
5. ♂
6. ♄
7. ♄
8. ♄
9. ♃
10. ☉♂
11. ☽
12. ☽

Day Hours
☉ 7:17 AM
♀ 8:01 AM
☿ 8:46 AM
☽ 9:31 AM
♄ 10:15 AM
♃ 11:00 AM
♂ 11:45 AM
☉ 0:29 PM
♀ 1:14 PM
☿ 1:59 PM
☽ 2:43 PM
♄ 3:28 PM

Night Hours
♃ 4:13 PM
♂ 5:28 PM
☉ 6:44 PM
♀ 7:59 PM
☿ 9:15 PM
☽ 10:30 PM
♄ 11:46 PM
♃ 1:01 AM
♂ 2:17 AM
☉ 3:32 AM
♀ 4:48 AM
☿ 6:03 AM

Day of ☉
Hour of ♀

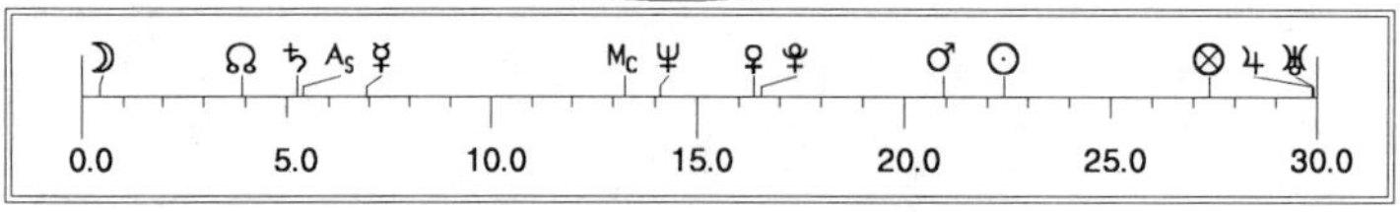

Table of Essential Dignities

Points	Ruler	Exalt.	Trip.	Terms	Face	Detr.	Fall	Score	Solar	Quality of Degree
☉	♂	--	♂	☿	♀	♀	☽	- 5p	Ori.	Fem., Smokey, Deep
☽	♀	☽ +	☽ +	♀	☿	♂	--	+ 7	Ori.	Fem., Dark
☿	♂	--	♂	♃	♂	♀	☽	- 5p	Ori. Beams	Fem., Light, Fort.
♀	♀ +	♄	☿	♃	♄	♂	☉	+ 5	Ori.	Masc., Light
♂	♃	☋	♃	♄	♄	☿	--	- 5p	Occ.	Fem., Smokey
♃	♃ +	☋	♃ +	♂	♄	☿	--	+ 8	Occ.	Masc., Light, Deep
♄	☿	☿	☽	☿	☉	♃	♀	- 5p	Ori.	Fem., Light
♅	☿	☊	☿	♂	☉	♃	--	--	Occ.	Fem., Void, Deep
♆	♀	♄	☿	♃	♄	♂	☉	--	Ori.	Fem., Light, Fort.
♇	☉	--	♃	♀	♃	♄	--	--	Occ.	Fem., Smokey
☊	♀	☽	☽	♀	☿	♂	--	--	Ori.	Fem., Light
☋	♂	--	♂	♂	♂	♀	☽	--	Ori.	Masc., Light
As	☉	--	♃	♄	♄	♄	--	--	--	Fem., Dark, Deep
Mc	♂	☉	♃	♀	☉	♀	♄	--	--	Masc., Dark
⊗	♄	--	☿	♂	☽	☉	--		Ori.	Fem., Light

Pl.	Antiscia
☉	7°♒35'
☽	29°♌34'
☿	23°♒03'
♀	13°♓37'
♂	9°♑03'
♃	0°♑07'
♄	24°♈44'
♅	0°♋04'
♆	15°♓52'
♇	13°♉26'
☊	26°♌04'
As	24°♉36'
Mc	16°♍42'
⊗	2°♏36'

J. Lee Lehman, Ph.D. - P.O. Box 501107 - Malabar FL 32950 - (407) 728-2277 Fax -2244

OLDTIME1

(C) 1992 Astrolabe, Inc.

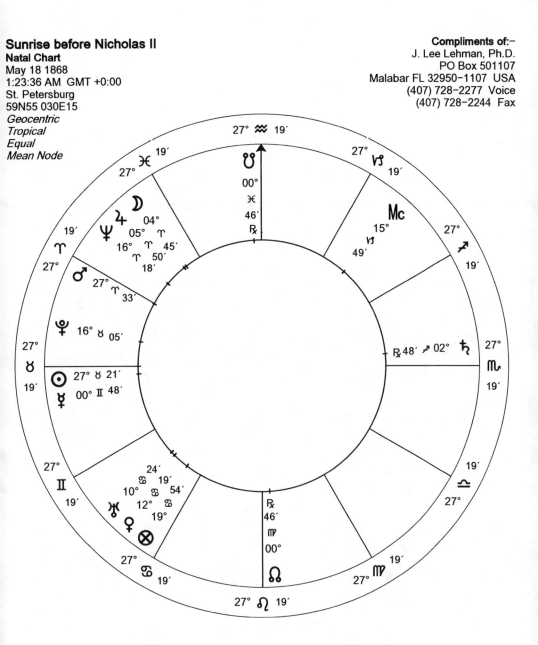

Sunrise before Nicholas II
Natal Chart
May 18 1868
1:23:36 AM GMT +0:00
St. Petersburg
59N55 030E15
Geocentric
Tropical
Equal
Mean Node

Compliments of:-
J. Lee Lehman, Ph.D.
PO Box 501107
Malabar FL 32950-1107 USA
(407) 728-2277 Voice
(407) 728-2244 Fax

333

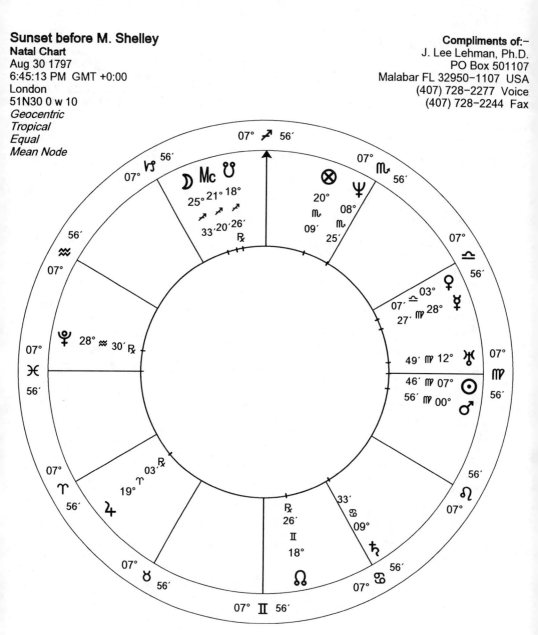

Compliments of:−
J. Lee Lehman, Ph.D.
PO Box 501107
Malabar FL 32950−1107 USA
(407) 728−2277 Voice
(407) 728−2244 Fax

Sunset before M. Shelley
Natal Chart
Aug 30 1797
6:45:13 PM GMT +0:00
London
51N30 0 w 10
Geocentric
Tropical
Equal
Mean Node

Aleister Crowley	23:30:00 UT	Oct. 12, 1875
Leamington Spa, England	52°N 14'00"	1°W 30'00"
Regiomontanus	0:48:30 S.T.	J.D. = 2406174.4791
Natal Chart	R.A.M.S. = 13:24:30	Obl. = 23°27'20"
Tropical	No Ayanamsha	Geocentric Ecliptic

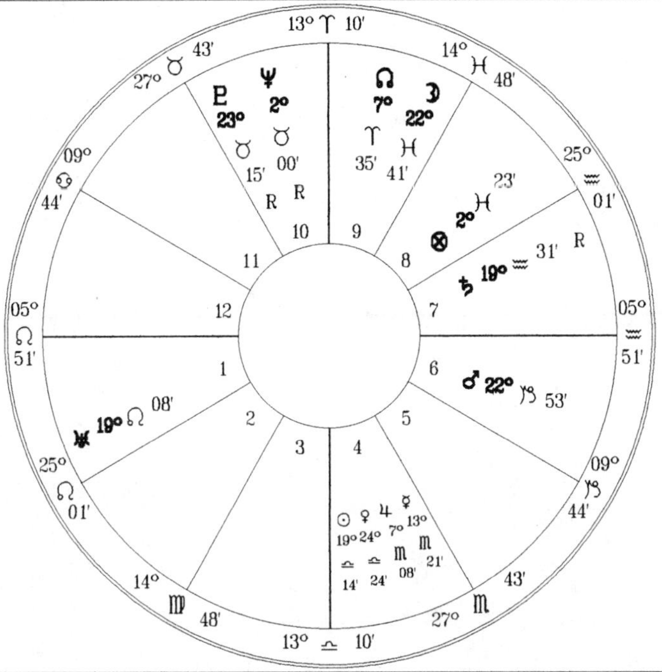

Almutens of Houses
1. ☉
2. ☉
3. ☿
4. ♀ ♄
5. ♂
6. ♄
7. ♄
8. ♄
9. ♃
10. ☉ ♂
11. ☽
12. ♃

Day Hours	
☽	6:25 AM
♄	7:20 AM
♃	8:14 AM
♂	9:09 AM
☉	10:03 AM
♀	10:58 AM
☿	11:52 AM
☽	0:47 PM
♄	1:41 PM
♃	2:36 PM
♂	3:30 PM
☉	4:25 PM
Night Hours	
♀	5:19 PM
☿	6:25 PM
☽	7:31 PM
♄	8:36 PM
♃	9:42 PM
♂	10:47 PM
☉	11:53 PM
♀	0:59 AM
☿	2:04 AM
☽	3:10 AM
♄	4:16 AM
♃	5:21 AM

Day of ☽
Hour of ♂

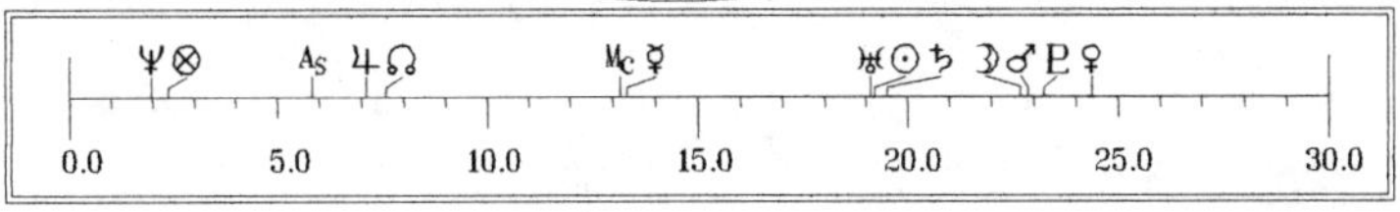

Table of Essential Dignities

Points	Ruler	Exalt.	Trip.	Terms	Face	Detr.	Fall	Score	Solar	Quality of Degree
☉	♀	♄	☿	☿	♄	♂	☉ -	- 9p	Ori.	Masc., Dark, Deep
☽	♃	♀	♂ m	♂	♂	☿	☿	+ 3	Ori.	Masc., Void
☿	♂	--	♂	♃	☉	♀	☽	- 5p	Occ.	Fem., Void
♀	♀ +	♄	☿	♂	♃	♂	☉	+ 5	Occ. Comb.	Fem., Light
♂	♄	♂ +	☽ m	♂ +	☉	☽	♃	+ 9	Ori.	Masc., Void
♃	♂	--	♂	♃ +	♂	♀	☽	+ 2	Occ.	Fem., Light
♄	♄ +	--	☿	♀	☿	☉	--	+ 5	Ori.	Masc., Light, Fort.
♅	☉	--	♃	♃	♃	♄	--	--	Ori.	Fem., Smokey
♆	♀	☽	☽	♀	☿	♂	--	--	Occ.	Fem., Dark
♇	♀	☽	☽	♄	♄	♂	--	--	Occ.	Fem., Light, Deep
☊	♂	☉	♃	♀	♂	♀	♄	--	Ori.	Masc., Light
☋	♀	♄	☿	♀	☽	♂	☉	--	Ori. Beams	Fem., Dark
As	☉	--	♃	♄	♄	♄	--	--	--	Fem., Dark, Deep
Mc	♂	☉	♃	♀	☉	♀	♄	--	--	Masc., Dark
⊗	♃	♀	♂	♀	♄	☿	☿		Ori.	Masc., Dark

Pl.	Antiscia
☉	10°♓46'
☽	7°♎19'
☿	16°♒39'
♀	5°♓36'
♂	7°♐07'
♃	22°♒52'
♄	10°♏29'
♅	10°♉52'
♆	28°♌00'
♇	6°♌45'
☊	22°♍25'
As	24°♉09'
Mc	16°♍49'
⊗	27°♎37'

J. Lee Lehman, Ph.D. - P.O. Box 501107 - Malabar FL 32950 - (407) 728-2277 Fax -2244

OLDTIME1

(C) 1992 Astrolabe. Inc.

Catherine de Medici	04:15:20 UT	Apr. 13, 1519
Florence	43°N 46'00"	11°E 15'00"
Regiomontanus	18:21:04 S.T.	J.D. = 2275964.6803
Natal Chart	R.A.M.S. = 1:20:45	Obl. = 23°30'07"
Tropical	No Ayanamsha	Geocentric Ecliptic

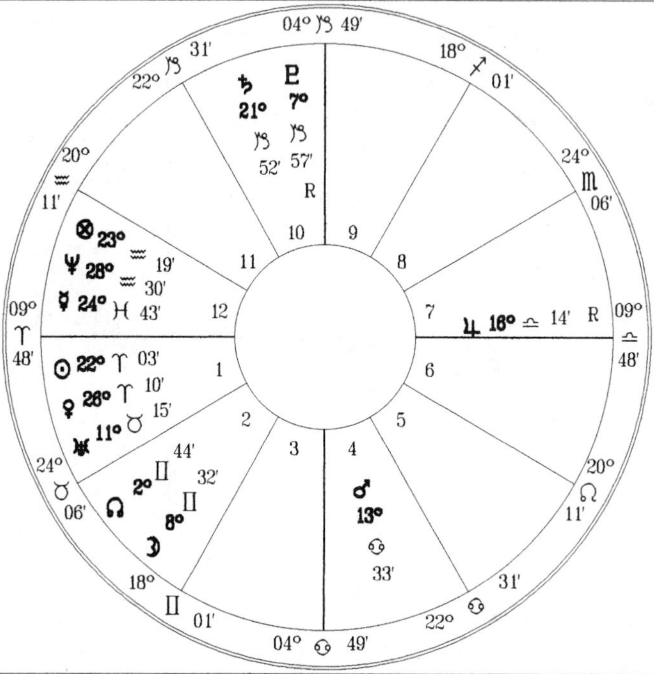

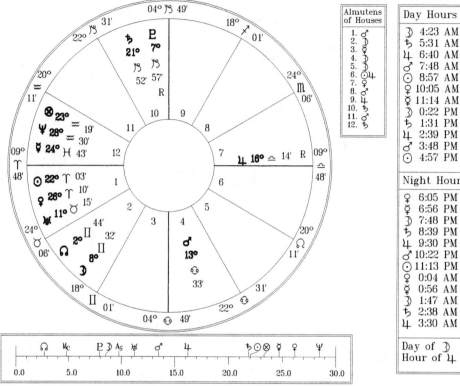

Almutens of Houses
1. ♂
2. ☽
3. ☿
4. ☽
5. ☽
6. ☉♃
7. ♀
8. ♂
9. ♃
10. ♄
11. ♂
12. ♄

Day Hours
☽ 4:23 AM
♄ 5:31 AM
♃ 6:40 AM
♂ 7:48 AM
☉ 8:57 AM
♀ 10:05 AM
☿ 11:14 AM
☽ 0:22 PM
♄ 1:31 PM
♃ 2:39 PM
♂ 3:48 PM
☉ 4:57 PM
Night Hours
♀ 6:05 PM
☿ 6:56 PM
☽ 7:48 PM
♄ 8:39 PM
♃ 9:30 PM
♂ 10:22 PM
☉ 11:13 PM
♀ 0:04 AM
☿ 0:56 AM
☽ 1:47 AM
♄ 2:38 AM
♃ 3:30 AM
Day of ☽
Hour of ♃

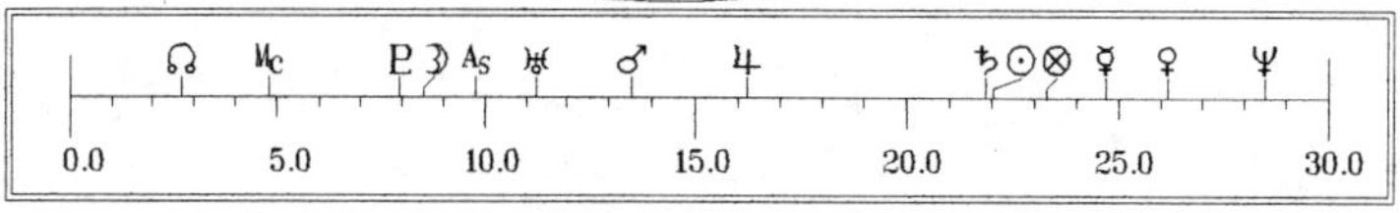

Pl.	Antiscia
☉	7°♍57'
☽	21°♋28'
☿	5°♎17'
♀	3°♍50'
♂	16°♊27'
♃	13°♓46'
♄	8°♐08'
♅	18°♌45'
♆	1°♏30'
♇	22°♐03'
☊	27°♋16'
As	20°♍12'
Mc	25°♐10'
⊗	6°♏41'

Table of Essential Dignities

Points	Ruler	Exalt.	Trip.	Terms	Face	Detr.	Fall	Score	Solar	Quality of Degree
☉	♂	☉ +	♃	♂	♀	♀	♄	+ 4	Occ.	Masc., Void, Deep
☽	☿	☊	☿	♃	♃	♃	--	− 5p	Occ.	Masc., Light
☿	♃	♀	♂	♂ m	♂ m	☿ −	☿ −	− 6	Ori.	Fem., Void
♀	♂	☉	♃	♄	♀ +	♀ −	♄	− 4	Occ. Comb.	Masc., Light
♂	☽	♃	♂ +	☿ m	☿ m	♄	♂ −	+ 2	Occ.	Masc., Dark, Lame
♃	♀	♄	☿	♃ +	♄	♂	☉	+ 2	Ori.	Masc., Light
♄	♄ +	♂	☽	♂	☉	☽	♃	+ 5	Occ.	Masc., Dark, Deep
♅	♀	☽	☽	☿	☽	♂	--	--	Occ.	Fem., Void, Deep
♆	♄	--	☿	♂	☽	☉	--	--	Ori.	Fem., Light, Deep
♇	♄	♂	☽	☿	♃	☽	♃	--	Occ.	Masc., Light
☊	☿	☊ +	☿	☿	♃	♃	--	--	Occ.	Fem., Light
☋	♃	☋ +	♃	♃	☿	☿	--	--	Occ.	Fem., Light
As	♂	☉	♃	♀	♂	♀	♄	--	--	Masc., Dark
Mc	♄	♂	☽	♀	♃	☽	♃	--	--	Masc., Dark
⊗	♄	--	☿	♃	☽	☉	--		Ori.	Fem., Void, Deep

J. Lee Lehman, Ph.D. - P.O. Box 501107 - Malabar FL 32950 - (407) 728-2277 Fax -2244

OLDTIME1

(C) 1992 Astrolabe. Inc.

Muhammad Ali	18:30:00 CST	Jan. 17, 1942
Louisville, KY	38°N 15'00"	85°W 46'00"
Regiomontanus	2:34:06 S.T.	J.D. = 2430377.5211
Natal Chart	R.A.M.S. = 19:47:10	Obl. = 23°26'49"
Tropical	No Ayanamsha	Geocentric Ecliptic

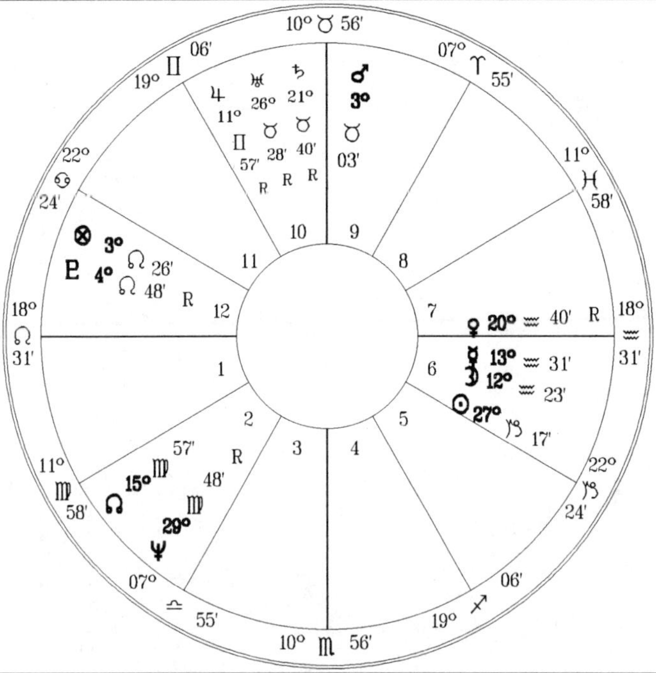

Almutens of Houses
1. ☉
2. ♀
3. ♀
4. ♂
5. ♃
6. ♂
7. ♄
8. ♃
9. ♂
10. ☽
11. ☿
12. ☽

Day Hours	
♄	6:58 AM
♃	7:47 AM
♂	8:37 AM
☉	9:26 AM
♀	10:15 AM
☿	11:04 AM
☽	11:53 AM
♄	0:43 PM
♃	1:32 PM
♂	2:21 PM
☉	3:10 PM
♀	3:59 PM
Night Hours	
☿	4:49 PM
☽	5:59 PM
♄	7:10 PM
♃	8:21 PM
♂	9:32 PM
☉	10:42 PM
♀	11:53 PM
☿	1:04 AM
☽	2:15 AM
♄	3:25 AM
♃	4:36 AM
♂	5:47 AM

Day of ♄
Hour of ☽

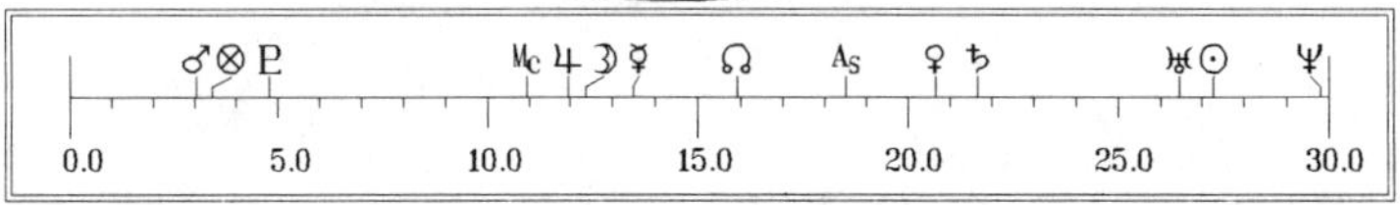

Pl.	Antiscia
☉	2°♐43′
☽	17°♏37′
☿	16°♏29′
♀	9°♏20′
♂	26°♌57′
♃	18°♋03′
♄	8°♌20′
♅	3°♌32′
♆	0°♈12′
♇	25°♉12′
☊	14°♈03′
As	11°♉28′
Mc	19°♌03′
⊗	26°♉34′

Table of Essential Dignities

Points	Ruler	Exalt.	Trip.	Terms	Face	Detr.	Fall	Score	Solar	Quality of Degree
☉	♄	♂	☽	♄	☉ +	☽	♃	+ 1	Ori.	Masc., Dark, Lame
☽	♄	--	☿	♀	☿	☉	--	− 5p	Occ. Beams	Fem., Dark
☿	♄	--	☿ +	♀	☿ +	☉	--	+ 4	Occ. Beams	Fem., Light
♀	♄ m	--	☿	♃	☽	☉	--	+ 5	Occ.	Masc., Light
♂	♀	☽	☽	♀	☿	♂ −	--	−10p	Ori.	Fem., Light
♃	☿	☊	☿	♃ +	♂	♃ −	--	− 3	Ori.	Masc., Light, Deep
♄	♀ m	☽	☽	♃	♄ +	♂	--	+ 6	Ori.	Fem., Light
♅	♀	☽	☽	♂	♄	♂	--	--	Ori.	Masc., Light, Fort.
♆	☿	☿	☽	♂	☿	♃	♀	--	Occ.	Masc., Dark
♇	☉	--	♃	♄	♄	♄	--	--	Occ.	Masc., Dark, Fort.
☊	☿	☿	☽	♃	♀	♃	♀	--	Occ.	Fem., Light, Deep
☋	♃	♀	♂	☿	♃	☿	☿	--	Occ.	Fem., Dark
As	☉	--	♃	♀	♃	♄	--	--	--	Fem., Smokey, Fort.
Mc	♀	☽	☽	☿	☽	♂	--	--	--	Masc., Void
⊗	☉	--	♃	♄	♄	♄	--		Occ.	Masc., Dark

J. Lee Lehman, Ph.D. – P.O. Box 501107 – Malabar FL 32950 – (407) 728–2277 Fax –2244

OLDTIME1

(C) 1992 Astrolabe. Inc.

George Foreman	21:15:00 CST	Jan. 10, 1949
Marshall, TX	32°N 33′00″	94°W 23′00″
Regiomontanus	4:18:41 S.T.	J.D. = 2432927.6357
Natal Chart	R.A.M.S. = 19:21:13	Obl. = 23°26′45″
Tropical	No Ayanamsha	Geocentric Ecliptic

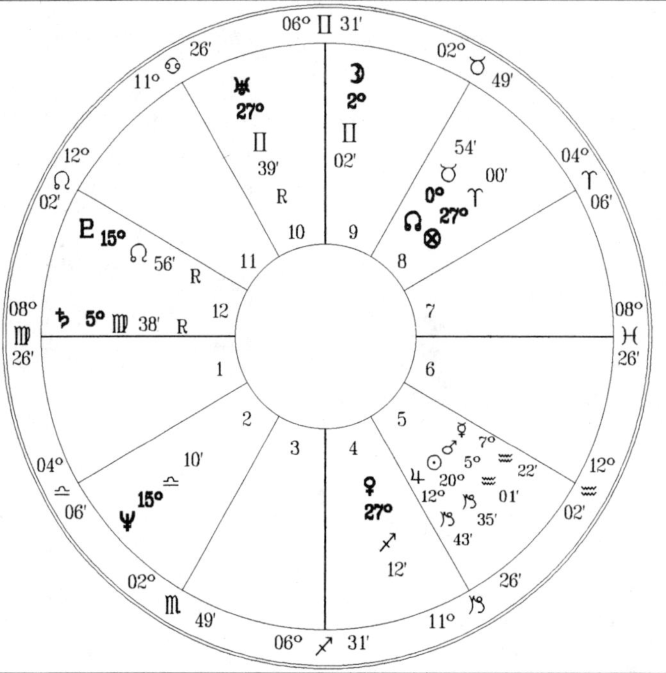

Almutens of Houses
1. ☿
2. ♄
3. ♂
4. ♃
5. ♂♄
6. ♄
7. ♃
8. ♂
9. ☽♀
10. ☿
11. ♃
12. ☉

Day Hours	
☽	7:20 AM
♄	8:11 AM
♃	9:02 AM
♂	9:53 AM
☉	10:44 AM
♀	11:35 AM
☿	0:25 PM
☽	1:16 PM
♄	2:07 PM
♃	2:58 PM
♂	3:49 PM
☉	4:39 PM

Night Hours	
♀	5:30 PM
☿	6:39 PM
☽	7:49 PM
♄	8:58 PM
♃	10:07 PM
♂	11:16 PM
☉	0:25 AM
♀	1:34 AM
☿	2:44 AM
☽	3:53 AM
♄	5:02 AM
♃	6:11 AM

Day of ☽
Hour of ♄

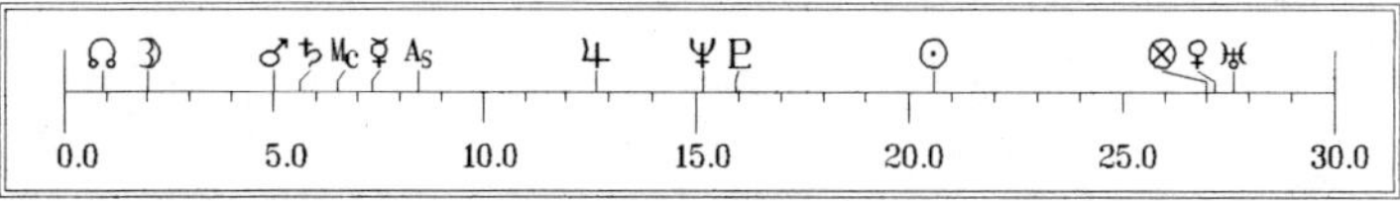

Pl.	Antiscia
☉	9°♐25′
☽	27°♋58′
☿	22°♏38′
♀	2°♑48′
♂	24°♏59′
♃	17°♐17′
♄	24°♈22′
♅	2°♋21′
♆	14°♓50′
♇	14°♉04′
☊	29°♌06′
As	21°♈33′
Mc	23°♋28′
⊗	3°♍00′

Table of Essential Dignities

Points	Ruler	Exalt.	Trip.	Terms	Face	Detr.	Fall	Score	Solar	Quality of Degree
☉	♄	♂	☽	♂	☉ +	☽	♃	+ 1	Ori.	Masc., Dark
☽	☿	☊ m	☿	☿	♃	♃	--	+ 4	Ori.	Fem., Light
☿	♄ m	--	♀ +	☿ +	♀	☉	--	+10	Occ. Beams	Fem., Light
♀	♃	☋	♃	♂	♄	☿	--	− 5p	Ori.	Masc., Light
♂	♄	--	☿	♄	♀	☉	--	− 5p	Occ. Beams	Fem., Light
♃	♄	♂	☽	♃ +	♂	☽	♃ −	− 2	Ori. Comb.	Fem., Smokey, Fort.
♄	☿ m	☿	☽	☿	☉	♃	♀	+ 5	Occ.	Fem., Light
♅	☿	☊	☿	♂	☉	♃	--	--	Ori.	Fem., Void
♆	♀	♄	☿	♃	♄	♂	☉	--	Occ.	Masc., Light
♇	☉	--	♃	♀	♃	♄	--	--	Occ.	Fem., Smokey
☊	♀	☽ m	☽	♀	☿	♂	--	--	Ori.	Fem., Dark
☋	♂	--	♂	♂	♂	♀	☽	--	Ori.	Masc., Dark
As	☿	☿	☽	♀	☉	♃	♀	--	--	Masc., Void
Mc	☿	☊	☿	☿	♃	♃	--	--	--	Masc., Dark
⊗	♂	☉	♃	♄	♀	♀	♄		Ori.	Masc., Light

J. Lee Lehman, Ph.D. – P.O. Box 501107 – Malabar FL 32950 – (407) 728–2277 Fax –2244

OLDTIME1

(C) 1992 Astrolabe. Inc.

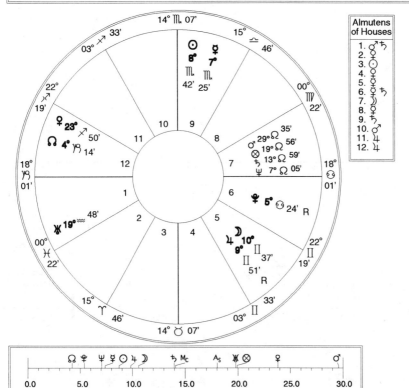

Union Carbide	12:00:00 EST	Nov. 1, 1917
Albany NY	42°N 39'00"	73°W 45'00"
Regiomontanus	14:46:38 S.T.	J.D. = 2421534.2086
Natal Chart	R.A.M.S. = 14:41:37	Obl. = 23°27'00"
Tropical	No Ayanamsha	Geocentric Ecliptic

Almutens of Houses

1. ♂ ♄
2. ♀ ♀
3. ⊙
4. ☿ ♀
5. ☿ ♄
6. ☿
7. ☽
8. ♀
9. ♄
10. ♂ ♂
11. ♃
12. ♃

Day Hours

♃ 6:28 AM
♂ 7:20 AM
⊙ 8:12 AM
♀ 9:03 AM
☿ 9:55 AM
☽ 10:47 AM
♄ 11:38 AM
♃ 0:30 PM
♂ 1:22 PM
⊙ 2:13 PM
♀ 3:05 PM
☿ 3:57 PM

Night Hours

☽ 4:48 PM
♄ 5:57 PM
♃ 7:05 PM
♂ 8:14 PM
⊙ 9:22 PM
♀ 10:31 PM
☿ 11:39 PM
☽ 0:47 AM
♄ 1:56 AM
♃ 3:04 AM
♂ 4:13 AM
⊙ 5:21 AM

Day of ♃
Hour of ♄

Table of Essential Dignities									
Points	Ruler	Exalt.	Trip.	Terms	Face	Detr.	Fall	Score	Solar	Quality of Degree
⊙	♂ m	--	♂ m	♃	♂	♀	☽	+ 8	Occ.	Fem., Void, Deep
☿	♂☿	☊	☿	♃	♂☿	☿	☽	- 5p	Occ.	Masc., Light, Fort.
☿	♃☿	☋	☿	♃	♂☿	♃	☽	- 5p	Ori. Comb.	Fem., Light
☿	♃ m	☋	☿ m	♄ m	♂ +	♃		+ 2	Occ.	Fem., Light, Deep
♃	☿	☊	☿	♃☿ +	♃ +	☿	♃ -	+11	Ori.	Masc., Light
♃	☿	☋	♀ m	♃♀ + m	♃♀ +	☿	♃ -	- 2	Occ.	Masc., Light
♄	☿	☋	☿	♃♀	♃♀	♄☉	♃ -	- 3	Ori.	Masc., Smokey
♄	☿	--	☿	♃♀	♃♀	--	--		Ori.	Masc., Light, Fort.
⚹	♄☉	♃♂	☿♀	♃♀	♃♀	☽	♂☉	--	Occ.	Fem., Dark
☿	♄☉	♃♂	☿♀	☿♃	♃♀	☽	♂☉	--	Occ.	Fem., Light
☊	♄☉	--	☿♀	♃♀	☽	--	♂	--	Occ.	Masc., Dark
A_S	♃	☋	♂♃	♃☿	♃	☿	♃	--		Fem., Light
M_C	♄☉	--	☿♀	♃♀	♄	--	☽	--		Masc., Light
⊗	⊙	--	⊙	♃	♂	♄	--		Ori.	Fem., Smokey

Pl.	Antiscia
⊙	21°♒18'
☽	19°♋23'
☿	22°♒35'
♀	6°♑10'
♂	0°⊙25'
♃	20°♋09'
♄	16°♉01'
⚹	10°♏12'
♀	22°♉55'
☿	24°♊36'
☊	25°♐46'
A_S	11°♐58'
M_C	15°♒53'
⊗	10°♉04'

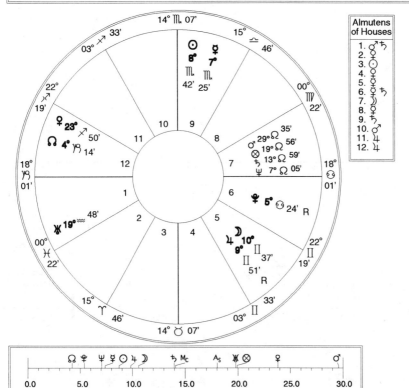

J. Lee Lehman, Ph.D. - P.O. Box 501107 - Malabar FL 32950 - (407) 728-2277 Fax -2244

OLDTIME1

(C) 1992 Astrolabe, Inc.

339

Union Carbide 1st Trade	10:00:00 EST	Mar. 1, 1926
NEW YORK CITY, NY	40°N 42'51"	74°W 00'23"
Regiomontanus	20:38:36 S.T.	J.D. = 2424576.1253
Natal Chart	R.A.M.S. = 22:34:38	Obl. = 23°26'56"
Tropical	No Ayanamsha	Geocentric Ecliptic

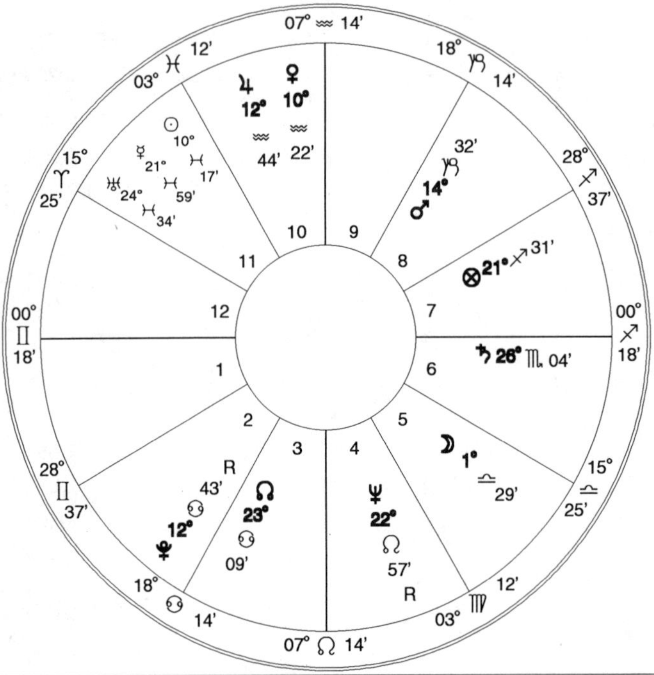

Almutens of Houses
1. ☿
2. ☿
3. ☽
4. ☉
5. ☿
6. ♄
7. ♃
8. ♃
9. ♂ ♄
10. ♄
11. ♀
12. ☉

Day Hours
☽ 6:31 AM
♄ 7:27 AM
♃ 8:24 AM
♂ 9:20 AM
☉ 10:16 AM
♀ 11:13 AM
☿ 0:09 PM
☽ 1:05 PM
♄ 2:02 PM
♃ 2:58 PM
♂ 3:54 PM
☉ 4:50 PM

Night Hours
♀ 5:47 PM
☿ 6:50 PM
☽ 7:54 PM
♄ 8:57 PM
♃ 10:01 PM
♂ 11:05 PM
☉ 0:08 AM
♀ 1:12 AM
☿ 2:15 AM
☽ 3:19 AM
♄ 4:22 AM
♃ 5:26 AM

Day of ☽
Hour of ♂

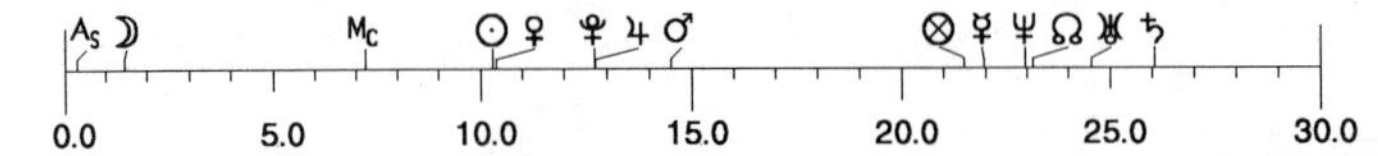

Table of Essential Dignities

Points	Ruler	Exalt.	Trip.	Terms	Face	Detr.	Fall	Score	Solar	Quality of Degree
☉	♃	♀	♂	♃	♃	☿	☿	- 5p	Ori.	Fem., Light
☽	♀	♄	♄	♄	☽ +	♂	☉	+ 1	Occ.	Masc., Light
☿	♃	♀	♂	♂	♂	☿ -	☿ -	-14p	Occ. Beams	Masc., Light
♀	♄	--	♄	☿	☿	☉	--	- 5p	Ori.	Fem., Dark
♂	♄ m	♂ +	♀	♃	♂ +	☽	♃	+10	Ori.	Fem., Smokey
♃	♄	--	♄	♀	♀	☉	--	- 5p	Ori.	Fem., Dark
♄	♂ m	--	♂	☿	☿	♀	☽	+ 5	Occ.	Masc., Void, Deep
♅	♃	♀	♂	♂	♂	☿	☿	--	Occ. Beams	Fem., Void
♆	☉	--	☉	♃	♂	♄	--	--	Ori.	Fem., Void, Deep
♇	☽	♃	♂	♃	☿	♄	♂	--	Ori.	Masc., Dark, Lame
☊	☽	♃	♂	♀	☽	♄	♂	--	Ori.	Fem., Light
☋	♄	♂	♀	♂	☉	☽	♃	--	Ori.	Masc., Void, Deep
As	☿	☊	♄	☿	♃	♃	--	--	--	Fem., Light
Mc	♄	--	♄	☿	♀	☉	--	--	--	Fem., Light
⊗	♃	☋	☉	♄	♄	☿	--		Ori.	Fem., Smokey

Pl.	Antiscia
☉	19° ♎ 43'
☽	28° ♓ 31'
☿	8° ♎ 01'
♀	19° ♏ 38'
♂	15° ♐ 28'
♃	17° ♏ 16'
♄	3° ♒ 56'
♅	5° ♎ 26'
♆	7° ♉ 03'
♇	17° ♊ 17'
☊	6° ♊ 51'
As	29° ♋ 42'
Mc	22° ♏ 45'
⊗	8° ♑ 29'

J. Lee Lehman, Ph.D. - P.O. Box 501107 - Malabar FL 32950 - (407) 728-2277 Fax -2244

OLDTIME1

(C) 1992 Astrolabe, Inc.

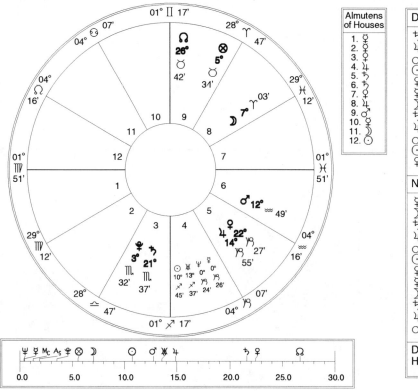

J. Lee Lehman, Ph.D. - P.O. Box 501107 - Malabar FL 32950 - (407) 728-2277 Fax -2244

OLDTIME1

(C) 1992 Astrolabe, Inc.

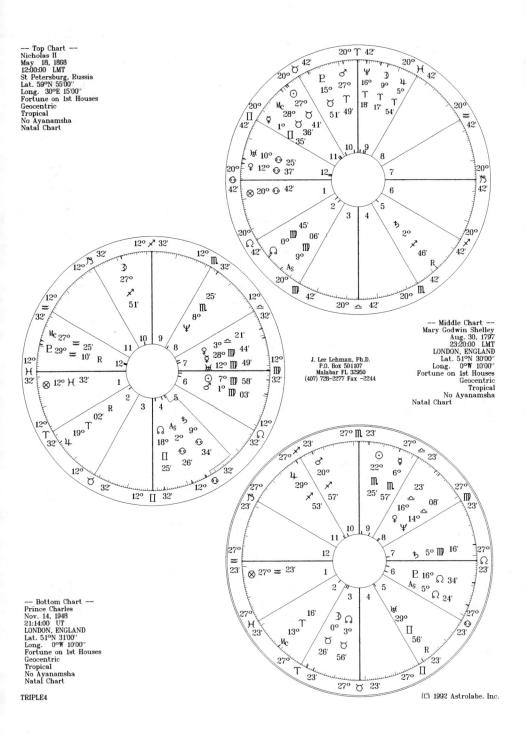

-- Top Chart --
Nicholas II
May 18, 1868
12:00:00 LMT
St Petersburg, Russia
Lat. 59°N 55'00"
Long. 30°E 15'00"
Fortune on 1st Houses
Geocentric
Tropical
No Ayanamsha
Natal Chart

J. Lee Lehman, Ph.D.
P.O. Box 501107
Malabar FL 32950
(407) 728-2277 Fax -2244

-- Middle Chart --
Mary Godwin Shelley
Aug. 30, 1797
23:20:00 LMT
LONDON, ENGLAND
Lat. 51°N 30'00"
Long. 0°W 10'00"
Fortune on 1st Houses
Geocentric
Tropical
No Ayanamsha
Natal Chart

-- Bottom Chart --
Prince Charles
Nov. 14, 1948
21:14:00 UT
LONDON, ENGLAND
Lat. 51°N 31'00"
Long. 0°W 10'00"
Fortune on 1st Houses
Geocentric
Tropical
No Ayanamsha
Natal Chart

TRIPLE4

(C) 1992 Astrolabe, Inc.

342

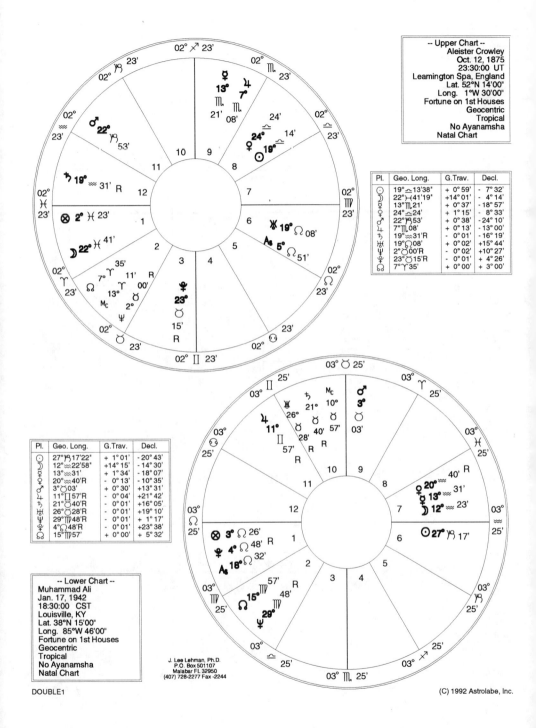

-- Upper Chart --
Aleister Crowley
Oct. 12, 1875
23:30:00 UT
Leamington Spa, England
Lat. 52°N 14'00"
Long. 1°W 30'00"
Fortune on 1st Houses
Geocentric
Tropical
No Ayanamsha
Natal Chart

Pl.	Geo. Long.	G.Trav.	Decl.
☉	19°≏13'38"	+ 0° 59'	- 7° 32'
☽	22°⨽41'19"	+14° 01'	- 4° 14'
☿	13°♏21'	+ 0° 37'	-18° 57'
♀	24°≏24'	+ 1° 15'	- 8° 33'
♂	22°♑53'	+ 0° 38'	-24° 10'
♃	7°♏08'	+ 0° 13'	-13° 00'
♄	19°♒31'R	- 0° 01'	-16° 19'
♅	19°♌08'	+ 0° 02'	+15° 44'
♆	2°♉00'R	- 0° 02'	+10° 27'
♇	23°♉15'R	- 0° 01'	+ 4° 26'
☊	7°♈35'	+ 0° 00'	+ 3° 00'

Pl.	Geo. Long.	G.Trav.	Decl.
☉	27°♑17'22"	+ 1° 01'	- 20° 43'
☽	12°♒22'58"	+14° 15'	- 14° 30'
☿	13°♒31'	+ 1° 34'	- 18° 07'
♀	20°♒40'R	- 0° 13'	- 10° 35'
♂	3°♉03'	+ 0° 30'	+13° 31'
♃	11°♊57'R	- 0° 04'	+21° 42'
♄	21°♉40'R	- 0° 01'	+16° 05'
♅	26°♉28'R	- 0° 01'	+19° 10'
♆	29°♍48'R	- 0° 01'	+ 1° 17'
♇	4°♌48'R	- 0° 01'	+23° 38'
☊	15°♍57'	+ 0° 00'	+ 5° 32'

-- Lower Chart --
Muhammad Ali
Jan. 17, 1942
18:30:00 CST
Louisville, KY
Lat. 38°N 15'00"
Long. 85°W 46'00"
Fortune on 1st Houses
Geocentric
Tropical
No Ayanamsha
Natal Chart

J. Lee Lehman, Ph.D.
P.O. Box 501107
Malabar FL 32950
(407) 728-2277 Fax -2244

DOUBLE1

(C) 1992 Astrolabe, Inc.

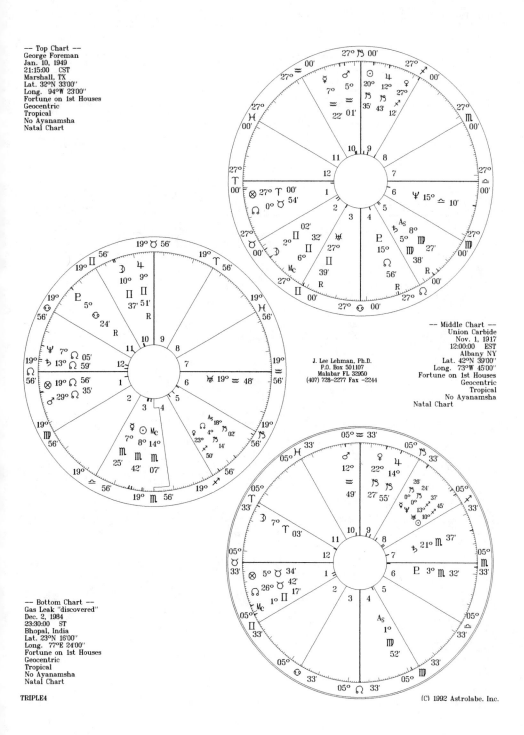

--- Top Chart ---
George Foreman
Jan. 10, 1949
21:15:00   CST
Marshall, TX
Lat. 32°N 33'00''
Long. 94°W 23'00''
Fortune on 1st Houses
Geocentric
Tropical
No Ayanamsha
Natal Chart

--- Middle Chart ---
Union Carbide
Nov. 1, 1917
12:00:00   EST
Albany NY
Lat. 42°N 39'00''
Long. 73°W 45'00''
Fortune on 1st Houses
Geocentric
Tropical
No Ayanamsha
Natal Chart

--- Bottom Chart ---
Gas Leak "discovered"
Dec. 2, 1984
23:30:00   ST
Bhopal, India
Lat. 23°N 16'00''
Long. 77°E 24'00''
Fortune on 1st Houses
Geocentric
Tropical
No Ayanamsha
Natal Chart

J. Lee Lehman, Ph.D.
P.O. Box 501107
Malabar FL 32950
(407) 728-2277 Fax -2244

TRIPLE4

(C) 1992 Astrolabe, Inc.

344

Camille Paglia	18:57:00 EST	Apr. 2, 1947
Endicott, NY	42°N 06'00"	76°W 03'00"
Regiomontanus	7:34:43 S.T.	J.D. = 2432278.4982
Natal Chart	R.A.M.S. = 0:41:56	Obl. = 23°26'46"
Tropical	No Ayanamsha	Geocentric Ecliptic

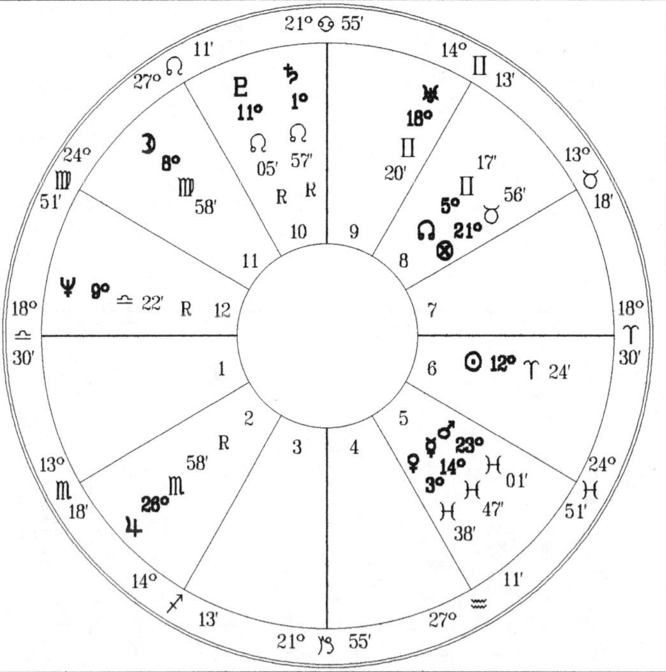

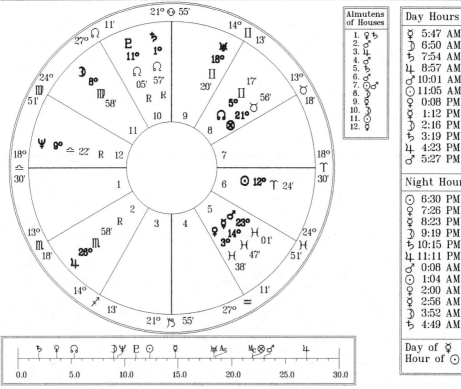

Almutens of Houses
1. ♀♄
2. ♂
3. ♃
4. ♂
5. ♄
6. ♂
7. ☉♂
8. ☽
9. ☿
10. ☽
11. ☉
12. ☿

Day Hours	
☿	5:47 AM
☽	6:50 AM
♄	7:54 AM
♃	8:57 AM
♂	10:01 AM
☉	11:05 AM
♀	0:08 PM
☿	1:12 PM
☽	2:16 PM
♄	3:19 PM
♃	4:23 PM
♂	5:27 PM

Night Hours	
☉	6:30 PM
♀	7:26 PM
☿	8:23 PM
☽	9:19 PM
♄	10:15 PM
♃	11:11 PM
♂	0:08 AM
☉	1:04 AM
♀	2:00 AM
☿	2:56 AM
☽	3:52 AM
♄	4:49 AM

Day of ☿
Hour of ☉

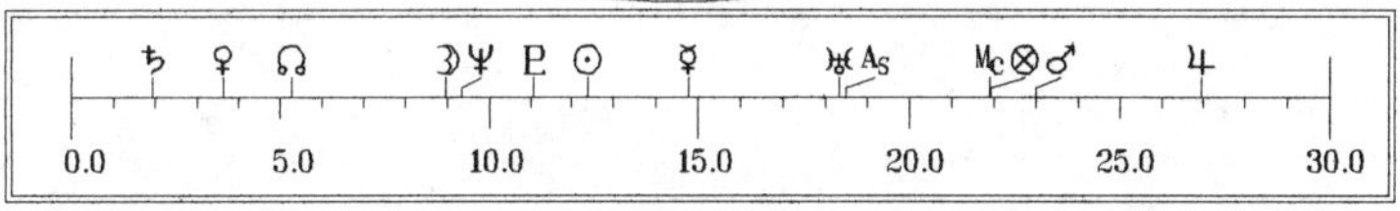

Table of Essential Dignities

Points	Ruler	Exalt.	Trip.	Terms	Face	Detr.	Fall	Score	Solar	Quality of Degree
☉	♂	☉ +	♃	♀	☉ +	♀	♄	+ 5	Ori.	Masc., Dark
☽	☿	☿	☽ +	♀	☉	♃	♀	+ 3	Ori.	Masc., Void
☿	♃	♀	♂	☿ +	♃	☿ –	☿ –	– 7	Ori.	Fem., Dark
♀	♃	♀ +	♂	♀ +	♄	☿	☿	+ 6	Ori.	Masc., Dark, Deep
♂	♃ m	♀	♂ +	♂ +	♂ +	☿	☿	+11	Ori.	Fem., Void, Deep
♃	♂ m	--	♂	☿	♀	♀	☽	+ 5	Occ.	Masc., Void, Deep
♄	☉	--	♃	♄ +	♄ +	♄ –	--	– 2	Ori.	Masc., Dark, Fort.
♅	☿	☊	☿	♀	♂	♃	--	--	Occ.	Fem., Light
♆	♀	♄	☿	♀	☽	♂	☉	--	Ori.	Fem., Dark
♇	☉	--	♃	☿	♃	♄	--	--	Ori.	Masc., Smokey
☊	☿	☊ +	☿	☿	♃	♃	--	--	Occ.	Masc., Dark
☋	♃	☋ +	♃	♃	☿	☿	--	--	Occ.	Masc., Light
As	♀	♄	☿	♃	♄	♂	☉	--	--	Masc., Dark
Mc	☽	♃	♂	♀	☽	♄	♂	--	--	Masc., Light
⊗	♀	☽	☽	♃	♄	♂	--		Occ.	Fem., Light

Pl.	Antiscia
☉	17°♍36'
☽	21°♈02'
☿	15°♎13'
♀	26°♎22'
♂	6°♎59'
♃	3°♒02'
♄	28°♉03'
♅	11°♋40'
♆	20°♓38'
♇	18°♉55'
☊	24°♋43'
As	11°♓29'
Mc	8°♊05'
⊗	8°♌04'

J. Lee Lehman, Ph.D. – P.O. Box 501107 – Malabar FL 32950 – (407) 728–2277 Fax –2244

OLDTIME1

(C) 1992 Astrolabe. Inc.

Ludwig II of Bavaria	23:38:48 UT	Aug. 24, 1845
Munich, Bavaria	48°N 09'00"	11°E 33'00"
Regiomontanus	22:37:25 S.T.	J.D. = 2395168.4854
Natal Chart	R.A.M.S. = 10:12:24	Obl. = 23°27'34"
Tropical	No Ayanamsha	Geocentric Ecliptic

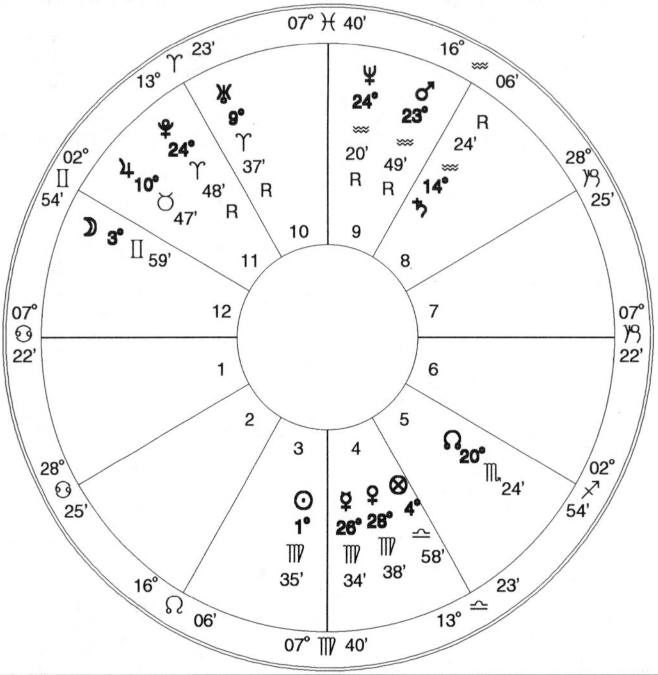

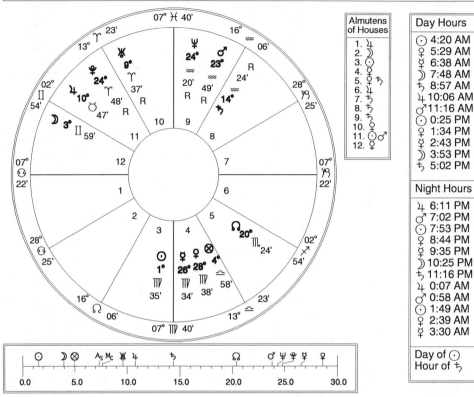

Almutens of Houses
1. ♃
2. ☽
3. ☉
4. ☿
5. ♀ ♄
6. ♃
7. ♄
8. ♄
9. ♄
10. ♀
11. ☉ ♂
12. ☿

Day Hours
☉ 4:20 AM
♀ 5:29 AM
☿ 6:38 AM
☽ 7:48 AM
♄ 8:57 AM
♃ 10:06 AM
♂ 11:16 AM
☉ 0:25 PM
♀ 1:34 PM
☿ 2:43 PM
☽ 3:53 PM
♄ 5:02 PM

Night Hours
♃ 6:11 PM
♂ 7:02 PM
☉ 7:53 PM
♀ 8:44 PM
☿ 9:35 PM
☽ 10:25 PM
♄ 11:16 PM
♃ 0:07 AM
♂ 0:58 AM
☉ 1:49 AM
♀ 2:39 AM
☿ 3:30 AM

Day of ☉
Hour of ♄

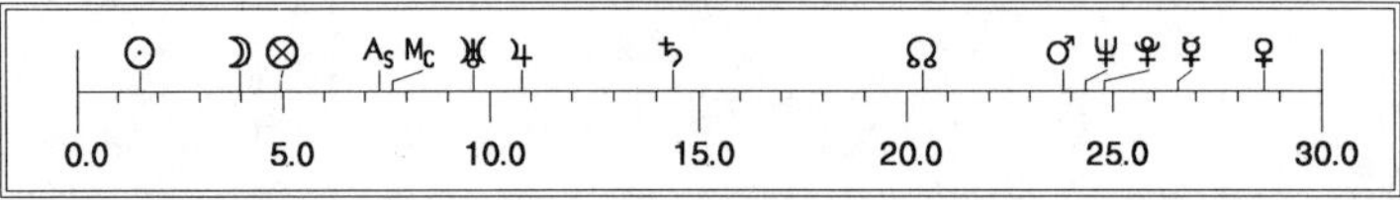

Table of Essential Dignities

Points	Ruler	Exalt.	Trip.	Terms	Face	Detr.	Fall	Score	Solar	Quality of Degree
☉	☿	☿	☽	☿	☉ +	♃	♀	+ 1	Occ.	Fem., Dark
☽	☿	☊	☿ m	☿	♃ m	♃	--	+ 4	Ori.	Fem., Light
☿	☿ +	☿ +	☽ m	♂	☿ +	♃	♀	+13	Occ.	Masc., Void
♀	☿	☿	☽	♂	☿	♃	♀ -	- 9p	Occ.	Masc., Dark
♂	♄	--	☿	♃	☽	☉	--	- 5p	Ori.	Fem., Void, Deep
♃	♀	☽	☽	☿	☽ m	♂	--	+ 1	Occ.	Masc., Void
♄	♄ +	--	☿	♀	☿	☉	--	+ 5	Ori.	Fem., Light
♅	♂	☉	♃	♀	♂	♀	♄	--	Occ.	Masc., Dark
♆	♄	--	☿	♃	☽	☉	--	--	Ori.	Masc., Void
♇	♂	☉	♃	♂	♀	♀	♄	--	Occ.	Masc., Light
☊	♂	--	♂	♀	♀	♀	☽	--	Occ.	Fem., Light
☋	♀	☽	☽	♃	♄	♂	--	--	Occ.	Masc., Light
As	☽	♃	♂	♃	♀	♄	♂	--	--	Fem., Light
Mc	♃	♀	♂	♀	♄	☿	☿	--	--	Masc., Light
⊗	♀	♄	☿	♄	☽	♂	☉		Occ.	Masc., Light

Pl.	Antiscia
☉	28° ♈ 25'
☽	26° ♋ 01'
☿	3° ♈ 26'
♀	1° ♈ 22'
♂	6° ♏ 11'
♃	19° ♌ 13'
♄	15° ♏ 36'
♅	20° ♍ 23'
♆	5° ♏ 40'
♇	5° ♍ 12'
☊	9° ♒ 36'
As	22° ♊ 38'
Mc	22° ♎ 20'
⊗	25° ♓ 02'

J. Lee Lehman, Ph.D. - P.O. Box 501107 - Malabar FL 32950 - (407) 728-2277 Fax -2244

OLDTIME1

(C) 1992 Astrolabe, Inc.

Mantle, Mickey (C Data)	10:00:00 CST	Oct. 20, 1931
Spavinaw, OK	36°N 23'00"	95°W 03'00"
Regiomontanus	11:32:24 S.T.	J.D. = 2426635.1669
Natal Chart	R.A.M.S. = 13:52:36	Obl. = 23°26'53"
Tropical	No Ayanamsha	Geocentric Ecliptic

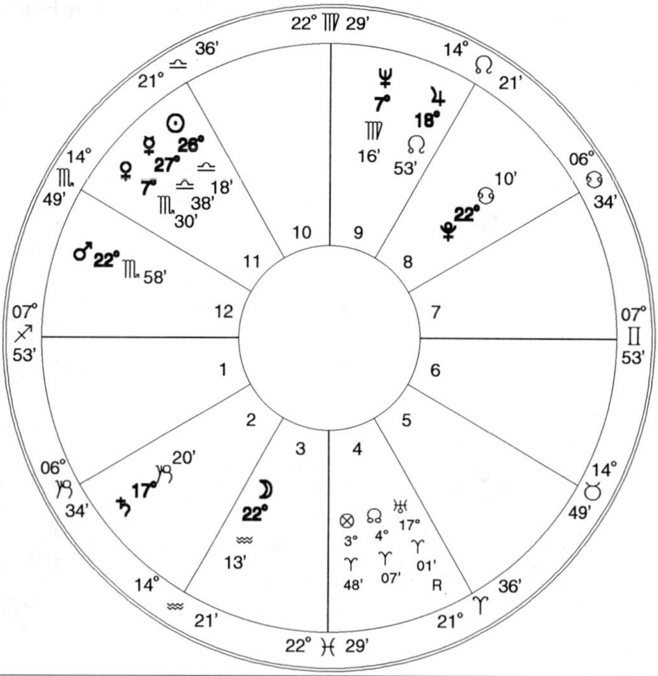

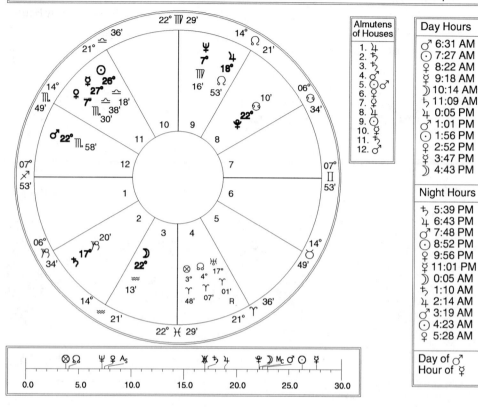

Almutens of Houses
1. ♃
2. ♄
3. ♄
4. ♂
5. ☉ ♂
6. ♀
7. ☿
8. ♃
9. ☉
10. ☿
11. ♄
12. ♂

Day Hours
♂ 6:31 AM
☉ 7:27 AM
♀ 8:22 AM
☿ 9:18 AM
☽ 10:14 AM
♄ 11:09 AM
♃ 0:05 PM
♂ 1:01 PM
☉ 1:56 PM
♀ 2:52 PM
☿ 3:47 PM
☽ 4:43 PM

Night Hours
♄ 5:39 PM
♃ 6:43 PM
♂ 7:48 PM
☉ 8:52 PM
♀ 9:56 PM
☿ 11:01 PM
☽ 0:05 AM
♄ 1:10 AM
♃ 2:14 AM
♂ 3:19 AM
☉ 4:23 AM
♀ 5:28 AM

Day of ♂
Hour of ☿

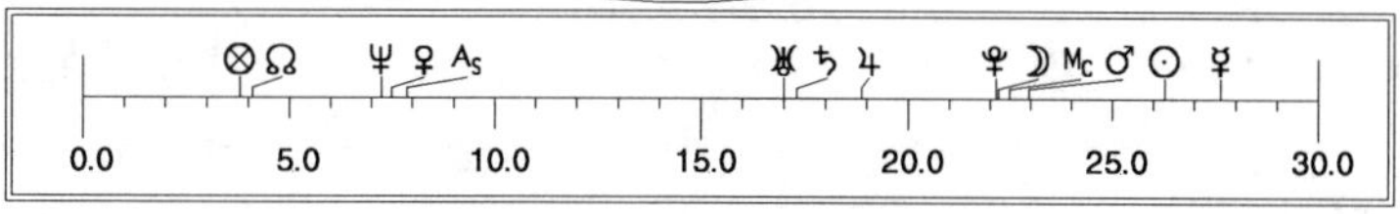

Table of Essential Dignities

Points	Ruler	Exalt.	Trip.	Terms	Face	Detr.	Fall	Score	Solar	Quality of Degree
☉	♀	♄	♄	♂	♃	♂	☉ -	- 9p	Ori.	Fem., Light
☽	♄	--	♄	♃	☽ +	☉	--	+ 1	Ori.	Fem., Void
☿	♀	♄	♄	♂ m	♃	♂	☉	+ 2	Occ. Comb.	Masc., Void
♀	♂	--	♂	♃ m	♂ m	♀ -	☽	- 2	Occ. Beams	Fem., Light
♂	♂ +	--	♂ +	☿ m	♀ m	♀	☽	+11	Occ.	Fem., Smokey, Deep
♃	☉	--	☉	♀ m	♃ +	♄	--	+ 3	Ori.	Fem., Smokey, Fort.
♄	♄ +	♂	♀	♃	♂	☽	♃	+ 5	Occ.	Fem., Light
♅	♂	☉	☉	☿	☉	♀	♄	--	Ori.	Fem., Light
♆	☿	☿	♀	♀	☉	♃	♀	--	Ori.	Fem., Light, Deep
♇	☽	♃	♂	♀	☽	♄	♂	--	Occ.	Masc., Light, Deep
☊	♂	☉	☉	♃	♂	♀	♄	--	Ori.	Masc., Light
☋	♀	♄	☉	♄	☽	♂	☉	--	Ori.	Masc., Light
As	♃	☋	☉	♃	☿	☿	--	--	--	Masc., Light, Lame
Mc	☿	☿	♀	♄	☿	♃	♀	--	--	Masc., Void
⊗	♂	☉	☉	♃	♂	♀	♄		Ori.	Masc., Light

Pl.	Antiscia
☉	3° ♓ 42'
☽	7° ♏ 47'
☿	2° ♓ 22'
♀	22° ♒ 30'
♂	7° ♒ 02'
♃	11° ♉ 07'
♄	12° ♐ 40'
♅	12° ♍ 59'
♆	22° ♈ 44'
♇	7° ♊ 50'
☊	25° ♍ 53'
As	22° ♑ 07'
Mc	7° ♈ 31'
⊗	26° ♍ 12'

J. Lee Lehman, Ph.D. - P.O. Box 501107 - Malabar FL 32950 - (407) 728-2277 Fax -2244

OLDTIME1

(C) 1992 Astrolabe, Inc.

Mantle's Liver Transplan	04:00:00 EDT	June 8, 1995
DALLAS, TX	32°N 47'00"	96°W 49'00"
Regiomontanus	18:37:41 S.T.	J.D. = 2449876.8340
Natal Chart	R.A.M.S. = 5:04:57	Obl. = 23°26'24"
Tropical	No Ayanamsha	Geocentric Ecliptic

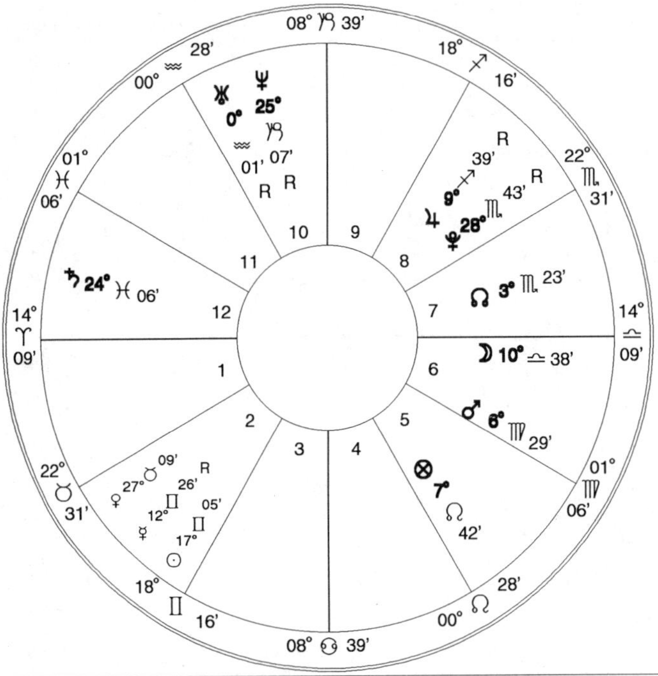

Almutens of Houses
1. ☉♂
2. ☽
3. ☿
4. ♃
5. ☉
6. ☿
7. ☿ ♄
8. ♂
9. ♃
10. ♄
11. ♄
12. ♀

Day Hours	
☿	7:19 AM
☽	8:30 AM
♄	9:41 AM
♃	10:53 AM
♂	0:04 PM
☉	1:15 PM
♀	2:26 PM
☿	3:37 PM
☽	4:49 PM
♄	6:00 PM
♃	7:11 PM
♂	8:22 PM
Night Hours	
☉	9:33 PM
♀	10:22 PM
☿	11:11 PM
☽	12:00 PM
♄	0:49 AM
♃	1:37 AM
♂	2:26 AM
☉	3:15 AM
♀	4:04 AM
☿	4:52 AM
☽	5:41 AM
♄	6:30 AM

Day of ☿
Hour of ☉

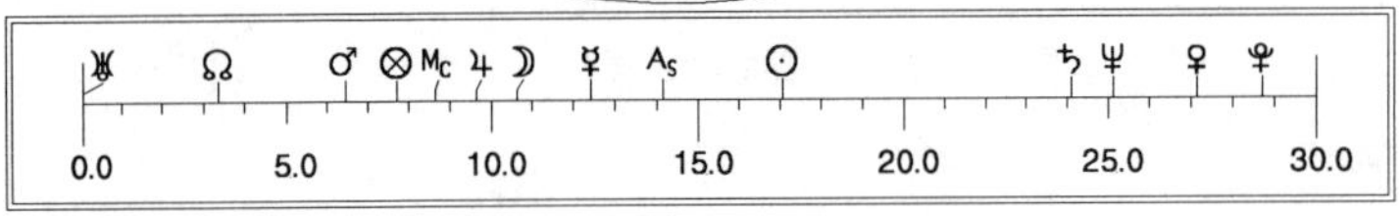

Table of Essential Dignities

Points	Ruler	Exalt.	Trip.	Terms	Face	Detr.	Fall	Score	Solar	Quality of Degree
☉	☿	☊	☿	♀	♂ m	♃	--	+ 1	Occ.	Fem., Light
☽	♀	♄	☿	♀	♄	♂	☉	- 5p	Ori.	Fem., Light
☿	☿ +	☊	☿ +	♃	♂	♃	--	+ 8	Ori. Comb.	Masc., Void
♀	♀ +	☽	☽	♂	♄	♂	--	+ 5	Ori.	Masc., Light
♂	☿	☿	☽	☿	☉ m	♃	♀	+ 1	Occ.	Fem., Light
♃	♃ +	☋	♃ +	♀	☿	☿	--	+ 8	Ori.	Masc., Dark
♄	♃	♀	♂	♂	♂	☿	☿	- 5p	Ori.	Fem., Void
♅	♄	--	☿	♄	♀	☉	--	--	Occ.	Masc., Smokey, Deep
♆	♄	♂	☽	♄	☉	☽	♃	--	Occ.	Masc., Dark, Lame
♇	♂	--	♂	♄	♀	♀	☽	--	Ori.	Masc., Void
☊	♂	--	♂	♂	♂	♀	☽	--	Ori.	Masc., Light
☋	♀	☽	☽	♀	☿	♂	--	--	Ori.	Fem., Light
As	♂	☉	♃	☿	☉	♀	♄	--	--	Masc., Dark
Mc	♄	♂	☽	☿	♃	☽	♃	--	--	Masc., Light
⊗	☉	--	♃	☿	♄	♄	--		Occ.	Fem., Dark

Pl.	Antiscia
☉	12°♋55'
☽	19°♓22'
☿	17°♋34'
♀	2°♌51'
♂	23°♈31'
♃	20°♑21'
♄	5°♎54'
♅	29°♏59'
♆	4°♐53'
♇	1°♒17'
☊	26°♒37'
As	15°♍50'
Mc	21°♐21'
⊗	22°♉18'

J. Lee Lehman, Ph.D. - P.O. Box 501107 - Malabar FL 32950 - (407) 728-2277 Fax -2244

OLDTIME1

(C) 1992 Astrolabe, Inc.

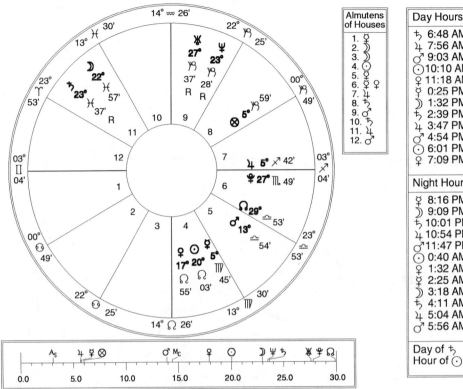

Mantle's Death	01:10:00 CDT	Aug. 13, 1995
DALLAS, TX	32°N 47'00"	96°W 49'00"
Regiomontanus	21:07:36 S.T.	J.D. = 2449942.7576
Natal Chart	R.A.M.S. = 9:24:51	Obl. = 23°26'23"
Tropical	No Ayanamsha	Geocentric Ecliptic

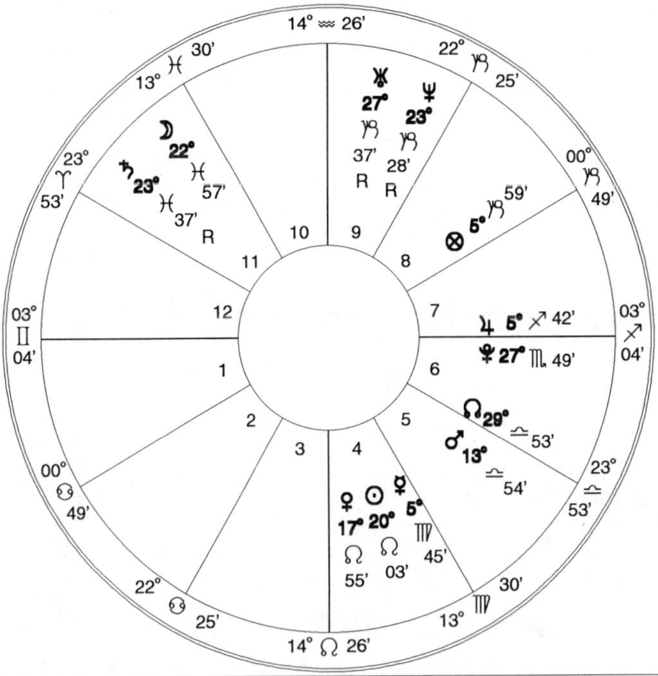

Almutens of Houses

1. ☿
2. ☽
3. ☽
4. ☉
5. ☿
6. ☿ ♀
7. ♃
8. ♄
9. ♂
10. ♄
11. ♃
12. ♂

Day Hours

♄ 6:48 AM
♃ 7:56 AM
♂ 9:03 AM
☉ 10:10 AM
♀ 11:18 AM
☿ 0:25 PM
☽ 1:32 PM
♄ 2:39 PM
♃ 3:47 PM
♂ 4:54 PM
☉ 6:01 PM
♀ 7:09 PM

Night Hours

☿ 8:16 PM
☽ 9:09 PM
♄ 10:01 PM
♃ 10:54 PM
♂ 11:47 PM
☉ 0:40 AM
♀ 1:32 AM
☿ 2:25 AM
☽ 3:18 AM
♄ 4:11 AM
♃ 5:04 AM
♂ 5:56 AM

Day of ♄
Hour of ☉

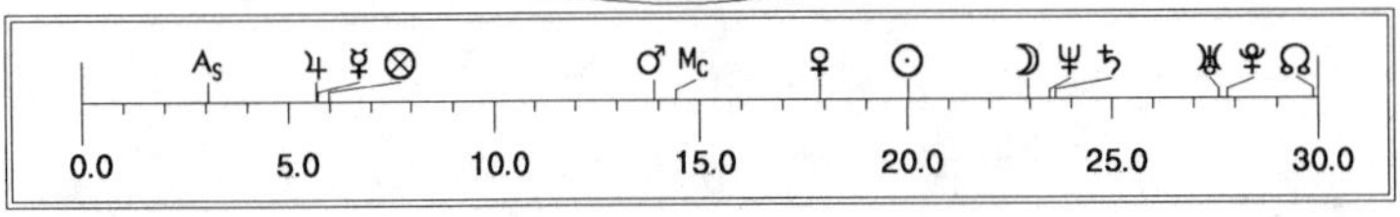

Table of Essential Dignities

Points	Ruler	Exalt.	Trip.	Terms	Face	Detr.	Fall	Score	Solar	Quality of Degree
☉	☉ +	--	♃	♃	♂	♄	--	+ 5	Ori.	Fem., Void
☽	♃	♀	♂	♂	♂	☿	☿	- 5p	Occ.	Masc., Void
☿	☿ +	☿ +	☽	☿ +	☉	♃	♀	+11	Occ. Beams	Fem., Light
♀	☉	--	♃	♀ +	♃	♄	--	+ 2	Ori. Comb.	Fem., Smokey, Lame
♂	♀	♄	☿	♃	♄ m	♂ -	☉	- 4	Occ.	Fem., Light
♃	♃ +	☋	♃ +	♃ +	☿	☿	--	+10	Ori.	Masc., Light
♄	♃	♀	♂	♂	♂ m	☿	☿	+ 1	Occ.	Fem., Void, Deep
♅	♄	♂	☽	♄	☉	☽	♃	--	Ori.	Masc., Dark, Lame
♆	♄	♂	☽	♂	☉	☽	♃	--	Ori.	Masc., Void, Deep
♇	♂	--	♂	♄	♀	♀	☽	--	Ori.	Masc., Void, Lame
☊	♀	♄	☿	♂	♃	♂	☉	--	Occ.	Masc., Void, Deep
☋	♂	☉	♃	♄	♀	♀	♄	--	Occ.	Masc., Void
As	☿	☊	☿	☿	♃	♃	--	--	--	Fem., Light
Mc	♄	--	☿	♀	☿	☉	--	--	--	Fem., Light
⊗	♄	♂	☽	♀	♃	☽	♃		Ori.	Masc., Dark

Pl.	Antiscia
☉	9° ♉ 57'
☽	7° ♎ 03'
☿	24° ♈ 15'
♀	12° ♉ 05'
♂	16° ♓ 06'
♃	24° ♑ 18'
♄	6° ♎ 23'
♅	2° ♐ 23'
♆	6° ♐ 32'
♇	2° ♒ 11'
☊	0° ♓ 07'
As	26° ♋ 55'
Mc	15° ♏ 34'
⊗	24° ♐ 01'

J. Lee Lehman, Ph.D. - P.O. Box 501107 - Malabar FL 32950 - (407) 728-2277 Fax -2244

OLDTIME1

(C) 1992 Astrolabe, Inc.

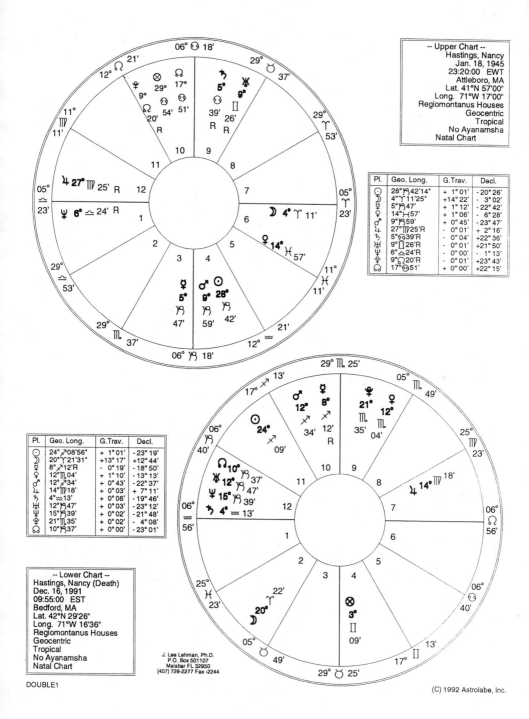

Upper Chart

-- Upper Chart --
Hastings, Nancy
Jan. 18, 1945
23:20:00 EWT
Attleboro, MA
Lat. 41°N 57'00"
Long. 71°W 17'00"
Regiomontanus Houses
Geocentric
Tropical
No Ayanamsha
Natal Chart

Pl.	Geo. Long.	G.Trav.	Decl.
☉	28°♑42'14"	+ 1°01'	-20°26'
☽	4°♈11'25"	+14°22'	- 3°02'
☿	5°♑47'	+ 1°12'	-22°42'
♀	14°♓57'	+ 1°06'	- 6°28'
♂	9°♑59'	+ 0°45'	-23°47'
♃	27°♍25'R	- 0°01'	+ 2°16'
♄	5°♋39'R	- 0°04'	+22°36'
♅	9°♊26'R	- 0°01'	+21°50'
♆	6°♎24'R	- 0°00'	- 1°13'
♇	9°♌20'R	- 0°01'	+23°43'
☊	17°♋51'	+ 0°00'	+22°15'

Lower Chart

Pl.	Geo. Long.	G.Trav.	Decl.
☉	24°♐08'56"	- 23°19'	-23°19'
☽	20°♈21'31"	+13°17'	+12°44'
☿	8°♐12'R	- 0°19'	-18°50'
♀	12°♏04'	+ 1°10'	-13°13'
♂	12°♐34'	+ 0°43'	-22°37'
♃	14°♍18'	+ 0°03'	+ 7°11'
♄	4°♒13'	+ 0°06'	-19°46'
♅	12°♑47'	+ 0°03'	-23°12'
♆	15°♑39'	+ 0°02'	-21°48'
♇	21°♏35'	+ 0°02'	- 4°08'
☊	10°♑37'	+ 0°00'	-23°01'

-- Lower Chart --
Hastings, Nancy (Death)
Dec. 16, 1991
09:55:00 EST
Bedford, MA
Lat. 42°N 29'26"
Long. 71°W 16'36"
Regiomontanus Houses
Geocentric
Tropical
No Ayanamsha
Natal Chart

DOUBLE1

J. Lee Lehman, Ph.D.
P.O. Box 501107
Malabar FL 32950
(407) 728-2277 Fax -2244

(C) 1992 Astrolabe, Inc.